Life-Span Developmental Psychology

Psychology

INTERVENTION

CONTRIBUTORS

STEPHEN S. AMATO

PAUL B. BALTES

JOCHEN BRANDTSTÄDTER

MICHAEL J. CHANDLER

N. CHRISTIANSEN

J. CLEMENT

STANLEY H. COHEN

DAVID B. CONNELL

STEVEN J. DANISH

B. DE PAREDES

WILLIAM J. FREMOUW

M. G. HERRERA

FRANCES DEGEN HOROWITZ

ARTHUR MATHIS

J. O. MORA

N. ORTIZ

WILLIS F. OVERTON

GEORGE PICKETT

HAYNE W. REESE

ANDREW L. REITZ

DANIEL I. RUBENSTEIN

RAYMOND E. SANDERS

KERMIT K. SCHOOLER

HARVEY L. STERNS

RALPH R. TURNER

L. VUORI

D. WABER

M. WAGNER

DIANA S. WOODRUFF

LIFE-SPAN DEVELOPMENTAL PSYCHOLOGY

INTERVENTION

Edited by

RALPH R. TURNER and HAYNE W. REESE

Department of Psychology
West Virginia University
Morgantown, West Virginia

1980

ACADEMIC PRESS

A Subsidiary of Harcourt Brace Jovanovich, Publishers

New York   London   Toronto   Sydney   San Francisco

ACADEMIC PRESS, INC.
111 Fifth Avenue, New York, New York 10003

United Kingdom Edition published by
ACADEMIC PRESS, INC. (LONDON) LTD.
24/28 Oval Road, London NW1 7DX

Library of Congress Cataloging in Publication Data

West Virginia University Conference on Life–Span
    Developmental Psychology, 6th, 1978.
    Life–span developmental psychology.

    Proceedings of the conference held in Morgantown,
W. Va., May 31–June 3, 1978.
    Includes bibliographies and indexes.
    1. Developmental psychology––Congresses.
2. Psychology, Applied––Congresses. I. Turner,
Ralph R. II. Reese, Hayne Waring, 1931–
III. Title.
BF712.5.W47 1978   155   80–10479
ISBN 0–12–704150–8

PRINTED IN THE UNITED STATES OF AMERICA

80 81 82 83   9 8 7 6 5 4 3 2 1

Contents

THEORETICAL AND POLITICAL ISSUES

1. Relationships between Life-Span Developmental Theory, Research, and Intervention: A Revision of Some Stereotypes

Jochen Brandtstädter

2. Models, Methods, and Ethics of Intervention

Hayne W. Reese and Willis F. Overton

3. Intervention in Life-Span Development and Aging: Issues and Concepts

Paul B. Baltes and Steven J. Danish

4. Life-Span Intervention as a Symptom of Conversion Hysteria

Michael J. Chandler

5. The Politics of Public Intervention

George Pickett

ENVIRONMENTAL AND BIOPHYSICAL INTERVENTION

6. The Impact of the Planned Environment on the Elderly

Kermit K. Schooler and Daniel I. Rubenstein

7. Multiple Impacts and Determinants in Human Service Delivery Systems

Stanley H. Cohen

8. Effects of Nutritional Supplementation and Early Education on Physical and Cognitive Development

M. G. Herrera, J. O. Mora, N. Christiansen, N. Ortiz, J. Clement, L. Vuori, D. Waber, B. De Paredes, and M. Wagner

9. Is Genetic Counseling Intervention?

Stephen S. Amato

10. Intervention in the Psychophysiology of Aging: Pitfalls, Progress, and Potential

Diana S. Woodruff

EDUCATIONAL AND DEVELOPMENTAL INTERVENTION

11. Intervention and Its Effects on Early Development: What Model of Development Is Appropriate?

Frances Degen Horowitz

12. The Preschool Child or the Family?: Changing Models of Developmental Intervention

Ralph R. Turner, David B. Connell, and Arthur Mathis

13. Intervention for Delinquency: Art or Science?

William J. Fremouw and Andrew L. Reitz

14. Training and Education of the Elderly

Harvey L. Sterns and Raymond E. Sanders

List of Contributors

Numbers in parentheses indicate the pages on which the authors' contributions begin.

STEPHEN S. AMATO (185), Department of Pediatrics, West Virginia University Medical Center, Morgantown, West Virginia 26506

PAUL B. BALTES (49), College of Human Development, The Pennsylvania State University, University Park, Pennsylvania 16802

JOCHEN BRANDTSTÄDTER (3), Lehrstuhl für Psychologie I, Universität Erlangen-Nürnberg, Nürnberg, West Germany

MICHAEL J. CHANDLER (79), Department of Psychology, The University of British Columbia, Vancouver, B. C. Canada V6T 1W5

N. CHRISTIANSEN (149), Department of Nutrition, Harvard School of Public Health, Boston, Massachusetts 02115

J. CLEMENT (149), Department of Nutrition, Harvard School of Public Health, Boston, Massachusetts 02115

STANLEY H. COHEN (125), Department of Psychology, West Virginia University, Morgantown, West Virginia 26506

DAVID B. CONNELL (249), Abt Associates Inc., Cambridge, Massachusetts 02138

STEVEN J. DANISH (49), College of Human Development, Division of Individual and Family Studies, The Pennsylvania State University, University Park, Pennsylvania 16802

B. DE PAREDES (149), Columbia Institute of Family Welfare, Bogota, Columbia

WILLIAM J. FREMOUW (275), Department of Psychology, West Virginia University, Morgantown, West Virginia 26506

M. G. HERRERA (149), Department of Nutrition, Harvard School of Public Health, Boston, Massachusetts 02115

FRANCES DEGEN HOROWITZ (235), Department of Human Development and Family Life, University of Kansas, Lawrence, Kansas 66045

ARTHUR MATHIS (249), Abt Associates Inc., Cambridge, Massachusetts 02138

J. O. MORA (149), Department of Nutrition, Harvard School of Public Health, Boston, Massachusetts 02115

N. ORTIZ (149), Department of Nutrition, Harvard School of Public Health, Boston, Massachusetts 02115

WILLIS F. OVERTON (29), Department of Psychology, Temple University, Philadelphia, Pennsylvania 19122

GEORGE PICKETT (93), West Virginia Department of Health, Charleston, West Virginia 25305

HAYNE W. REESE (29), Department of Psychology, West Virginia University, Morgantown, West Virginia 26506

ANDREW L. REITZ (275), Pressley Ridge School, Pittsburgh, Pennsylvania 15224

DANIEL I. RUBENSTEIN (103), School of Social Work, Syracuse University, Syracuse, New York 13210

RAYMOND E. SANDERS (307), Department of Psychology, University of Akron, Akron, Ohio 44325

KERMIT K. SCHOOLER (103), School of Social Work, Syracuse University, Syracuse, New York 13210

HARVEY L. STERNS (307), Department of Psychology, and Institute for Life-Span Development and Gerontology, University of Akron, Akron, Ohio 44325

RALPH R. TURNER* (249), Department of Psychology, West Virginia University, Morgantown, West Virginia 26506

L. VUORI (149), Department of Nutrition, Harvard School of Public Health, Boston, Massachusetts 02115

D. WABER (149), Department of Nutrition, Harvard School of Public Health, Boston, Massachusetts 02115

M. WAGNER (149), Institute of Nutrition, Justus Liebig University, Giessen, West Germany

DIANA S. WOODRUFF (197), Department of Psychology, Temple University, Philadelphia, Pennsylvania 19122

* Present Address: Abt Associates Inc., Cambridge, Massachusetts 02138.

Preface

The West Virginia University Conferences on Life-Span Developmental Psychology have helped to shape, define, and encourage the implementation of this theoretical and methodological perspective. The first two conferences specifically emphasized these theoretical and methodological issues, whereas the next three emphasized empirical evidence and detailed theoretical analyses. The series as a whole had provided detailed explication of life-span models and methods, and discussion of the first two of the three general aims of the life-span approach—the description and explanation of life-span development. Across the series of conferences, however, interest in the third aim—modification or optimization of life-span development—became increasingly apparent. That interest was reflected in the theme of the sixth conference: the theory and practice of intervention as viewed from the life-span perspective.

We retained our organizational system from the conference, in which the papers were presented as a series of symposia, to structure this book of the proceedings. Many of the papers were subsequently revised to reflect the thoughtful and often lively discussions that occurred at these symposia. The themes dealt with three broadly defined areas: theoretical and political issues in intervention; environmental and biophysical intervention; and educational and developmental intervention.

The selection of topics reflects current trends in the field. For example, several papers in the first section deal with the relation between theory and practice; a topic of perennial concern, judging from the attention it also received in the fourth life-span conference. The life-span perspective on environmental and biophysical intervention provides a strong cautionary note about possible long-term side effects—a worthy contribution even if it were the only one in this area. The life-span educational intervention papers reflect the current trend toward continuing education, particularly among the older population, and concomitant interest in revision of elementary school curricula to provide more effective "anticipatory socialization." And developmental intervention is a particularly pressing concern; from the vantage point of a decade of experience with large-scale intervention in early childhood—Head Start—we can now anticipate problems that were not foreseeable without such experience. As programs expand to other age periods, the early introduction of the life-span perspective can help in the development of coherent programs, rather than, for example, separate plans for children and the elderly. Although the individual papers vary in their relative emphasis on academic and practical concerns, both the academician and the practitioner will find valuable information in each paper.

Acknowledgments

Like each of the preceding conferences, the Sixth West Virginia University Conference on Life-Span Developmental Psychology was dependent on an intricate network of cooperating individuals and institutions. We thank them all, including those we name here and those whose names we may have inadvertently omitted. We are especially indebted to Ray Koppelman, vice president for Energy Studies, Graduate Programs, and Research, for his continuing intellectual support of these conferences and for his administrative efforts and skills in obtaining financial support for them. We also thank Roger Maley and Jon Krapfl, former chairman and chairman, respectively, of the Department of Psychology, West Virginia University, for somehow managing to complete the financial underpinnings of the sixth conference. The graduate students in our life-span program have always contributed overwhelmingly to the success of the conferences through their generous hospitality, unflagging good spirits, and plain hard work. They include Alfreda Antonucci, Christina Arco, Linda Boulter, Karen Fuchs, Carol Giesen, James Killarney, Bonnie Kwiatkowski, Elizabeth McConnell, and Gale Richardson. We are also indebted to Renate Benkert, who translated one of the papers. For her assistance in the final preparation of the manuscript, we thank Kristina Grafton. Finally, the junior editor acknowledges with gratitude his truly junior status with respect to the distribution of the editorial work load.

PART I

THEORETICAL AND POLITICAL ISSUES

Relationships between Life-Span Developmental Theory, Research, and Intervention: A Revision of Some Stereotypes

JOCHEN BRANDTSTÄDTER

UNIVERSITY OF ERLANGEN-NÜRNBERG
NÜRNBERG, WEST GERMANY

I. Introduction

In the history of developmental psychology, the past two decades will probably be recognized not only as a time of great expectations and challenges, but also as one of frustrated hopes. Large-scale intervention programs were designed to break through cycles of disadvantage and to alleviate developmental deficiencies. However, the target variables of developmental interventions often proved to be far more change-resistant than expected.

Various interpretations have been offered for the often disappointing evaluative results, especially in the area of compensatory education. The theoretical rationale of the programs has been called in question (e.g., Jensen, 1969). Failures were attributed to insufficient implementation procedures (e.g., Weikart, 1972), but they were also explained away by studies that pointed to the methodological pitfalls of the evaluation procedures (e.g., Campbell & Erlebacher, 1970; Zimiles, 1970).

This potpourri of arguments seems to be more characteristic of the inter-

LIFE-SPAN DEVELOPMENTAL PSYCHOLOGY
Intervention

play among developmental theory, research, and intervention than of the received streamlined model, according to which theories are "applied" in intervention and "tested" (confirmed or falsified) by evaluating interventional results. It seems that this model is incorrect or at least oversimplified. Such metatheoretical simplifications, however, lead to specific deficiencies in the design of intervention and evaluation programs as well as in the interpretation of observed results. The object of this chapter is to give a more realistic and differentiated account of the relationships and interfaces among developmental psychological theory, research, and intervention. In particular, the following stereotyped views will be examined more closely: (a) the stereotype that developmental psychology can only contribute to technical decisions and not to decisions concerning the goals of guided human development; (b) the stereotype that technical decisions are implied by or can be formally deduced from developmental theories; (c) the stereotype that intervention is the touchstone of developmental psychological theories.

II. The Contribution of Developmental Psychological Research and Theory to Decisions about Developmental Goals

According to general opinion, the contribution of developmental psychology to developmental planning confines itself to technological aids. Decisions about developmental goals—as simplifying arguments frequently claim—involve value questions, and, therefore, they are not in the competence range of empirical human and social sciences but are subjects of politics, religion, moral philosophy, or perhaps personal conscience. This stereotype, which is widely accepted among politicians and developmental scientists, serves to keep psychologists away from the higher levels of developmental policymaking.

The philosophical and historical backgrounds of this stereotype have been previously discussed elsewhere (Brandtstädter, 1977; Brandtstädter & Montada, 1979). This chapter attempts to further revise the stereotype by showing that developmental psychology can provide valuable assistance in the selection of developmental goals in at least two ways: (a) by assessing the feasibility and compatibility of proposed developmental goals and (b) by predicting developmental consequences and side effects of goal-oriented developmental interventions. Some methodological and theoretical problems related to these tasks will also be discussed.

A. Assessment of the Feasibility and Compatibility of Developmental Goals

Assessment of the feasibility and compatibility of developmental objectives is one of the key problems of rational developmental planning. Disregarding this problem obviously results in material costs; more important, striving for developmental goals that are outside individual behavioral and developmental possibilities may impose considerable stress on the individuals involved. The difficulties of differentiating between unfeasible and feasible "utopias" should not be underrated.

1. The Limited Use of Descriptive Statistical Information

Statistical developmental norms or descriptive developmental functions provide an initial, albeit insufficient, information base for judgments about the feasibility of developmental goals. Descriptive statistics of this type are always functionally related to prevailing developmental conditions and antecedents, and they may be drastically altered if the relevant conditions change. If they are uncritically accepted as indicators of developmental potentials and limitations of given age groups or developmental stages, developmental statistics easily become self-fulfilling prophecies. Fortunately, developmental psychologists have become aware of this problem and its implications for various stages of the life span (see Nardi, 1973; Neugarten, Moore, & Lowe, 1965).

Similar reservations apply to correlational data sets, at least as long as the data have not been connected with a theoretical model that offers an explanation for them. For instance, Bloom's (1964) longitudinal correlation data, per se, warrant no conclusions about age-specific ranges of intraindividual variability or about *critical periods* in intellectual development. If certain developmental features at particular stages of the life span exhibit intraindividual variability or stability to a greater or lesser extent, this finding needs to be relativized to given developmental conditions. Hypotheses about Age × Treatment-Interactions, which are presupposed in the assumption of critical periods, can be tested only when educational or interventional treatments are applied across the whole life span—something that is hardly the case in the present educational system. As long as it is based entirely on descriptive statistical evidence, the concept of critical period is misleading and may even have the effect of desensitizing educators and politicians to the developmental potentials of certain age groups.

In relation to the problem of assessing developmental goals, the *heredity-environment* question is routinely raised. The preceding arguments are also relevant to this question. The educational and political relevance of statistical *heritability coefficients,* which are, as is well known, specific to the tests, persons, and environmental conditions sampled, seems to be generally overrated—curiously enough, even by inveterate environmentalists. Hereditary determination of a developmental attribute does *not* preclude external modification; for example, congenital myopia can easily be corrected with optical devices. On the other hand, the assumption that the environment-related portions of the phenotypic variance of the attribute in question are, so to speak, at the free disposal of the educator or intervenor is just as erroneous. Many factors contributing to environmental variance (for example, certain prenatal conditions or climatic factors) do not lend themselves easily to manipulative control (cf. Merz & Stelzl, 1977). In order to prevent such erroneous interpretations and conclusions, one should perhaps conceive of heritability coefficients as parameters of theoretical and interventional ignorance. Without going into technical details (e.g., see Ehrman, Omenn, & Caspari, 1972), it can be maintained that the utility of heritability statistics with respect to the assessment of the feasibility of developmental goals is just as limited as the utility of other descriptive statistics. To answer questions of feasibility, developmental theories that specify the conditions of inter- and intraindividual variability of the target variables in question are needed. In other words, we must formulate theories that yield explanations for descriptive developmental statistics.

2. *Compatibility of Developmental Goals*

The problem of compatibility of multiple developmental goals (i.e., the problem of feasibility of aggregate goals) deserves special consideration because intervention programs, especially in the field of education, often do not strive for isolated developmental attributes. Rather, they attempt to realize target types, which technically represent vectors in a multidimensional attribute space. For example, the prevalent target type of educational and interventional endeavors is characterized by attributes such as creativity, independence, achievement orientation, willingness to accept responsibility, social empathy, and principled moral orientation. Usually, little attention is given to the question of whether the desired attributes compiled in the "bag of virtues" (Kohlberg & Mayer, 1972) are mutually compatible or simultaneously realizable. Compatibility questions can only be answered on the basis of logical, semantical, and theoretical analyses. A simple physical example may serve to expound the problem: the oscillation frequency and the length of a pendulum cannot be independently varied. According to the pendulum law, only a subset of all logically possible combinations of values in length and oscillation frequency is realizable. The fact that relatively little is known about the compatibility of psychological variables points to nomological deficiencies of actual research in developmental psychology. The notorious tendency of developmental psychology to divide itself into isolated research areas—one needs only to think of the disintegration of research in the cognitive and affective domains of development—and the corresponding lack of cross-domain theorizing seriously impede compatibility analyses.

It should be clear from the previous discussion that correlational data provide no safe evidence for assessing the compatibility of developmental attributes. Functional incompatibility implies a negative covariation between attributes, but the reverse does not hold true. For example, descriptive evidence that creative writers score above average in the clinical scales of the Minnesota Multiphasic Personality Inventory (MMPI) (Barron, 1969), should not be interpreted as indicative of a functional incompatibility between creativity and mental health, as long as there is no causal model to explain the observed relationships. At this point, it should be evident that judgments about the feasibility of developmental goals and target types are to be relativized to the present state of knowledge. With advances in developmental psychology, the lines of demarcation between feasible and unfeasible utopias usually change.

3. A Model of Restrictions for Developmental Interventions

The selection and realization of developmental goals are subject not only to logical and nomological restrictions, but also to further paralogical and paratheoretical constraints. For example, it often happens that limitations of technological knowledge preclude the manipulation of antecedent conditions that are known to be relevant to the achievement of a given developmental goal; furthermore, legal and ethical restrictions have to be observed. Figure 1.1 shows a simple model of the different types of restrictions pertinent to developmental goal planning and intervention (cf. Rapp, 1977).

Various aspects of the model may give rise to discussion. For example, there might be some doubt that the action constraints imposed by political and legal restrictions are indeed narrower than those imposed by limitations in temporal and material resources. In addition, moral philosophers might argue that ethical restrictions should be represented separately from legal and political restrictions. Furthermore, the model does not represent the dynamic interdependence among the various restrictions (e.g., interdependence among technological developments, scientific knowledge, material resources, and social need systems). These interesting issues cannot be elaborated in the present context. More important, however, is the extent to which the various restrictions should be accepted as invariant or

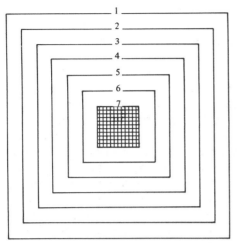

(1) Logical constraints
(2) Developmental laws
(3) State of developmental psychological knowledge
(4) Technological modification potential
(5) Individual and social demands and needs
(6) Material and temporal resources
(7) Political, legal and ethical restrictions

Figure 1.1. A model of restrictions on developmental goal planning and intervention. The central area (hatched) represents the set of developmental goals that are realizable, desirable, and permitted at a given time.

as alterable. With regard to the general aim of optimizing human development, it certainly would be a fatal (and fatalistic) mistake to accept all restrictions as naturally given. Indeed, only restrictions 1 and 2 can be considered invariant; restrictions 3 to 7 are more or less open to change and modification. From a historical developmental perspective, these restrictions (3–7) can be regarded as the result of social and political decision processes, which, in turn, are influenced by hypothetical and quasi-theoretical premises such as anthropological assumptions and "naive" or prescientific conceptions of human development. Such implicit premises and assumptions can and should be made explicit and subjected to scientific criticism. The critical historical reconstruction of the various normative constraints that limit the action space for developmental intervention seems to be a necessary condition for a more comprehensive approach to the problems of optimizing human development.

With regard to the scope of the model given in Figure 1.1, it should be added that the model applies not only to scientifically planned interventions, but also to naive interventions as they occur in the everyday context of education and socialization. Parents, teachers, and educational politicians have their own subjective models of theoretical, technological, and normative action constraints for developmental interventions; the modification of such implicit action-relevant models may be a very efficient, albeit more indirect, mode of developmental intervention. For example, the revision of stereotyped assumptions concerning the developmental and behavioral potential of the elderly may have a much more powerful impact on developmental processes than any direct intervention program.

B. Predicting the Consequences of Developmental Interventions

Along with the problem of assessing the feasibility and compatibility of intervention goals, the prediction of outcomes of developmental interventions is among the central problems of rational intervention planning. Two different types of prediction can be distinguished: (a) *technical predictions* that focus on the prospective efficiency of an intervention with respect to intended outcomes and (b) predictions concerning possible side effects of intervention that are not directly intended but are still relevant to the decision to intervene. We will call predictions of the first type *convergent* and those of the second type *divergent* (cf. the distinction between *formal prediction* and *forecast,* Finan, 1962).

1. Convergent Predictions

The fact that theory-based interventions often fail to produce the desired results frequently gives rise to lamentations about the limited applicability or external validity of psychological theories or research findings. However, the assumption that external validity (Campbell & Stanley, 1963) is a main criterion for evaluating theoretical constructions is hardly tenable. First, the external validity of theoretical assumptions or research findings cannot be judged a priori; it is always pragmatically related to generalization intents (cf. Cornbach, Gleser, Nanda, & Rajaratnam, 1972). Second, it should be noted that theories usually do not refer to concrete systems but to idealized models of concrete systems (cf. Bunge, 1967). Gravitational theory, for example, disregards many factors (friction, air pressure, etc.) that influence the falling of physical bodies *in situ*. One can test theories that refer to idealized systems only under specific ideal conditions. This should not be regarded as a defect; nevertheless, we are still faced with the problem of how to derive valid technical predictions from idealized theoretical models. Basically, there are two different ways to deal with this problem:

1. The first approach is to reduce the complexity of the action field to the complexity of the technical prediction model (*assimilative solution*). This strategy of "technically reconstructing the everyday world according to the model of experimental reality [Groeben & Westmeyer, 1975, p. 133]" is quite common in technology. For example, if the behavior of technical systems is to be made reliable and predictable, the environment of the system (i.e., the totality of external factors influencing the system's

behavior) must be systematically structured and reduced. Within the field of intervention, the inherent problems of this strategy stem from the fact that developmental interventions should be evaluated not only with regard to isolated objectives, but also with regard to the whole set of accepted developmental goals. In order to achieve an isolated developmental goal, it may be technically advisable to take the target persons out of their natural and familiar ecological contexts and move them to specially designed environments; however, this strategy might well be detrimental to or incompatible with other developmental goals. Thus, especially in the field of intervention, technical means–end considerations have to be complemented by a careful scrutiny of possible side effects. The fact that intervention programs (especially in the field of compensatory education) were often insensitive to possible adverse side effects (labeling processes, alienation effects, etc.) has contributed considerably to the rise of anti-intervention resentments (cf. the concept of *radical nonintervention,* Schur, 1973). In short, theoretical knowledge relevant to the design of intervention technologies is not sufficient for responsible decisions about the use of these technologies. Additional theoretical knowledge is required for generating divergent predictions (see Section III of this chapter).

2. Raising the complexity of technical prediction models to the complexity of the action field (*accommodative solution*) is the second approach to the problem. In this case, system-specific nuisance variables that affect the behavior of the target person and may counteract interventional treatments are not eliminated; they are explicitly taken into account in the design of intervention programs. The *triadic model* of behavior modification in the natural context proposed by Tharp and Wetzel (1969) might be considered as a prototypic example. Its basic idea consists of analyzing the social reinforcement network for a given target person and restructuring it through direct and indirect controls so that a positive reinforcement balance for a desired behavior is achieved. The main advantage of this accommodative approach is that it minimizes the risk of relapses that frequently occur when a target person is transferred from a reduced therapeutic setting back to his natural milieu; the use of this approach reduces the sharp demarcation between the therapeutic and the natural setting. With regard to possible side effects, however, the same caveats apply to this approach that apply to any other types of intervention.

2. Divergent Predictions

The predictive assessment of possible adverse consequences and side effects often proves to be the most intricate part of intervention planning. Prediction requires very diversified theoretical knowledge and (as the term *divergent prediction* connotes) an investigatory approach that typically involves *divergent thinking*. To deal with this type of prediction, it may be advantageous to draw on system-analytic decision techniques (e.g., decision trees, cross-impact analyses, multiattribute utility analyses; cf. Böhret, 1975; Edwards, Guttentag, & Snapper, 1975).

The problem of divergent prediction is of particular importance for life-span developmental psychology. Traditionally, the scope of developmental intervention planning in education and psychology was restricted to the earlier periods of life; possible developmental consequences for middle and older age groups were not considered. The crises that can be actually observed in the later periods of the life span (cf. Datan & Ginsberg, 1975) may be at least partially viewed as unwanted (and, because of insufficient theoretical background knowledge, as unforeseen) side effects of this limited planning perspective. If one extends his scope over the entire life span, sequences of developmental tasks have to be designed in such a way that the realization of developmental objectives for a given age level enhances, or at least does not impede, the achievement of developmental objectives for succeeding age levels. This is a special variant of the aforementioned compatibility problem that involves the compatibility of developmental goals staggered across developmental stages. With regard to the present condition of developmental psychology, however, the possibility of prognosticating intermediate and long-term consequences of developmental interventions seems to be rather limited. This holds true not only for the prediction of psychological consequents from psychological antecedents (see Kohlberg, LaCrosse, & Ricks, 1972), but all the more for the prediction of sociological, economic, and political consequences from developmental psychological data. Undoubtedly, there is a lack of valid theoretical models relevant to predictions of the latter type, which are of the utmost importance to educational and developmental policy. The development of such models evidently requires increased collaboration between developmental psychology and related human and social sciences.

It should be added at this point that the decision to intervene requires both a predictive assessment of possible intervention outcomes and a valuation of the anticipated outcomes. Such valuations are usually made on the basis of some tacitly assumed "model of optimal development." At present, the social and human sciences in general and developmental psychology in particular have little to contribute to the explication and critical evaluation of such tacit normative assumptions. Attempts to develop a system of social indicators that could give more precise meanings to such broad and pervasive aims as "quality of life" and "happiness" have not yet moved beyond the early stages (cf. Bauer, 1966; Sheldon & Freeman, 1970). In the decades to come, it will be one of developmental psychology's most challenging and exacting tasks to contribute to the construction and critique of scientifically founded models of optimal human development, which alone can yield criteria for the comprehensive planning and evaluation of developmental intervention (cf. Brandtstädter, 1977; Brandtstädter & Schneewind, 1977).

III. Interfaces between Theory and Technology

It is commonly said that developmental theories are "applied" in intervention. Behind this use of the word often stands the assumption that technologies can be derived from theories or are implied by them. This stereotype obstructs our perspective on a number of problems that intervene in the process of bringing theory into action. The following sections of this chapter will discuss this position and its inherent weaknesses and then consider what I believe is a more adequate model of the theory-technology relationship.

A. The Axiomatic–Deductive Technology Model and Its Limitations

The assumption that a deductive argument leads from theory to technology is based on a supposed structural analogy between technological arguments and scientific explanations (see the traditional explication of Hempel & Oppenheim, 1948). To quote Popper (1972), "from a logical point of view, both the derivation of predictions and the technical application of scientific theories may be regarded as mere inversions of the basic scheme of scientific explanation [p. 353]." Table 1.1 gives a schematic representation of the assumed analogies among technical application of scientific theory, prediction, and explanation (cf. Prim & Tilman, 1975).

In a footnote that has evidently received less attention than the previously quoted statement, Popper added a reservation: "This analysis should not be interpreted as implying that the technologist or the engineer is concerned only with '*applying*' theories which are supplied by the pure scientist. On the contrary, the technologist and the engineer are constantly faced with *problems to be solved* [1972, p. 353; emphasis in the original]." Let us consider these problems more closely in relation to the model represented in Table 1.1.

The *axiomatic–deductive technology model* shown in the table presupposes that technological objectives are formulated in theoretical language. This is usually not the case, especially in the field of developmental intervention, frequently, the developmental objectives prescribed or pro-

Table 1.1

Assumed Structural Analogies among Explanation, Prediction,
and Technology—Axiomatic-Deductive Technology Model

Model elements	Explanation	Prediction	Technology
Antecedents	To find	Given	To find (as means)
Laws	To find	Given	To find
Consequents	Given (as "explanandum")	To find (as "projectandum")	Given (as "realisandum")

posed by educators or politicians must first be theoretically explicated, which is often a difficult if not unsolvable task. Certainly, it would be very restrictive to exclude all developmental objectives from consideration for which precise theoretical explications were not available. If such a restriction existed, a number of very nonspecific (but not meaningless) target concepts of optimal development—such as "happiness," "freedom," and "autonomy"—would have to be rejected. Presumably, satisfactory solutions to the explication problem can be reached only through the interchange of scientific and extrascientific concepts and theories, as well as through ordinary language analyses.

A further objection to the axiomatic–deductive technology model results from the fact that there are many successful technologies, the effectiveness of which cannot be scientifically explained. Indeed, phenomenological low-level hypotheses—which treat the system as "black box" and state only input–output contingencies, without any reference to causal mechanisms—often suffice to control the behavior of systems efficiently (cf. Bunge, 1967). Without a doubt, there were successful educators long before developmental psychology established itself as a science. Historical analyses show that only loose interrelationships exist between developments in pure science and developments in technology (e.g., see Ayres, 1968). Of course, it should not be overlooked that with only low-level technological knowledge, the applicability range of a technology cannot be sharply defined. Often, this results in overgeneralizations with corresponding failures or in ritual fixations of functionally irrelevant elements of the technological action pattern (for example, consider the therapeutic ceremony of orthodox psychoanalysis). Moreover, the flexible adaptation of technical action patterns to changing situational demands is reduced. (It should be noted, with reference to transfer in problem solving, that the importance of understanding basic solution principles was already pointed out by Judd in 1908.) Our formerly successful educator may suddenly be helpless if, instead of children, he faces a target group of adults. Abortive attempts at applying a hitherto successful technology generally lead to an increased interest in gaining deeper theoretical insights into the conditions of success; thus, the programmatic challenges of "life-long learning" and "recurrent education" may also stimulate basic research in learning and developmental psychology. All of this, however, does not alter the fact that a deeper understanding of causal mechanisms is neither necessary nor sufficient for successful technical action; in the domain of technology, phenomenological low-level theories may even be preferred to deeper and more sophisticated ones because of their greater operational simplicity.

A third major objection to the axiomatic–deductive technology model is that technological problems are only partially solved by the derivation of a statement about relevant antecedent conditions in achieving a desired effect. The important question about how these antecedent conditions are to be realized remains unanswered. For example, labeling theory suggests that the social isolation of mongoloid children may be caused by certain "deviant" features of external appearance (eyelid folds, receding chin, etc.). However, labeling theory says nothing about how these physiognomic attributes can be changed; at this point, the psychological problem changes into a surgical one. Problem shifts like this one are quite typical in the implementation of intervention programs, especially in preventive intervention. It is evident from these arguments that a theory is not a technological problem solving device; at best, theories provide the input for action systems whose output produces the desired developmental effects. Developmental psychologists have to get accustomed to the idea that the competence to explain developmental processes does not imply the competence to control them, and they must recognize that in many cases the last technological problem is solvable only in cooperation with other disciplines.

Finally, special ethical and deontological issues are involved in the transition from theory to action. The system of premises underlying technical decisions is not to be considered as purely descriptive, as is the case with explanations and predictions, but as a mixed, normative–descriptive system that combines hypothetical (theoretical) assumptions and value judgments (see also the psychological expectancy value models of decision behavior; e.g., Mitchell & Biglan, 1971). This poses a question about the validity of *practical conclusions* based on premises systems including normative components. With regard to the acceptability of normative premises, this question involves an ethical evaluation; with regard to the formal validity of practical conclusions, it touches upon the logic of norms (e.g., see Von Wright, 1963). Thus, developmental interventions are only partially determined by theoretical assumptions and can only be partially evaluated on theoretical grounds.

All of these characteristic problems involved in the transition from theory to technological action are not represented by the axiomatic–deductive technology model; therefore, this model may be considered deficient or at least limited in scope.

B. An Alternative to the Axiomatic–Deductive Technology Model

Starting in part from similar considerations, Bunge (1967) has suggested a conception of technology that gives a more differentiated picture of the interfaces between theory and technology than the axiomatic–deductive model. It will be discussed here briefly.

At the core of Bunge's technology model are the concepts *nomopragmatic statement* and *rule*. Nomopragmatic statements are *if–then* statements that correspond structurally to nomological statements; however, the *if* component of a nomopragmatic statement is distinctive because it does not refer to an event but to an action. According to Bunge, the following two technical rules correspond to a nomopragmatic statement of the $A \rightarrow B$ type: (*a*) *B* per *A* (colloquially phrased, "*B* through *A*" or "To the end *B* use the means *A*") and (*b*)–*B* per–*A* ("To prevent *B* do not do *A*").

Obviously, technical rules do not provide all of the information relevant to concrete action. For example, consider the technical rule "To increase the probability of occurrence for reaction *x*, reinforce *x*." Which stimuli should be selected as reinforcers in the concrete case? Bunge explicitly deals with this implementation or specification problem in distinguishing between *substantive* and *operative* technologies. Whereas substantive technologies yield general rules for producing some desired effect, operative technologies supply decision aids for the effective implementation of substantive–technological rules in the concrete action context. Thus, the aforementioned technical rule can count as an element of a substantive technology of behavior modification, whereas specific implementation strategies (interviews and observational studies to identify effective reinforcers for specific persons and situations, principles of contingency management etc.; cf. the behavior therapy stratagems described by Blackham & Silberman, 1975) form part of the corresponding operative technology of behavior modification.

The relationships among nomological statements, nomopragmatic statements, and technical rules are explicitly conceived by Bunge not as logical but as pragmatical relationships. This is a radical departure from the axiomatic–deductive model. Bunge (1967) specifies the relations with the following pragmatic metarule: "If '$A \rightarrow B$' is a law formula, try the rules '*B* per *A*' or '$-B$ per $-A$' [p. 135]." This rule suggests the tentative acceptance of technical rules in the light of accepted law formulas, but it does not obligate us to adopt them. In this context, Bunge points out that law formulas and, correspondingly, technical rules are corrigible; furthermore, he reminds us of the fact that theories usually refer to more or less idealized models of concrete systems, so that the rules may be inefficient in the concrete case. According to Bunge, technical rules do not have truth values but effectiveness values (e.g., effective, ineffective, and indeterminate). Since the effectiveness of a rule may be ruined (e.g., as a result of operative–technological faults), the truth of a law formula does not warrant the effectiveness of the rule based on it; even less can we infer the truth of a law formula from the effectiveness of the rule. This argument warns us not to confound the phases of theory testing and intervention practice and not to overestimate the theoretical contribution of the latter.

IV. Intervention Practice as a Touchstone of Developmental Psychological Theory?

It is often asserted that if intervention fails to produce the theoretically predicted results, then the pertinent theory should be rejected or at least revised. Verbally, at least, the majority of psychologists seems to adhere to this "falsificationist" position. There are, of course, more or less naive and sophisticated variants of this view. Naive falsificationists assert that theories should always be rejected in the light of application failures. They do not bother about the question of why intervention has failed, and they overlook the fact that there is more than just one possible answer to this question. More sophisticated advocates of this position claim that only data gathered within carefully controlled research designs can provide a stringent test of a theoretical hypothesis. Unfortunately, this methodological reservation opens the door to dodging the falsificationist ideal by habitually attributing practical failures to some uncontrolled external disturbance, methodological deficiency, etc. This defensive attitude seems to be particularly preferred when one's own theory is at stake.

The previous reflections have already highlighted some problems inherent in the falsificationist position by demonstrating that no logical tracks lead from theory to practice and back again. And, in addition, that, generally, one does not "apply" merely single theoretical hypotheses but rather a heterogeneous cluster of theoretical, substantive–technological and operative–technological assumptions. This seriously complicates inferences about the quality of single elements within this cluster. Thus, a naive falsificationist position is hardly tenable. However, if even within carefully controlled "true experiments" we cannot claim to have achieved a perfect internal validity in the sense of having excluded all possible alternative interpretations to observed interventional effects (cf. Gadenne, 1976), then the sophisticated version of the falsificationist position would also seem to lack an easy defense. Indeed, the program of "methodological falsificationism" is no longer unanimously accepted within the philosophy of science. Let us first discuss these developments and their implications with regard to the question of whether theories are empirically testable.

A. The "Falsification Crisis"

Popper (1935) has shown that there can be no conclusive empirical verification of theories because inductive generalizations from even a great number of favorable instances cannot be logically justified. For inductive verification, he substituted the program of methodological falsificationism. According to this conception, knowledge progresses in the interplay between daring theoretical conjectures and relentless refutations. This received methodological conception has come under serious attack:

1. As Kuhn (1967) has shown, there is ample evidence from the history of science that theories are not instantaneously abandoned in the light of unfavorable evidence or anomalies; more important, in retrospect this tenacity often proved to be fruitful and justified. Only when anomalies (or failure-induced frustrations) abound, can a scientific revolution replace the old theoretical system with a new one. This critical point, however, cannot be determined methodologically. According to Kuhn (1970), scientific revolutions and paradigm shifts do not conform to a logic of research; rather, they have to be explained psychologically.

2. Empirical as well as systematical analyses have shown that observations and measurements always involve theoretical or hypothetical components (see Lenk, 1975; Suppe, 1974; and any textbook about the psychology of perception). The "hard fact" ideology founders because any observation presupposes the implicit or explicit acceptance of certain "interpretative" theories or hypotheses (theoretical assumptions about measurement, object–indicator hypotheses, assumptions concerning the functioning of observation tools, etc.). These interpretative assumptions form a protective belt around the structural core of the theory, against which falsification assaults can be deflected (cf. the concept of *negative heuristics,* Lakatos, 1970). Thus, "It is not that we propose a theory and Nature may shout NO, rather, we propose a maze of theories, and Nature may shout INCONSISTENT [Lakatos, 1970, p. 130]." Popper, of course, was aware of the fact that observations are impregnated with theories, but he perhaps underrated the dangers that this fact brings about for a falsificationist position.

3. The received view of theories as systems of statements (*statement view*) has been opposed by a *nonstatement view* (NSV) (see Sneed, 1971). According to the NSV, theories can be differentiated into (*a*) a nonsemantical, mathematical structural core and (*b*) an extension of the structural core based on special laws, which entails the intended applications of the structural core. Only the core extension can be subjected to empirical tests. So far, the NSV has been strictly explicated only for mature physical theories (see Stegmüller, 1973; for an interesting attempt to apply the NSV to psychological research programs, see Herrmann, 1976).

We cannot digress further into the historical and methodological backgrounds of the falsification crisis. Let us instead consider some everyday examples from psychology that highlight some facets of the falsification problem.

1. A psychoanalyst hypothesizes that his client unconsciously wishes to kill his father. When his client opposes this interpretation, the psychoanalyst does not consider his hypothesis as refuted but tries to explain the opposition as resistance.

2. A behavior therapist attempts to reinforce a child's behavior with candy rewards. When this does not work, he by no means despairs of his learning theory but tries again, using a toy car as a reinforcer.

3. A psychologist who adheres to a theory of instinctive aggression is confronted with the experimental finding that children under certain conditions imitate aggressive behaviors of adult models. He maintains that the children's behavior should not be interpreted as aggression but simply as play.

4. Two psychologists discuss the significance of genetic versus environmental factors in cognitive development. One points to the correlation between socioeconomic variables and intelligence variables as favoring an environmentalist position. The other sketches a causal model that explains these correlations as spurious.

5. An experimental psychologist tries to test the assumption that fluid intelligence functions cannot be changed by training. Using a spatial ability test as a measure of fluid functioning, he succeeds in demonstrating that spatial test performance can be significantly improved by a specially designed training program. It is argued that the training procedure might have affected only performance factors that are extraneous to ability.

6. A life-span developmental psychologist maintains that, contrary to the biological decrement model, there is no significant age decline of intellectual competence. He suggests that findings from cross-sectional studies indicating intellectual decline might be explained by

cohort effects. Faced with similar findings from longitudinal studies, he formulates the hypothesis that the observed decrements might be accounted for by age-related changes in test-taking attitudes.

This list of examples, which could easily be extended, shows that it is a common practice in psychology to defend hypotheses and theories against unfavorable evidence and that the most diversified strategies (and tricks) are used in this context. However, not all strategies of defense appear to be equally admissible and justified.

The most common strategy for defending a hypothesis is to explain away unfavorable evidence by introducing some ad hoc hypothesis. There is nothing basically wrong about this strategy, as long as the ad hoc hypothesis can be subjected to independent tests (cf. Bunge, 1967). That is, the claim that the observed anomalies might be caused by instrument errors or other interfering factors has to be supported by evidence independent of the observed anomalies (cf. the concept of orthogonal operations in Garner, Hake, & Eriksen, 1956). In Example 1, it is questionable whether this criterion is met, for it is difficult to see how the hypothesis of resistance could be tested without drawing on precisely the same evidence that the hypothesis tries to explain. In contrast, in Examples 5 and 6 the ad hoc hypotheses are independently testable. Such independently testable defense arguments may have a positive heuristic function; as is well known, an observed anomaly in the perihelion of the planet Uranus did not lead to a rejection of gravitational theory but rather to the discovery of Pluto. Likewise, the attempt to defend the perhaps initially intuitive assumption of a nondecrement model of intelligence development has led to valuable findings concerning sensory and intellectual functioning in the elderly (e.g., see Baltes, Cornelius, & Nesselroade, 1978; Birren & Schaie, 1977). Certainly, the case is not yet decided; the decrement model can in turn be defended against unfavorable evidence (e.g., by the ad hoc assumption of biased sampling or design weaknesses or by specifying the model's validity range). For an interesting discussion pertinent to this point, see the Baltes–Schaie versus Horn–Donaldson controversy (Schaie, 1974; Baltes & Schaie, 1974; Horn & Donaldson, 1976; Baltes & Schaie, 1976; Horn & Donaldson, 1977; Schaie & Baltes, 1977). After all, the decision to retain or reject a theoretical conception ultimately does not depend on the number of nonassimilable anomalies; rather, "only a new theory with a radically new intellectual design drives the last nail into the coffin of the old theory [Stegmüller, 1973, p. 252]."

With regard to Example 2 above, it can further be shown that certain types of theoretical statements are immune to falsification from the start, at least as long as they are not combined with additional interpretative assumptions. Thus, the theoretical statement "For all r: if r is a reaction, and r is reinforced, then the probability of occurrence of r is increased" cannot be falsified as long as the term *reinforcer* is applied only to classes of stimuli that function in the theoretically prescribed manner. Therefore, it is misleading to speak of the "application" of learning theory in intervention: theoretical statements of the aforementioned type are indeed applied only in connection with *idiographic reinforcement hypotheses* (cf. Westmeyer, 1976), which may be formulated by drawing on additional assumptions from motivational or developmental psychology or on the basis of experimental or observational evidence. This is in some sense analogous to the previously mentioned structural core expansion referred to by proponents of the nonstatement view (see Herrmann, 1976). Under such circumstances, inefficient application attempts such as the one described in Example 2 blame the user rather than the theory. In a similar vein, attempts to refute the assumption that fluid intellectual capacity cannot be changed by training procedures (see Example 5) will turn out to be futile if this assumption is an essential element of the rules for identifying fluid performances. Because of semantical weaknesses in the theory of "fluid" and "crystallized" intelligence (Cattell, 1971; Horn, 1966, 1976), we are not quite sure about this point, but there are reasons to assume that the language game inherent in this theory prohibits the application of the term *fluid* to performance variables that are sensitive to training or dependent on previous learning. In this case, experiments of the type mentioned in Example 5 (for more concrete examples, see Plemons, Willis, & Baltes, 1978; Roether, Galow, Göbner, Henkel, Köpcke, & Köpcke, 1977) at best may suggest a revision of certain construct–indicator hypotheses that belong to the semantical part, but not to the structural core, of the pertinent theory.

Within the philosophy of science, the falsification crisis has lead to a reconsideration of the question of whether theories are testable. Bunge (1973) has suggested a well-balanced proposal to deal with this problem; he avoids the deleterious consequence of dropping the "testability" criterion at all but at the same time takes into account that there are different types of theories with different degrees of testability. He suggests that in evaluating scientific theories, one should consider not only *empirical testability* but also *conceptual testability* or testability "as to consistency with the bulk of antecedent knowledge [Bunge, 1973, p. 39]." Starting from this distinction, he develops the following taxonomy of theories:

1. *Specific theories* or *theoretical models* (Type I theories): Theories of this type have a clear-cut and narrow reference class (*species*); all of the basic symbols of the theory have factual content. Type I theories are conceptually as well as empirically testable. As examples, Bunge quotes particle mechanics or stochastic models of maze learning.

2. *Generic interpreted theories* (Type II theories): The basic symbols of these theories have a factual interpretation; the reference class is a *genus* with several *species*, each of which are representable by a Type I theory. A Type II theory is conceptually testable but by itself empirically untestable. However, if it is adjoined to a model object, it can be transformed into a Type I theory that is empirically testable. Bunge's examples include classical mechanics and synthetical evolution theory. Piaget's theory of the development of the object concept, theories of operant conditioning (without idiographic reinforcement hypotheses), and statistical models in genetic psychology could be considered as psychological examples. (Presumably, most psychological theories belong to this category.)

3. *Generic semi-interpreted theories* (Type III theories): Most symbols of these theories have no factual interpretation; the reference class is a whole *family* of *genera*. Theories of this type are only conceptually testable; however, they can eventually be interpreted through a Type II theory and thus become vicariously empirically testable. Information theory and game theory are mentioned as examples by Bunge. As developmental psychological examples, one could consider Piaget's general developmental theory with the core concepts of equilibrium, adaptation, assimilation, and accommodation or his theory of groupings for classification and seriation operations. Mathematical change models (e.g., Markov chain models) would be another example in developmental psychology.

According to Bunge (1973), only conceptual testability is necessary for a theory to qualify as scientific. This conclusion is supported by the existence of theories that are generally "stuff free," and therefore empirically untestable, but nevertheless have proven to be of tremendous heuristic value (e.g., information theory and general systems theory). Not included in the taxonomy are metaphysical assumptions, which are neither conceptually nor empirically testable, but which nevertheless may be of heuristic value for the construction of theories (in the stricter sense of the aforementioned taxonomy) and therefore should not be generally excluded from science. To this category belong prototheoretical development conceptions as discussed by Reese and Overton (1970) (e.g., organismic, mechanistic, and dialectical views of development). In the various hot debates about the adequacy of these views, developmental psychologists often overlook the fact that an evaluation of such metaphysical conceptions makes sense only with reference to the theoretical constructions that are inspired by them.

B. Facets and Functions of Intervention Research

The first and basic aim of intervention is certainly the solution (alleviation, prevention) of developmental problems. It has been argued, however, that the application of knowledge to solve practical problems is but one function of intervention work and that we should not overlook the knowledge-generation potential of intervention (e.g., Baltes & Willis, 1977; Brandtstädter, Fischer, Kluwe, Lohmann, & Wiedl, 1974). Indeed, interventions can and should, as far as possible, be conceptualized and designed as experiments (Campbell, 1969); that is, intervention programs should be combined with evaluation research. With regard to the knowledge-generating function of intervention, however, the preceding considerations lead me to add some qualifying remarks.

In opposition to some "action researchers," I think that the phases of theory construction, theory testing, and practical intervention should not be confounded, even though they are interdependent. For ethical as well as methodological reasons, the field of developmental intervention work is not a very suitable place for testing theories. First, intervention work should be based on the best available knowledge; to design large-scale intervention programs on the basis of theoretical and technological assumptions that are not yet sufficiently corroborated through previous research is to play a questionable game of chance. Theories and technologies should be tested in low-risk situations before they are "applied" in high-risk environments. Furthermore, we should notice that the aforementioned basic difficulties of testing theoretical hypotheses become aggravated when we move from *basic* to *applied* research contexts. It is known that the possibilities of utilizing "truly experimental" randomized control group designs in applied intervention and evaluation research are limited for practical, methodological, and ethical reasons (cf. Boruch, 1974); instead, preexperimental and quasi-experimental designs (in the sense of Campbell & Stanley, 1963) prevail. It should be added, however, that the basic difficulties in drawing theoretical conclusions from intervention studies are not intrinsically related to questions of experimental design. More frequently, these difficulties arise from the fact that the treatments in practical intervention are usually highly complex. Since the planning and implementation of intervention programs involve not only theoretical hypotheses but also a variety of additional substantive–technological and operative–technological assumptions (see previous discussion), the results observed in evaluation research generally cannot be related to theoretical hypotheses in a stringent and clear-cut way. In applied intervention research, action programs, not theories, are put to test. To quote again from Bunge (1967): "The doctrine that practice is the touchstone of theories relies on a misunderstanding of both practice and theory: on a confusion between practice and experiment, and on an associated confusion between rule and theory. The question 'does it work?', pertinent as it is with regard to things and rules, is impertinent in respect of theories [p. 129]."

Much confusion about the functions of intervention research could be avoided by differentiating among different types of intervention-related research activities; these activities are interrelated, but nonetheless they should not be confounded conceptually and practically. More specifically, it is important to distinguish among:

1. *Basic research,* which is primarily directed toward the construction and testing of theories that may be relevant to developmental intervention. Basically, this category of intervention-related research entails all developmental psychological research activities.

2. *Technology research,* which is oriented toward the development of intervention techniques and strategies and yields substantive-technological as well as operative-technological rules relevant to the solution (alleviation, prevention) of developmental problems. Technology research is only partially dependent on basic research.

3. *Implementation research,* which basically assesses the system-specific conditions and constraints relevant to the successful use of intervention techniques and strategies developed within technology research. Implementation research is intimately tied to the planning of concrete action programs and is characterized by an idiographical–diagnostical approach (which resembles what has been called *context evaluation* by Stufflebeam, 1969).

4. *Evaluation research,* which provides feedback information about the functioning (*formative evaluation, process evaluation*) and about the effects and side effects (*summative evaluation, product evaluation*) of intervention programs in action. If a program, which has been designed by drawing on information from the aforementioned research areas, turns out (or seems) to be ineffective, this finding may trigger troubleshooting designed to locate the critical components of the program or the critical elements in the cluster of hypotheses on which the program has been based. An advisable sequential strategy of troubleshooting would be to first reexamine the evaluative procedures themselves, then restudy the procedures used and data gathered in implementation research, and finally critically reexamine the results of previous technology research. Only if a revision or replication of these antecedent research phases yields no information relevant to explaining the observed evaluation results and to redesigning the program, is one justified in doubting the basic theoretical assumptions. Thus, there are strong safeguards that screen off theories from unfavorable evidence gathered in evaluation research.

At this point, some final remarks concerning the psychology of intervention research may be added. The aforementioned historical analyses have shown that psychological (motivational, ideological, political) factors already play an important part in basic research and theorizing (for psychological examples, see Pastore, 1949; Sherwood & Nataupsky, 1968; see also Brandtstädter & Reinert, 1973). It can be supposed that such factors are even more influential in the more application-oriented phases of intervention research. Especially in evaluation research, the conclusions that are drawn from evaluative findings often seem to be a function of personal involvement and of political and ideological predilections. For example, it has been observed that in explaining observed intervention failures, external evaluators or critics prefer to focus on presumed theoretical flaws, whereas internal evaluators (i.e., evaluators involved in program planning and implementation) prefer to attribute failures to factors that lie outside of their responsibility (e.g., insufficient financial funding or lack of time; cf. McDill, McDill, & Sprehe, 1972). From the previous discussion, we can infer that the main reason for the intrusion of psychological (political, ideological, motivational) factors into the process of data interpretation is that data are open to multiple interpretations. The larger the number of possible alternative interpretations for observed intervention effects, the more likely it is that the choice of a particular interpretation alternative will assume the character of a motivated decision. As we have seen, the interpretative ambiguity of data gathered in evaluation research is especially high. Of course, data may be more or less ambiguous, depending partly on the research design used. For example, correlational data sets are particularly susceptible to ideologically biased interpretations since they conform to various causal models. But even data gathered within "true" experimental designs may be open to widely different interpretations (cf. Gadenne, 1976). It should be parenthetically noted that there is not only a falsification crisis but also a crisis of significance testing (cf. Cronbach, 1975; Lykken, 1968). Since the validity of data interpretations depends less on the number than on the plausibility of possible alternative interpretations, projective distortions and arbitrariness in data interpretation can finally be obviated only by potent theoretical arguments. However, there is presumably no methodology that completely rules out psychological (ideological, political, motivational) factors in the interpretation of research data. If this is the case, intervention researchers should be that much more sensitized to motivational and ideological biases. Otherwise, we run the risk that developmental research, theory, and intervention drift toward paths that diverge from the objective of optimizing human development across the life span.

ACKNOWLEDGMENT

I am grateful to Renate Benkert for her valuable help in the English translation of this chapter.

REFERENCES

Ayres, R. V. *Technological forecasting and long-range planning*. New York: McGraw-Hill, 1968.

Baltes, P. B., Cornelius, S. W., & Nesselroade, J. R. Cohort effects in developmental psychology. In J. R. Nesselroade & P. B. Baltes (Eds.), *Longitudinal research in the behavioral sciences: Design and analysis*. New York: Academic Press, 1978.

Baltes, P. B., & Schaie, K. W. Aging and IQ: The myth of the twilight years. *Psychology Today*, 1974, *40*, 35–38.

Baltes, P. B., & Schaie, K. W. On the plasticity of intelligence in adulthood and old age: Where Horn and Donaldson fail. *American Psychologist*, 1976, *31*, 720–725.

Baltes, P. B., & Willis, S. L. Toward psychological theories of aging and development. In J. E. Birren & K. W. Schaie (Eds.), *Handbook of the psychology of aging*. New York: Van Nostrand Reinhold, 1977.

Barron, F. *Creative person and creative process*. New York: Holt, Rinehart & Winston, 1969.

Bauer, R. A. (Ed.). *Social indicators*. Cambridge, Mass.: M.I.T. Press, 1966.

Birren, J. E., & Schaie, K. W. (Eds.). *Handbook of the psychology of aging*. New York: Van Nostrand Reinhold, 1977.

Blackham, G. J., & Silberman, A. *Modification of child and adolescent behavior*. Belmont, Calif.: Wadsworth, 1975.

Bloom, B. S. *Stability and change in human characteristics*. New York: Wiley, 1964.

Böhret, C. *Grundriß der Planungspraxis*. Opladen: Westdeutscher Verlag, 1975.

Boruch, R. F. Contentions about randomized experiments for evaluating social programs. In H. W. Riecken & R. F. Boruch (Eds.), *Proceedings of the 1974 SSRC conference on social experiments*. Washington, D.C.: Science Technology and Policy Office, National Science Foundation, 1974.

Brandtstädter, J. Gedanken zu einem psychologischen Modell optimaler Entwicklung. In J. Schneider & M. Schneider-Düker (Eds.), *Interpretationen der Wirklichkeit. Ernst E. Boesch zum 60. Geburtstag*. Saarbrücken: ssip-Schriften, 1977.

Brandtstädter, J., & Montada, L. Normative Implikationen der Erziehungsstilforschung. In K. A. Schneewind & T. Herrmann (Eds.), *Theorien, Methoden und Anwendungen der Psychologie elterlichen Erziehungsverhaltens*. Göttingen: Hogrefe, 1979.

Brandtstädter, J., & Reinert, G. Wissenschaft als Gegenstand der Wissenschaft vom menschlichen Erleben und Verhalten: Überlegungen zur Konzeption einer Wissenschaftspsychologie. *Zeitschrift für Allgemeine Wissenschaftstheorie*, 1973, *4*, 368–379.

Brandtstädter, J., & Schneewind, K. A. Optimal human development: Some implications for psychology. *Human Development*, 1977, *20*, 48–64.

Brandtstädter, J., Fischer, M., Kluwe, R., Lohmann, J., Schneewind, K. A. & Wiedl, K. H. Entwurf eines heuristisch–taxonomischen Schemas zur Strukturierung von Zielbereichen pädagogisch–psychologischer Forschung und Lehre. *Zeitschrift für Entwicklungspsychologie und Pädagogische Psychologie*, 1974, *6*, 1–18.

Bunge, M. *Scientific research II: The search for truth*. Berlin: Springer, 1967.

Bunge, M. *Method, model and matter*. Boston: Reidel, 1973.

Campbell, D. T. Reforms as experiments. *American Psychologist*, 1969, *24*, 409–429.

Campbell, D. T., & Erlebacher, A. E. How regression artifacts in quasi-experimental evaluations can mistakenly make compensatory education look harmful. In J. Hellmuth (Ed.), *Compensatory education: A national debate* (Vol. 3). New York: Brunner & Mazel, 1970.

Campbell, D. T., & Stanley, J. C. Experimental and quasi-experimental designs in research on teaching. In N. L. Gage (Ed.), *Handbook of research on teaching*. Chicago: Rand McNally, 1963.

Cattell, R. B. *Abilities: Their structure, growth and action.* Boston: Houghton Mifflin, 1971.

Cronbach, L. J. Beyond the two disciplines of scientific psychology. *American Psychologist,* 1975, *30,* 116–127.

Cronbach, L. J., Gleser, G. C., Nanda, N., & Rajaratnam, N. *The dependability of behavioral measurements: Theory of generalizability for scores and profiles.* New York: Wiley, 1972.

Datan, N., & Ginsberg, L. H. (Eds.). *Life-span developmental psychology: Normative life crises.* New York: Academic Press, 1975.

Edwards, W., Guttentag, M., & Snapper, K. A decision–theoretic approach to evaluation research. In E. L. Struening & M. Guttentag (Eds.), *Handbook of evaluation research* (Vol. 1). London: Sage, 1975.

Ehrman, L., Omenn, G. S., & Caspari, E. (Eds.). *Genetics, environment, and behavior.* New York: Academic Press, 1972.

Finan, J. L. The system concept as a principle of methodological decision. In R. M. Gagné (Ed.), *Psychological principles in system development.* New York: Holt, Rienhart, & Winston, 1962.

Gadenne, V. *Die Gültigkeit psychologischer Untersuchungen.* Stuttgart: Kohlhammer, 1976.

Garner, W. R., Hake, H. W., & Eriksen, C. W. Operationism and the concept of perception. *Psychological Review,* 1956, *63,* 149–159.

Groeben, N., & Westmeyer, H. *Kriterien psychologischer Forschung.* München: Juventa, 1975.

Hempel, C. G., & Oppenheim, P. Studies in the logic of explanation. *Philosophy of Science,* 1948, *15,* 135–175.

Herrmann, T. *Die Psychologie und ihre Forschungsprogramme.* Göttingen: Hogrefe, 1976.

Horn, J. L. Integration of structural and developmental concepts in the theory of fluid and crystallized intelligence. In R. B. Cattell (Ed.), *Handbook of multivariate experimental psychology.* Chicago: Rand McNally, 1966.

Horn, J. L. Human abilities: A review of research and theory in the early 1970's. *Annual Review of Psychology,* 1976, *27,* 437–485.

Horn, J. L., & Donaldson, G. On the myth of intellectual decline in adulthood. *American Psychologist,* 1976, *31,* 701–719.

Horn, J. L., & Donaldson, G. Faith is not enough: A response to the Baltes–Schaie claim that intelligence does not wane. *American Psychologist,* 1977, *32,* 369–373.

Jensen, A. R. How much can we boost IQ and scholastic achievement? *Harvard Educational Review,* 1969, *39,* 1–123.

Judd, C. H. The relation of special training to general intelligence. *Educational Review,* 1908, *36,* 28–42.

Kohlberg, L., LaCrosse, J., & Ricks, D. The predictability of adult mental health from childhood behavior. In B. Wolman (Ed.), *Manual of child psychopathology.* New York: McGraw-Hill, 1972.

Kohlberg, L., & Mayer, R. Development as the aim of education. *Harvard Educational Review,* 1972, *42,* 449–496.

Kuhn, T. S. *The structure of scientific revolutions.* Chicago: University of Chicago Press, 1967.

Kuhn, T. S. Logic of discovery or psychology of research? In I. Lakatos & A. Musgrave (Eds.), *Citicism and the growth of knowledge.* London and New York: Cambridge University Press, 1970.

Lakatos, I. Falsification and the methodology of scientific research programmes. In I. Lakatos & A. Musgrave (Eds.), *Criticism and the growth of knowledge.* London and New York: Cambridge University Press, 1970.

Lenk, H. *Pragmatische Philosophie.* Hamburg: Hoffmann & Campe, 1975.

Lykken, D. T. Statistical significance in psychological research. *Psychological Bulletin,* 1968, *70,* 151–159.

McDill, E. L., McDill, M. S., & Sprehe, J. T. Evaluation in practice: Compensatory education. In P. H. Ross & W. Williams (Eds.), *Evaluating social programs: Theory, practice, and politics.* New York: Seminar Press, 1972.

Merz, F., & Stelzl, I. *Einführung in die Erbpsychologie.* Stuttgart: Kohlhammer, 1977.

Mitchell, T. R., & Biglan, A. Instrumentality theories: Current uses in psychology. *Psychological Bulletin,* 1971, *76,* 432–454.

Nardi, A. H. Person-perception research and the perception of life-span development. In P. B. Baltes & K. W. Schaie (Eds.), *Life-span developmental psychology: Personality and socialization.* New York: Academic Press, 1973.

Neugarten, B. L., Moore, J. W., & Lowe, J. C. Age norms, age constraints, and adult socialization. *American Journal of Sociology,* 1965, *70,* 710–717.

Pastore, N. *The nature–nurture controversy.* New York: Kings Crown Press, 1949.

Plemons, J. K., Willis, S. L., & Baltes, P. B. Modifiability of fluid intelligence in aging: A short-term longitudinal training approach. *Journal of Gerontology,* 1978, *33,* 224–231.

Popper, K. R. *Logik der Forschung.* Wien: J. Springer, 1935.

Popper, K. R. *Objective knowledge: An evolutionary approach.* Oxford: Oxford University Press, 1972.

Prim, R., & Tilman, H. *Grundlagen einer kritisch–rationalen Sozialwissenschaft.* Heidelberg: Quelle & Meier, 1975.

Rapp, F. Technische Handlungen und ihre Realisierungsmöglichkeiten. In H. Lenk (Ed.), *Handlungstheorien-interdisziplinär* (Vol. 4). München: Fink, 1977.

Reese, H. W., & Overton, W. F. Models of development and theories of development. In L. R. Goulet & P. B. Baltes (Eds.), *Life-span developmental psychology: Research and theory.* New York: Academic Press, 1970.

Roether, D., Galow, V., Göbner, B., Henkel, H., Köpcke, H., & Köpcke, K. F. Entwicklungspsychologische Aspekte der intellektuellen Lernfähigkeit im Erwachsenenalter. *Zeitschrift für Psychologie,* 1977, *185,* 128–148.

Schaie, K. W. Translations in gerontology—from lab to life: Intellectual functioning. *American Psychologist,* 1974, *29,* 802–807.

Schaie, K. W., & Baltes, P. B. Some faith helps to see the forest: A final comment on the Horn and Donaldson myth of the Baltes–Schaie position on adult intelligence. *American Psychologist,* 1977, *32,* 1118–1120.

Schur, E. M. *Radical nonintervention: Rethinking the delinquency problem.* Englewood Cliffs, N.J.: Prentice-Hall, 1973.

Sheldon, E. B., & Freeman, H. E. Notes on social indicators: Promise and potential. *Policy Science,* 1970, *1,* 97–111.

Sherwood, J. S., & Nataupsky, M. Predicting the conclusions of negro–white intelligence research from the biographical characteristics of the investigator. *Journal of Personality and Social Psychology,* 1968, *8,* 53–58.

Sneed, J. D. *The logical structure of mathematical physics.* Dordrecht: Reidel, 1971.

Stegmüller, W. *Probleme und Resultate der Wissenschaftstheorie und analytischen Philosophie* (Vol. II, 2). Berlin: Springer, 1973.

Stufflebeam, D. L. Evaluation as enlightenment for decision making. In W. H. Beatty (Ed.), *Improving educational assessment and an inventory of measures of affective behavior.* Washington, D.C.: National Education Association, 1969.

Suppe, F. The search for philosophic understanding of scientific theories. In F. Suppe (Ed.), *The structure of scientific theories.* Urbana: University of Illinois Press, 1974.

Tharp, R. G., & Wetzel, R. J. *Behavior modification in the natural environment*. New York: Academic Press, 1969.

Von Wright, G. H. *Norm and action: A logical enquiry*. London: Routledge & Kegan Paul, 1963.

Weikart, D. P. Relationship of curriculum, teaching and learning in preschool education. In J. Stanley (Ed.), *Preschool programs for the disadvantaged: Five experimental approaches to early childhood education*. Baltimore: Johns Hopkins University Press, 1972.

Westmeyer, H. Grundlagenprobleme psychologischer Diagnostik. In K. Pawlik (Ed.), *Diagnose der Diagnostik*. Stuttgart: Klett, 1976.

Zimiles, H. Has evaluation failed compensatory education? In J. Hellmuth (Ed.), *Compensatory education: A national debate* (Vol. 3). New York: Brunner & Mazel, 1970.

CHAPTER 2

Models, Methods, and Ethics of Intervention

HAYNE W. REESE
WEST VIRGINIA UNIVERSITY
MORGANTOWN, WEST VIRGINIA

WILLIS F. OVERTON
TEMPLE UNIVERSITY
PHILADELPHIA, PENNSYLVANIA

If the term *intervention* has one meaning in psychology, that meaning is not readily apparent. One indication of the multiplicity of meanings is the multiplicity of terms used to denote intervention, including correction, education, enrichment, prevention, rehabilitation, remediation, service delivery, stimulation, supplementation, therapy, training, and treatment. The terms are further multiplied by such adjectives as educational, medical, nutritional, and psychological; moreover, the last term is subdivided into such aspects as cognitive, intellectual, and social.

Intervention is clearly a complex area, but it is also an area with ill-defined boundaries and contents. Our purpose in this chapter is to try to clarify the nature of this area by analyzing its relation to "pure" science and by examining the models, goals, methods, and ethics of intervention—what it is, why it is done, how it is done, and whether it should be done.

I. Boundaries: Relation to "Pure" Science[1]

Precise definitions of the difference between basic or "pure" science and applied science have been suggested, but all have been challenged as either

[1] Much of the material in this section was presented by Willis F. Overton in a symposium at the meeting of the Society for Research in Child Development, Philadelphia, March 1973.

29

LIFE-SPAN DEVELOPMENTAL PSYCHOLOGY
Intervention

not clear-cut or not useful. Nevertheless, the belief that they differ persists, and questions have been raised about the relation between them. We shall confine our discussion to the relation between pure *theory* and applied *practice,* thereby avoiding some of the ambiguities of the larger basic–applied distinction.

There are four logically possible orientations to the relation between theory and practice: (*a*) theory is not functionally related to practice; (*b*) theory generates practice; (*c*) practice generates theory; (*d*) theory and practice interact reciprocally, each generating and generated by the other. The point of exploring these four possible orientations is not to settle any historical or contemporary arguments but to provide a framework within which rational discussion of intervention might proceed.

Before turning to the exploration of these orientations, it is important to understand the modern conception of the role of common sense experience in science. This conception is crucial because science and social programs are not necessarily related, even though common sense experience underlies science, and even though it is in the crucible of everyday experiences that social programs are generated. Virtually all contemporary philosophers of science agree that science is deeply rooted in common sense experience and represents a means of critically reflecting upon, specifying, elaborating, and explaining common sense (e.g., Pepper, 1942; Rychlak, 1968; Toulmin, 1963; Wartofsky, 1968). As Ernest Nagel (1967) has expressed it, "All scientific inquiry takes its departure from common sense belief and eventually supports its findings by falling back on common sense [p. 6]." Thus, the legitimate business of science is to be critical of common sense and to refine it in order to arrive at reflected knowledge. On this theme there is virtually universal agreement. However, once this goal has been set, it is obvious that there are multiple possible means for its realization. With regard to these means, we find ourselves in the realm of deep-rooted value commitments.

One position concerning the path from everyday experiences to reflected knowledge asserts that the initial step is the acceptance of certain basic concepts that are universally given or freely created. The acceptance of these basic concepts leads to their employment in the construction of theory and research methods, which are ultimately applied to the field of common sense experience. This, of course, is the idealist–rationalist philosophical approach. Perhaps its purest form is exhibited in Weimer's (1973) proposal that the Platonic approach to understanding the everyday phenomena of memory and language still provides the best available explanation of these phenomena.

A second conception of the pathway from common sense experience to reflected knowledge entails a realist–empiricist philosophical commitment rather than an idealist–rationalist one. As one pre-eminent representative of the approach has expressed it, this type of study begins with a "common sense exploration of the field [Skinner, 1950, p. 215]." It then proceeds by discovering antecedent variables that ostensibly control behavior. Refined knowledge ultimately consists of observed correlations between behavior and controlling stimulus events.

The point in examining these two different approaches to the relationship between common sense experience and reflected knowledge is to indicate that such philosophical commitments color the orientations that different individuals take toward the distinction between theory and practice. We are not asserting that all who hold to the view that theory generates practice are necessarily rationalists, nor that all who maintain that practice generates theory are necessarily radical empiricists. Rather, we are asserting that each philosophical commitment has an extended influence and that the orientation one selects concerning theory and practice is not a matter of superficial preferences, as some scientists have maintained (cf. Spiker, 1966). With these thoughts in mind, we now turn to the four possible orientations.

The first view, that theory is unrelated to practice, is traceable to the ancient Greek separation of the *head* and the *hands,* that is, the "separation of the functions of theoretical explanation and practical know-how [Wartofsky, 1968, pp. 26–27]." Only the upper or leisure class of society could afford the luxury of knowledge for its own sake; therefore, the separation of theoretical and practical knowledge became a sign of privilege (Wartofsky, 1968).

An example of this position can be found by comparing the work of the Babylonians and the Ionians in the field of astronomy. The Babylonians were masters at the practical matter of calculating the date and time of various astronomical events. However, they totally lacked any theoretical system to explain these events. In contrast, the Ionians had a rich theoretical system of interpretation and speculations that involved virtually no predictions (Toulmin, 1963). The unproductiveness of this extreme separation of theory from practice (and vice versa) is suggested by the fact that neither of these cultures produced a viable science (Kaplan, 1961). The contemporary manifestation of this early approach can be seen in all distinctions between pure science and applied science; current distinctions, however, usually reflect one of the other orientations instead of absolute separation. Perhaps the last of the "great men" in psychology who explicitly took a position favoring the absolute separation of theory from practice was Titchener, who had little sympathy for both application specifically and common sense experience generally (Heidbreder, 1933).

The second view, that theory generates practice, has a certain rationalist flavor to it, as already noted. One example of this orientation in the natural sciences is the "new" world of quantum mechanics and relativity created by theorists such as Planck, Bohr, and Einstein. (However, we have some concern that, upon a deeper analysis, these scientists may be better examples of the fourth position, which will be described later.) These were people who, sensing difficulties in their contemporary intuitive Newtonian world, freely created a world that *might be* and only later discovered it matched a world that *is* (Pylyshyn, 1972). Some 40 years after Einstein's creation of the special relativity theory, its application was observed in the cities of Hiroshima and Nagasaki (Clark, 1971).

In the field of linguistics and psychology, the most explicit rationalists of our time are Chomsky and some of his followers in the psycholinguistic movement (Pylyshyn, 1972; Weimer, 1973). Here we see a situation in which theory seems to be developing most productively, yet little application has emerged so far. It should be noted in passing that this lack of application is not entirely due to Chomsky's nativist position regarding language structure, for although such structures are considered to be given, their activation in the context of language experience admits the possibility of applications. Clearly, theory is here viewed as primary, and although practice is not disvalued (as it often is with explicit separation of realms) it is left for a later time and possibly other hands. This situation highlights two problems involving the view that theory generates practice. First, such a view has a tendency to fall prey to the impulse to generate greater and greater elaborations of smaller and smaller issues. Functionally, this orientation may ultimately dissolve itself into a new separation of head and hands. The second problem is that the all but exclusive focus on theory and basic research frequently leaves application to others who are not as prepared for the difficult job of translating theory into practice. Among the many unfortunate effects of this problem is an ultimate negative reflection on the theory; people fail to see that it is the translation that is defective and instead attribute failures to the theory.

Before leaving the view that theory generates practice, let us consider the orientation called *general behavior theory,* or the *learning theory viewpoint,* or, more specifically, the *Hull–Spence tradition.* This orientation is certainly characterized by a bent toward theory and basic research over practice, yet the label *rationalist* is as certainly inappropriate. Perhaps this group constitutes the exception. However, it is more plausible that this group illustrates the difference between entailment and preference. The rationalist orientation entails the view that theory generates practice; the Hull–Spence orientation merely reflects a preference for problems of theoretical import over problems of practical import. In the Hull–Spence orientation, as in that of Skinner, theory originates in experience—the third view to be considered.

In considering the third possible view—that practice generates theory—we need not leave psychology to find examples. This orientation is well represented by the perspective that has variously been described as the *experimental analysis of behavior, functional analysis of behavior, operant analysis, applied behavior analysis,* or *behavior modification.* The approach is based on Skinner's work, which has called for the establishment of a technology of behavior (Skinner, 1971). In contrast to the second approach, which maintains that control follows from prediction, the third approach asserts that control leads to prediction. As mentioned earlier, the basic stance taken by proponents of the latter view is that through the application of principles of reinforcement, we will ultimately arrive at laws that will stand forth as observed correlations. Although the operant approach is the best contemporary example of this view, it should be noted that Watson also expected the work of psychology to proceed along the lines of application (Heidbreder, 1933).

The danger that this orientation entails is the reverse of that of the preceding orientation. That is, the danger of the second orientation (theory generates practice) is that reflected knowledge may not reach back to common sense experience, and the danger of the third orientation is that common sense experience may never reach forward to reflected knowledge. According to Deitz (1978), the latter danger is real: "The field seems to be shifting from *applied* behavior analysis to *applying* behavior analysis [p. 807]." His point is that the technology being applied does not yet have a sufficiently well-established knowledge base; moreover, because of this shift in purpose, the necessary knowledge base will not be acquired. (See also Birnbrauer, 1979; Hayes, Rincover, & Solnick, 1979.)

The fourth possible orientation asserts that there are *reciprocal interactions* constantly occurring between theory and practice. The results of these interactions may be felt over various time spans from the immediate to the long-range. This orientation must be clearly differentiated from the preceding two, for it is not a simple sum of them. To clarify this contrast, we will again examine the possible paths between common sense experience and reflected knowledge. On the one hand, the rationalist maintains that knowledge begins with given concepts or theory and proceeds to a critical view of common sense or application. On the other hand, the radical empiricist asserts that knowledge begins with common sense experience or application and proceeds to concepts or theory. However, both the rationalist and the empiricist imply a linear chain or linear causal sequence. The fourth orientation rejects this linear sequence and substitutes a philosophical commitment much closer to the principles described by Kant and Hegel. Kant proposed that all knowledge is based on experience and that this experience is of two types: experience of the basic given categories of mind and experience of the senses. Hegel carried this proposition a step further by proposing a developmental dimension or dialectic in which there is a constant struggle or interaction between components. Such interactions cannot be decomposed into unidirectional influences or into circular chains of a turn-by-turn linear type (Baltes & Reese, 1977). New levels are reached on the basis of these interactions, and, in turn, they lead to new interactions. Thus, each stage of reflected knowledge is taken to be the product of a dialectic between mind and common sense experience.

In terms of our primary focus, we might borrow from Kant's famous aphorism and say that the banner slogan of this fourth position is the assertion that *theory without application is empty, and application without theory is blind.* Using an analogy, we might also say that science, in its development, proceeds like the human organism: There are continual assimilations and accommodations within the theory–practice matrix. The clearest modern statement of this orientation was Mao Tse-tung's, and the clearest example of implementation was in the People's Republic of China after the Cultural Revolution of 1966–1969 (Reese, 1978).

The concept of *interaction* is central to understanding this alternative, but *interaction* varies widely in meaning from group to group (Overton & Reese, 1973). In the present context, it retains its dictionary meaning of *reciprocal action;* that is, theory and practice act upon each other. The term *reciprocal interaction* has been introduced—a bit redundantly—to emphasize that the focus of this orientation stays on the interaction as a unit and not on one of the part processes.

II. The Nature of Intervention

A classification of interventions as *primary, secondary,* and *tertiary prevention* was introduced by Caplan in 1964, and has now become so commonplace that discussions of it can reasonably omit citing Caplan as a reference (as in Clarizio & McCoy, 1976, pp. 515–516). Primary prevention is designed to prevent the development of some disorder; secondary prevention involves treatment of the disorder to correct it, cure it, or arrest its further development; and tertiary prevention involves rehabilitation to help the affected person adjust to the disorder. Enrichment programs for at-risk infants are intended to be preventive; Head Start was intended to be corrective; and programs in some prisons are intended to be rehabilitative.

Baltes and Danish (Chapter 3 of this volume) use the terms *enrichment* and *optimization* to refer to rehabilitation or tertiary prevention, but Horowitz and Paden (1973) used the term *enrichment* as a substitute for primary prevention. This flexibility of characterization illustrates the main problem with Caplan's system: It refers to the goals of intervention, not to models, methods, or morals of intervention. Baltes and Danish and Horowitz and Paden were referring to methods, but, as noted by Baltes and Danish, models influence choice of methods, and therefore model issues precede methodological issues.

A. Models

Government interventions seem to work in a fragmented way. For example, at the same time that the United States Department of Health, Education and Welfare was scheduled to spend $30 million on an antismoking campaign in 1978, the United States Department of Agriculture planned to spend some $600 million subsidizing the growing of tobacco. Similarly, legislation relevant to the elderly has been fragmented with respect to the age period and problem addressed; it also has been politically situational and crisis oriented (Kerschner & Hirschfield, 1975). In short, the approach has been piecemeal and pragmatic. In these respects, legislators have been like practitioners. Many observers have noted that practitioners tend to deal with single aspects of development, such as the cognitive or intellectual (Brandtstädter, Chapter 1 of this volume; McCluskey & Arco, in press), and Brandtstädter argues that their approach is also pragmatic. According to Brandtstädter, technologists and engineers are often viewed as practitioners *applying* pure theories, but they are actually problem solvers who may be purely pragmatic. In working with input–output regularities without necessarily worrying about explaining them, technologists are like the circus-dog trainer who is concerned about *whether* the dogs will go through the hoop, not *why*.

Approaches that are piecemeal and pragmatic seem especially liable to produce unwanted side effects, or "unforeseen consequences," as Chandler (Chapter 4 of this volume) calls them. For example, drug therapy is the major form of treatment of behavior disorders, but it is not guided by theory and it is rife with unwanted side effects, some of which are not always recognized (Baxley & LeBlanc, 1976; Berger, 1978; Sroufe, 1975; Weiss & Santelli, 1978). According to Baltes and Danish (this volume), intervention efforts that are guided by a theory are less likely to produce unwanted effects and are more likely to produce the wanted effect. In contrast, Brandtstädter (this volume) points out that theoretical predictions of the effects of intervention can err because theories are idealizations and may lack external validity. Furthermore, no articulated theory predicted such unwanted effects as the carcinogenic effects of saccharine ingestion and cigarette smoking or the teratogenic effect of taking thalidomide during the first trimester of pregnancy.

Nevertheless, planned intervention is always based on "theory" to some extent, for it is conceived consistently with at least a low-level phenomenological theory or a set of "input-output regularities" and it is also conceived consistently with some general model of reality. As implied in the preceding section, the model of reality will determine how the formal relation between theory and practice is conceptualized, and this in turn will influence the nature of the intervention, including its goals, methods, and targets.

Even if the adopted model of reality is implicit—as it seems likely to be for most legislators and practitioners—it influences the choice of methods. A deficit model or the "psychology of more" (Looft, 1971; Riegel, 1973) has often been the model that implicitly influences American intervention efforts, including the now past escalation of American involvement in Vietnam, the continuing proliferation of the capacity for nuclear overkill, increases in the numbers of police officers and judges as a means of dealing with increasing crime rates, and increases in special education programs as a means of dealing with increasing unease about minority groups. This model or partial model tends to imply that the problem needing attention is some kind of quantitative deficiency: The power to intervene in foreign affairs is underestimated by our enemies, military strength is too low, the number of personnel is insufficient, technical skills need to be acquired. It also implies that doing more will overcome the deficit; in fact, when the initial action produces no change, those concerned may call for more and more intervention (Baltes & Danish, this volume).

The deficit model also encourages the conceptualization of lower-class and minority groups as *sub*cultures rather than *co*cultures (McCandless, 1970), and the conceptualization of their ambiance as "cultural deprivation" (Tulkin, 1972). If the problem is deprivation, then the solution is enrichment—the addition of something missing (Horowitz & Paden, 1973). This notion is apparent in Maier's (1978) definition of the helping process as: "A series of socially engineered intervention activities in which the practitioner (the helper) deliberately *introduces* specifically structured events into the experience of an individual or group of individuals, or into an organizational context, in order to facilitate ordinary developmental processes [p. 195; emphasis added]."

One problem with these characterizations of intervention is that primary prevention does not always involve enrichment or addition; it often involves subtraction. For example, reducing the sound level in a premature infant's incubator would be a subtractive intervention of the preventive type.

Another problem is that some interventions involve substitution rather than addition or subtraction. For example, if a mother is judged unfit and her children are taken from her and placed in foster homes, the unfit mothering is not merely subtracted; rather, fit mothering is intended to be substituted. Another example is provided by Lawson, Daum, and Turkewitz's (1977) study of the ecology of a neonatal intensive-care unit, which suggests that the infants in such units "may suffer from an inappropriate *pattern* rather than an inadequate *amount* of stimulation [p. 1633; emphasis added]." Thus, intervention in the ecology of such a unit should involve not addition or subtraction but substitution, not quantitative change but qualitative change.

However, the major problem is related to the distinction between the *deficit* and *difference* models of the target of intervention. The deficit model represents the individual as deficient in some way and the difference model represents the individual as perhaps well socialized in his or her own culture but not well socialized from the perspective of another culture. Under the deficit model, something that everyone should have is missing or weak, and the individual is defective. Under the difference model, the individual is not defective but lacks something that would be useful under certain circumstances. (The *developmental-lag model* is a version of the deficit model: The something that is missing or weak is slow in developing but will eventually appear.)

It might be argued that the distinction disappears if it is viewed from a relativistic perspective. For example, in replying to a critique by Sroufe (1970), Bee, Streissguth, Van Egeren, Leckie, and Nyman (1970) suggested that the deficit model is entirely appropriate if *deficit* is defined as specific to situational requirements: "an individual who is unable to read, by this definition, would have a deficit in those situations in which reading was required [p. 147]." Similarly, most intervenors who deal with language competence support the deficit model with the argument that public education requires proficiency in standard English. Although it is doubtful that arguments such as these will satisfy those committed to the difference position, they are important because they illustrate a universal feature of model employment—the continuing effort to assimilate other models to one's own perspective.

Conflict between the deficit and difference models may be inherent in all highly developed technological democracies. On the one hand, as Horowitz and Paden (1973) pointed out, a technological society fosters the deficit model of its constituent nondominant cultures. Such a society requires certain technical skills of its citizens, and, consequently, these skills are included in the values of the dominant culture. Individuals who fail to acquire such skills will not have equality of opportunity in this society; they will be deficient. On the other hand, the pluralistic social philosophy of the United States implies the difference model of constituent nondominant cultures. A people may view cultural assimilation, which is the goal of intervention under the deficit model, as tantamount to cultural annihilation and may therefore opt for limited cultural assimilation in order to preserve its own cultural identity. Such a choice would be accepted in a society that has adopted the difference model. In presenting this contrast, however, Horowitz and Paden may have overstated the case for the latter option, which seems to be more a part of the ideal self of the dominant white middle-class culture of the United States than part of its real self. At best, this culture seems more often to *tolerate* cocultures rather than to *accept* them; it harbors sentiments about deficiency even when expressing beliefs about difference (cf. Tulkin, 1972).

B. Goals

Under both the deficit and the difference models, intervention is aimed at acquiring something that is missing and needed for some purpose or at strengthening something that is too weak for some purpose. In other words, intervention in both cases is situationally constrained; the intent is not merely to change, but to change for some specific purpose. This purpose is more likely to be stated explicitly when the difference model has been adopted. When the deficit model has been adopted, an overarching purpose—the purpose of cultural homogenization—is automatically implied, and, for those who adopt the deficit model, this purpose is reasonable and sufficient.

Two alternative goals of intervention can appear in both models. The goal may be to optimize development: "The natural course of events will insure adequate development; enrichment just makes it better [Horowitz & Paden, 1973, p. 335]." Alternatively, the goal may be to prevent inadequate development: The natural course of events is deficient for some purpose and intervention is needed to prevent inadequate development. (Note that only the first goal appears in Maier's [1978] definition of the helping process: "to facilitate ordinary developmental processes.") The issue, then, is not about what is done but rather about its ultimate purpose. The choice between cultural homogenization and cultural diversity is an issue of values—a humanistic or political issue. The purpose of intervention must be determined by the conception of what is desirable, which is a matter of values. This reliance on values cannot be avoided by using norms or statistical averages to specify purposes (Boesch, 1964; Brandtstädter, Chapter 1 of this volume; Horowitz & Paden, 1973).

Statistical norms are inadequate as specifications of the goals of intervention. It has been pointed out many times that statistical norms indicate what *is*, not what *is possible* or what *should be;* they are descriptive, not prescriptive (e.g., Brandtstädter, this volume). Cultural norms are not entirely satisfactory either, even if they are idealizations rather than culture-specific statistical norms. First, behavior may be pathological and yet culturally normal (Cameron & Magaret, 1951). Second, one might argue that the goals of intervention should be principled rather than merely socially convenient. However, cultural relativity seems to stop well short of the highest levels of morality and ethics as formulated in Kohlberg's (1973) analysis. Cultural relativity seems to be consistent with Stage 5 morality, which is based on notions of social contract, but it also appears to be consistent with Stage 4 morality, which is based on notions of law and order. It is certainly short of Stage 6 morality, which is based on universal principles, and it is far short of the hypothetical Stage 7 morality, which is based on cosmic principles.

Functional norms have also been used, explicitly or implicitly, to specify the goals of intervention. For example, Cameron and Magaret (1951, p. 4) defined behavior as pathological when it renders the individual persistently tense, dissatisfied, incompetent, or ineffectual. A problem with this view is that although the reference is clearly to *functions* of behaviors, some of the functions may be culturally defined. Behavior is incompetent or ineffective when it is inadequate or unsuitable for a particular purpose. However, cultural relativity may be involved in the definition of adequate or suitable levels of functioning, as well as in the specification of relevant purposes. Similarly, tension and dissatisfaction may refer to expectations or beliefs about desirable levels of functioning, and desirability is likely to be defined culturally. Thus, functional norms may be reduced to cultural norms.

Natural norms of various kinds have been described. For example, Horowitz and Paden (1973) mentioned biological norms and Simpson (1949) tried to derive ethical principles from laws of cultural evolution. The morality of Kohlberg's Stages 6 and 7 may also fit this category. However, cultural relativity always seems to be lurking behind these cosmologies. For example, in Kohlberg's Stage 6 the value of a human life is derived from the purportedly universal human value of respect for the individual; however, this seems to be a Western value and it seems to relegate all dissenting beliefs to lower stages of morality—in other words, a deficit model.

Thus, it appears that at some levels the distinction between the deficit and difference models is not clear-cut and that the distinction is limited in usefulness. Undeniably, the homogenization versus diversity issue is politically important, and we do not belittle political importance. Intervention occurs in the everyday world of practical politics, and a careless choice of words can undermine the best plans for intervention. However, the distinction is less useful for discussions among dispassionate professionals.

Finally, it is important to consider that without cultural relativity, which we have seen is questionable as a determinant of intervention goals, the plausibility of the difference model depends on the domain of reference. It is highly plausible when applied to intellectual and cognitive domains, in which it has been influential among some behaviorists at least since the publication of Ferguson's behavioral theory of intelligence in 1954. However, the difference model seems hard to maintain when the behaviors are destructive, whether they are aimed at others as in child abuse or aimed at self as in suicide or as in the self-destructive behaviors of some retarded and psychotic children.

C. Methods

1. Levels of Intervention

In our previous quotation from Maier (1978), reference was made to interventions aimed at the individual, at a group of individuals, or at their organizational context. Baltes and Danish (Chapter 3 of this volume) also discuss these levels of intervention and add a fourth one that could be characterized as sociological. As Baltes and Danish put it, the problem that needs attention involves the individual who does not fit within the established norms (individual level of analysis); or the problem is interpersonal difficulties (small-group level of analysis); or the problem is outside the realm of persons or small groups and results from societal or community actions (community–society level of analysis).

It seems obvious that these different conceptions of the problem will lead to differences in methods of intervention. Current models of child abuse provide an example (see Burgess, 1978; Parke & Collmer, 1975). At the individual level, the psychiatric model attributes child abuse to personality disorders of the parents, which leads to attempts to remedy these disorders. At the community–society level, the sociological model attributes child abuse to features of the social environment or culture, which leads to recommendations of social reform such as the elimination of poverty. However, when the third current model of child abuse is considered, it becomes apparent that the level of intervention is not the determinant of the nature of the intervention. The third model, the social–situational or social–interactional model, attributes child abuse to environmental events, both interpersonal and physical, that elicit and maintain punitive behavior in parents. This model leads to the use of behavior modification techniques at the individual level, including training in nonpunitive management behavior, anger control, and social skills (which reduce the social isolation that characterizes many abusing individuals and their families). Thus, at the individual level, the psychiatric model leads to one kind of intervention and the social–situational model leads to another; different *kinds* of intervention can be used at the same *level* of intervention.

Similarly, the same kind of intervention can be used at different levels. For example, in behavior modification, which is the major individual-oriented intervention, the only kinds of change in behavior are quantitative; the change is either an *increase* or a *decrease* (e.g., Baer & Sherman, 1970; Risley & Baer, 1973). Behaviors are classified as desirable or undesirable, and they are characterized as too low or too high in strength. Intervention is aimed at modifying the strength of behaviors through reinforcement, punishment, or extinction. In other words, the treatment is additive or subtractive; it involves presentation or withdrawal of a stimulus, or no change in stimulation. Even when it seems that the intent is to change the topography of a behavior by shaping, the change is understood to be quantitative (Baltes & Reese, 1977).

At the community–society level, intervention in the behavioral systems approach is aimed at changing institutions or organizations, which are conceptualized as collections of contingencies. The argument is that institutions have most of the power in a society; therefore, the most efficient way to change individuals is to change the institutions. The reason for changing an institution is to change the way it manages contingencies applied to individuals, and the way to effect change in an institution is to manage the contingencies that control it. Thus, with the behavioral approach, the treatment at both the individual and community–society levels is additive or subtractive (or involves no change in stimulation).

2. The Behavioral versus Cognitive Distinction

The distinction between behavioral and cognitive models provides another way to classify types of intervention. According to Avila, Combs, and Purkey (1977), the older view in the helping professions was that

[W]hat helped the client, student, or patient was what the helper did or said. As a consequence, helpers conceived of their tasks as "diagnosing and treating," "teaching the facts," "giving advice," or exerting some overt or covert form of direction. . . . With further study and experience, it has become apparent that the specific acts or behavior employed by the helper are far less important to the helping process than the nature of the relationships established between helper and helpee. The processes of helping are much more than mechanical questions of input and output. . . .The success of the helping professions is dependent upon change in personal meaning [p. xii].

The "older view" is clearly behavioristic, but Avila *et al.* did not express it in the best possible way. In behavior modification (in its technical sense), the variable that causes change is either stimulation that is entirely noncontingent (in the case of extinction) or stimulation that is contingent on the target behavior (in the case of reinforcement and punishment). The role of the helper is not to change the behavior of the helpee but to manage the contingency between behavior and stimulation. It makes no theoretical difference whether this contingency is controlled directly by the helper, as in the classic work by Lovaas with schizophrenic children (e.g., Lovaas, 1967), or is controlled directly by the helpee on instructions from the helper, as in covert conditioning (e.g., Cautela, 1971).

The newer perspective claimed by Avila *et al.* contains clear hints of *cognitivism,* in the sense of the term that includes transactionism and humanism and contrasts with behaviorism.

The behavioral model is consistent with the mechanistic world view and the cognitive model is consistent with organicism or contextualism. The world view affects the conception of what changes as a result of intervention, and it also influences the nature of the intervention. Consistent with the mechanistic model, the behavioral approach involves treatment of specific behaviors by means of environmental manipulations, specifically the management of contingent environmental events. The target behavior need not be objectively observable (Cautela, 1971; Reese, 1971), but it must be observable by whoever manages the contingencies. Side effects are attributed to generalization or to response classes. Generalization occurs spontaneously but will disappear if the contingency management continues (because discrimination will occur). Response classes result from prior learning (Baer, 1976), but they will break down if the responses they contain are given differential consequences. In short, intervention effects are highly specific or can be made highly specific through appropriate management of contingencies. The techniques are effective in education (Sherman & Bushell, 1975), in psychotherapy (Baer & Sherman, 1970), and, apparently, as tools for normal development (Risley & Baer, 1973).

Although the behavioral approach has most often been associated with the deficit model, it is also consistent with the difference model, as mentioned earlier in connection with Ferguson's (1954) behavioral theory of intelligence. However, when the deficit model is interpreted behaviorally, it is important to note that it is the behavior that is stigmatized and not the person who exhibits the behavior. As Baer (1976) said, the person is merely the unfortunate host of undesirable or ineffective behaviors.

Another feature of the behavioral model is that it is additive—not only in the sense of interpreting interventions as addition or subtraction of environmental events, but also in the sense of combining behaviors.

Behaviors can be linked into chains, but the meaning of the combination is found by examining the parts, not by looking for any emergent quality of the whole.

In contrast, in the cognitive model the whole is a system of interrelated parts, and its meaning is found not in the parts but in their interrelations. This model implies that social behavior can be understood only if its relation to cognitive behavior is also considered. This view is apparent in McCluskey and Arco's (in press) argument that "It is crucial that the intervention promote all aspects of the child's development, not just the cognitive and intellectual [p. 47]." Particularly if the contextualistic brand of cognitivism is adopted, the historical context of behavior needs to be considered. Thus, Baltes and Danish (Chapter 3 of this volume) suggest that the intervenor needs to consider the past, present, and future conditions and contexts of aging; as a result, intervention into aging may actually occur much earlier in the life span. In contrast, behaviorally oriented intervenors are concerned with the here and now—the present environmental contingencies that are maintaining the behavior. They deny that the past has any direct influence unless the maintaining contingencies remain effective, and they deny that etiology has implications for treatment (e.g., Baer & Sherman, 1970).

D. Ethics

McCluskey and Arco (in press) questioned the ethics of intervention programs aimed solely at the child: "Programs must be designed so that the family unit, rather than a single child, is the target for intervention. The detrimental effects of isolating the child from this all-important social unit may cause irreparable harm for all members concerned [p. 48]." They further argued, in agreement with Sroufe (1970) and with Horowitz and Paden (1973), that "tampering with the culture and social structure of . . . families could have very dangerous consequences for both the individual families involved and the society at large [p. 48]." This position is self-evident from the cognitive perspective, but is not at all obvious from the behavioral perspective. If the intervenor has adopted a behavioral model, there is no ethical requirement that the family unit be treated. In fact, there is no family *unit* as such, but only members of a particular kind of group. However, if the intervenor has adopted a cognitive model, then, as McCluskey and Arco argued, there is an ethical demand that treatment not be limited to the child. Extending the argument to the larger developmental picture, one could say that treatment should not be limited to any one member of the family unit, be it hospitalized infant, retarded child, incarcerated parent, or institutionalized grandparent.

Genetic counseling provides specific examples. According to Murray (1975), psychological problems may be produced in a family with "no affected children, when a high risk for giving birth to such children is revealed to the parents [p. 174]." Murray also listed other ethical problems, including (a) counseling about sexual activity when, as is often the case, the genetic counselor does not have training in this kind of counseling; (b) the effect of counseling when the genetic counselor's personal interest is the effects of reproduction on genetic defects in the gene pool rather than the individual client; (c) the issue of whether full disclosure should be given before it is relevant (Murray's example is telling parents their child has sickle cell anemia before the disease is clinically manifested). This kind of information may be emotionally damaging to the parents, or it might cause them to use unfortunately different child-rearing practices.

All of these ethical concerns pale in light of the largest issue, which arises not as a consequence of intervention but as a consequence of intervention research. Interventions often come to an end because of political or other expediencies, and one would be justified in asserting that "at least they had a few good years." However, when the intervention is terminated because a research project has been completed, the ethics of the entire intervention must be questioned.

III. Concluding Comments

We have argued that the distinction one makes between "pure" science and application, or theory and practice, or science and technology, is influenced by deeply held commitments that determine how these realms are related to each other. The boundary is blurred from the position of the behavior analysts because of their emphasis on the individual organism and their rejection of the hypothetico–deductive method and any "strongly held" hypotheses (Deitz, 1978). However, the boundary is also blurred from a dialectical orientation—including Hegel's idealistic dialectics and Marx's and Mao's materialistic dialectics—because the domains interact in such a way that analytically separating them distorts their meaning and function.

These underlying convictions also influence the way intervention itself is conceptualized. We noted that the deficit model tends to be associated with behavioral orientations and the difference model with cognitive orientations, but these associations are matters of preference and are not imposed by underlying convictions. For example, Ferguson's (1954) behavioral theory of intelligence is one of the best examples of a difference model, and Flavell's (1970) cognitive analysis of memory development clearly reflects a deficit model. However, the underlying convictions influence the selection of *methods* and *targets* of intervention and, to a large extent, affect interpretations of the *ethics* of intervention.

The danger of failing to recognize the underlying convictions is that the bases for selecting methods and targets and for judging ethics become blurred. In conclusion, we would suggest that the primary danger is a failure to realize that "You can't do just one thing" (see Willems, 1973); there are no effects without side effects; purpose must be tempered by context.

A working sundial was invented thousands of years before the development of geometrical optics led to the explanation of how it works by application of the scientific principles of the rectilinear propagation of light. But do we need to know why it works? Do we need theory and research to tell us that hunger is bad, regardless of findings on the psychological effects of malnutrition?

REFERENCES

Avila, D., Combs, A. W., & Purkey, W. W. Preface. In D. Avila, A. W. Combs, & W. W. Purkey (Eds.), *The helping relationship sourcebook* (2nd ed.). Boston: Allyn & Bacon, 1977.

Baer, D. M. The organism as host. *Human Development,* 1976, *19,* 87–98.

Baer, D. M., & Sherman, J. A. Behavior modification: Clinical and educational applications. In H. W. Reese, & L. P. Lipsitt (Eds.), *Experimental child psychology.* New York: Academic Press, 1970.

Baltes, M. M., & Reese, H. W. Operant research in violation of the operant paradigm? In B. C. Etzel, J. M. LeBlanc, & D. M. Baer (Eds.), *New developments in behavioral research: Theory, method, and application.* Hillsdale, N. J.: Lawrence Erlbaum Associates, 1977.

Baxley, G. B., & LeBlanc, J. M. The hyperactive child: Characteristics, treatment, and evaluation of research design. In H. W. Reese (Ed.), *Advances in child development and behavior* (Vol. 11). New York: Academic Press, 1976.

Bee, H. L., Streissguth, A. P., Van Egeren, L. F., Leckie, M. S., & Nyman, B. A. Deficits and value judgments: A comment on Sroufe's critique. *Developmental Psychology,* 1970, *2,* 146–149.

Berger, P. A. Medical treatment of mental illness. *Science,* 1978, *200,* 974–981.

Birnbrauer, J. S. Applied behavior analysis, service, and the acquisition of knowledge. *Behavior Analyst,* 1979, *2,* 15–21.

Boesch, E. E. Die diagnostische Systematisierung. In R. Heiss (Ed.), *Psychologische Diagnostik* (Vol. 6). Göttingen: Hogrefe, 1964.

Burgess, R. L. Child abuse: A behavioral analysis. In B. B. Lahey & A. E. Kazdin (Eds.), *Advances in child clinical psychology.* New York: Plenum, 1978.

Cameron, N., & Magaret, A. *Behavior pathology.* Boston: Houghton Mifflin, 1951.

Caplan, G. *Principles of preventive psychiatry.* New York: Basic Books, 1964.

Cautela, J. R. Covert conditioning. In A. Jacobs & L. B. Sachs (Eds.), *The psychology of private events: Perspectives on covert response systems.* New York: Academic Press, 1971.

Clarizio, H. F., & McCoy, G. F. *Behavior disorders in children* (2nd ed.). New York: Crowell, 1976.

Clark, R. W. *Einstein: The life and times*. New York: World, 1971.

Deitz, S. M. Current status of applied behavior analysis: Science versus technology. *American Psychologist*, 1978, *33*, 805–814.

Ferguson, G. A. On learning and human ability. *Canadian Journal of Psychology*, 1954, *8*, 95–112.

Flavell, J. H. Developmental studies of mediated memory. In H. W. Reese & L. P. Lipsitt (Eds.), *Advances in child development and behavior* (Vol. 5). New York: Academic Press, 1970.

Hayes, S. C., Rincover, A., & Solnick, J. V. Trends in applied behavior analysis. *American Psychologist*, 1979, *34*, 642. (Comment)

Heidbreder, E. *Seven psychologies*. New York: Appleton-Century-Crofts, 1933.

Horowitz, F. D., & Paden, L. Y. The effectiveness of environmental intervention programs. In B. M. Caldwell & H. N. Ricciuti (Eds.), *Review of child development research* (Vol. 3). Chicago: University of Chicago Press, 1973.

Kaplan, A. *The new world of philosophy*. New York: Random House, 1961.

Kerschner, P. A., & Hirschfield, I. S. Public policy and aging: Analytic approaches. In D. S. Woodruff & J. E. Birren (Eds.), *Aging: Scientific perspectives and social issues*. New York: Van Nostrand, 1975.

Kohlberg, L. Continuities in childhood and adult moral development revisited. In P. B. Baltes & K. W. Schaie (Eds.), *Life-span developmental psychology: Personality and socialization*. New York: Academic Press, 1973.

Lawson, K., Daum, C., & Turkewitz, G. Environmental characteristics of a neonatal intensive-care unit. *Child Development*, 1977, *48*, 1633–1639.

Looft, W. R. The psychology of more. *American Psychologist*, 1971, *26*, 561–565.

Lovaas, O. I. A behavior therapy approach to the treatment of childhood schizophrenia. In J. P. Hill (Ed.), *Minnesota symposia on child psychology* (Vol. 1). Minneapolis: University of Minnesota Press, 1967.

McCandless, B. R. Socialization. In H. W. Reese & L. P. Lipsitt (Eds.), *Experimental child psychology*. New York: Academic Press, 1970.

McCluskey, K. A., & Arco, C. M. B. Stimulation and infant development. In J. G. Howell (Ed.), *Modern perspectives in the psychiatry of infancy*. New York: Brunner/Mazel, in press.

Maier, H. W. *Three theories of child development* (3rd ed.). New York: Harper & Row, 1978.

Murray, R. F. Commentary II. In K. W. Schaie, V. E. Anderson, G. E. McClearn, & J. Money (Eds.), *Developmental human behavior genetics: Nature–nurture redefined*. Lexington, Mass.: Lexington Books, 1975.

Nagel, E. The nature and aim of science. In S. Morganbesser (Ed.), *Philosophy of science today*. New York: Basic Books, 1967.

Overton, W. F., & Reese, H. W. Models of development: Methodological implications. In J. R. Nesselroade & H. W. Reese (Eds.), *Life-span developmental psychology: Methodological issues*. New York: Academic Press, 1973.

Parke, R. D., & Collmer, C. W. Child abuse: An interdisciplinary analysis. In E. M. Hetherington (Ed.), *Review of child development research* (Vol. 5). Chicago: University of Chicago Press, 1975.

Pepper, S. C. *World hypotheses*. Berkeley: University of California Press, 1942.

Pylyshyn, Z. Competence and psychological reality. *American Psychologist*, 1972, *27*, 546–552.

Reese, H. W. The study of covert verbal and nonverbal mediation. In A. Jacobs & L. B. Sachs (Eds.), *The psychology of private events: Perspectives on covert response systems*. New York: Academic Press, 1971.

Reese, H. W. Dialectics in theory and educational practice. Paper presented at the meeting of the American Psychological Association, Toronto, August 1978.

Riegel, K. F. Developmental psychology and society: Some historical and ethical considerations. In J. R. Nesselroade & H. W. Reese (Eds.), *Life-span developmental psychology: Methodological issues*. New York: Academic Press, 1973.

Risley, T. R., & Baer, D. M. Operant behavior modification: The deliberate development of behavior. In B. M. Caldwell & H. N. Ricciuti (Eds.), *Review of child development research* (Vol. 3). Chicago: University of Chicago Press, 1973.

Rychlak, J. F. *A philosophy of science for personality theory*. New York: Houghton Mifflin, 1968.

Sherman, J. A., & Bushell, D., Jr. Behavior modification as an educational technique. In F. D. Horowitz (Ed.), *Review of child development research* (Vol. 4). Chicago: University of Chicago Press, 1975.

Simpson, G. G. *The meaning of evolution*. New Haven: Yale University Press, 1949.

Skinner, B. F. Are theories of learning necessary? *Psychological Review,* 1950, *57,* 193–216.

Skinner, B. F. *Beyond freedom and dignity*. New York: Random House, 1971.

Spiker, C. C. The concept of development: Relevant and irrelevant issues. In H. W. Stevenson (Ed.), Concept of development. *Monographs of the Society for Research in Child Development,* 1966, *31* (5, Serial No. 107).

Sroufe, L. A. A methodological and philosophical critique of intervention-oriented research. *Developmental Psychology,* 1970, *2,* 140–145.

Sroufe, L. A. Drug treatment of children with behavior problems. In F. D. Horowitz (Ed.), *Review of child development research* (Vol. 4). Chicago: University of Chicago Press, 1975.

Toulmin, S. *Foresight and understanding*. New York: Harper & Row, 1963.

Tulkin, S. R. An analysis of the concept of cultural deprivation. *Developmental Psychology,* 1972, *6,* 326–339.

Wartofsky, M. W. *Conceptual foundations of scientific thought*. Toronto: Macmillan, 1968.

Weimer, W. B. Psycholinguistics and Plato's paradoxes. *American Psychologist,* 1973, *28,* 15–33.

Weiss, B., & Santelli, S. Dyskinesias evoked in monkeys by weekly administration of haloperidol. *Science,* 1978, *200,* 799–801.

Willems, E. P. Behavioral ecology and experimental analysis: Courtship is not enough. In J. R. Nesselroade & H. W. Reese (Eds.), *Life-span developmental psychology: Methodological issues*. New York: Academic Press, 1973.

CHAPTER 3

Intervention in Life-Span Development and Aging: Issues and Concepts[1]

PAUL B. BALTES
STEVEN J. DANISH
THE PENNSYLVANIA STATE UNIVERSITY
UNIVERSITY PARK, PENNSYLVANIA

I. Introduction

This chapter is more a catalog of ideas than a comprehensive discussion of a topic. However, such a catalog is useful because the emerging fields of life-span development and aging are at a critical juncture.[2] As is true for most scientific progressions, the initial focus in life-span development and aging has been one of description rather than explanation and modification. At present, the dominant theme of identifying the course and varia-

---

[1]Preparation of this chapter was supported, in part, by a grant from the U. S. National Institute on Aging (No. 5 RO1 AG00403–02) to Paul B. Baltes and Sherry L. Willis. It was first presented at a conference on Gerontological Intervention sponsored by the German Volkswagen Foundation and held at Heidelberg in February 1978.

A modified version of this chapter has been translated into German and appeared in the *Zeitschrift für Entwicklungspsychologie und Pädagogische Psychologie,* 1979, *11,* 112–140.

[2]The terms *life-span development* and *aging* are, for the most part, used interchangeably in the present manuscript. This decision reflects the fact that this paper was initially written for a gerontological audience. In addition, this decision reflects the authors' views that aging begins at birth and that aging change is not only change towards deterioration. In principle, the term *life-span development* is used by the authors as the overarching concept; that is, what other researchers might label *aging* is seen as one component included in the concept of *life-span development.*

LIFE-SPAN DEVELOPMENTAL PSYCHOLOGY
Intervention

tion of development from a life-span perspective is being supplemented with vigorous efforts aimed at intervention, both on theoretical and action-oriented levels. The purpose of this chapter is to provide researchers with an appropriate framework for guiding and evaluating life-span and gerontological intervention work as it evolves over the next decade.

Most of the ideas presented in this chapter have been discussed earlier in other contexts such as early childhood education or mental health. However, it is our view that the following presentation provides a new context for these ideas. The initial development of the ideas expressed here are the result of Baltes' venture into the arena of gerontological intervention in which he organized and edited a symposium on *Strategies for Psychological Intervention in Old Age* (Baltes, 1973). This chapter updates and expands these preliminary thoughts. The major additions resulted from an effort to integrate these ideas with the concept of intervention as used in the human services field, to relate intervention to the larger context of social policy and health delivery, and to view intervention within the framework of theory construction and the field of human development. Human development, as we see it, is a multidisciplinary and multiprofessional emphasis that deals with the study and modification of human development through the life span (including aging) and within the context of a changing society (Frank, 1963; Baltes, Reese, & Nesselroade, 1977).

II. Intervention and Conceptions of Development

A. *Definition of Intervention*

The concept of *intervention* does not have a singular meaning. In this chapter, it is defined as "a programmatic attempt at alteration [Baltes, 1973a, p. 4]" or, as Urban (1976) put it, "as planned intrusive inputs into an organized network of active and ongoing processes." In the context of human development and gerontology, this definition can be further specified by stating that the attempt at alteration involves the course of development and aging. Gerontological intervention in psychology, then, deals with programmatic attempts aimed at modification of the course of psychological aging.

Additional specifications of the concept are possible and necessary in order to prevent an uncritical use of the term intervention. Intervention is not an isolated concept. It gains its meaning in at least two contexts: that of theories about individual development and societal functioning and that of values and norms about what is desirable. In other words, as soon as one moves to the *when, how,* and *what for* aspect of intervention, theoretical and value issues become important.

B. Conceptions of Development and Intervention

Let us first illustrate issues of theory: If one considers the usual criteria applied to describe developmental processes (e.g., Wohlwill, 1973), the course of development can be modified in terms of a variety of indicators. Rate, directionality, maxima, minima, variability, and length are examples of quantitative criteria. Other criteria, usually developed within a qualitative concept of development (Overton & Reese, 1973), involve such attributes as the sequencing of stages, the seriation of developmental tasks, or the notion of end states. These examples demonstrate that implementing the concept of intervention always involves an alignment with a theoretical knowledge base concerning development and aging. Without clear relationships to theory, we may be left asking the question, "Intervention: why, how, and for what purpose?"

With regard to issues of values and norms, our argument is that any decision to intervene presupposes a dimension of quality of functioning—a decision about what is and what should be. Furthermore, there is a value question involving evolutionary perspectives and social change (or involving social stability). Some researchers, particularly community psychologists and sociologists, have argued that the theoretical and value context provided by theories of individual development is not the only matter of importance. On the contrary, they argue that the concept of intervention is also related to general notions of societal functioning and social stability versus change. In that case, contextual information about intervention derives its rationale from two systems: one set related to conceptions of individual development, the other to conceptions of societal structure and functioning.

Let us further illustrate the need to consider jointly conceptions of individual development and societal functioning. Basing their study on earlier work by Matilda Riley and her colleagues (Riley, 1976; Riley, Johnson & Foner, 1972; see also Neugarten & Datan, 1973), Baltes, Cornelius, and Nesselroade (1979) have presented a conception of development that illustrates joint consideration of conceptions of individual and societal development. In related papers, Baltes and Willis (1979) have shown how such a conception is based on empirical research, using the domain of intellectual behavior as a sample case, and Baltes, Reese, and Lipsitt (in press) have elaborated this position with a focus on life-span developmental psychology. Figure 3.1 illustrates. The upper part of the figure summarizes major prototheoretical conceptions of development, determinants, and three sets of influence systems operating during and on development. The lower part of the figure is designed to accentuate the fact that successive cohorts age during different epochs. Therefore, distinct cohorts may respond to and interact with different patterns of factors associated with the three classes of influence systems.

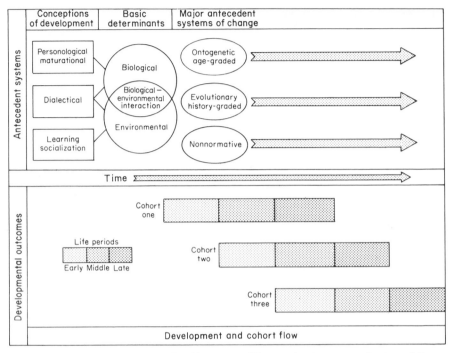

Figure 3.1. Illustration of relationships among life-span development, cohorts, and three major influence systems: ontogenetic (age-graded), evolutionary (history-graded), and nonnormative (nondevelopmental). The figure is taken from Baltes, Cornelius, and Nesselroade (1979). The lower part of the figure is an adaptation of the age–cohort stratification model presented by Matilda W. Riley (e.g., Riley *et al.,* 1972).

The ellipses at the center of the upper part of Figure 3.1 represent the core of life-span thinking. They illustrate the three distinct influence systems that operate jointly in the control and production of aging for any given cohort. Influences that covary systematically with chronological age are labeled *age-graded,* those that covary systematically with biocultural change are labeled *evolutionary history-graded,* and those that do not occur in any general or universal fashion (in terms of frequency, patterning, and timing) are labeled *nonnormative.* Examples of nonnormative influences would be area- and period-specific events such as wars and economic depressions or other kinds of idiosyncratic life events such as career change, migration, unemployment, divorce, or accidents. The reader interested in a more detailed and up-to-date discussion of this framework may want to consult Baltes, Reese, and Lipsitt (in press).

Figure 3.1 illustrates some important considerations for the field of life-span intervention. It shows that conceptions of aging differ widely;

moreover, it suggests that gerontological intervention needs to consider views, factors, mechanisms, and procedures that are formulated within a dialectic provided by the two time trajectories mentioned earlier (individual and social) and within the framework provided by the three influence systems (age-graded, history-graded, and nonnormative).

The multicausality (age-graded, history-graded, nonnormative) of development represented in Figure 3.1 has a counterpart on the descriptive level. Because life-span development is multicausally determined, the nature of psychological development and aging can vary markedly in terms of direction, rate of change, onset, differences between individuals, and categories of behavior. Such a pluralistic view of the descriptive nature of individual ontogeny is expressed in Figure 3.2. Figure 3.2 summarizes the product of the multiple influences on development and aging represented in Figure 3.1.

The product consists of *behavior-change processes* or *developmental functions*. These developmental functions (see Wohlwill, 1973) are representations of intraindividual change and interindividual differences or similarities in quantitative and qualitative change (Baltes, Reese, & Nesselroade, 1977). They can be described in terms of such concepts as rate, sequentiality, directionality, maxima, minima, and dimensionality. Which indicators are chosen to describe developmental functions is, in part, a reflection of the underlying metamodel of development (Overton & Reese, 1973) and the behavior class considered.

There are two central themes depicted in Figure 3.2 (A). First, when viewed within a life-span developmental framework, developmental functions can exhibit multiple directions and trajectory characteristics. Second, developmental functions often show larger interindividual variability with increasing age. This position is occasionally labeled as *differential aging*. Differential aging (see part D of this section) is used here to indicate that there is much diversity on the intraindividual level (across situations and behaviors) as well as on the level of interindividual differences (within and between cohorts).

Figure 3.2 (B) supplements the differential view of life-span development expressed in Figure 3.2 (A). It illustrates the notion of *discontinuity* associated with *life course-grading* (Neugarten & Datan, 1973). The proposition underlying Figure 3.2 (B) is that life-span development is not usefully conceptualized as a unitary, life-long cumulative process. Although such unidimensional processes may exist, there are a large number of alternative life-span trajectories that exhibit discontinuity and life course-grading. The concepts of discontinuity and life course-grading imply two features that are characteristic of behavior-change processes. First, behavior-change processes do not necessarily represent changes along

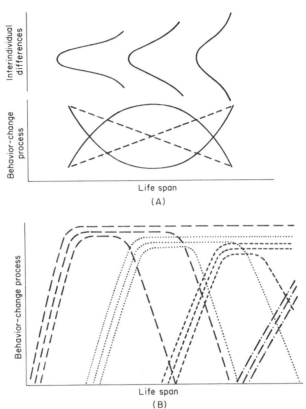

Figure 3.2. Selective examples of life-span developmental processes: (A) multidimensionality, multidirectionality, and age-correlated increases in interindividual variability and (B) notions of life course-grading and discontinuity. Developmental functions (behavior-change processes) differ in terms of onset, duration, and termination when charted in the framework of the life course; moreover, they involve both quantitative and qualitative aspects of change.

an invariant continuum of measurement, nor are they always completely predictable from ontogenetically earlier phenomena. Second, behavior-change processes do not always extend across the entire life span; they do not all originate at birth and terminate at death. Following Havighurst's (1972) concept of developmental tasks and Neugarten's conception of age gradation (e.g., Neugarten & Hagestad, 1976), the notion is that the life course of individuals represents a pattern of behavior-change processes that differ in terms of onset, duration, and termination (see also Hollingsworth, 1927). This view is further strengthened by such concepts as nonnormative and history-graded events and demands, which are represented in Figure 3.1. In fact, life-span developmentalists (e.g., Baltes, 1968; Huston-Stein &

Baltes, 1976; Neugarten, 1969) are impressed with the relative magnitude of discontinuity and heterogeneity that the life courses of individuals seem to display. The extent to which the issue of discontinuity can be pushed is still open to question. However, it is clear that simple, unitary, and cumulative developmental processes are insufficient when it comes to the task of representing the complexity of life-span development.

The concept of intervention is necessarily modified by such formal characteristics of developmental and gerontological theories and by the nature of theories and models formulated for specific classes of developmental or aging behavior. For example, Weinert (1979) has presented a thoughtful discussion of the interfaces among the nature of the concept of development, the specific substantive theory, and conceptions of intervention (see also Sigel, 1972). Although Weinert's discussion deals with a specific cluster of intervention techniques in the fields of child development and education, his discussion can be easily generalized to the fields of life-span development and gerontology.

C. Some Historical Observations on the History of Gerontology: From Description to Explanation and Modification

In gerontology, the general notion of intervention is a somewhat recent development. Moreover, it is apparent that the notion of intervention work is not sufficiently accepted or understood. An example is a recent critique of the concept of intervention by Birren and Renner (1977).

In its formative decades, gerontology was very concerned with descriptive identification of the nature of aging. For the most part, researchers were impressed with the normative aspects of aging, notably ontogenetic decline. Perhaps Kastenbaum (1968) described this trend most eloquently. He said that researchers in gerontology until the 1960s were largely satisfied with "counting and classifying the wrinkles of aged behavior [p. 282]." This focus on the description of age deficits (see also Lehr, 1972) was probably a necessary and valid step in creating a body of knowledge in the field of gerontology.

Since the 1960s, however, there has been a growing concern with the reasons for the why of psychological aging and with the question of whether it is necessary. Questions of why, of course, usually lead to causal–analytic work, including that related to manipulative–experimental research. Such research deals with the study of the conditions and mechanisms of aging and is aimed at explanation (Baltes & Willis, 1977; Labouvie, 1973).

The step from the explanation of aging to its modification or intervention is a relatively small one, and it touches on the interface between basic and applied research. As soon as one accumulates evidence on explanatory factors, one's tendency is to rearrange these factors if they lead to undesirable outcomes; thus, intervention is born. Furthermore, as evidence on explanation accumulates, the question of *why* is somewhat altered. It deals not only with the *why* of an *existing* phenomenon (i.e., aging as it is observed), but also with questions of invariance versus modifiability (plasticity) of aging and of existing versus necessary versus alternate conditions. Thus, the explanatory study is directed toward examining the conditions under which alternative forms of psychological aging could occur. This is an emerging theme in the current scene of research on psychological aging.

In our view, the question of the *why and how of diverse forms of aging* is the more advanced one in the development of a science (Baltes & Baltes, 1977; Baltes & Willis, 1977) and is indicative of the progress in modern gerontology, with regard to both theory and practice. In relation to theory, the question helps distinguish between necessary and sufficient conditions (McCall, 1977), between what is and what is possible; moreover, it provides for information on ecological contingencies of behavioral phenomena. In relation to practice, the question generates a new intellectual climate of optimism, suggests the possibility of redesigning the aging process, and gives practitioners an emerging set of tools for intervention. In short, it is in the interface between knowledge generation and knowledge application which is inherent in intervention work, where the dialog between theory and practice is most vigorous and mutually satisfying.

D. Some Salient Features of Aging Processes: Differential Aging and Plasticity

In the past, much of psychological aging has been seen as a normative–general decline in the sense of deterioration or movement toward less adaptive capacity. In this framework, the general intervention goal would be the deceleration or even the halting of such a decline phenomenon.

The 1970s, however, saw the initiation of many efforts aimed at providing us with a more differentiated and less monolithic view of the aging process. A new picture of differential and multidirectional patterns of aging is emerging. This picture evidences the following features (see Baltes, 1979; Baltes & Willis, 1979):

1. Psychological aging is not a simple unidirectional process; it includes

dimensions of multidimensionality, multilinearity, and multidirectionality.

2. People exhibit dramatic interindividual differences in the timing and level of aging change; there is comparatively little universality and homogeneity.

3. Psychological aging not only exhibits large interindividual variability, it also is not fixed for individuals; in addition, there is much intraindividual plasticity in the nature of aging.

These general features of multidimensionality, multidirectionality, interindividual variability, and intraindividual plasticity have been observed in diverse domains of behavior including personality (e.g., Thomae, 1976, 1979) and intellectual abilities (Baltes & Schaie, 1976; Baltes & Willis, 1979; Labouvie-Vief & Chandler, 1978). On the one hand, these features are promising for intervention considerations. If aging is diverse and modifiable, there is the potential for redesign. On the other hand, these features seem to contradict simple developmental theories of biological growth that traditionally have focused on such features as unidirectionality, fixed sequentiality, a single end-state orientation, and irreversibility. Thus, the emerging pattern of differential aging poses new challenges for developmental theories and theory-based intervention. For example, there is a growing concern for formulating alternative conceptions of adult development and aging that include developmental conceptions of biological growth only as a special case (e.g., Baltes, 1979; Hultsch & Plemons, 1979; Lehr, 1975; Löwe, 1977; Thomae, 1979).

As mentioned earlier, the concept of differential aging is related to the processes represented in Figures 3.1 and 3.2. The high incidence of large variability and multidirectionality in aging phenomena is probably due to the fact that the three major sources of influences (age-graded, history-graded, nonnormative) do not operate in the same combination at different segments of the life span. For example, if history-graded and nonnormative influences operate at a comparatively higher intensity in adulthood and advanced age (in contrast with a relative preponderance of age-graded influences in childhood), then the occurrence of large variability and multidirectionality of behavior change in the second part of the life span is a likely outcome.

The general implication of the concept of differential aging for intervention is that much of human development and gerontological intervention needs to be *differential intervention*. Differential intervention is based on the assumption that the pathways of development and aging (their origins, sequences, and outcomes) can differ markedly for different behaviors and people and, therefore, intervention treatments in gerontology are not always normative.

III. Basics of Intervention Action

A. Functions of Intervention: Knowledge Application and Knowledge Generation

Some of the previous observations have already implied that intervention work has implications for both theory and practice. It is necessary to illustrate further the nature of this relationship because, in the past, it has been occasionally assumed that intervention is merely the application of knowledge derived from the study of existing phenomena or the blind search for applicable and effective treatment programs (e.g., Birren & Renner, 1977). In contrast, we would argue that the task of altering the course of development based on existing knowledge about determining factors and processes of aging (knowledge application) is only *one* of the functions of intervention work. The other function of intervention work is the generation of new knowledge. The function of generating knowledge follows from the rationale that intervention always implies some scheme of systematic variation of conditions. Therefore, intervention is analogous to one important feature of explanatory–analytic research (the classical analogue is the experiment), which is usually designed to produce knowledge about cause–effect sequences. As one considers the treatments associated with interventive action, it is important to recognize that variation of antecedent conditions in intervention can include situations or antecedent conditions that are not usually encountered in the prevalent ecological context.[3]

In this vein, Baltes and Willis (1977) have suggested that intervention work does not only involve the application of knowledge, but also plays an important part in the generation of new knowledge about the range of aging phenomena. They reason that "naturalistically" occurring aging phenomena are only a subset of possible aging phenomena. Accordingly, intervention efforts represent an important vehicle for increasing

---

[3]To illustrate in another context: A researcher interested in examining the effect of temperature on water would not be able to study water in its full spectrum of states if the study were restricted to the temperature range usually available in the prevalent geographic ecology, for example, in West Germany. Therefore, the range of temperature would be broadened in the laboratory, etc. Similarly, in gerontology, researchers will not be able to examine a large spectrum of "possible" aging unless they find or produce conditions that differ more markedly from each other than those existing in the prevalent ecology of a given cultural entity.

knowledge. "The nature of psychological aging changes not only with a changing biocultural context, but also with the range of intervention programs which researchers and social planners are able to create [Baltes & Willis, 1977, p. 147]."

The two functions of intervention, knowledge generation and knowledge application, lead to some similarities and differences in approach when they are related to theory and practice. However, it is their joint consideration that makes a focus on intervention a powerful avenue for advancing the fields of human development and gerontology, both as a science and as a profession. Considering the functions of intervention separately—either as a form of knowledge generation or as a form of knowledge application (e.g., Birren & Renner, 1977)—would make the concept of intervention less desirable. One should also note that intervention should not be considered only as a set of known strategies or as an established technology to be used for applying or generating new knowledge; intervention is also part of a distinct, *evolving* body of knowledge about intervention. Therefore, intervention does not represent merely the application of a context-specific theory on development and aging.

B. Taxonomic Considerations on Intervention

Let us now concentrate on the second major function of intervention work—the function of altering the course of development and aging. A number of taxonomic considerations have been developed that are helpful in organizing the field. One set deals with generic strategies of intervention, another deals with a review of concrete modes of action in terms of intervention targets and intervention treatments.

1. Generic Strategies

Several reviews are available that summarize generic strategies of intervention. Works by Kessler and Albee (1975), Brandstädter and Von Eye (1979), and Cowen (1973) are examples. Generic strategies are defined here by their general properties in relation to timing and intent of intervention. In many respects, these generic strategies are independent of the specified intervention context (target behavior, intervention technology). However, this is an oversimplification.

One taxonomic distinction that has acquired widespread use in the behavioral sciences is primarily based on work by Caplan (1964), a psychiatrist who described the distinctions among *primary, secondary,* and *tertiary prevention.* Primary prevention involves steps taken to prevent the occurrence of a disease or another form of dysfunction. The key strategy is to counteract harmful circumstances before they have a chance to produce illness or dysfunctioning. Frequently, but not necessarily, primary prevention is a communal or societal conception of intervention; therefore, it is often directed at a population rather than at individuals. Secondary prevention involves early treatment of an existing problem and is designed to reduce the intensity and duration of the problem, both at the level of an at-risk population and at the level of individual functioning. Tertiary prevention is designed to increase the likelihood that a normal level of functioning can be approximated and that a reoccurrence of the problem can be minimized. Caplan's concepts of primary, secondary, and tertiary prevention are not free from controversy (e.g., Kessler & Albee, 1975). This is the reason that Wagenfeld (1972), for example, suggests that we consider a return to pre-Caplan terminology. An example of pre-Caplan terminology would be the distinctions among *prevention, treatment,* and *rehabilitation.*

Another set of distinctions occasionally used are those among *preventive, corrective,* and *enriching* (or *optimizing*) *intervention* (Baltes, 1973). In this classification, the term *enriching intervention* possesses what is perhaps a novel feature. It not only connotes a concern with dysfunction and its prevention or correction, but also states explicitly a counterpart orientation—that of maximizing human potential. Thus, the term *enriching* introduces a new dimension and conception, involving the optimization of human development. The concepts of enrichment and optimization have strong support from researchers in the field of human development and education. In this instance, human development is defined not only as the *passive* study of naturally occurring development, but also as the *active* study of the conditions that promote optimal functioning. Thus, the term *human development* begins to carry both passive (how does it look?) and active (how does one promote it?) connotations.

Whichever specific terminology one choses, it is important in the field of gerontological intervention to recognize that aging is not a static event but a process involving patterns of events. The process view, which is perhaps best illustrated in a life-span approach to aging, makes it clear that intervention efforts should be process-oriented. The terms *prevention, enrichment,* and *optimization* convey this process-oriented view on intervention.

Moreover, taxonomic efforts at delineating intervention strategies make it clear that there is a direct, though often subtle, relationship between intervention and the theoretical context formulated for the target of intervention efforts. Enrichment, prevention, treatment, and rehabilitation always presuppose an implicit or explicit theory or model of the "natural" or "desirable" state or course of the target phenomenon. Examples of these implicit or explicit theories include a theory of behavioral development, a theory of ideal societal functioning, or a value-based conception (including values based on nonscientific criteria such as religion) of the ideal. In this context, it is important to recognize that such implicit or explicit theoretical or model conceptions are not always based on a formulated scientific theory. They may also represent implicit prescientific belief systems about behavior, people, and society. In the clinical psychology literature (e.g., Boesch, 1964), this situation is expressed in efforts to delineate alternative norm conceptions such as *statistical, functional,* and *ethical.*

2. Modes of Intervention Action

The interplay between presupposed models of development and intervention is also evident in presentations on concrete modes of intervention technologies. In the German literature on educational psychology, Brandt-städter and his colleagues (1974) and Weinert (1979) have discussed the relationship between theory and conceptions of intervention in a comprehensive and thoughtful manner.

The term *modes of intervention action* refers to concrete technologies of implementation. In psychology, these technologies involve such parameters as the target behavior, setting, mechanism, and timing, and duration of intervention. Examples of such heuristic taxonomic efforts in psychological gerontology are provided by Gottesman, Quarterman, and Cohn (1973) and Eisdorfer and Stotsky (1977). Gottesman *et al.* base their exposition on clinical gerontology on distinctions among self-treatment, noninstitutional social treatment, individual psychological therapies, group treatments, and institutional treatments. Eisdorfer and Stotsky add to this catalog physical interventions involving various forms of medical treatments.

In the foreword to the 1973 symposium on Strategies for *Psychological Intervention in Old Age,* Baltes (1973) has presented a taxonomic model based on work by Jacobs (1972). This taxonomic scheme is illustrated in Table 3.1. Table 3.1 is not intended to be comprehensive, but it is illustrative of the diversity of possible intervention activities. It focuses on several parameters of intervention, including generic *goals* of intervention (e.g., alleviation, prevention, enrichment), *targets, settings,* and *intervention mechanisms.* Another useful heuristic scheme has been developed by Rappaport (1977) in the context of social intervention. The spectrum of such schemes would be easily expanded by the consideration of additional items suggested from other disciplinary orientations such as medicine, economics, or sociology.

Rappaport's contribution also explicitly demonstrates how the development and choice of a particular intervention strategy is dependent, in large part, on the values and goals of the intervenor or is inherent in theoretical conceptions. He identifies four parameters of social intervention: *values and goals, levels of analysis, conceptions* of intervention, and *strategies or*

Table 3.1

Parameters of Psychological Intervention Strategies: Examples [a]

Goal	Target behavior	Setting	Mechanism
Enrichment	Cognition	Laboratory	Training–practice
Prevention	Language	Family	Social learning
Alleviation	Intellectual abilities	Classroom	Psychotherapy
	Social interactions	Senior citizen center	Environmental change
	Motivational states	Hospital	Health delivery
	Personality traits	Community	Economic support
	Attitudes	Macroecology	

[a] From Baltes (1973) based on Jacobs (1972). See also Birren and Woodruff (1973) for further illustrations of the present scheme.

tactics of intervention (see Rappaport, 1977, Table VI-I, pp. 164–166). Furthermore, Rappaport illustrates that these parameters have a major effect on where and how one intervenes. For example, the nature of intervention depends on whether one views social problems as a function of the inability of some people to fit within the established norms (individual level of analysis), as the result of interpersonal difficulties (small-group level of analysis), as the creation of organizations that fail to implement the desirable goals of a social institution (organizational level of analysis), or as the result of societal or community actions that are outside the realm of persons or groups (community–society level of analysis).

In a later section, we will discuss at greater length the relationship between values and intervention. At this point, it is sufficient to recognize that not only theories of behavior and development but also values (implicit or explicit) play an important role in constructing heuristic schemes of intervention action.

IV. Human Gerontology and Intervention

In the following section, an attempt is made to formulate some general considerations on intervention in the field of human gerontology. Many of these considerations follow from our discussion in the previous sections of this chapter.

A. Theories of Aging and Intervention

It has been previously stated that the type of intervention work espoused in this chapter suggests an active interplay between theory development and intervention, particularly if a long-term process such as aging is the target for intervention. The key assumption is that unless intervention efforts are guided by a precise and usable theoretical and human development-oriented framework, they are likely either to be ineffective or to run the risk of incurring negative side effects (see Danish, 1977; Urban, 1976).

1. Developmental Process and Intervention

A first set of considerations relates metatheoretical and theoretical features of the concepts of development and aging to intervention. Theoretical concepts of development and aging specify the nature (direction, sequence, etc.) of a behavior-change process. Thus, definitions of development and aging single out which behavior-change processes are properly labeled as constituting development and aging (Baltes, Reese, & Lipsitt, 1980; Baltes & Willis, 1977; Birren & Renner, 1977; Lerner, 1976). In child development literature, for instance, the biology-oriented growth concept of development (Harris, 1957) specifies that in order for a behavior-change process to be labeled as *development,* it needs to be characterized as unidirectional, sequential, qualitative–structural, irreversible, and endstate oriented. Piaget's theory of cognitive development is a good example. If one has such a theoretical position on development and a related concrete theory, it is possible to deduce guidelines and constraints for the design of intervention.

Guidelines and constraints that are derived from theoretical propositions about the nature of development involve statements about the potential *range* of modifiableness, *goals* or optimization targets of intervention efforts, the scope of intervention *transfer* effects, and *strategies* for the design of intervention programs—especially as they relate to *timing* and *packaging* of treatments (Baltes & Willis, 1977, p. 145). Thus, depending on the nature of the development theory (Overton & Reese, 1973; Weinert, 1978), distinct modes of diagnosis, treatment, and evaluation are derived.

The form and number of specifications and constraints associated with distinct theories of behavior change vary in their implications. Consider, for example on a metatheoretical level, the implications for intervention derived from the acceptance of either a mechanistic or an organismic model of development (Reese & Overton, 1970). Organismic models contain a series of prescriptions for the *when, how,* and *toward what* of intervention. At the same time, they imply firm constraints on the possible range of intervention effectiveness as well as on the possible negative side effects (e.g., Kohlberg, 1968; Wohlwill, 1970). On the other hand, mechanistic models are less rich in terms of development-oriented guiding principles. Although they still can suggest powerful intervention treatments, these are more likely of the concurrent static kind. Accordingly, "interventionists of the mechanistic kind show less concern for the metatheoretical sacredness and/or power of a system of fixed and sequential regulatory principles of developmental behavior-change or for the contextual system of transfer effects [Baltes & Willis, 1977, p. 146]."

When it comes to developmental intervention, however, the two key perspectives that are practically always mentioned are the existence of a *process* and a *context* in which behavior change occurs (Urban, 1976, 1978). On the descriptive level, processes involve series of states and behavior-change transitions. In addition, on the explanatory level, processes involve aggregations and cumulations of antecedent factors (i.e., histories of determining factors). This is the reason why developmentally oriented researchers propagate the use of historical (time-ordered) paradigms in the description and explanation of development or aging (Baltes, Reese, & Nesselroade, 1977). Note again that it is the existence of a process (which is at least somewhat predictable) that makes it possible to go beyond alleviative treatment and to consider prevention and enrichment. Thus, if a long-term process is well understood, it is possible to engineer conditions early in the series that would optimize its unfolding in desirable directions.

With regard to the context of development and aging, the basic notion (which does not apply to strictly personological, intraorganismic models) is that behavior change is usefully conceptualized as part of a person–environment system and that, in the long run, it always reflects an interactive property involving organism–environment interchanges. Accordingly, ecological perspectives (Baltes & Baltes, 1977; Bronfenbrenner, 1977) and systems perspectives (Urban, 1978) are introduced as promising theoretical conceptions. In child development literature, for example, Sigel (1972) has presented some insightful comments on the role of ecological contexts (such as parental homes) in the design of school-based intervention programs in cognitive development.

2. Examples of Theory–Intervention Interface: Models and Influences

Figure 3.1, which was presented earlier, is useful in illustrating some of the relationships between theoretical models of development (aging) and intervention on a generic level. Although Figure 3.1 does not represent concrete intervention programs, it suggests that intervention in development and aging varies according to one's theoretical world view and research emphasis.

With regard to intervention design, one of the major implications of Figure 3.1 is that intervention needs to consider the joint impact of all influence systems (age-graded, history-graded, nonnormative) in order to be developmental, preventative, and optimizing. Moreover, it is likely that nonnormative influences (e.g., accidents, career changes, personal life crises) are the ones most difficult to approach from a preventative and optimizing point of view. In other words, the less one knows prospectively about the likelihood and sequence of developmental events the less one is in a position to intervene in a preventative fashion. However, preventative intervention is still a possibility if it entails generic skills or resources related to dealing effectively with the unexpected. For example, Danish (1977) has described a life-development training program in which various life skills are taught. These life skills are assumed to be helpful across a variety of normative and nonnormative influences. They would enable one to be more prepared for future life events (nonnormative and normative) and would thus contribute to the "supplies" that Caplan (1964) finds essential for primary prevention.

Figure 3.1 also illustrates some multidisciplinary perspectives and represents relationships between individual and historical change. Multidisciplinary perspectives are emphasized because it is important to recognize that a comprehensive view of intervention needs to consider the interaction and joint impact of environmental and biological systems—not only at a given point in time but also in their trajectories over time. With regard to historical change, Figure 3.1 suggests that intervention targets and sequences are not invariant over historical time; moreover, it implies that the aging of individuals is part of a dynamic system of generational interaction and transmission, both in terms of continuity and discontinuity. In other words, both the aging of a given cohort and intervention into aging processes are codefined by the behavior of preceding and succeeding cohorts. Rutter and Madge's (1976) *Cycles of Disadvantage* and Riley's (1976) age-cohort stratification model are persuasive illustrations of the need to consider the individual life course and aging in the dynamic context of historical change and intergenerational relations (see also Bengtson & Black, 1973; Riegel, 1976). In other words, intervention action is not only aimed at ontogenetic life courses but also at intergenerational transmission and the course of social change.

3. Specific Theories of Aging

Another illustration of the interface between theory and intervention follows from the consideration of specific substantive theories of aging. If aging theories differ in their substance and explanation, they provide different knowledge bases from which to design intervention and different answers to basic questions involving intervention work: Why does the problem exist? In which direction should it be modified? How can the intervention be designed not only to be effective immediately, but also to optimize future aging and to prevent future dysfunctions and negative side effects?

Since Cowdry (1942), for example, we can distinguish between two general theoretical views of aging. The *involutionary-process* conception regards aging as leading to cumulative "aging" products and modifications of cells, tissues, and fluids. The other view, which is more *environmentally-oriented,* conceptualizes aging as structural alterations due to input defects such as infections, traumas, or nutritional disturbances. Intervention designs would differ according to which view one chose. Similarly, Birren (e.g., Birren & Renner, 1977) divides theories about aging into three groups: accident (wear and tear), genetic, and counterpart theories. Each of these theories would require distinct strategies of intervention.

To give one concrete example: Theories on intellectual aging vary according to the relative emphasis they place on biological–maturational and environmental factors and according to their relative focus on linear versus multilinear trends and on stability versus plasticity. Accordingly, intervention efforts in gerontological intelligence differ in terms of their substantive emphasis (e.g., experiential–educative versus biological treatments) and their relative emphasis on the need for consideration of life-long processes (Baltes & Labouvie, 1973; Baltes & Schaie, 1976; Eisdorfer & Stotsky, 1977; Labouvie-Vief, 1976).

B. Life-Span Development View of Aging and Intervention

A central theme of this paper is that a broadly defined developmental approach to intervention in aging is desirable, from both a conceptual and a pragmatic point of view. This approach makes intervention work an active contributor to theory building. At the same time, a developmental framework can provide the knowledge base necessary for practice, particularly if preventative and optimizing intervention efforts are at stake. In such a case, intervention efforts are planned as part of an explicit theory (or theories) of human behavior and societal functioning (Danish, 1977).

1. Aging as Part and Outcome of Life-Span Processes

A life-span approach to aging is perhaps the most explicit expression of a developmental orientation. A life-span view of aging (e.g., Baltes, 1979; Lerner & Ryff, 1978; Riley, 1979) suggests that:

1. Aging is part of the overarching process of life-span development.
2. Aging is the result of complex antecedents involving the biological and experiential life history of individuals.
3. Intervention into aging needs to consider the past, present, and future conditions and contexts in which aging occurs.

A number of specific considerations are implied by a life-span view of aging. For example, a life-span view makes it apparent that the locus of intervention is not necessarily the aging and aged. On the contrary, in line with a preventative and optimizing orientation, much of the intervention work needs to occur earlier in the life span. Adulthood, due to its temporal proximity to aging in the life sequence, is perhaps the key period when gerontological intervention might be most effective.

A life-span-oriented posture toward gerontological intervention does not deny, in principle, the need for concurrent treatment of existing dysfunctions in the elderly. In fact, the model presented in Figure 3.1 suggests that at least one set of influences (nonnormative) on aging cannot be fully predicted at earlier states in the life span, particularly at the level of individual functioning. A life-span view of gerontological intervention does suggest, however, that a major portion of intervention resources should be invested in the control of processes that antedate the occurrence of aging per se, thereby reducing the magnitude and intensity of aging dysfunctions.

The need to consider preaging periods in gerontological intervention concerns not only treatments on the individual level but also macrolevel interventions as evidenced in social policy and medical services systems. Thus, social policy for the aged is often best examined in policies dealing with the adult and the young. This future orientation might detract from the current needs of the elderly. At the same time, however, a life-span distribution of intervention efforts appears to be the only intervention strategy that, in the long run, is apt to use resources in an optimal manner by being able to tackle problems before they occur or even by preventing their occurrence.

2. Society, Social Change, and Aging

A life-span view of aging also makes it clear that gerontological intervention cannot be isolated from intervention efforts aimed at other age cohorts or at other indicators of social structure such as sex, social class, or occupation.

The work by Riley and her colleagues (1972; 1976) and other sociologists such as Guillemard (1977) is perhaps most explicit on this point. Consider, for example, the major domains of individual life: family, occupation, education, leisure, and health. These categories form a constellation in which individuals participate throughout their lives in varying degrees, profiles, and patterns. Furthermore, societies differ in their allocation of time to these activities, both on an absolute level and according to such indicators as age, sex, and social class. It is important to recognize that the status and role of the aged is part of a larger societal pattern involving family life, education, occupation, leisure, and health. As a consequence, decisions on resources necessary for gerontological intervention require attention to other age cohorts, and it is desirable to make these decisions in the larger context of societal functioning and the individual life course.

Consider the example of education (see Baltes & Willis, 1979; Schaie & Willis, 1978). In the past, most educational resources have been invested in the first part of the life span. On the other hand, research on gerontological intelligence and the obsolescence created by rapid social change suggest a life-span approach to the distribution and design of educational experiences and systems. Redistributing education throughout the life span is the key strategy, not simply increasing education for the aged. Another example that illustrates the role of the larger context of society in gerontological intervention deals with retirement policies and the extension of the human life span (see Neugarten & Havighurst, 1976, 1977, for a discussion of some of the core issues in social policy and social ethics in this realm).

It is therefore important to recognize that gerontological intervention takes place in the context of a larger system provided by the individual life course and by the macrostructure of society. In fact, it has been argued occasionally that "primary prevention in many areas may require social and political changes [Kessler & Albee, 1975, p. 576]" and that a major source of resistance to the use of primary prevention is the need for making major social system changes. This view is most forcefully presented by Marxist sociologists (e.g., Guillemard, 1976, 1977) and by behavioral scientists such as Watzlawik, Weakland, and Fisch (1974). These studies conclude that, other claims notwithstanding, the beneficiaries of social or individual intervention in gerontology are often not the elderly (especially not the poor elderly) but the service provider (e.g., gerontologists) or the cohort of younger adults. To illustrate this point, Guillemard (1977) analyzes French social policies on aging. She attempts to demonstrate that recent French policy on aging, which promotes an independent and activity-oriented model for the elderly, has been implemented under the guise of humanitarianism. She argues, however, that this policy of independent living for the elderly tends to serve the ruling class (including the upper-class elderly), while it dooms the majority of (poor) elderly who, for psychological and economic reasons, are unable to live up to this new standard of independent aging.

A multilevel and contextual view is also expressed by Watzlawick *et al.* (1974). Their work refers to three solution errors in intervention: (*a*) action is necessary but not taken; (*b*) action is taken but not necessary; (*c*) an error of "logical typing" occurs. Logical typing errors are most relevant to the present situation. One kind of logical typing error takes place when a *system* level problem is taken care of by an *individual* level solution. It establishes a "Game without Ends" in which all intervention efforts lead to no change because the wrong kind of intervention is used. As a result, more and more interventions are called for without success.

Aging is a social problem often dealt with by logical typing errors. Rappaport's (1977) discussion of these errors with regard to mental health services can be easily applied to gerontological services. These services are usually designed to increase independence and effective functioning; however, the intervention processes often serve to enhance the service recipients' tendency to be dependent and nonfunctioning, or even incompetent. This outcome is similar to that described in Guillemard's (1977) analysis of French policies on aging. Such strategies often entail a "blaming the victim" posture (Ryan, 1971) because they assume that the service delivery system is intact and blame the service recipient for being unable to benefit and adapt.

Whether or not the specific contentions of these authors are correct, their arguments sensitize us to the facilitating or interfering role that the existing social and economic structure in a given society might play. Moreover, this line of reasoning is apt to raise our level of consciousness about side effects of gerontological intervention efforts, particularly about the possibility of covert beneficiaries and covert societal benefits that accrue from chronic intervention failures.

V. Promise and Reality: Some Caveats

In the behavioral sciences, the current scene is one of optimism and promise resulting from the rapidly growing body of knowledge about aging. This optimism extends to the task of intervention. Based on evidence about the variability, plasticity, and ecological relativity of aging (Baltes & Baltes, 1977; Baltes & Willis, 1979; Lehr, 1975), the design and implementation of gerontological intervention is becoming more than a dream. However, we need to be careful not to confuse intent with realization. The body of knowledge dealing with the study of the conditions under which diverse forms of aging occur and can be produced is preliminary and fragmented. In addition, there is a dearth of literature on the relationship between theory and practice, on intervention technology, and on the role of ethics in identifying targets for intervention and in selecting treatment programs.

In our view, this early stage in the art of intervention work is frustrating. However, it is a necessary step in the evolution of gerontology as a science and profession. A move from description to explanation and suggestions for intervention is desirable from the perspective of scientific development, but this move is accompanied by a new set of philosophical, ethical, and political issues and conflicts (Looft, 1973). The seductive simplicity of certain intervention goals and strategies is not always desirable in itself, and it is necessary to examine these goals and strategies in the context of ethical and political contingencies. The excitement generated by early intervention work easily outruns its actual long-range benefits. Therefore, this concluding section summarizes suggestions for priorities in future work and contains a list of caveats.

A. Context of Intervention

We have emphasized that it is necessary not only to attend to immediate intervention effectiveness but also to consider the larger context. This larger context goes beyond the individuals serving as intervention targets and extends to their life space (e.g., the family), the societal and institutional context in which the intervention occurs, the professionals involved in the delivery of intervention, and the nature of theories about development and aging. The larger context also includes those individuals who compete for intervention services.

The complexity of the intervention context is apparent. The design and evaluation of intervention work must consider such contextual ramifications whenever possible. Two additional examples will be given here to illustrate issues related to this complexity.

1. Values and Intervention

One implication that is derivable from the complexity of the intervention context relates to the existence of a multitude of value-related criteria inherent in decisions on the *when, how,* and *to what end* of intervention.

In a given situation, several value perspectives can be confluent or discrepant in terms of priorities and goals. Consider, for example, the issue of competing requests for intervention resources at the societal level. Any allocation of societal resources to preventative gerontology might be in conflict with alternative intervention targets involving children and youth or with medical gerontological services. Another example is the design of geriatric hospitals for the purpose of ward management efficiency versus their design for the purpose of maintaining independence in the aged patient (see Barton, 1978; Barton, Baltes, & Orzech, in press).

The issue of value conflict is easily apparent when one attempts to articulate the notion of *optimal aging* in individuals. In the medical sciences, the criterion of lengthening life has a long tradition as a valuable general goal for intervention work aimed at optimization, on the level of both research and research application. Behavioral scientists have not yet agreed on a similar guiding principle. Life-satisfaction measures come closest;

however, the assessment of life satisfaction in aging is at a preliminary stage, and this is only partly for reasons of measurement validity (e.g., Larson, 1978). The assessment of life satisfaction also involves metajudgments about what is desirable on a personal, professional, societal, and philosophical level. Moreover, length of life and life satisfaction do not always correlate well. This is particularly true for advanced age and situations of death and dying. Discussions surrounding euthanasia and the maintenance of low levels of biological life in extreme situations of extended illness are good illustrations of such value conflicts and of the lack of a normative correlation between length of life and life satisfaction.

2. Systems Effects and Transfer Effects

Another issue that is easily overlooked also results from the contextual complexity of intervention work. As previously illustrated in Figures 3.1 and 3.2, theories of development and aging are rarely unidimensional; they are often aimed at holistic conceptions of individuals. Furthermore, theories of development and aging always incorporate statements about time-ordered processes (sequences) and the personal context (life-space) in which individual aging takes place. Thus, adherents of the developmental approach to aging have a tendency to view the individual as a system that is always changing in and interacting with an environmental context (e.g., Urban, 1978; Willems, 1973).

Accordingly, the perspective on gerontological intervention suggested by a developmental orientation is one that focuses on time trajectories, patterns of intervention treatments and intervention effects, and patterns of intervention targets. If intervention work has a sole or primary focus on a specific (both in terms of substance and point in time) intervention goal and a single individual, it easily overlooks side effects produced or neglected by the intervention action. For example, making nursing home patients more independent and active can result in nursing staff resistance if the staff is more interested in custodial care than rehabilitative work. Or, if one focuses solely on the dying patient in the design of intervention efforts, it is likely that problems surrounding the patient's family members will be overlooked or even aggravated. Finally, if one is concerned primarily with the biological health aspect of an individual's life, it is likely that important dimensions of his or her psychological life will remain unattended.

The definition and assessment of system effects or side (transfer) effects is aided by a theoretical, multivariate, and multidisciplinary orientation toward development. In the long run, a firm body of knowledge dealing with a developmental, contextual, and holistic conception of life-span development is a necessary prerequisite to intervention. The lack of this prerequisite is the reason that system effects or side effects are rarely well articulated and often overlooked in the beginning stages of intervention work.

B. Need for Evaluation

Intervention action is not necessarily effective, nor is it always effective in anticipated forms. Thus, intervention work requires a component of evaluation. This is particularly true when the knowledge base for intervention work is at the frontier of science in a given field, as is often the case in gerontology.

Knowledge is never final; frontier knowledge, moreover, is evolving and undergoing rapid change. Therefore, effects and effect patterns need continuous evaluation (Urban, 1976). In fact, as the interface between intervention research and intervention practice is being articulated more fully, a new body of methodologies (e.g., Struening & Guttentag, 1975) is evolving that deal specifically with evaluation methodology. In literature on human services, the terms *Research and Demonstration* (R & D) and *Research Program Planning and Evaluation* (RPP&E), which respond to this movement and quest for evaluation as a necessary ingredient in intervention work, have become part of the standard terminology. Furthermore, specific concepts and positions have been advanced that aim at specifying unique features of evaluation methodology.

For instance, the terms *formative evaluation* (aimed at examining the process of intervention) and *summative evaluation* (aimed at providing information on the overall product of intervention) have been proposed. On a more general level, a distinction between *basic research* (empirical) and *evaluation research* has been discussed. This distinction is primarily related to the goals and procedures involved in both approaches to research. Basic research is aimed at advancing scientific knowledge; evaluation research is aimed at establishing the worth, effectiveness, and efficiency of intervention (Scriven, 1972; Suchman, 1967). However, because our own view focuses jointly on knowledge generation and knowledge application, we would make the distinction between basic research and evaluation research one of emphasis rather than qualitative difference. This is particularly true if a theory-based approach to intervention is chosen. Thus, when intervention functions as a knowledge-generation mechanism in a theory-based approach, the evaluation process becomes the vehicle for assessing whether and how intervention follows from theory. Moreover, the outcome of the evaluation would be used to test or modify the precision, scope, and employability of a theory.

The key points of this section are that evaluation and intervention action are inextricably linked and that evaluation efforts will benefit from an explicit and aggressive stance on the need for a theory-based developmental and contextual framework. Effective evaluation cannot be an afterthought (Danish & Conter, 1978). Moreover, evaluation efforts will benefit from an explicit search for overt and covert value judgments. In the field of gerontology, an explicit focus on theory-based conceptions and value presuppositions is especially pertinent because there is a lack of tradition in gerontological intervention. This lack presents both an opportunity for productive action and a risk of unintended errors. We must compensate for this lack of tradition, for, when we consider intervention in human development and aging, we need to be not only vigorous and relevant but also more often right than wrong.

Summary

Written from the perspective of the behavioral sciences, this chapter presents a catalog of issues and concepts surrounding the relationship between intervention and life-span development within the context of aging. First, an effort is made to define intervention and to delineate alternative conceptions in the context of human development and gerontology. Intervention is defined as always including the systematic study of the conditions under which human development and aging can be modified. Three sets of developmental conditions or influences on development and aging (and correlated possibilities for intervention) are delineated: age-graded, history-graded, and nonnormative influences.

The next section identifies some of the dimensions of intervention work such as taxonomic distinctions among generic emphases of intervention (e.g., corrective, preventative, optimizing), the role of value assumptions inherent in the decision to intervene, and distinctions among different modes (strategies, tactics) of intervention. It is pointed out that intervention is always related, either implicitly or explicitly, to theories of development and aging. Such theories, because they differ not only in precision and scope but also in assumptions and explanatory principles, suggest distinct modes of attack involving the when, the end, and the how of interventive action. Subsequently, intervention is discussed as it applies to the field of gerontology, both as a science and a profession. It is argued that intervention is a necessary ingredient to both gerontological research and gerontological practice.

Major themes of the chapter include a concern with a life-span approach to the design of intervention and a concern with viewing intervention efforts in the context of a changing society. Thus, it is asserted that gerontological intervention efforts, for example, will benefit if they view aging as a process and as the outcome of life history and if they consider the nature of aging in the context of societal structure and functioning. Relationships of intervention to larger macrolevel conditions are also mentioned. Thus, existing social and economic structures are not always supportive of gerontological intervention—especially of the prevention–optimization kind—particularly if intervention requires major changes in the existing social system that are related to income, health, education, employment, and leisure. A concluding section deals with caveats and the need to distinguish between promise and reality. Examples are given to identify some of the costs and benefits of intervention and to identify the issues in evaluation. Finally, general caution in the wake of intellectual enthusiasm about intervention work is encouraged.

ACKNOWLEDGMENTS

We owe thanks to several colleagues at The Pennsylvania State University who have alerted us to many of the issues presented here, most notably Anthony D'Augelli, Donald H. Ford, Donald L. Peters, H. B. Urban, Fred W. Vondracek, and S. L. Willis. In addition, Judy K. Plemons, Carol A. Ryff, and Ellen Skinner offered helpful comments on our earlier version of this chapter.

REFERENCES

Baltes, M. M., & Baltes, P. B. The ecological relativity and plasticity of psychological aging: Convergent perspectives of cohort effects and operant psychology. *Zeitschrift fur Experimentelle und Angewandte Psychologie,* 1977, *24,* 179–197.

Baltes, P. B. Longitudinal and cross-sectional sequences in the study of age and generation effects. *Human Development,* 1968, *11,* 145–171.

Baltes, P. B. (Ed.). Strategies for psychological intervention in old age: A symposium. *The Gerontologist,* 1973, *13,* 4–38.

Baltes, P. B. Life-span developmental psychology: Some converging observations on history and theory. In P. B. Baltes & O. G. Brim, Jr. (Eds.), *Life-span development and behavior* (Vol. 2). New York: Academic Press, 1979.

Baltes, P. B., Cornelius, S. W., & Nesselroade, J. R. Cohort effects in developmental psychology. In J. R. Nesselroade & P. B. Baltes (Eds.), *Longitudinal research in the study of behavior and development.* New York: Academic Press, 1979.

Baltes, P. B., & Labouvie, G. V. Adult development of intellectual performance: Description, explanation, modification. In C. Eisdorfer & P. Lawton (Eds.), *The psychology of adult development and aging.* Washington: American Psychological Association, 1973.

Baltes, P. B., Reese, H. W., & Lipsitt, L. P. Life-span developmental psychology. *Annual Review of Psychology,* 1980, *31,* 65–110.

Baltes, P. B., Reese, H. W., & Nesselroade, J. R. *Life-span developmental psychology: Introduction to research methods.* Monterey, Calif.: Brooks/Cole, 1977.

Baltes, P. B., & Schaie, K. W. On the plasticity of intelligence in adulthood and old age: Where Horn and Donaldson fail. *American Psychologist,* 1976, *31,* 720–725.

Baltes, P. B., & Willis, S. L. Toward psychological theories of aging and development. In J. E. Birren & K. W. Schaie (Eds.), *Handbook of the psychology of aging.* New York: Van Nostrand-Reinhold, 1977.

Baltes, P. B., & Willis, S. L. Life-span developmental psychology, cognitive functioning, and social policy. In M. W. Riley (Ed.), *Aging from birth to death.* Boulder, Colo.: Westview Press, 1979.

Barton, E. M. *The social ecology of the nursing home: A naturalistic study of staff reinforcement contingencies for resident behavior.* Unpublished doctoral dissertation, The Pennsylvania State University, College of Human Development, 1978.

Barton, E. M., Baltes, M. M., & Orzech, M. G. On the etiology of dependence in older nursing home residents during morning care: The role of staff behavior. *Journal of Personality and Social Psychology,* in press.

Bengtson, V. L., & Black, K. D. Intergenerational relations in socialization. In P. B. Baltes & K. W. Schaie (Eds.), *Life-span developmental psychology: Personality and socialization.* New York: Academic Press, 1973.

Birren, J. E., & Renner, V. J. Research on the psychology of aging: Principles and experimentation. In J. E. Birren & K. W. Schaie (Eds.), *Handbook of the psychology of aging.* New York: Van Nostrand-Reinhold, 1977.

Birren, J. E., & Woodruff, D. Human development over the life-span through education. In P. B. Baltes & K. W. Schaie (Eds.), *Life-span developmental psychology: Personality and socialization.* New York: Academic Press, 1973.

Boesch, E. E. Die diagnostische Systematisierung. In R. Heiss (Ed.), *Psychologische Diagnostik* (Vol. 6). Göttingen: Hogrefe, 1964.

Brandtstädter, J., Fischer, M., Kluwe, R., Lohmann, J., Schneewind, K. A., & Wiedl, K. H. Entwurf eines heuristisch–taxonomischen Schemas zur Strukturierung von Zielbereichen padagogisch-psychologischer Forschung und Lehre. *Zeitschrift fur Entwicklungspsychologie und Pädagogische Psychologie,* 1974, *6,* 1–18.

Brandtstädter, J., & Von Eye, A. Pädagogisch–psychologische Praxis zwischen Prävention und Korrektur. In J. Brandtstädter, G. Reinert, & K. A. Schneewind (Eds.), *Pädagogische Psychologie.* Stuttgart: Klett-Cotta, 1979.

Bronfenbrenner, U. Toward an experimental ecology of human development. *American Psychologist,* 1977, *32,* 518–531.

Caplan, G. *Principles of preventive psychiatry.* New York: Basic Books, 1964.

Cowdry, E. V. *Problems of aging.* Baltimore: Williams & Wilkins, 1942.

Cowen, E. L. Social and community interventions. *Annual Review of Psychology,* 1973, *24,* 423–472.

Danish, S. J. Human development and human services: A marriage proposal. In I. Iscoe, B. L. Bloom, & C. B. Spielberger (Eds.), *Community psychology in transition.* New York: Halsted, 1977.

Danish, S. J., & Conter, K. R. Intervention and evaluation: Two sides of the same community coin. In L. Goldman (Ed.), *Research methods for counselors.* New York: Wiley, 1978.

Eisdorfer, C., & Stotsky, B. A. Intervention, treatment, and rehabilitation of psychiatric disorders. In J. E. Birren & K. W. Schaie (Eds.), *Handbook of the psychology of aging.* New York: Van Nostrand-Reinhold, 1977.

Frank, L. K. Human development: An emerging scientific discipline. In A. J. Solnit & S. A. Provence (Eds.), *Modern perspectives in child development.* New York: International Universities Press, 1963.

Gottesman, L. E., Quarterman, C. E., & Cohn, G. M. Psychosocial treatment of the aged.

In C. Eisdorfer & M. P. Lawton (Eds.), *The psychology of adult development and aging.* Washington, D.C.: American Psychological Association, 1973.

Guillemard, A. M. *La politique d'integration de la vieillesse.* Paris: Centre d'Etude des Mouvements Sociaux, 1976.

Guillemard, A. M. *A critical analysis of governmental policies on aging from a Marxist sociological perspective: The case of France.* Unpublished manuscript, Center for the Study of Social Movements, Paris, 1977.

Harris, D. B. (Ed.). *The concept of development.* Minneapolis: University of Minnesota Press, 1957.

Havighurst, R. J. *Developmental tasks and education.* New York: McKay, 1972.

Hollingworth, H. L. *Mental growth and decline.* New York: Appleton, 1927.

Hultsch, D. F., & Plemons, J. K. Life-span development and significant life events. In P. B. Baltes & O. G. Brim, Jr. (Eds.), *Life-span development and behavior* (Vol. 2). New York: Academic Press, 1979.

Huston-Stein, A., & Baltes, P. B. Theory and method in life-span developmental psychology: Implications for child development. In H. W. Reese (Ed.), *Advances in child development and behavior* (Vol. 11). New York: Academic Press, 1976.

Jacobs, A. Strategies of social intervention: Past and future. In A. Jacobs & W. Spradlin (Eds.), *The group as agent of change.* Chicago: Aldine, 1972.

Kastenbaum, R. Perspectives on the development and modification of behavior in the aged: A developmental–field perspective. *The Gerontologist,* 1968, *8,* 280–283.

Kessler, M., & Albee, G. W. Primary prevention. *Annual Review of Psychology,* 1975, *26,* 557–591.

Kohlberg, L. Early education: A cognitive–developmental view. *Child Development,* 1968, *39,* 1013–1062.

Labouvie, G. V. Implications of geropsychological theories for intervention: The challenge for the seventies. *The Gerontologist,* 1973, *13,* 10–14.

Labouvie-Vief, G. V. Toward optimizing cognitive competence in later life. *Educational Gerontology,* 1976, *1,* 75–92.

Labouvie-Vief, G. V., & Chandler, M. Cognitive development and life-span developmental theories: Idealistic versus contextual perspectives. In P. B. Baltes (Ed.), *Life-span development and behavior* (Vol. 1). New York: Academic Press, 1978.

Larson, R. Thirty years of research on the subjective well-being of older Americans. *Journal of Gerontology,* 1978, *33,* 109–125.

Lehr, U. *Psychologie des Alterns.* Heidelberg: Quelle, 1972.

Lehr, U. Die psychologischen Veränderungen im Alter als Voraussetzung der Rehabilitation. *Aktuelle Gerontologie,* 1975, *5,* 291–304.

Lerner, R. M. *Concepts and theories of human development.* Reading, Mass.: Addison-Wesley, 1976.

Lerner, R. M., & Ryff, C. D. Implementation of the life-span view of human development: The sample case of attachment. In P. B. Baltes (Ed.), *Life-span development and behavior* (Vol. 1). New York: Academic Press, 1978.

Looft, W. R. Reflections on intervention in old age: Motives, goals, and assumptions. *The Gerontologist,* 1973, *13,* 6–10.

Löwe, H. *Einführung in die Lernpsychologie des Erwachsenenalters.* Berlin: VEB Deutscher Verlag der Wissenschaften, 1977.

McCall, R. B. Challenges to a science of developmental psychology. *Child Development,* 1977, *48,* 333–344.

Neugarten, B. L. Continuities and discontinuities of psychological issues into adult life. *Human Development,* 1969, *12,* 121–130.

Neugarten, B. L., & Datan, N. Sociological perspectives on the life cycle. In P. B. Baltes & K. W. Schaie (Eds.), *Life-span developmental psychology: Personality and socialization.* New York: Academic Press, 1973.

Neugarten, B. L., & Hagestad, G. Age and the life course. In R. Binstock & E. Shanas (Eds.), *Handbook of aging and the social sciences.* New York: Van Nostrand-Reinhold, 1976.

Neugarten, B. L., & Havighurst, R. J. (Eds.). *Social policy, social ethics, and the aging society.* Chicago: University of Chicago, Committee on Human Development, 1976.

Neugarten, B. L., & Havighurst, R. J. (Eds.). *Extending the human life span: Social policy and social ethics.* Chicago: University of Chicago, Committee on Human Development, 1977.

Overton, W. F., & Reese, H. W. Models of development: Methodological implications. In J. R. Nesselroade & H. W. Reese (Eds.), *Life-span developmental psychology: Methodological issues.* New York: Academic Press, 1973.

Rappaport, J. *Community psychology: Values, research and action.* New York: Holt, Rinehart, & Winston, 1977.

Reese, H. W., & Overton, W. F. Models of development and theories of development. In L. R. Goulet & P. B. Baltes (Eds.), *Life-span developmental psychology: Research and theory.* New York: Academic Press, 1970.

Riegel, K. F. The dialectics of human development. *American Psychologist,* 1976, *31,* 689–700.

Riley, M. W. Age strata in social systems. In R. Binstock & E. Shanas (Eds.), *Handbook of aging and the social sciences.* New York: Van Nostrand-Reinhold, 1976.

Riley, M. W. (Ed.). *Aging from birth to death.* Boulder, Col.: Westview Press, 1979.

Riley, M. W., Johnson, W., & Foner, A. (Eds.). *Aging and society* (Vol. 3). New York: Russell Sage Foundation, 1972.

Rutter, M., & Madge, N. *Cycles of disadvantage.* London: Heinemann, 1976.

Ryan, W. *Blaming the victim.* New York: Random House, 1971.

Schaie, K. W., & Willis, S. L. Life-span development: Implications for education. *Review of Research in Education,* 1978, *6,* 120–156.

Scriven, M. The methodology of evaluation. In C. H. Weiss (Ed.), *Evaluating action programs: Readings in social action and education.* Boston: Allyn & Bacon, 1972.

Sigel, I. E. Developmental theory: Its place and relevance in early intervention programs. *Young Children,* 1972, *37,* 364–372.

Struening, E. L., & Guttentag, M. (Eds.). *Handbook of Evaluation Research.* Beverly Hills, Calif.: Sage Publications, 1975.

Suchman, E. A. *Evaluation research: Principles and practices in public service and social action programs.* New York: Russell Sage Foundation, 1967.

Thomae, H. (Ed.). Patterns of aging: Findings from the Bonn Longitudinal Study of Aging. *Contributions to Human Development* (Vol. 3). Basel: Karger, 1976.

Thomae, H. The concept of development and life-span developmental psychology. In P. B. Baltes & O. G. Brim, Jr. (Eds.), *Life-span development and behavior* (Vol. 2). New York: Academic Press, 1979.

Urban, H. B. *Issues in human development intervention.* Unpublished manuscript, The Pennsylvania State University, College of Human Development, 1976.

Urban, H. B. The concept of development from a systems perspective. In P. B. Baltes (Ed.), *Life-span development and behavior* (Vol. 1). New York: Academic Press, 1978.

Wagenfeld, M. P. The primary prevention of mental illness. *Journal of Health and Social Behavior,* 1972, *13,* 195–203.

Watzlawick, P., Weakland, J. H., & Fisch, R. *Change: Principles of problem formation and problem resolution.* New York: Norton, 1974.

Weinert. F. Uber die mehrfache Bedeutung des Begriffes "entwicklungsangemessen" in der pädagogisch-psychologischen Theorienbildung. In J. Brandtstädter, G. Reinert, & K. A. Schneewind (Eds.), *Pädagogische Psychologie*. Stuttgart: Klett-Cotta, 1979.

Willems, E. P. Behavioral ecology and experimental analysis: Courtship is not enough. In J. R. Nesselroade & H. W. Reese (Eds.), *Life-span developmental psychology: Methodological issues*. New York: Academic Press, 1973.

Wohlwill, J. F. The age variable in psychological research. *Psychological Review,* 1970, *77,* 49–64.

Wohlwill, J. F. *The study of behavioral development*. New York: Academic Press, 1973.

CHAPTER **4**

Life-Span Intervention as a Symptom of Conversion Hysteria

MICHAEL J. CHANDLER
THE UNIVERSITY OF BRITISH COLUMBIA
VANCOUVER, BRITISH COLUMBIA

I. Introduction

Other contributors to this volume detail particular attempts to psychologically intervene with persons located at various points along the life span or discuss the theoretical rationale and procedural means for carrying out such interventions. This chapter is more cautionary in its purpose and attempts to raise questions about the *ends* that guide such intervention efforts rather than the *means* by which they might be carried out. Discussions of this genre—which presume to talk ethics, but often present sophisms or attempt to escape from decision making into the alibi of moral uncertainty—tend, almost uniformly, to be aggravatingly smug and to function as wet blankets upon an otherwise upbeat spirit of reform. The present chapter will not prove to be an important exception to this general rule. However, it will argue that although most contemporary social science intervention efforts bristle with good intentions, their manipulations commonly lack carefully considered adequacy criteria for justifying the value system that they tacitly express; consequently, these manipulations often have the approximate status of attempted religious or political conversions. Although the choice of ends is always *eo ipso* an

79

LIFE-SPAN DEVELOPMENTAL PSYCHOLOGY
Intervention

ethical matter, this chapter will further argue that socio-psychological intervention with the elderly is an especially hazardous moral terrain. Some broad consensus probably exists to the effect that children should be helped to become adults, and intervention efforts toward this end are not commonly called into question. However, it is much less obvious what young adults should become, and the potential for tyranny and intolerance toward alternate ways of being is very real. In the absence of any divinely revealed moral truth regarding the proper goals of aging, any prospective manipulations or exercises of power in the name of reform must be thought about very carefully.

In this case, minimal care would seem to require that: (*a*) intervention efforts have an explicit target; (*b*) the chosen targeted behaviors show some demonstrable need of reform; (*c*) the prospective interventionists have some practicable theory to guide their conversionary efforts. In the pages that follow, I will attempt to clarify these three prerequisites to responsible interventions and then consider each in turn as they apply to contemporary efforts at life-span intervention.

Any impulse to intervene—to effect some sort of change in other persons—would seem to require, as a *first* condition, the ability to reliably identify some enduring, nontrivial dimension of difference between persons or groups of persons. Without meeting this minimal (and I hope noncontroversial) condition, it would be impossible to imagine what was to be changed into what, and change efforts would have nowhere to begin or end. Although this point may seem so obvious as to be hardly worth mentioning, it would appear that at least in the area of adult development, so few enduring, nontrivial age-related differences have been reliably identified that the prospective interventionist might be hard-pressed to know where to begin.

The *second* precondition to responsible intervention would appear to be the explicit detailing of some evaluative framework within which those individual differences that have been observed can be judged as being more or less desirable. Without some such defensible value orientation, there is no basis for regarding one different way of being as any better or worse than another, and there is no authority or motivation for attempting any kind of systematic intervention. Persons familiar with the apparently glaring handicaps suffered by the sick or elderly or disenfranchised may regard this concern as unnecessarily academic. Surely, it would seem self-evident that it is better to be independent rather than dependent, to usually remember rather than usually forget, to be flexible rather than rigid, or to be fast rather than slow. In the following sections of this chapter, I will argue against some of these supposedly self-evident assumptions, and try to document what appears to be a growing sense of disillusionment among developmentalists with the value framework within which age-related changes have traditionally been evaluated.

If one were successful in reliably establishing the existence of more than a single way of being, and if one could locate these differences within some acceptable value framework that permitted the judgment that one of those ways of being was better than another, the hopeful interventionist would still need some practicable theory about growth and development as a *third* prerequisite to intervention. The difficulty here is that the major prompts and occasions for developmental change, as envisioned by most contemporary developmental theories, tend to be in the hands of biological, epigenetic, or formistic processes that are thought to lie outside the usual sphere of influence of the behavioral scientist. What, if anything, is to be done about this kind of institutionalized impotence will be the focus of the concluding remarks of this chapter.

Having previewed the major points that I feel are prerequisite to any responsible attempts at intervention, I will now consider them in turn with the aim of trying to determine, at least to my own satisfaction, whether there is still room for well-reasoned life-span intervention. In further illustrating these points, I will try, as far as I am able, to draw upon the research literature concerning the development of adult and aged persons—both because it seems more consistent with the interests of this volume and because some of the problems I will try to underscore have arisen in studies focused upon this portion of the lifespan.

II. Identifying Potential Targets for Intervention

Turning to what I have characterized as the first prerequisite to responsible intervention research, I will first take up the question of what, if any, nontrivial differences have been demonstrated that reliably distinguish among persons located at different points along the adult portion of the life span. The purpose of this optimistic agenda is to establish whether there are at least two ways of being adult so that the hopeful interventionist will have one thing that potentially can be turned into something else.

Superficially, the task seems ridiculously simple. It is usually assumed that to be "old" is to be such things as slow, forgetful, easily confused, or of small consequence. In contrast, being an adult that is "not old" commonly implies being productive, responsible, and generally in charge of things. However, as soon as one attempts to move beyond such easy age stereotypes, the simplicity of the task seems merely superficial. My own reading of the available literature suggests that practically nothing of consequence can be incontrovertibly shown to distinguish the old from the not-so-old, with the possible exception of sensory–motor slowing (Labouvie-Vief & Chandler, 1978). Some things, which at first seemed to discriminate among persons of different ages, actually turned out upon closer inspections to be artifactual consequences of the particular cohort into which a person was born, instead of actually having to do with longevity per se. Similarly, other apparent differences have been traced to other brands of sampling bias resulting from the fact that persons who are ill or institutionalized or at death's door (and who are therefore only incidently old) are more easily corralled for research purposes than are sounder and more independent or free-living persons of the same age (Riegel & Riegel, 1972). Thus, what initially passed as age-related differences often proved, on closer inspection, to be health-related or class-related distinctions potentially relevant to persons of any age.

In addition to these artifactual differences resulting from cavalier methods of subject selection, other counterfeit differences have been traced to equally unwise decisions about the choice of measurement strategies (Labouvie-Vief & Chandler, 1978). The point here is more subtle, but only slightly more so. It has been observed that older people tend to be even less enchanted than the young with being told precisely what to do and how to do it; moreover, they generally dislike bookish, abstract, or childish tasks of low meaningfulness. When given laboratory tasks of this genre, they often perform poorly—more poorly than it turns out they are able—and are regularly surpassed by their younger, more compliant, and test-wise counterparts. Such differences are of course real, but they are not real in the sense that the authors of these comparative studies typically had in mind. Borrowing from Heider's (1959) phenomenological characterization of behavior, these studies set out to determine what the elderly *can* and *cannot* do, only to learn what they were and were not willing to *try*. In other words, research instruments intended to capture differences in competence often succeeded only in snaring more trivial differences in performance. These distinctions are real enough, but they are not the sort of distinctions upon which important theories of aging can be built. Recent intervention studies (Labouvie-Vief, 1978), which have demonstrated how easily such differences can be washed out with warm-up effect or with a little cajoling and good will, underscore the ephemeral quality of these shallow age-related distinctions. My purpose here is not to choose sides in the stormy debate about whether or not intellectual decline in adulthood is mythical (Horn & Donaldson, 1976; Schaie & Baltes, 1977), but to emphasize the point that whatever differences might exist between the old and the not-so-old, these differences are rather hard to come by and do not jump out at the potential interventionist at every turn.

Some rather convincing evidence does seem to support the contention that there are reliable stylistic differences in the way that the old and the young organize, categorize, or go about remembering things (Labouvie-Vief, 1978). It seems equally clear, however, that these types of differences do not intuitively order themselves along some dimension of good or bad, or more or less adequate. Deciding how those age-related differences that do exist arrange themselves in any evaluative sense, which is our next category of concern, will not be a simple matter.

III. Ethical Considerations in the Formulation and Acceptance of Intervention Goals

The second precondition to the responsible undertaking of intervention research was previously defined as the explicit framing of some value or standard by means of which one way of being adult could be considered better or worse than another. It is, of course, entirely possible to detect different ways of thinking, feeling, or behaving without becoming embroiled in any normative or evaluative considerations regarding these pluralistic ways of being. Such differences can be noted and simply left alone. However, as soon as we elect to act upon these observed differences in order to convert or reform one possible way of being into another, we necessarily leave behind the plane of value neutrality. The criteria that determine the proper attitudes toward action are always ethical (Pepper, 1970), and it is consequently impossible to undertake any intervention program in an ethically neutral way. In short, the interventionist, having disapprovingly concluded that the way a person *is* is not the way he or she *ought* to be, becomes a moralist and proselytizer for a conversionary cause. My point is not to question whether things should be otherwise (directionality is by definition a feature of guided change) but to underscore the fact that such ethical considerations are inescapable and to lobby for a reflective scrutiny of our reformist agendas.

Faced with the recognition that all interventions entail ethical considerations, some authors have concluded that the logic behind all interventions can be ultimately reduced to arbitrary, elitist value biases that indefensibly ride roughshod over the unique cultural forms and behavior patterns of nondominant groups. Although it may prove that all intervention efforts do ultimately resolve themselves into exercises in Procustean bed-fitting, the history of developmental theory is marked by numerous claims for less arbitrary or capricious standards for formulating and evaluating change.

Except among developmentalists of the most mechanistic, antecedent-consequent sort, change is not commonly regarded as some ad hoc process of blind ontogenetic extension. Instead, most contemporary psychologists picture children as being swept along toward inevitable maturity by power-ful, universal forces. Within such idealistic accounts, stages in the process of human development are conceptualized as imperfect or progressive categories, teleologically aimed at, and ultimately realized in, the fixed goal or end state of maturity. Moreover, change is construed as inherently direc-tional, growth is understood as progress, and adulthood is regarded as suc-cess. The laws and principles of development generated in this idealistic context are prescriptive rather than simply descriptive, and adulthood takes on the role of a kind of Platonic absolute (Labouvie-Vief & Chandler, 1978).

Organismic and other developmental views similar to those just outlined, offer, therefore, a restricted but nevertheless widely employed evaluative framework for judging certain kinds of behavior in relation to others. Ac-cording to such schemes, individual differences, which are also developmental, are not morally neutral or arbitrary (Kohlberg, 1971) but can be evaluatively ordered in terms of their relative desirability. Within this evaluative framework, intervention goals that mirror the usual out-comes of "normal" development may be regarded as nonarbitrary and self-justifying. On essentially these grounds, Kohlberg (1971), for example, has argued that facilitating "natural" development is a very different mat-ter from attempting to inculcate arbitrary cultural beliefs and that, conse-quently, the only ethically acceptable forms of intervention are those that operate to stimulate development. The rationale for this argument is that if a particular way of being is the common end point of natural development, then eventually being that particular way not only *is* but *ought* to be the case.

Closely related to this is-to-ought assertion is the corollary assumption that the progressive categories or stages that approximate the idealized end state of natural development unfold in a linear, single sequence progression (Van den Daele, 1969) and that these stages can also be ordered in terms of their relative merit and be chosen as progressive goals in related interven-tion efforts. Implicit or explicit allegiance to these assumptions has pro-vided the directionality and moral authority for a whole range of therapeutic and educational interventions, including attempts to train or retrain such things as moral judgments (Turiel, 1974), conservation skills, seriation, classificatory abilities (Miller, 1976), and social role-taking skills (Chandler, 1973).

This idealistic rationale, if it can be defended against close criticism, pro-vides a justificatory framework for the defense of whole families of evaluative and intervention strategies; it holds out the potential for elevating our good intentions above the level of arbitrary value bias and locating them on a more lofty and self-justifying "natural" plane. Because of these sweeping implications, one would be well advised, before accepting these views to note and critically evaluate the assumptions on which they rest and the implications that they carry. This task will be the agenda of section IV of this chapter, which will attempt to isolate and evaluate in some detail each of the several parts of these broad assumptions and, through approaching them in this more systematic way, will try to arrive at some conclusions regarding their acceptability.

IV. Developmental Theory as a Vehicle for Generating Intervention Strategies

The following assumptions are implicitly or explicitly contained within most contemporary accounts of developmental progress: (a) the goal of early development is a single, universal end state of idealized maturity, the apogee of this progressive development occurs at a point well in advance of the end of the life span, and all changes subsequent to the accomplishment of this final stage are consequently decremental and lack the positive, progressive, prescriptive quality of earlier growth; (b) the route to maturity is a universal, unidirectional, single-sequence process; and (c) this fixed course and outcome of development is at least tacitly understood not only by developmental theorists but also by all of those people who follow these prescriptive obligations in the course of their development. Having summarized these assumptions, I will now attempt to detail and discuss the problems of each of them in turn.

A. Monistic and Pluralistic Views of Development

First, as suggested earlier, organismic accounts of development tend to be inherently idealistic because they define stages in the course of human development as imperfect or progressive categories aimed at, and only ultimately realized in, a fixed ideal goal or end state. Developmental research undertaken from this perspective becomes a kind of ontological ballistics, tracking growth along a unilinear trajectory toward its idealized apogee in adulthood (Labouvie-Vief & Chandler, 1978).

The obvious advantages and disadvantages of such a monistic view of maturity are practically the same. Prior to adulthood, it seems clear that growing up is a universal requirement, and any hesitancy or misdirection in carrying out this task can be confidently branded as deviancy. Although ready cures are not always available, what such a cure would look like when accomplished is clear. These apparent benefits of maintaining such an idealistic view are quickly offset, however, as soon as attention is redirected toward the latter two-thirds of the life span. Only a discipline historically preoccupied with the almost exclusive study of childhood could have had the shortsightedness to locate the presumptive end of development so close to its beginning. The negative consequence of this seemingly perverse choice has been to leave the larger part of life-span development free-floating and without theoretical guidance.

As one might suspect, this problem has not gone unnoticed by developmentalists with life-span interests, and several different sorts of solutions have been suggested. Some theorists such as Flavell (1970) have proposed dichotomous solutions whereby early and late development are regarded as discontinuous and are best understood in terms of qualitatively different explanatory models. Others (e.g., Dulit, 1972) have attempted to get additional mileage out of available organismic models by accepting the usually identified end state of development but arguing that this goal is commonly approached much more slowly and tentatively and by a more meandering course than is usually supposed. The common research strategy among exponents of this tradition is to demonstrate that the formal, idealized qualities associated with developmental maturity are neither universally achieved nor uniformly practiced by most adults. In contrast, other authors such as Erikson (1968) and Neugarten (1969) have sought to finesse the solution to the problem by postulating additional stages in the course of adult development. In these stage models, the notion of a terminal end state is accepted in principle, but, through the introduction of additional stages or categories, it is located much closer to the end than to the beginning of the life span. Finally, others (Chandler, 1977; Labouvie-Vief, 1977; 1978; Labouvie-Vief & Chandler, 1978; Reese, 1973), have become sufficiently disenchanted with the limitations inherent in organismic models to argue that they should perhaps be abandoned altogether.

With regard to the available alternatives proposed as substitute strategies for organismic models, some investigators (e.g., Reese, 1973) have argued that the increasingly heavy influence of environmental factors in shaping the course of adulthood calls for a shift from organismic to more mechanistic models. My own preferred substitute for idealized organicism is what Pepper (1970) has termed *contextualism*. For those unfamiliar with Pepper's writings, contextual models refer to a family of theories that share many features in common with more familiar organismic accounts. Both emphasize the centrality of change, the importance of qualitative as opposed to quantitative shifts, and the role of dialectical tensions in providing the impetus for development. However, contextual and organismic theories differ importantly with respect to the assumptions that they make regarding the directionality and ultimate outcome of change. In contrast to the progressive claims made by organismic models, contextual theories regard change as simply that and make no assumptions that such variations serve to achieve any particular goal or idealized end state. According to Pepper, the omission of this central idealistic assumption is sufficient to cause the progressive categories of organismic models to undergo a general revision in the direction of contextualism. A contextualist, in short, is an organicist who has peered into the Platonic cave and found it empty (Labouvie-Vief & Chandler, 1978). The price of this lost idealism is high. What it is that persons of various ages should be or should not be changing into becomes indeterminate, and our aristocratic sense that we, as mature behavioral scientists, constitute the proper standard to which others should be held, is lost. What is gained by this shift toward contextualism, however, is the acquisition of a conceptual framework that enables us to appreciate the unique socio-historical context within which particular persons live, that makes us free to regard the changes of adulthood as developmental in the same fashion as changes in childhood, and that allows us to avoid branding all life-span changes after 16 as automatic deficits.

B. Single Sequence Development

The second burdensome and seemingly unnecessary feature of most contemporary organismic accounts of development is their portrayal of growth as a linear, universal, single-sequence affair. This concept of growth not only requires that everyone arrive at the same developmental destination but also insists that everyone reach this common terminus by precisely the same route. Of course, it is at least technically possible to imagine a single, universal outcome of development that is approximated by a great variety of avenues. However, the two views are usually bracketed together, and universal *goals* are most commonly presumed to be achieved by universal *means*.

Although the assumption of universality concerning either the ends or the means of development greatly simplifies the task of sorting through and evaluating the tremendous variety of ways in which persons manage to be, the cost of this assumption is high. For example, this kind of simplification has traditionally been achieved at the cost of promoting models that spiral to unnecessarily lofty and impractical levels of alienated abstraction. Furthermore, in order to sustain what I would regard as the illusion of universality, organismic developmental theorists have been forced to practice a kind of narrow ethnocentrism that judges cultures other than their own to be arrested in their approach to more local brands of developmental universals.

If, as recent cross-cultural studies (e.g., Buck-Morss, 1975) suggest, persons who grow up in different social and historical contexts not only approach qualitatively different end points, but also proceed to wherever it is they are going by qualitatively different routes, then the *process* of growth becomes as evaluatively indeterminate as its *outcome*. From the perspective of the would-be interventionist, this procedural indeterminacy closes off still another avenue to responsible action. Perhaps one could get by without knowing the ultimate consequences of normal development as long as the course by which this still open-ended process unfolded was itself clear and unambiguously universal. Under these minimal conditions, there would still be grounds for assuming that later was better and for intruding therapeutically whenever development seemed to be taking a different turn or slowed in its progress. However, if the grounds for assuming a universal developmental sequence are missing (as they appear to be), then intervention is all but "game over." If few nontrivial differences between persons of various ages have been demonstrated, and if the course and outcome of development are so indeterminate that no universal standard of value exists for assessing the relative merits of those few age differences that have been well documented, where and why is intervention to begin?

Incredible as it would seem in any other context, the usual solution to this dilemma is to assert that informed answers to these seemingly crucial questions are not required in order to get underway. This counter-intuitive, "wise child" argument rests upon the debatable assumption that people know where they ought to be going and how they should be getting there, even if behavioral scientists do not. This third assumption of organismic models is rooted in an image of development as the unwinding of some well-programmed, built-in epigenetic time clock that runs without recourse to conscious human invention. Furthermore, this presumptive ground plan is thought to be auto-regulative, and growth is imagined to reflect, in its diachronic course, a self-righting moment sufficient to allow it to recover its natural directionality from all but the most persistent of environmental assaults.

To the extent that some such self-guidance system does operate to canalize growth along a prefigured course, the task of the interventionist is greatly simplified. Under these conditions, the role of the therapist or educator is somewhat analogous to that of a person pushing someone in a wagon; all that is required is effort, and the problem of steerage is left in the hands of the passenger. Something like this is what Kohlberg (1971) apparently had in mind when he suggested that efforts to "facilitate" development are our only available, ethically acceptable means of intervention.

While there is something comforting about substituting wisdom of the body for our own ignorance about development, there is also something especially hazardous about abdicating responsibility for the consequences of our own actions by relying too heavily on the guiding hand of epigenetic fate. If the directionality and self-righting moment of development were all that reliable, there would be no need for intervention in the first place. In the absence of information to the contrary, a safer, even if less optimistic, assumption is that any therapeutic lever big enough to move people can probably move them in any direction. The existence of whole families of introgenetic or physician-induced disorders speaks to the fact that intervention efforts often prove to be double-edged swords and that therapeutic backlashes are not altogether uncommon. If concern for these issues is carried over into the avenue of life-span developmental intervention, there is little cause to be comfortable with plans for pushing blindly from the rear in the hope that someone is driving.

In summary, I have argued that, given the present state of our art, we are hard pressed to identify nonartifactual and nontrivial psychological differences between persons at different positions along the adult portion of the life span. Even when such process or outcome differences have been reliably identified, we appear to lack the moral means of establishing an unbiased standard by which we can confidently say that any one of these alternative ways of being is better or worse than any other. Finally, even if we could establish *where* and *why* intervention should begin, the *how* of such prospective treatment efforts would elude us. At least from the perspective or organismic models, responsibility for theoretically meaningful variations among persons is always traceable to large-scale developmental forces that lie beyond the apparent sphere of human influence. It is on these grounds that I have questioned the moral authority on which life-span intervention rests and have suggested that a number of invidious comparisons can be made between such treatment efforts and other equally ideologically based attempts at religious and political conversion.

V. Conclusion

Certain of the issues raised in the preceding pages—specifically those concerned with the adequacy of the theoretical and empirical base of our work—can be addressed within the usual context of traditional psychological practice. If important differences do exist that distinguish the elderly from persons of less advanced age, proper attention to subject selection and measurement strategies will bring these differences to the surface. Similarly, if mainstream, child-centered theories of development are not properly addressed to the issues of aging, then, as other contributors to this volume have demonstrated, it is possible and perhaps obligatory that new conceptual models be found. What is not so easily addressed, however, is the remaining issue concerning the identification of some acceptable ethical framework that could serve to justify any intervention effort we might mount. The difficulty here seems deeply rooted in a broadly shared meta-science that permits reason to work in the value-neutral realm of *means* but sets the choice of *ends* beyond the boundaries of rational science (Unger, 1975). As long as social scientists are prepared to languish in this awkwardly "gerrymandered" space of supposed ethical neutrality, where facts are regarded as prophylactically isolated from impregnation by values, a certain pristine illusion can be maintained. The cost of this virginal posture, however, is high. Unless we are engaged in a barren quest for knowledge—in which knowing is dichotomized from deciding—we are not free to act, at least on our own agendas, without becoming mechanics and manipulators in a cause that we do not avow. The rub, of course, is that the distinction between knowing a thing and evaluating it seems inescapable, and none of the machinery of our present science appears to lend us any special expertise in the business of evaluating. Knowledge, we seem convinced, is neutral toward the purposes of specific individuals.

One potential avenue to the seemingly closed character of knowledge is signaled by advocates of what is sometimes referred to as the *hermeneutic–dialectic* tradition of metascience (Radnitzky, 1970). In this view, the search for some *universal* standard of rational morality necessarily excludes a decision to favor the goals of any single individual simply because he or she happens to want them. Under these conditions, a morality of reason could not be devoted to the promotion of any substantive end except the end of freedom (Unger, 1975). On these grounds, theorists such as Habermas (1971) find a foothold for defining an *emancipatory* ethic in which progress lies in the *autonomy* of the individual and tolerance of alternative ways of being is seen in all circumstances as more humane than the tyranny of attempts to impose any particular substantive way of being. K. O. Apel (cited by Radnitzky, 1970) further extended this ground plan by urging that the emancipatory interest be made into a categorical imperative according to which individuals should adopt as their own existential interest the emancipation of others.

Whether a value-explicit view of this sort of personally supportable and, perhaps more critically, whether it can survive the kind of particularization required to employ it as a guide to concrete attempts at life-span intervention, remain open questions. It is my own view, however, that without this or some similar value commitment, social science intervention will remain a conversionary exercise of an unnamed and unexamined faith.

REFERENCES

Buck-Morss, S. Socio-economic bias in Piaget's theory and its implication for cross-culture studies. *Human Development,* 1975, *18,* 35–49.

Chandler, M. J. Egocentrism and anti-social behavior: The assessment and training of social perspective-taking skills. *Developmental Psychology,* 1973, *9,* 1–6.

Chandler, M. J. Social cognition and life-span approaches to the study of child development. In H. W. Reese (Ed.), *Advances in child development and behavior* (Vol. 11). New York: Academic Press, 1977.

Dulit, E. Adolescent thinking à la Piaget: The formal stage. *Journal of Youth and Adolescence,* 1972, *1,* 281–301.

Erikson, E. H. *Youth and crisis.* New York: W. W. Norton, 1968.

Flavell, J. H. Cognitive changes in adulthood. In P. B. Baltes & L. R. Goulet (Eds.), *Life-span developmental psychology: Research and theory.* New York: Academic Press, 1970.

Habermas, J. *Knowledge and human interests.* Boston: Beacon Press, 1971.

Heider, F. *The psychology of interpersonal relations.* New York: Wiley, 1959.

Horn, J. L., & Donaldson, G. On the myth of intellectual decline in adulthood. *American Psychologist,* 1976, *31,* 701–719.

Kohlberg, L. From is to ought: How to commit the naturalistic fallacy and get away with it in the study of moral development. In T. Mischel (Ed.), *Cognitive development and epistemology.* New York: Academic Press, 1971.

Labouvie-Vief, G. Adult cognitive development: In search of alternative interpretations. *Merrill-Palmer Quarterly,* 1977, *23,* 227–263.

Labouvie-Vief, G. Personality and socialization in later life. In M. E. Lamb (Ed.), *Social and personality development.* New York: Holt, Rinehart & Winston, 1978.

Labouvie-Vief, G., & Chandler, M. J. Cognitive development and life-span developmental theory: Indealistic versus contextual perspectives. In P. B. Baltes (Ed.), *Life-span development and behavior* (Vol. 1). New York: Academic Press, 1978.

Miller, S. Extinction of Piagetian concepts: An updating. *Merrill-Palmer Quarterly,* 1976, *22,* 257–281.

Neugarten, B. L. Continuities and discontinuities of psychological issues into adult life. *Human Development,* 1969, *13,* 121–130.

Pepper, S. C. *World hypotheses* (2nd ed.). Berkeley: University of California Press, 1970.

Radnitzky, G. *Contemporary schools of metascience.* Copenhagen: Scandinavian University Press, 1970.

Reese, H. W. Life-span models of memory. *The Gerontologist,* 1973, *13,* 472–478.

Riegel, K. G., & Riegel, R. M. Development, drop, and death. *Developmental Psychology,* 1972, *6,* 306–319.

Schaie, K. W., & Baltes, P. B. Some faith helps to see the forest: A final comment on the Horn and Donaldson myth of the Baltes–Schaie position on adult intelligence. *American Psychologist,* 1977, *32,* 1118–1120.

Turiel, E. Conflict and transition in adolescent moral development. *Child Development,* 1974, *45,* 14–29.

Unger, R. *Knowledge and politics.* New York: Free Press, 1975.

Van den Daele, L. D. Quantitative models in developmental analysis. *Developmental Psychology,* 1969, *1,* 303–310.

CHAPTER 5

The Politics of Public Intervention

GEORGE PICKETT
WEST VIRGINIA DEPARTMENT OF HEALTH
CHARLESTON, WEST VIRGINIA

The English language is infamous for its richness, its nuances and shadings. It confounds those who speak another primary tongue. The advantages of American "plagiarism" are demonstrated by our ability to borrow from many tongues and to create whole new images out of words intended for another purpose. Even our current mania for reductionism—for cutting down our vocabulary to a few monosyllabic grunts accompanied by shrugs—cannot offset our penchant for linguistic invention. Yet, in one peculiar area, we seem to lack facility. We simply cannot handle the concepts of intervention. We have the verb *intervene,* the noun *the intervenor* or *the interventionist,* and even the adjective *intervening;* but I cannot find a commonly accepted word for the object of intervention—a word to describe the person or group we are meddling with. Depending on who the "we" (the intervenor) is and how we feel about the object of our intervention, it or they are called variously the *others, targets, victims,* or *miscreants.* In order to avoid pejorative intimations, it may be best to speak of the objects of intervention as either *voluntary* or *involuntary clients.*

LIFE-SPAN DEVELOPMENTAL PSYCHOLOGY
Intervention

I. The Difficulties of Public Intervention

Not being a linguist, I am not sure how other cultures deal with the problem. But I suspect that this difficulty is peculiarly American. Surely, very few countries can have agonized so much over the politics of intervention. Not intervention in the sense of war, of course; that is a unique situation. At least in current times, it is well understood that interventions in the form of war are very dangerous. They are characterized by the same sense of rectitude and the same propaganda as the more benign forms of intervention, but at least we recognize that a lot of people will get hurt and we seem to be getting serious about disarmament (although one questions whether this has more to do with ethics than economics).

But name another country that has gone through the throes of prohibition. Name another country where the majority of the people think that pistols are unnecessary and dangerous and that their sale and ownership ought to be controlled; yet this same country seems paralyzed at the prospect of simple registration. Name another country whose first known form of social insurance was Mothers' Insurance that has yet to cope with general health insurance. Name another country that thinks that advertising charges for treatment of the mind or body is unethical but at the same time insists on complete disclosure for insulation, candy bar additives, and politicians.

It is difficult to understand just when Americans will tolerate intervention and when they will not. It has a great deal to do with who the interventionist is, who the client is, and what the intervention entails.

If interventions are looked at in terms of power, it seems that those who are in control of the levers of life have more to say about interventions than those who are not. Twenty-nine percent of our population is under the age of 17. We cater to that group a great deal. Our largest industry—education—is concerned with it; television is almost preoccupied with it and seemingly wishes to hurry it into the next age bracket. Yet that group has very little direct power in deciding who will be the intervenors and who will be the clients. By and large, they are involuntary clients themselves.

Those 65 and over constitute 10% of the population, and although they are increasingly militant, they too are more likely to be the clients, voluntary or involuntary, of the groups in power.

Those aged 25-64 make up 46% of the population—nearly half. And if you add a few precocious teenagers and a few potent elders, they probably make up the majority of our population. But even beyond their sheer numbers, they are in the power positions: they raise and control the kids; they manage the factories and bureaucracies; they invest and steal our money; and they make, break, and enforce our laws.

More than anything else, the ability to intervene is a question of power, and we intervene more directly and more significantly with those who have less power than we do—with children and the elderly and those we can label "gravely disabled or a threat to themselves or others."

II. Life-Span Intervention: When Is It Acceptable?

Consider the areas and issues for which we will condone intervention and those for which we will not. Let us begin with pregnancy. There are all kinds of clinical, social, and juridical interventions related to getting pregnant, who can get pregnant, and how you can get pregnant; moreover, as intervenors, most of us have been active, personally or professionally, in the process of conception. But as clients—those who were conceived—we had nothing to say about it. Although courts may argue about when we become living beings with rights (whether we want them or not), no court has argued that a single germ cell has any rights at all. We do intervene in conception. We inhibit germ cell development, growth, travel, and maturation; we strain them through filters, condoms, foams, and home remedies. But until two germ cells meet, the ethical and philosophical questions of intervention do not really exist. From that point on, however, until the final act of intervention—burial or cremation—public intervention is practiced and socially sanctioned.

It seems as if we can hardly wait to intervene. Many years ago we started doing blood tests on the mother to see if she had syphilis. Once the baby is born, we test it for syphilis and now give additional tests for such conditions as phenylketonuria and hypothyroidism. With somewhat less coercion, we have looked for anemia, tuberculosis, and acne and have engaged in all sorts of protective procedures for the newborn: circumcision, silver nitrate in the eye, heel prints, birth certificates, etc. Now we are sticking optical scopes into the uterus to peer at it, sample its fluids, and test its adequacy. We have been treating the baby *in utero* for some time, and we may soon see overt attempts at intrauterine psychotherapy. These are all interventions that we perform on others either to protect them or to protect the rest of society from them.

But there are also a number of early social and juridical interventions that we practice in order to protect the interventionists. For example, we have decided that having a baby is both an unnatural and a natural act—an event characterized by disability and normality. We are loath to call it a disability from the standpoint of the employer or the insurance agent, but we have made it illegal for anyone to assist a woman during childbirth and then have granted a special license to certain kinds of people to do just that.

When you suggest that birth is a natural process and that a midwife can be hired to help, you are told, "No, it is a medical problem." But bosses and insurance companies don't agree; you usually cannot use sick leave time for childbirth. So the clients—the voluntary one (the mother) and the involuntary one (the baby)—are the objects of a variety of interventions: clinical, social and juridical. The result is a loss of self-control, presumably in the interest of better health and cheaper payrolls.

Then there comes a period of greater ambivalence. Once the baby is born, the only generally accepted intervenor is the parent or guardian. *Public* interventions are slow to gain acceptance. It is true that we have made a number of social decisions that result in the baby or the preschool child getting shots or having its eyes or ears tested, but these interventions do not inconvenience the parental intervenor very much; they are usually free and they usually terrify the child, not the parent. It is easy to witness this in an immunization clinic. The mothers (usually) herd the kids ahead till they get to the shot giver, saying:

"Hold Still."
"It won't hurt."
"Because your brother already had his shots."
"Get up off the floor or I'll tell the doctor to stick you twice."

Then, having deftly administered the dose, the shot giver looks up at the mother and says, "How about you, shouldn't you get a booster?"

"Oh, well, no, I haven't time. . . ."
"Oh, I've had all my shots. . . ."
"My doctor told me I was allergic to shots. . . ."
"I have a pacemaker. . . ."
"Are you crazy!? This is for kids!"

The great swine flu fiasco was a classic example. The Secretary of Health, Education, and Welfare and his associates were so sure of their power as intervenors that they were confident that 90% of us would line up. You can barely get 90% of our kids immunized when they are being volunteered by their parents, and they only constitute a fraction of our total population. Anyone who thinks that 90% of America's adults will become voluntary clients to be stuck by a needle for a disease they fully expect to get anyway simply does not understand the politics and psychodynamics of successful interventions. We can sanction interventions, even in our own lives, when we can be convinced that they are intended to protect society generally, but we will not comply when we are told it is for our own good!

Generally, childhood is a period for which we tolerate almost all kinds of parental intervention, but we have a very difficult time trying to understand how to deal with our children becoming involuntary clients of nonparental intervention. We seem to draw property lines around certain parts of our lives, and our children are one of them. It isn't that we don't want to intervene; we can scarcely suppress the urge to weigh, measure, test, and influence our children. We do sanction compulsory education, making the children involuntary clients. But we solved that problem more than a hundred years ago by saying that it was their right to be educated—no matter how badly—and it would be illegal to deprive them of this intervention. (A growing number of parents are not so sure about that now.) Even here, our ambivalence—perhaps our insecurity—is manifest. Sex education is still a problem. It is a problem when it *is* done and when it *isn't* done. We also get concerned about religion, four letter words, and respect for the flag.

Generally, we hesitate to endorse public interventions during childhood. As neighbors or as professional intervenors, we have to wait until the problem gets so bad that the child is clearly a danger to itself or others—a fire setter or a throat cutter—and then we can accept intervention. We do not do it very effectively. Much of this problematic behavior is labeled *acting out,* and much of it stems from the same kinds of etiologic factors; however, depending on the form it takes, we may label the child *delinquent, incorrigible,* or *sick.* Our most recent euphemism is *status offender,* though it is not clear whose status is being offended. Until recently, our intervention differed according to the nature of the offending behavior. Now we have homogenized the process, and, presumably to protect the rights of the child (but also, one suspects, to protect the business of lawyers), we have decided that the client has a right to counsel. Instead of a rational and thoughtful attempt to figure out what is wrong and what is needed, diagnosis and treatment have been made into an adversary process. Intervention has become a win or lose contest, and the winner is usually the hired intervenor, not necessarily the client or society. It is hard to be optimistic about the future of this process.

It is interesting that we tolerate, even endorse, the injection of a vaccine but become socially anarchic about telling children where babies come from. We do not hesitate to test children's hearing or examine their teeth, but we are fearful about testing their minds. These reservations do not apply only to parents; professional intervenors also have mixed feelings about certain kinds of interventions. In another setting, however, these fears and reservations are reversed. The public health nurse, making a home visit, usually refrains from making a diagnosis or prescribing a treatment for a physical malady (we now prefer to call these processes assessment and planning). But the nurse can quite comfortably advise the mother about toilet training a possibly retarded child, even though a word may be more potent than a scalpel in influencing future development.

It seems that much of our willingness to accept intervention has to do with the status of the intervenor. If we have been taught that certain knowledge is quite scientific and that only certain people have it (usually licensed people), we may be more likely to accept the proposed intervention, even though there may be very little basis for our assumptions.

Acceptance of intervention probably also hinges on our need to be able to tolerate dependence. If you have made up your mind to take your lump to a surgeon, you have probably already made up your mind to accept surgery. Rightly or wrongly, as clients we believe in the infallibility of the surgeon because we have to believe in it. You cannot stretch out on the table and be anesthetized unless you have accepted this maximum form of intervention. In this case, we have given up all power to another and must justify that act by complete acceptance. Perhaps *reconciliation* is the better word; trust is implied, but in fact it is probably absent, which results in a love–hate relationship from the beginning.

This sort of "bonding" does not occur as dramatically with an internist and is still less prevalent with a mental interventionist. Although Americans are fascinated by mental intervention, we obviously do not accept the assumptions of special knowledge and professional licensure. We condone all sorts of counseling or mind meddling. We even assign school children to school counselors without any concern for their qualifications, and we allow ministers, bartenders, and those we used to call *nonprofessionals* (we now call them the *new professionals*) to engage in the diagnosis and treatment of mental problems. Still more recently, we have turned to do-it-yourself treatment of the mind.

As clients, we are much less likely to accept the authority of the mental interventionist than the power of the surgeon. There are probably reasons for this difference: our acceptance or rejection of a special knowledge relationship and the amount of fear we feel about the planned target. We *seem* to be more comfortable with someone attacking an appendix than with someone probing our emotions. Perhaps this comfortableness is only an appearance resulting from the fact that commitment to the intervention has to be in wholes, not halves, with surgery. With mind intervention, we can increase or decrease the commitment more easily and our fears are thus less troubling; that is, it is easier to live with than to suppress them, as is necessary when undergoing surgery. Our fears are also less troubling because we know that more is understood about the appendix than about the mind.

III. The Politics of Public Intervention: Some Guidelines

The issues considered in the previous section suggest some guidelines for understanding the politics of *public* intervention. First, the assumption of infallibility is an important ingredient, even though it is increasingly hard to come by. We accept the measles vaccine for children partly because we believe it works. We are less receptive to the influenza vaccine partly because we are not convinced of its infallibility. Of course, our acceptance also depends on who makes the decision for whom to get the shot. As a society, we have endorsed the assertion that suicide is an insane act, and thus we sanction and applaud intervention.

The maintenance of individuality—of self-control—is a second important ingredient. Voluntary client status with a therapist is acceptable. We can see a dentist and endure all sorts of trauma and indignity. However, fluoridating our water supplies is a very different act of intervention for two reasons: (*a*) we become involuntary clients and (*b*) the relationship between intervenor and client is not individualized. In this case, we cannot see the intervenor, and, because we lack that relationship, our fears have no manageable outlet. You cannot love or hate a fluoride ion. It is probably easier to accept involuntary client status when the relationship with the intervenor is at least an individualized one. Without that relationship, our fears more readily give way to fantasies about "them" and what "they" are going to do to me.

Third, the role of power in intervention is very complex. Perhaps the safest thing to do is to try and describe it by a theory of political imbalance. If we assume that those involved in the intervention decision all have certain hypothetically equal powers (meaning that they are all between 18 and 64 years of age and are not legally institutionalized) then we can assume that those with a sharply defined interest of high intensity can usually beat a much larger group with a more diffuse interest of less intensity. Gun control is a classic example. So is the virtual ban on research in controlled drinking for alcoholics or the three-way struggle over gay rights—the gays, the antigay's, and most of the rest of us.

Finally—at least for now—there is the question of whose rights are being jeopardized. We had a major problem in the United States in trying to intervene in cigarette-smoking habits until many nonsmokers decided that their job was not to save the smoker but to save themselves. Then they became aggressive intervenors who have steadily expanded the concept as well as the geography of nonsmoking. As another example, we insist that drivers be licensed to protect us (although we have not dealt well with relicensing), but we have found it difficult to cope with interventions designed to protect the involuntary client (the driver) himself. Remember the struggles over automobile ignition-locking devices and seat belts and the great statehouse squabbles over helmets for motorcyclists.

We can isolate, by quarantine or commitment, someone whom we can define as dangerous to us, but we have not learned the ethics of requiring treatment. In theory, we can lock up people who have syphilis or tuberculosis until they are no longer infectious, but we cannot force them to accept treatment. It is now even more complicated to deal with mental illness. The issue of requiring treatment without consent is very confused, but you cannot restrain a client without treating that person in some way. Thus, we can intervene on our own behalf (which makes us clients and interventionists at the same time), but we cannot make the client the object of our concern.

IV. Conclusion

The politics of public intervention are complex and poorly understood. Some of its ingredients are the knowledge base and its security or infallibility, the degree of personalization involved, the power balance and theories about political imbalances, and the common-law concept of the police power of the state (that is, our right to be protected from the acts of others, especially if the other ingredients are interacting in such a way as to make laws possible).

In many ways we have already intervened too much, and we threaten to intervene even more—professionally and publicly. We have allowed special groups to intrude deeply into our lives. Doctors, lawyers, accountants, architects, and many others have mystified the simple, made special the commonplace, and reserved to themselves the right to intervene. As technology and the knowledge base (or what we call special knowledge) expands, the urge to intervene grows. Fortunately, our would-be clients are now fighting back—not very successfully so far, but the signs are promising. Of course, if the clients win in the end, they will become the new interventionists. In this constant struggle between would-be interventionists and reluctant, suspicious clients, the missing ingredient is ethics, not technology. Although we have done research on the phenomenon, we have failed to understand that it is *not* a scientific issue, but an ethical one.

High intervention drives always accompany high technology. Our technology has clearly surpassed our more primitive ethical knowledge. Even at the risk of retarding scientific development, we might be wise to retard the implementation of technology while we try to expand our ethical expertise.

PART **II**

ENVIRONMENTAL AND BIOPHYSICAL
INTERVENTION

The Impact of the Planned Environment on the Elderly

KERMIT K. SCHOOLER
DANIEL I. RUBENSTEIN
SYRACUSE UNIVERSITY
SYRACUSE, NEW YORK

> *The term [environment] is rarely used with precise meaning. Perhaps this is partly because the term is so all-inclusive; the tendency to think of it as including everything produces a certain vagueness. As the term is ordinarily used, environment refers to the conditions, circumstances, and influences surrounding and affecting the individual. Evidently, then, environment is everything outside the person that influences him in some way. If we say that environment causes behavior, we are saying that everything surrounding the person causes his behavior. But what the social scientist wants to do is to be able to pick out of the total environment those specific elements or factors that caused some specific event or form of behavior.*
>
> —McKee, 1973

Our concern here is "to pick out of the total environment those specific elements" that may be examined in order to analyze their impact. To accomplish this task, we will recognize the fact that some aspects of environment are properties of the social structure and their impact is broad, is not global, whereas the effects of other aspects of the environment are best observed and measured primarily as the responses of single, separate individuals. The first section of this chapter, which employs a social-structured perspective, deals with the impact of the planned environment

LIFE-SPAN DEVELOPMENTAL PSYCHOLOGY
Intervention

on the aggregate class of older people; the second section of this chapter deals with those effects of the planned environment that are primarily observable on an individual-to-individual basis.

I. Analyzing Planned Impact at the Societal Level

A. Structural Framework Models

One of the earliest proponents of using a structural framework at the societal level for studying the effects of planned impact on the well-being of the aggregate elderly population was Walter M. Beattie, Jr. (1977), who proposed that a *life-cycle* and *intergenerational* framework be employed for defining the role and specifying the location of programmatic planned impact in the form of services for the elderly. His model identifies specific levels of services for the aging as related to identifiable, predictable conditions of older persons. These progressively decremental conditions of stages require the organization of planned services that include: (*a*) basic services meeting the needs of all persons; (*b*) adjustment and integrative services that permit the older person to retain and utilize his or her capacities, to adjust to new roles, and to remain an active participant in the community; (*c*) supportive services that enable an elderly person to remain in his or her habitat; (*d*) congregate and shelter care for those who can no longer fully care for themselves; (*e*) protective services that protect civil and personal rights when the elderly are no longer able and capable. The work of Sheldon Tobin (1975) reflects a simpler, collapsed model including; (*a*) community programs for the comparatively well elderly; (*b*) programs that prevent unnecessary and premature institutionalization among the impaired elderly; (*c*) institutional programs for older persons whose functioning necessitates such care. These two models and other related structured schemes derive from a perception of the aging process from a decremental perspective and, for that reason, are not entirely applicable to the purposes of the present discussion. Less dependent on a decremental perspective and more environmentally responsive is the environmental schema developed by Lowy (1975), which includes: (*a*) services to the aged living in the community and in congregate care facilities: (*b*) age-integrated versus segregated services; (*c*) categorical versus comprehensive services; (*d*) social utilities and social intervention programs and services; (*e*) auspice of service (governmental and nongovernmental). A more dynamic perspective is one that perceives the environment as institutional forces that act upon the elderly and, in turn, are acted upon by the elderly. Rosow (1977) describes this type of environment as composed of "major institutional forces at work which systematically undermine the position of older people in

American Society, depreciate their status, limit their participation, and channel them from the mainstream of social life [p. 79]." Moreover, he asserts that this environmental impact (the progressive corrosion of the status of the aged) accelerates with modernity. Rosow (1977) further explains that "analysis has shown that seven major institutional factors govern the status of older people in all societies. In addition to certain patterns of social obligation, these concern various resources that old people command and functions they perform. The changes in modern American life have undermined these possible institutional supports and have relegated the aged to a weak position [p. 79]." These seven institutional forces (determinants of status) are property ownership, strategic knowledge, productivity, mutual dependence, tradition and religion, kinship and family, and community life.

Notwithstanding the insightfulness of the several aforementioned models, their applicability for use in assessing planned impact is limited. The impact of the environment they describe is unplanned, and the outcomes are expressed as responses; that is, as evolutionary social change. If the environment is conceptualized as made up of the components of planned social organization (social institutions), it is then possible to assess the planned impact of that environment. Kamerman and Kahn (1976) provide a feasible model for that purpose in their conceptualization of the six human services. Since our society recognizes income security, health, employment, housing, and personal social services as essential to human welfare, they will be the specific elements of the planned environment whose impact is to be assessed in this analysis, although the importance of housing policy will be subsumed under the discussion of noninstitutional environment in the latter half of this chapter. (Institutionalized education is also considered to be essential to human welfare. However, since education is primarily focused on socializing the young into society, it will not be dealt with here. This in no way minimizes the significance that institutionalized education can play in the life and development of older persons.)

B. Income

Every person should have an adequate wage or access to basic income supports. Since only about 2.9 million or 13% of older people in the United States were in the labor force in 1977 (3% of the U.S. labor force) (U.S. Department of Health, Education and Welfare—Office of Human Development, 1977), the greater number of the elderly rely on income support other than wages. Retired workers receiving private pensions, as estimated by the Social Security Administration in 1973, were a little over 6 million (Schulz, 1976), with an average of $2000 per person per year. The major source of income support is the Social Security System, which administers Old Age Survivors and Disability Insurance (OASDI) grants and Supplementary Security Income (SSI) payments. At the end of September 1977, 21 million persons over 65 were in receipt of OASDI. Their average monthly grants were $240. In addition, 2 million aged persons were receiving federally administered SSI payments of less than $200 per month (U.S. Department of Health, Education and Welfare—Social Security Administration, 1978). Over 90% of all people in the United States aged 65 or older are either drawing Social Security benefits or will be eligible to do so upon retirement (Bechill, 1977, p. 23).

Currently, the economic environment is not adequate to sustain the older person in meeting basic human needs with dignity. During 1975, there were 3.3 million persons aged 65 or older with incomes below the poverty level; that is, 15.3% or roughly one of every seven elderly persons. In near poverty were 2.2 million persons over 65. In aggregate, then, 5.5 million persons aged 65 or over, were in or near poverty.

The economic environment of the elderly is both planned and unplanned. Although earnings, assets, and retirement benefits do play a role in financing the later years (Viscusi & Zeckhauser, 1978), these sources of income are relatively fixed, whereas prices for the necessities of food and shelter are variable. The importance of the Social Security System's impressive contribution to financing the later years becomes apparent. Pechman (1978) reminds us that: "The Social Security System is perhaps the most successful social program ever enacted by the U.S. government [p. 31]." Efforts to correct and improve the system's adequacy continue.

Consistent changes in the economic environment of the elderly are difficult to discern. In the short run, we are witnessing evidence of some improvement and alleviation. These changes can be noted as (a) efforts toward maintaining the elderly as wage earners in the work force, as evidenced by the recent passage of a policy that extends the minimum age for forced retirement; (b) the recent achievement of guaranteed investment of private pensions with the developing impetus for providing portability; (c) the continuous improvement of income maintenance payments (Social Security and SSI) with the potentiality of Social Security being supported from the general revenue. However, although in the long run it is likely that the income and other financial resources of most of the future elderly will be greater than they are for the elderly of today, we will still have to deal with the continuing existence of large numbers of the elderly who are in or near poverty (U.S. Department of Health, Education and Welfare—Administration on Aging, 1978).

If the elderly as a class are ever to achieve the goal of income security with dignity in the later years, our planned environment will necessarily include the provision for an adequate federal benefit floor, as a universal provision for all persons.

C. Health

The person who enters the later years in good health, and with the means of maintaining it, possesses a major source of well-being for the years ahead. This truism notwithstanding, a gloomy future can be predicted if we examine the present environment of physical well-being. In a national sample of 11,153 persons age 58–63 and over, who participated in a 10-year study of the retirement process by the Office of Research and Statistics of the Social Security Administration, it was found that 35% of the people in the sample had a health condition that limited the kind or amount of work they could do. For 13%, the condition was severe enough to preclude their working altogether. Sixty-one percent were free of any kind of health condition that limited how well they could move or that affected the kind or amount of work they could do. Despite these disabilities, 8 out of 10 people in the sample said their health was equal to or better than that of other people their age. Motley (1976) noted "that American people age 58–63 were satisfied with their health [p. 23]." It is not unusual for surveys of self-reported health to show these differences between feelings and conditions. Barney and Neukom (1977), reporting a prevalence study of 470 persons aged 55 and older, found that most older people have established sources of health care, are more or less content with it, and are accepting of their declining health.

Nonetheless, about one in five Americans aged 65 and older requires multiple, intensive, and often extensive social and health-care services. Nearly 5% of the population aged 65 and older reside in institutions. Approximately 45% of persons aged 65 and older have some limitation on activity due to one or more chronic conditions, and 39% of these have *major* limitations on activity due to those conditions. About one in four older persons is hospitalized each year. This is twice the rate of hospitalization for persons under age 65. It is also known that older people utilize physician's services, drugs, eyeglasses, and other health-related appliances at a much higher rate than younger persons (Policy statement, *Public Welfare*, 1977). These findings, however, are not indicative of a lack of effort to respond to the concern for health service availability. In 1956 the concern for the elderly produced vendor payments under Old Age Assistance. In 1957 the Forand bill proposed 120 days of hospitalization, nursing home care, and surgery for those eligible for Social Security. The Kerr–Mills Act of 1960 provided federal grants to the states for health services to the poor and elderly (see

Stevens, 1971). In 1965 major progress was made with the establishment of Medicare and Medicaid (Titles 18 and 19 of the Social Security Act).

As Lewis, Fein, and Mechanic (1976) have observed, these historical intervention efforts were intended to serve as financing mechanisms that would in no way affect either the supply or organization of service. However, along with the current belief that health-care financing is more than adequate, a focus on accessibility and availability of medical services is developing. According to Mechanic (1972):

> As medicine has demonstrated greater efficacy, all segments of the population have gained a greater appreciation of the high standard of medical care possible in the United States. With heightened expectations, the failure to find accessible and responsive services has become a bitter pill to swallow, especially among more deprived groups who see their difficulties as one more manifestation of their exclusion from the mainstream of American society. Innumerable studies support these perceptions by demonstrating that the poor have a greater prevalence of illness, disability, chronicity, and restriction of activity because of health problems than those of higher status and that they have less accessibility to many health services and receive lower quality care [p. 80].

Despite concerns, interests, and efforts of the elderly and other special interest groups, the health system has been rigid and self-serving. The programs of the present health-care providers are unequal, unplanned, and uncoordinated; consequently, they serve the elderly poorly. The concept of entitlement or the belief that persons in need ought to receive medical care is more a desire than a reality.

By 1975, the average annual health-care bill for a person age 65 or older in the United States was $1360 (U.S. Department of Health, Education and Welfare—Public Health Service, 1976). This is a price that the elderly can ill afford. There is a growing feeling that a national health insurance program should be viewed as a statutory right and that the time for implementation is past due.

D. Employment

> *In our work-oriented society all persons are expected to be productive wage earners. In most cases, gainful employment is a necessary but not a sufficient condition for a person to see himself and to be considered by others a responsible and respected member of the community. In addition, the kind of job the person holds helps to determine both self-image and status in society. In short, work is a major life task and unless a person performs it adequately, the person is a failure by his or her own standards and by those of society—*PFOUTS, 1978, p. 203.

Jobs fulfill the functions of providing income, socialization, and status—essential conditions that are needed in the later years. Yet our society continues to encourage the elderly to leave the labor market. Amendments to the Social Security Act permit males to retire at the age of 62 if they so desire. Those who choose to stay in the labor market past the age of 65 are penalized by deductions from Social Security payments. As previously noted, persons over 65 comprise only 3% of the work force in the United States. With the new extension of the forced retirement age, a small rise in this percentage could be expected. Although many may feel that with adequate pensions or social security the elderly would not choose to work, Ginzberg (1978) observes that this notion proves false when one becomes aware of the "pressure that older people are putting on Congress to make sure that they can work [p. 31]."

The recognition of this concern of the elderly found its expression in the Job Opportunities Program, Title X of the Public Works and Economic Development Act. Its purpose was to provide emergency financial assistance to stimulate, maintain, or expand job-creating activities in urban and rural areas that suffer from unusually high levels of unemployment. It was recommended that work activities should include home repair, winterization, homemaker and chore services, outreach, and renovation of facilities for senior citizen or multiservice centers. The current program supports 4811 jobs in 71 projects at a cost of $21 million. A significant study has been undertaken to determine whether temporary employment opportunities, as provided under Title X, have a measurable impact on the employed elderly (i.e., on their quality of life, self-esteem, social participation, job satisfaction, and job performance) and an impact on the agencies where they are placed and on the social service network within the communities where the projects are administered (Foundation for Applied Research, 1977). The multistaged probability sample included almost half of the funded projects and one-sixth of the workers ($N = 862$). The study found that federal job programs are justified primarily in terms of financial benefits received by enrollees. However, although it was found that the income had a beneficial impact on the lives of the workers, a majority of the workers had derived extensive psychological and social benefits from employment, which in many cases were more important than the increased income. The study also found that the workers had an important impact on the effectiveness of the host agencies. Furthermore, it was reported that evidence from all indicators strongly supported the conclusion that employment had resulted in a variety of powerful benefits for nearly all of the Title X workers, including job satisfaction, increased self-esteem, enhanced social integration and participation, better financial position, greater happiness, and improved lives in general.

The environment of work is vital and necessary to many older people, yet it is a most deficient and neglected area. Ginzberg (1978) has observed that we are "still in the early stages of a fundamental revolution in which women and youth are the principal participants. Since 1945, three out of five jobs created in the U.S. have been taken by women. . . . Due to changes in demography, increasing numbers of youth have become available for work [p. 31]." The private sector has almost never been supportive of employment in the later years. On the contrary, the major opposition to extending forced retirement age came from the organizations representing industry and commerce. At present, it would appear that we have only the beginnings of a planned environment for meaningful work for persons in their later years. It is evident that if the elderly are to feel impact in this area, they must be provided with the opportunity for gainful employment in the public sector and the government must take strong action to remove barriers or impediments that obstruct older persons from meeting their economic, social, and status needs through employment.

E. Personal Social Services

The environment of the personal social services consists of the "public, quasi-public, and private interventions in social life—interventions which are no longer sporadic but more and more take the form of continuing activity, steered to influence and control a social process in a certain direction [Butterworth & Holman, 1975, p. 50]." The personal social services are an essential component of the total human service environment. They are a class of human services concerned with individuals and their internal and interpersonal adjustment and functioning. Their functions include facilitating access to all human services; specific therapeutic, helping, protective, and substitute care activities; and some developmental and socialization activities (Cleveland Foundation & American Public Welfare Association, 1978). More specifically, they consist of an array of community programs that provide caring to the aged individual such as transportation; nutrition programs (including preparation and delivery of meals for the homebound); services related to the management of the home (i.e., home help, chore services, and home repair); counseling; friendly visiting aid and escorts; community and multiservice centers; information, advice, referral, complaint, and advocacy services; day care and respite services; legal services; and protective services (Beattie, 1977). The personal social service system also includes those activities that are required to aid and support persons who can no longer care for themselves; that is, congregate and sheltered care for the frail or impaired elderly. These services address social problems or conditions that significantly affect older people and would result in undesirable consequences for the individual and society if they were ignored or avoided.

In the United States, note Kahn and Kamerman (1975) ordinary people "are being deprived of constructive solutions to problems in daily living, to those 'normal' problems that arise out of societal change. Indeed, the term 'problems' is probably inaccurate, since the programs involved represent appropriate, accepted responses to widely shared experiences. The lag will get worse and we will pay a price unless we can offer a more hospitable environment to social intervention [p. 171]."

Although a hospitable environment for personal social services needs to be further developed, there has been some ongoing activity. These social interventions are underfinanced, fragmented, uncoordinated, and not designed with a purposeful, central goal in mind; however, they do result in various impacts on the lives of older persons. Pihlblad, Hessler, and Freshley (1976), in an 8-year longitudinal study of 1700 persons, 65 years of age and older, residing in towns in Missouri with populations ranging from 250 to 5000, found improved changes in life satisfaction and health status and a maintenance of older persons' strong feelings of independence, their desire for independent living, their unwillingness to accept institutional care, and their desire to be independent of their children and family. Although in some instances these conditions were attributed to specific social activities and institutions, the major focus of the study was on suggesting and recommending planned activity to respond to the discovered needs (e.g., expansion of home health aid programs, visiting nurses, housing repair, recreation, and friendly visiting).

A number of evaluations of specific programs have unequivocally shown tremendous success in making impacts in the lives of older persons. The very popular and highly utilized nutrition programs are flourishing; senior centers are increasingly being recognized for their value and developing increasing support. Dial-a-Bus and other efforts to provide transportation on demand have opened doors and provided access to the lonely and isolated. The individual programs are many, and although their impacts may vary in different locales, it would be safe to say that these efforts are making meaningful impacts in the lives of older persons. Nevertheless, studies continue to point out the lack of services available to respond to the conditions of the elderly. In a transportation study, Bengtson, Torres-Gil, Newquist, and Simonian (1976), drawing on data from a probability sample of 1269 black, Mexican–American, and white Los Angeles County residents, age 45–74, and from a sample of 316 decision makers having jurisdictional responsibilities for Los Angeles County, found that the elderly have substantial mobility problems and a need for mobility; they also found that no major mode of transportation presently in existence satisfied the problems and needs of the elderly community. In another study, Rubenstein, Rosenberg, Perlstein, and Ward (1977) found that despite the need and desire of the elderly to participate in their religious institutions, there were numerous social and physical constraints that prevented them from doing so. A survey of services made available by the religious institutions in Syracuse, New York, found that opportunities for social participation by the elderly were minimal. The major constraints were impersonalization, ritual changes, youth orientation, and social change. A description of the physical characteristics of these religious institutions revealed that both poorly designed structures and upward social mobility restricted the elderly from full participation in their religious practices. The findings of Rubenstein *et al.* indicated a need for greater sensitivity to the religious concerns and physical conditions of the elderly and their environment.

Of all the programs intended to affect the elderly, those of long-term congregate care and institutionalization seem to be paramount and are surely the most visible in the public eye. After more than a century of neglect and abuse of those living in the congregate care environment, efforts are now being directed at remediation. The report presented by the Arden House Institute (1977) on continuity of long-term care may well be representative of the future trend. The Institute recommended that "greater state emphasis must be given to the social components in long-term care. Medical models are now well developed and dominant, and there must be action to bring the relatively neglected life support and social oriented services into parity with medical services. This better balance must also take the living environment into consideration [Arden House Institute, 1977, p. 7]."

Wilma Donahue (1978) posed the institutionalization issue when she asked, "What about our responsibility toward the abandoned elderly? [p. 102]." She went on to remind us, "The folly of closing mental hospitals needed for treatment of acute mental illness had been demonstrated, as had the efficicy of therapeutic settings [p. 110.]." Rose (1977), in his intensive exploration of this issue, was more hard-hitting: "We know of no evidence anywhere which suggests that those groups of people (placed ex-mental-health patients), those most likely to be placed in profit-motivated group residences, have benefited materially, socially, and/or psychologically from Department of Mental Hygiene practices [p. 2]." However, Donahue (1978), from her more forward-looking perspective, suggested that what is needed is nothing "more tangible than a presentiment that there is an undercurrent of opinion that may soon materialize in concrete form with far-reaching consequences [p. 110]."

Inasmuch as our society has a dual orientation toward the young (children and youths) and toward industrial productivity, it is not surprising that little or no social–environmental planning for the older person is found. The nation's population as a whole is becoming progressively older.

By the year 2036, 26% of the population will be over 60 (U.S. Department of Health, Education and Welfare—Administration on Aging, 1978). It may be expected by then that American society will address the development of an environment designed to respond to, and have an impact on, the changing needs of the older members of the changing society.

The planned environment for a better life in the later years is now negligible, and its impact is insignificant. With the advent of the Older Americans Act of 1965, a significant beginning was made. The need for further development of a purposive environment planned with and for the elderly can be summed up in the words of the Cleveland Project, which noted:

> What we have can be excused, explained historically. It may even have been predictable, given the elements in its development, a society reluctant to undermine individualism or to have government take on too much, responding one-at-a-time to problems, needs, groups which could no longer be ignored—but not wishing to create a precedent or to suggest permanence. The explanations are not acceptable as justifications. Clearly the services are needed because of the nature of modern life. They must be provided and provided well as an ongoing social responsibility. They enrich the society rather than undermine it [U.S. Department of Health, Education and Welfare—Administration on Aging, 1978].

II. The Effects of the Planned Environment on Individuals

In Section I of this chapter, the planned environment was conceptualized as consisting of an array of social institutions or components of social organization. At the societal—or macro—level, the impact of the planned environment was seen as the aggregate effect of social policy implementation. Policies regarding income maintenance, health-care organization and delivery, retirement and employment policy, social service availability and delivery, and housing, to name a few, are included in this scheme of interventions in the environment whose impact on a large number of older people can be assessed. But what of the direct impact of the proximate environment on the responses of the single individual? Is not a "micro" conceptualization also valid? This section of the chapter will be devoted to a discussion based on such a "micro" perspective and will focus on the effects of changes in the planned physical (residential) environment surrounding older people.

At first, one might conceive of an immobile elderly population, surrounded by an environment—however broadly defined—that is manipulated and changed. To be sure, such a conception could be the legitimate basis for environmental research. For example, imagine the older person in a room in which the level of illumination can be varied. Or, if not illumination, sound level or even wall colors might be varied. The elderly subject needs merely to stay put while the surrounding environment is changed. A moment's thought about the subject of environmental change, however, quickly reveals that in many, perhaps in most, instances in which the relevant environment is changed, it is changed in a place where the older person *is not;* and then after the change, the older person is moved, voluntarily or involuntarily, to the new environment. As one considers the impact of planned residential environment on the elderly, this statement concerning the *movement* of people from one environment to the other encompasses several fundamental aspects of the problem. First, one may be concerned with the consequences of differences between attributes of the two environments. Second, one may be concerned with consequences resulting from the movement from one environment to another, irrespective of the manner in which the two environments differ from each other. Third, the degree to which the change in the environment is voluntarily agreed to by the older person may itself have an impact on the lives of the elderly, irrespective of the changed attributes of the environment or whether or not mobility was required.

A. Environmental Change in Institutions

Attention will be given first to the study of environmental change at the institutional level. Although there is some evidence in the literature, going as far back as the 1940s, for the assertion that institutional environments have a negative impact on elderly people (Camargo & Preston, 1945), the current trend in research on the impact of institutions can be traced to Morton Lieberman's study (1961) on the relation between mortality rates and entrance into a home for the aged. In an effort to explain why mortality rates were significantly higher in the period shortly after people entered an institution than in the period just preceding entry during which they were on the waiting list, Lieberman examined records of those who survived and those who had died and attempted to determine the degree to which prior physical status could have accounted for the increased mortality rates. Analysis of the data led Lieberman to reject the notion that prior physical status was associated with the higher mortality rate, and thus provided both himself and later investigators with the rationale for the assumption or hypothesis that the difference in mortality rates might be accounted for by differences in attributes of the environments themselves.

Two years later, attention was still not being paid to attributes of the environment. However, Aldrich and Mendkoff (1963) introduced some concepts in their research that were to provide yet another link to research on institutional environment in the 1970s. In their study of the relocation of disabled persons consequent to the closing of an institution, Aldrich and Mendkoff were able to show that mortality rates were higher than previous experience would have suggested. It is even more significant, however, that in this study they also raised the question of the negative consequences of anticipation of relocation. Lack of statistical significance prevented them from drawing firm conclusions, although the data do tend to support the inference that anticipation of mobility is detrimental. Furthermore, they pointed out that nonpsychotics who expressed anger "were more likely to survive than patients who retreated from the conflict situation by regression or denial. . . ." In short, although Aldrich and Mendkoff did not address themselves to specific attributes of the environment, they did suggest the importance of debilitation to relocation and, in a more general way, laid the ground work for a theoretical framework involving psychological processes in interaction with environmental attributes.

For a period of several more years, research continued to focus on the relocation process and the attributes of the older person but did not attend to attributes of the environment or differences in attributes between the old and new environments. In an earlier review of this subject matter, Schooler (1976) made reference to a statement by Lieberman (1965), who postulated three ways of viewing the relocation process:

> One view stemming from the symbolic interaction position would consider the impact of institutionalization on the individual in terms of the personal meaning it has for him—it is traumatic or not because of its personally relevant symbolic meaning. . . . A second view of the problem is expressed by the continuity–discontinuity hypothesis which suggests that extensive change in the environment requires considerable adaptive capacity because a new environment demands new behavior patterns. . . . Thus, to move to a new environment is stressful to the extent that it requires relinquishing old patterns and roles and adopts new ones [p. 121].

It was observed then that Lieberman appeared to be ready to expand on a third viewpoint that would require attention to characteristics of the environment itself. But what seems to be the logical next step, from the vantage point of the 1970s, was not to be taken for several years. In the 1960s the objective of much of the research was to "identify the characteristics or combination of characteristics of the older person that would predict successful or unsuccessful adjustment to relocation [Schooler, 1976, p. 274]." However, there is evidence from the research of the 1960s that personal attributes that had predictive value in one environmental setting would be found to have no predictive value in another setting. Finally, in the 1970s there has been a beginning of research on institutional environments that has focused on the attributes of the environment itself as determinants of some criterion of well-being for the older person.

Lieberman (1974) summarizes some of his work by noting that "facilitative environments were those characterized by relatively high degrees of autonomy fostering, personalization of the patients and community integration [p. 500]." Moreover, he points out that "facilitative environments place the locus of control much more in the hands of the patients, differentiated among them and permitted them a modicum of privacy. Also, the boundaries between the institution and the larger community were more permeable than nonfacilitative environments . . . [p. 500]." Although such terms as "autonomy fostering" and "community integration" are not very precise, it is quite clear that Lieberman intends them to flow from the characteristics of the environment rather than the characteristics of the resident.

Another well-known investigator, Eva Kahana (1975), has developed and tested a theory pertaining to person-environment interaction that postulates that well-being will be associated with the degree of congruence between personal characteristics and characteristics of the environment. In her model, she identifies 7 major dimensions of congruence within which are 18 subdimensions. For each of these subdimensions, there is a statement of individual preference or need and a corresponding statement of an environmental attribute that is purported to be congruent to the individual attribute. Kahana has tested her model in three homes for the elderly. She finds that "in two out of three homes, congruence between individual's needs and the environment emerged as important and significant determinants of adjustment, when related in stepwise regression analysis to the Lawton Morale . . . [p. 200]." In the discussion of her research, however, Kahana (1975) notes:

> Specific dimensions of congruence which related to adjustment differed from home to home. The sub-dimension of privacy, motor control and stimulation proved to be important prediators of morale in. . . the two homes in which the congruence construct seemed to have the most explanatory power. The privacy subdimension was also among the best predictors of morale in the [third] home. Continuity with the past was an important predictor in [two of the homes] and change vs. sameness proved to be the best predictors of morale in [two of the homes].
>
> Thus, five out of eighteen sub-dimensions of congruence were shown to have an important role in explaining morale in at least two of the three homes. Privacy was among the best predictor in all three homes and motor control stimulation, continuity with the past and change vs. sameness appeared as best predictors in two out of three homes [p. 201].

For the purposes of this chapter, Kahana's study is significant in two ways. First, it is significant because it demonstrates that some characteristics, attributable to the environment itself, can be shown to be related to a measure of well-being among the elderly. Second, her study is significant because it suggests that those environmental attributes have predictive power in all settings. The latter point will be returned to later in this discussion.

This has been, at best, only a cursory review of some literature on the environmental impact of institutional living for the elderly. However, it is sufficient to suggest the following observation or conclusion: Over a period of two or two and one-half decades, research on institutions has tended to confirm that detrimental consequences of relocation sometimes ensue for some people and has suggested that characteristics of the milieu are sometimes associated with adaptation to the milieu. If it appears that this summary statement is somewhat ambiguous and certainly cautious, its intent has been realized.

B. Environmental Change and Elderly Individuals

The subject of environmental change and its impact on the noninstitutionalized elderly will be addressed in this section. Studies of this subject, similarly to studies of the institutional environment, have paid much attention to the negative effects of relocation rather than to the effects of the environmental characteristics themselves. For example, Marc Fried (1963), although he did not study the elderly in particular, conducted a substantial investigation of the consequences of relocating the residents of Boston's West End and found that very large numbers of those who were relocated involuntarily exhibited severe grief reactions even years after the move had taken place. Similar findings were noted several years later by Terreberry (1968) and by Kastler, Gray, and Carruth (1968). The authors of the latter study noted that "involuntary relocation was an especially stressful experience for older persons whose ties are generally firmly established and who, by the process of aging, may be more resistant to change than are younger persons [p. 279]." During this same period, Frances Carp (1966) was becoming involved in her now well-known study of the Victoria Plaza in San Antonio, Texas. Carp's study differs from those just alluded to in a number of significant ways, not the least of which is that, for all intents and purposes, the population she studied relocated voluntarily.

Victoria Plaza was one of the first residential sites developed expressly for the elderly with federal funding. By comparing those applicants for Victoria Plaza who were accepted for residence with those who were not accepted, Carp was able to show significant improvement consequent to, or at least subsequent to, the move to Victoria Plaza. Carp (1967) summarized her findings as follows: "Evidence of the dramatic effect of improved life setting on this group of older people was overwhelming and was similar for men and women. . . . Consistently, scores of residents improved, those of non-residents showed no change or slight decrement . . . they had fewer health complaints and among those they had, fewer were neurotic in type. . . . Unsuccessful applicants, initially similar to successful ones, exhibited a little difference in behavior or attitude [p. 106]." In an earlier review of this subject, Schooler pointed out that "whereas earlier studies on involuntary relocation and on institutionalization (which might be assumed to be involuntarily) predominantly showed the negative consequences of relocation/environmental change, most of Carp's movers, in contrast appear to improve [p. 279]."

In another study of the effects of relocation, Lawton and Yaffe (1970), comparing voluntary movers into a new apartment building with a comparable sample of nonmovers, also found that, after a year's time, the movers were more likely than the nonmovers to have improved in health but were also more likely to have declined. Several years later, Lawton and Cohen (1974) assessed the experiences of new tenants in five new housing sites with appropriate control groups and, in general, found data very consistent with Carp's results on Victoria Plaza; however, according to Lawton and Cohen, "the effect was less marked in the present research 1974 [p. 203]." This similarity between the two studies did not apply to a functional health variable. In this instance, Lawton and Cohen were obliged to report that although there is an overall favorable impact resulting from new housing, there is an apparent decline in functional health.

In still another study on the effects of relocation, Sherwood, Grier, Morris, and Sherwood (1972) evaluated a public housing project in New England designed primarily for the elderly and the physically handicapped and found that in comparison to matched control groups, there was a gain in a number of variables including self-rated health. Pursuing this line of research, Storandt, Wittles, and Botwinick (1975) attempted to determine whether the personal attributes that predicted adjustment to an institutional setting would retain their predictive power when applied to new tenants in a noninstitutional setting. A number of older people who voluntarily relocated to high-rise housing for the elderly were scored on cognitive, personality, health, and activity dimensions. It was subsequently found that the measures of cognitive and psycho–motor function rather than of personality, health, or activity predicted well-being approximately 1½ years later. Moreover, the predictors of poor adjustment in the relocation of the institutionalized elderly were not seen here as predictors in the present sample of healthy older adults. The research of Storandt et al. is one of several studies that are significant partly because they highlight the importance of differential adaptation. In other words, regardless of what the specific effect of environmental change might be, the magnitude and direction of that effect can be shown to vary with various personal characteristics.

Finally, some of Schooler's research (e.g., 1975) has been able to demonstrate, among other things, that within a vulnerable sample, defined as those who not only anticipate moving but also do move, morale declined most among those who experienced a deterioration in the quality of their environment. Additional analysis shows that "the change in environment can be separated from residential mobility and the effects of each can be separately determined [Schooler, 1975, p. 168]."

In summary, a review of the literature pertaining to environmental change and the well-being of the elderly, only a portion of which is represented in this presentation, supports the following conclusions:

1. Environmental change frequently means relocation, and relocation frequently, but not always, results in a decline.
2. Some environmental attributes and some personal attributes are associated with measures of well-being subsequent to a change in environment.
3. There are differential effects undoubtedly due to interaction between changes in environmental attributes and personal attributes of the older person.

C. Some Theoretical Considerations

This cursory review of the consequences of intervention on the environment of the older person leaves one with a mixture of feelings. On the one hand, one discovers that some interventions lead to predictable results. For example, environmental change in the form of relocation is frequently detrimental to the well-being of the older person. On the other hand, those interventions that can be demonstrated to be frequently detrimental or beneficial are never universally detrimental or beneficial. Clearly, the problem in prediction is that although some things seem to work, we really don't know why.

The best procedure for answering the question "Why?" is to develop a theory that can then be tested. To develop a theory in this instance, one must first decide on the most effective scale. It seems that it would be fruitless to invoke theories of human behavior on the grand scale—to invoke, for example, something spelled in capital letters such as LEARNING THEORY or MOTIVATION THEORY. On the other hand, it would also be foolish to develop a theory specific only to the success or failure of something such as a meals-on-wheels program. Of course, the answer lies in theories of the middle range. What is needed is a theory whose terms can define environment in relatively broad ways, whose terms can encompass a variety of interventions, and whose terms can define efficacy of intervention through a variety of responses on the part of the older individual. In 1975 Schooler attempted to adapt current theory to problems pertaining to change in residential environment. We believe that this theoretical approach can be useful in attempting to understand the efficacy of a variety of environmental changes.

In order to understand the usefulness of this theoretical development, it is first necessary to appreciate that older people, by and large, are a population at risk. It is commonplace to note, for example, that although the rates of change vary for individuals, advancing age is eventually accompanied by sensory losses, decrements in response rates, and certain forms of memory loss. In addition to these psychological changes, there are a number of biological decrements. Some might also consider as even more devastating the variety of social deficits accruing in old age, such as those described in Section I of this chapter. Moreover, older people are victimized by negative stereotypes and, in general, are considered to be members of a devalued class. Surely, this was not always so. Some writers, most notably David Hackett Fischer (1978), are optimistic regarding the prospects for the future of the elderly, but none deny that their current status is now, and is likely to be for the foreseeable future, denigrated and devalued. In summary, because of psychological, physiological, and social losses, older people, as a class, are vulnerable to a multitude of threatening and potentially injurious circumstances in their surrounding world.

It was recognition of the devalued status of the elderly and of their vulnerability to the insulting and potentially hazardous circumstances in their environment that led Schooler (1975) to attempt to explain response to environmental change in terms of coping with, and adapting to, stress. In short, he proposes that there is value in stress theory for predicting better than we have to date the success or failure of environmental intervention. This section of the chapter has tended to emphasize individual rather than societal responses. The differential success of social interventions may be explained on the grounds that insufficient attention is paid to individual differences (as opposed to class similarities) in trying to estimate the efficacy of any kind of programmatic intervention. In addition, it will become clear that the theoretical framework proposed here has a strong cognitive base. That is, it is fundamentally concerned with the process by which the events taking place in the environment, which are not part of the person, become incorporated into the person.

The theoretical statement proposed here is an adaptation of the theory developed by Richard Lazarus (1966). In its barest outline, Lazarus' theory states that a stressful situation is one in which circumstances in the real world are appraised by the individual as being threatening. The appraisal of threat is determined by two sets of circumstances: factors in the stimulus configuration itself and factors within the psychological structure of the individual. The appraisal of threat, as determined by these classes of factors, elicits coping behavior intended to reduce or eliminate the threatening aspects of the environment. Exactly which coping behaviors or processes are elicited from the individual's complete armamentarium of such processes is determined by what Lazarus calls *secondary appraisal,* which is dependent upon degree of threat, factors in the stimulus configuration, and various psychological factors such as ego resources, defensive dispositions, and patterns of motivation.

It should be pointed out here that environmental intervention as it is conceptualized in this chapter may itself be assessed as threatening (as in the case of residential relocation) or may be perceived as facilitating the coping process (as in the case of the establishment of health-related facilities). The point to be made is that irrespective of the place of the environmental intervention in terms of the theory, the important consideration in predicting efficacy of intervention is to relate that intervention to the individual appraisal of threat, or to the individual ability to cope with or adapt to an otherwise threatening or harmful situation. That is, when some environmental intervention (such as housing) can, in itself, be appraised as threatening, the efficacy of the housing development will be a function of the older person's ability to cope with that kind of change. At the same time, when some other circumstances (such as ill health) are assessed as threatening, the efficacy of a health-related intervention will depend on the manner in which the older person is able to see that the newly established service, such as it is, adds to his armamentarium of coping skills. In short, we need to adopt a theoretical frame of reference that permits us to view environmental intervention in relation to the response to stress.

What about research for the future? Rather than proposing a set of needed investigations, we will offer a few words of a more general nature, regarding a concerted research effort in this arena. First, a brief review of the first part of this section is in order: There have been a variety of interventions in the environment of the older person and the impact of those interventions has not been uniformly predictable. We contend that one of the principal reasons for this uneven success is that little systematic thought has been given to understanding or even proposing why the intervention ought to be successful. Such systematic thought is, of course, another name for theory. We further contend that much of the work purporting to determine the efficacy of various forms of environmental intervention, usually called evaluation research, is devoid of any semblance of underlying theory and could well profit from serious efforts to introduce theory. Neither the intentions of the investigators nor their capabilities are at fault. Apparently, it has not been considered sufficiently important to found one's evaluation research on good theory of the middle range. This principle, which must have been inculcated early in our careers, has been overlooked, but the remedy is simple: A concerted effort should be made to infuse future evaluative research with appropriate theoretical underpinnings. Second, a sharper focus should be brought to bear on underlying individual psychological and physiological processes. The traditional design, where there is indeed some design, is to treat the intervention as the independent variable, to measure outcome as either health or morale or some other measureable dependent variable, and perhaps to elaborate the design by attention to various demographic or social attributes. An attention to process, specifically psychological or physiological process, seems to be almost completely missing.

REFERENCES

Aldrich, C. K., & Mendkoff, E. Relocation of the aged and disabled: A mortality study. *Journal of the American Geriatrics Society,* 1963, *11,* 185–194.

Arden House Institute. *Report of the Arden House Institute on continuity of long-term care.* Report presented at the meeting of the State Communities Aid Association, New York, December 1977.

Barney, J. L., & Neukom, J. E. *Elderly users of health service.* Paper presented at the annual meeting of the Gerontological Society, San Francisco, November 1977.

Beattie, W. M., Jr. Aging and the social services. In R. H. Binstock & E. Shanas (Eds.), *Handbook of aging and the social sciences.* New York: Van Nostrand-Reinhold, 1977.

Bechill, W. D. *Policy statement on Social Security, Public Welfare,* 1977, *35*(2), 23.

Bengtson, V., Torres-Gil, F., Newquist, D., & Simonian, M. Transportation: The diverse aged. In National Science Foundation (Ed.), Washington, D.C.: U.S. Government Printing Office, 1976.

Butterworth, E., & Holman, R. (Eds.). *Social welfare in modern Britain.* Glasgow: William Collins, 1975.

Camargo, O., & Preston, G. H. What happens to patients who are hospitalized for the first time when over 65? *American Journal of Psychiatry,* 1945, *102,* 168–173.

Carp, F. M. *A future for the aged.* Austin: University of Texas Press, 1966.

Carp, F. M. The impact of environment on old people. *The Gerontologist,* 1967, *7,* 106–108.

Cleveland Foundation & American Public Welfare Association. *Personal social services delivery system.* Paper presented at the National Invitational Conference on Planning and Redesigning of Local Social Service Delivery, Cleveland, Ohio, May 1978.

Donahue, W. T. What about our responsibility toward the abandoned elderly? *The Gerontologist,* 1978, *18,* 102–111.

Fischer, D. *Growing old in America.* London: Oxford University Press, 1978.

Foundation for Applied Research. *The impact of employment programs on the older worker and the service delivery systems: Benefits derived and provided.* Washington, D.C.: Foundation for Applied Research, 1977.

Fried, M. Grieving for a lost home: Psychological costs of relocation. In L. Duhl (Ed.), *The urban condition*. New York: Basic Books, 1963.

Ginzberg, E. Employment goals vs. reality. *Public Welfare,* 1978, *36* (2),.

Kahana, E. A. Congruence model of person-environment interaction. In P. G. Windley, T. O. Byerts, & F. G. Ernst (Eds.), *Theory development in environment and aging.* Washington, D.C.: The Gerontological Society, 1975.

Kahn, A., & Kamerman, S. *Not for the poor alone*. Philadelphia: Temple University Press, 1975.

Kamerman, S., & Kahn, A. *Social services in the United States*. Philadelphia: Temple University Press, 1976.

Kastler, J. M., Gray, R., & Carruth, M. Involuntary relocation of the elderly. *The Gerontologist,* 1968, *8,* 276–279.

Lawton, M., & Cohen, J. The generality of housing impact on the well-being of older people. *Journal of Gerontology,* 1974, *29,* 194–204.

Lawton, M. P. and Yaffe, S. Mortality, morbidity, and voluntary change of residence by older people. *Journal of the American Geriatrics Society,* 1970, *18,* 823–831.

Lazarus, R. *Psychological stress and the coping process*. New York: McGraw-Hill Book Co. 1966.

Lewis, C., Fein, R., & Mechanic, D. *A right to health*. New York: Wiley, 1976.

Lieberman, M. A. Relationship of mortality rates to entrance to a home for the aged. *Geriatrics,* 1961, *16,* 515–519.

Lieberman, M. A. Factors in environmental change. In U.S. Dept. of Health, Education and Welfare, *Patterns of living and housing of middle-aged and older people*. Washington, D.C.: U.S. Government Printing Office, 1965, 117–125.

Lieberman, M. A. Relocation research and social policy. *The Gerontologist,* 1974, *14,* 494–500.

Lowy, L. Social welfare and the aging. In M. Spencer & C. Dorr (Eds.), *Understanding aging: A multidisciplinary approach*. New York: Appleton-Century-Crofts, 1975.

McKee, J. Heredity and environment. In J. M. Shepard (Ed.), *Kaleidoscope*. New York: Harper & Row, 1973.

Mechanic, D. *Public expenditure and health care*. New York: Wiley Interscience, 1972.

Motley, D. K. Health in the years before retirement. In U.S. Department of Health, Education and Welfare—Social Security Administration (Ed.), *Almost 65: Baseline data from the retirement history study*. Washington, D.C.: U.S. Government Printing Office, 1976.

Pechman, J. The social security system. In M. J. Boskin (Ed.), *The Crisis in social security*. San Francisco: Institute of Contemporary Studies, 1977.

Pfouts, J. H. *Vocational history of 309 arm, leg, and bilateral amputees of World War II*. Baltimore: Veterans Administration Outpatient Clinic, n.d. Quoted in D. Macarov. *The design of social welfare*. New York: Holt, Rinehart & Winston, 1978.

Pihlblad, C., Hessler, R., & Freshley, H. *The rural elderly and years later*. Columbus: University of Missouri–Columbia, 1976.

Policy statement on health care for the aging. *Public Welfare,* 1977, *35* (2), 59.

Rose, S. *Contradictions in deinstitutionalization policy and program*. Testimony prepared for the New York State Assembly Subcommittee on Aftercare, State University of New York, November 1977.

Rosow, I. Institutional position of the aged. In Steven Zair (Ed.), *Readings in aging and death: Contemporary perspectives*. New York: Harper & Row, 1977.

Rubenstein, D., Rosenberg, C., Perlstein, J., & Ward, D. *Social and physical conditions that keep the elderly out of institutions of religion*. Paper presented at the National Conference on Spiritual Well-Being of the Elderly, Atlanta, April 1977.

Schooler, K. K. *A comparison of rural and nonrural elderly on selected variables*. In *Rural environments and aging*. Washington, D.C. : Gerontological Society, 1975.

Schooler, K. K. Environmental change and the elderly. In I. Altman & J. Wohlwill (Eds.), *Human behavior and environment: Advances in theory and research.* New York: Plenum, 1976.

Schulz, J. *The Economics of Aging.* Belmont, Calif.: Wadsworth, 1976.

Sherwood, S., Grier, D., Morris, J., & Sherwood, C. *The Highland Heights experiment.* Washington, D.C.: U.S. Department of Housing and Urban Development, 1972.

Stevens, R. *American medicine and the public interest.* New Haven: Yale University Press, 1971.

Storandt, M., Wittles, I., & Botwinick, J. Predictors of a dimension of well-being in the re-located health aged. *Journal of Gerontology,* 1975, *30,* 608–612.

Terreberry, S. Household relocation: Resident's views. In E. Wolf & C. Lebeaux (Eds.), *Change and renewal in an urban community: Five case studies.* New York: Praeger, 1968.

Tobin, S. S., Social health services for the future aged, *The Gerontologist,* 1975, *1,* 32–37.

U.S. Department of Health, Education and Welfare—Administration on Aging, National Clearing House on Aging. *Some prospects for the future elderly population* (No. 3). Washington, D.C.: U.S. Government Printing Office, 1978.

U.S. Department of Health, Education and Welfare—Social Security Administration. *Social Security Bulletin,* 1978, *41* (April).

U.S. Department of Health, Education and Welfare—Office of Human Development, Administration on Aging, National Clearing House on Aging. *Facts about older Americans* (DHEW No. OHD 78-20006). Washington, D.C.: U.S. Government Printing Office, 1977.

U.S. Department of Health, Education and Welfare—Public Health Service, Health Resources Administration, National Center for Health Statistics. *Health—United States 1976* (DHEW No. HRA 76-1232). Rockville, Md.: U.S. Government Printing Office, 1976.

Viscusi, W. K., & Zeckhauser, R. The role of social security in income maintenance. In M. J. Boskin (Ed.), *The crisis in social security.* San Francisco: Institute of Contemporary Studies, 1978.

CHAPTER 7

Multiple Impacts and Determinants in Human Service Delivery Systems

STANLEY H. COHEN
WEST VIRGINIA UNIVERSITY
MORGANTOWN, WEST VIRGINIA

The provision of any human service occurs within a context (a system) of interrelated, interacting components. The client or the recipient of the service and the staff who imparts the service usually appear in the foreground whenever the system is observed. The background, however, is equally critical to the service delivery process, although its aspects are usually less visible and are sometimes overlooked. Included in the background are (a) the technology underlying the service (e.g., psychotherapeutic technique, transit vehicle design, educational program); (b) administrative and management personnel; (c) the existing pattern of human services into which the new system is introduced; (d) political and economic considerations; (e) the feedback among components and the consequences of this feedback on system change. Furthermore, any human service system has a life cycle during which all of the above components change over time.

When human service delivery is conceptualized as a *system* rather than as simply a program or intervention, its design, implementation, and evaluation become much more complicated. Decisions regarding program effectiveness require a multilevel, input–throughput–output analysis of each subsystem and subsystem interaction. In *human* service delivery, one must attend to and understand the *behavioral* phenomena underlying access to

125

LIFE-SPAN DEVELOPMENTAL PSYCHOLOGY
Intervention

and use of the system from both a learning and a developmental perspective. One has to recognize the developmental history of individuals in the potential target group in order to explain system performance. Knowledge about the physical and psychological characteristics of the target group and an assessment of the group's service needs are indispensable in the design of an adequate interface between the client and the service delivery system. The consequences to the client of his actions or inactions in the system must be monitored and evaluated. The results from this type of analysis lead to *conditional* statements about system effectiveness, not to the traditional dichotomous judgment of success or failure.

This chapter reports just such an analysis of a social action program intended to improve the mobility of handicapped and elderly citizens residing in West Virginia. The program offered eligible recipients low cost transportation tickets, analogous to foodstamps, which were redeemable for train, bus, and taxi rides. A multilevel, comprehensive evaluation of this program was undertaken at its inception and continued over a period of four years. The evaluation was designed to specify the behavioral changes that occurred in the eligible population in terms of (*a*) choice of transportation mode, (*b*) travel activities, (*c*) utilization of agency services, and (*d*) quality of life. The evaluation also represented an attempt to delineate a model for systems-level evaluation of social programs that could be generalized to other social programs that deliver transportation services to specific target populations.

I. Mobility and Human Service Delivery

In our society there is inseparable linkage between transportation systems and the delivery (and receipt) of virtually all human services, including education, welfare, health, and others. Except for certain outreach programs, recipients of services must somehow reach, or travel to, services centers if they are to obtain their benefits. In those instances where the service is simply a cash transfer, the recipient still has to travel to some agency in order to enroll, be certified, renew, or maintain eligibility in the program.

Thus, the quality of life in our society depends in large part on one's mobility. The structural and geographic arrangement of not only human service agencies but also job and shopping locations assume—and demand—that individuals can travel far distances efficiently to maintain their lives. When the distances are too far for walking and bicycling, *efficient* mobility requires mechanized conveyances such as the automobile, bus, taxi, train, and airplane. In just three generations, these means of travel (especially the automobile) have revolutionized our way of life.

This reshaping, of course, has had a profound impact on those individuals who, for reasons that will be described later, have not been able to physically or financially remain part of our transportation-derived society.

Although it is rather obvious that much of the human environment in the past 50 years has been designed with a high degree of mobility taken for granted, the rapid growth in human services that are targeted at special populations has occurred, for the most part, without this recognition. In fact, transportation services are most needed by precisely the same age, income, and geographic groups served by human services agencies. This result has contributed to the unfilled service gap in our society. Human service provision has proliferated since the advent of the Social Security System in the 1930s. Individuals in our country who have not benefited from "the Great Society" have subscribed in increasing numbers into a variety of health, education, and welfare programs. But access to these programs—as well as access to opportunities in the larger society—requires mobility. Unfortunately, public transportation has not kept pace. Transit ridership (confounded with availability, of course) has declined about 50% since 1940 (Revis, 1975). This figure would be even further reduced except for the increase in work commuting in metropolitan areas.

A striking contrast to the decline in public transit is the 250% rise in automobile ridership since 1940. Among the major factors attributed to this increase are the construction of highways (especially the federal interstate system), the growth of suburban areas surrounding existing population centers, the centralization and consolidation of services, and the separation of residential areas from commercial areas. The demise of the neighborhood grocery store and the rise of the one-stop shopping mall are obvious examples of this phenomenon.

This country has now witnessed three generations raised on private transportation—on the automobile. Although many argue for the opportunities provided by the automobile's instantaneous mobility, segments of our population clearly have been disenfranchised. Indeed, as income drops and physical ability diminishes, what arises is a group of individuals dependent on public transit. They are mostly elderly females, handicapped persons of all ages, and low-income workers who commute to their jobs. These are the individuals who have the most to win, or lose, with respect to transportation services in our country.

II. Mobility and the Aged

In 1971 the second White House Conference on Aging identified several problems faced by the elderly in our society. After health and income, transportation was one of the key issues at this meeting. A broad set of recommendations were formulated regarding transportation subsidies, coordination of services, system design, and driver licensing. Further analyses linking the goals of choice and mobility were highlighted in subsequent research reported in the Senate's Special Committee on Aging (Revis, 1975). Four categories of factors apparently relate to the loss of mobility experienced by the elderly: (a) income and the high cost of private transportation, (b) accessibility of transportation, (c) transit design, and (d) personal factors.

It has been estimated that although the elderly (individuals over the age of 60) constitute 14% of the population in the United States, 40% have incomes at or below the poverty level (Burkhardt, 1972). Living within the constraints of a low, fixed income, most of the elderly spend virtually all their income on food and housing. Those elderly persons (especially in rural areas) who maintain a high degree of mobility spend up to 60% of their income on transportation (Burkhardt, 1969). In any case, the aged in our society must adjust their transportation demands downward, at the expense of a reduced quality of life, or confront a changing lifestyle in other sectors if they are to afford their previous transportation levels. Either strategy is most unpleasant, and the negative consequences bear greatly on personal adjustment and well-being.

The changes in accessibility of transportation for the elderly are most dramatic. Walking and bicycling, the least expensive modes of mobility, are often incompatible with physical health or are impossible considering the distances to essential services destinations (Carp, 1971). As mentioned earlier, environmental arrangements often preclude travel except by mechanized vehicles. Private vehicles, automobiles, or taxicabs are too expensive. Indeed, the vast majority of the elderly are nondrivers; only 14% of the elderly population is licensed to drive (Revis, 1975) due to a variety of reasons. Many members in the present cohort have never driven; others let their licenses expire when they retire or begin to distrust their vision, reaction time, or motor coordination. Public transportation, although less expensive than private, is generally less than satisfactory in terms of convenience, availability, destinations served, and comfort. For the elderly, these inadequacies create an especially difficult situation. A simple shopping trip involves long waits, confusing transfers, and heavy packages—not to mention the transit design problems discussed in the next paragraph. Although many public transit riders are elderly, Hyde and Cohen (1978) found in their sample of 195 persons that 40% of the total trips made by the elderly on 20 different days over a 9-week period were taken in a friend's or relative's vehicle and that only 4% were taken in a bus or taxi.

Several researchers (Falcocchio & Cantilli, 1974; Golden, 1973) have noted the many features of the public transit system that make it unattractive to the elderly. Structural and informational deficiences appear to be among the most negative factors. The vehicles themselves present physical barriers to boarding and unboarding, and the limited space per person hinders the less agile older person. Decoding the routes and schedules of public transit vehicles sometimes requires information processing skills beyond the capacities of the aged, especially when they encounter public transportation systems for the first time. (The averseness of the first experience often stops further use of the system!) The difficulties associated with riding public transit systems by individuals of all ages are well documented in a series of studies reported by Carp (1972c) and Gelwicks (1970).

From a behavioral point of view, the last category related to loss of mobility—personal factors—is the most critical one. The process of aging causes several transitions in one's life: changes in income, family situation, and job role, to mention only a few. The shift from private transportation to "less private" transportation is another major disruption. It requires adapting to one's dependency on others versus self-sufficiency. The vulnerability of the aged to physical barriers and criminal assault (Falcocchio & Cantilli, 1974) and their seclusion from others strongly inhibit their mobility, in general, and their utilization of public transportation, in particular (Gurin, 1969; Sundeem & Mathiew, 1976). As Bissonnette (1978) has pointed out, going from private to public transportation is a large behavioral step in the life of an elderly person. This step is further exacerbated by one's developmental history and physical condition and by transit design and transit access. Without a thorough analysis of each of these four categories, the net attractiveness of any transportation system is destined to fail from the start.

Few would argue against the proposition that mobility is essential for the receipt of services. What is not as apparent is the effect mobility has on life satisfaction and well-being. Mobility itself is a social activity as well as a means of access to the larger society. Several studies have substantiated the importance of mobility for the aged. Revis (1975) suggested that transportation acts as an antidote for the process of aging and, by providing access to essential services, helps to sustain life goals. Immobility, according to Carp (1972a), is bound up with physical separateness and a subsequent lack of social integration into the community. Furthermore, Cutler (1972) found that mobility restrictions were highly related to life satisfaction. Elderly subjects in his sample who had their own means of transportation reported a higher life satisfaction than subjects without their own means. Taken together, these studies indicate the vital role transportation (and consequent mobility) plays in keeping the elderly in the mainstream of society and maintaining their functional well-being.

III. Travel Behavior and Transportation Needs of the Elderly

This section reviews the travel behavior of the elderly, who are viewed as a subpopulation. The research to date finds that the elderly, as a subpopulation, do not differ significantly from the general population in terms of travel frequency or destination, the only exception being work-related trips (see Ashford & Holloway, 1972; Hyde & Cohen, 1978; Patton, 1975; Revis, 1975). There are some subtle, but important, changes in the pattern of travel of the elderly that do need further consideration. Shopping trips and medical service trips show an increase in frequency. Travel is more likely to occur during nonpeak working–commuting hours. A large percentage of almost all kinds of travel is taken in vehicles owned by friends or relatives. Elderly persons who are physically able tend to walk to many destinations that are within one mile of their residences but use motorized vehicles for travel to more distant places. Affordable transportation is central to the elderly's choice of mode. Public transportation is seen as more costly, and less convenient, than travel in their own cars or in others' cars. Thus, the elderly, like the general population, view public transportation as attractive only when private transportation is not available.

Age, however, is an important factor in the design of a transportation system. Flexible, portal-to-portal service (Carp, 1972b) is necessary because walking with packages is more physically difficult for many elderly persons. Fixed public transportation routes either do not satisfy the elderly's need for recreational and social trips or require them to wait long periods at bus stops (Bell & Olsen, 1974). Personalized modes of public transportation are expensive; so the cost to the elderly rider, who has limited transportation resources, must be reduced in some manner. If public transportation is to meet the needs of tne elderly, it must be affordable, convenient, and comfortable in their eyes. Several systems targeted toward the elderly that have been implemented in the recent past are illustrated in the next section of this chapter.

IV. Review of Transportation Programs Designed for the Elderly

As of July 1974, there were slightly over 900 transportation projects serving the elderly in the United States (Revis, Eckman, Coit, Davidson, Revis, & Rechel, 1975). Most of these projects were funded in whole or in part through funds provided by the Department of Transportation, Urban Mass Transit Agency, Agency on Aging, Community Services Administration, and the Department of Health, Education and Welfare. Virtually all of them were local or regional in scope; many were in a demonstration phase of activity. The programs varied widely in number and type of vehicles, scheduling arrangement, fare structure, service capability, and integration with the general public transportation system.

With respect to scheduling arrangement, approximately 36% of the programs were demand-responsive (i.e., portal-to-portal, prearranged rides), 46% traveled fixed routes on a scheduled basis, 15% utilized volunteer drivers in private vehicles, and 3% consisted of contractual agreements with private taxicab companies that were reimbursed by public agencies. Many of the programs provided transportation to special services, mainly those related to health or welfare. Depending on the amount of grant funds available, fares ranged from no fare to a 75% reduction in fare. Those programs that were integrated with existing public transportation systems generally offered reduced-fare rides during off-peak hours or senior citizen discount cards. Several cities and states (Miami, Chicago, New York State, Pennsylvania) have subsidized public transportation programs for the elderly through lotteries or special taxes. Where state laws permit, school buses are utilized as carriers when they are not in service to transport students. More details about the structure of these programs are provided in the following examples.

Lift Line in Palm Beach County, Florida, uses minibuses to provide county-wide transportation over fixed routes. There is some limited radio-dispatched door-to-door service. Individuals who are disabled or receiving Aid to Families with Dependent Children (ADC) or Supplementary Security Income (SSI) funds may ride these vehicles at free fare. The system links low-income neighborhoods with social welfare and medical service facilities.

Seniors on the Move in Chicago, Illinois, provides free transportation to elderly individuals residing in the near South Side of Chicago. Vans transport between 300 and 400 passengers per month. An advance schedule service in combination with a demand-responsive dispatch tally about 80% shopping-related and 15% health-care-related trips.

One of the most geographically extensive programs is *Older Adults Transportation Service* (OATS). It encompasses an 84-county region in the State of Missouri. Elderly persons enroll on a membership basis and pay a 4.5¢ per mile fare. Small passenger vans travel the mostly long rural distances on a demand-responsive schedule and on some semifixed routes.

An example of a taxi-subscription system is *Project 33* in Arlington, Virginia. Elderly persons who register for the program obtain taxi rides anywhere within a fixed geographical area at a flat fare of 15¢ per trip. One van transports members free under certain conditions.

The four programs described here and the several hundred others with a similar purpose have delivered much needed transportation services to the elderly population. Many of these programs have not been carefully evaluated, so it is difficult to estimate with any great precision their impact on the target population. This alone is a point of considerable concern. In addition, however, analysis of these state-of-the-art programs reveals several inadequacies.

Most of these projects are ad hoc and do not integrate or coordinate their services with existing public transportation systems. This leads to transient demonstration programs that do not survive beyond their pilot funding period. Furthermore, many compete directly with existing systems for the same passengers and eventually deteriorate to such a low level of performance that continuation funds do not materialize.

Compared to the expressed needs of the elderly target population, these programs cannot offer the full array of mobility and accessibility required by any reasonable cost–effectiveness ratio. This problem is symptomatic of public transportation in general. Demand-responsive, portal-to-portal service is exceedingly expensive, but it attracts higher ridership. Semifixed route scheduling is less attractive to potential riders and generates lower revenues.

Free-fare and reduced-fare systems are subsidized through federal or local funding mechanisms. Such direct subsidies to providers lessens their accountability to the target group. Funding is generally not made contingent on the quality of provider service. Although providers may be subject to performance review, the delay in time between service-provision and service-evaluation obviates the effectiveness of the review procedures. On the other hand, a direct subsidy to the rider allows him or her to selectively seek out the best service provider for a given travel need.

One of the unintended negative consequences of any human service program targeted at special populations is its potential to stigmatize the "have nots" in society. Special transportation programs are no exception to this problem. One immediate result can be a lower utilization of the program by the target population. In the case of special transportation programs, many of the elderly view them as "welfare" and consequently refuse to participate in them. Although this consequence *rarely* can be eliminated entirely, it should be minimized whenever possible.

As with any human service, there is a bottom line: Who should pay for transportation programs? The short life of many of the projects attests to their fiscal vulnerability. Few transportation programs aimed at the elderly have considered the necessity of a long-term funding base. Given the low ridership of public transportation systems, none are able to continue service without special public revenue sources such as local taxes and lotteries.

Until public transportation secures a wider and larger ridership, special transportation programs must be associated with more stable funding arrangements than pilot grants.

With these critical observations in mind, West Virginia in concert with the federal government attempted to establish a statewide transportation system to serve the needs of its elderly population. The history, implementation, and evaluation of this project—the Transportation Remuneration Incentive Program—are detailed in the following section.

V. Goals and Design of the Transportation Remuneration Incentive Program

Plans for funding and implementing the Transportation Remuneration Incentive Program (TRIP) began in 1971 and culminated in 1974. These activities involved numerous individuals at the state and federal levels. From the beginning, the program was conceived as simultaneously meeting the transportation needs of West Virginia's population (in particular, those in more remote, rural areas) and reducing the special financial burden felt by low-income, handicapped, and elderly individuals in the state in securing adequate transportation. The experience of previous transportation programs in other states and of needs assessment surveys conducted in West Virginia during this period (TRIP Development Plan, 1974) provided many of the goals, assumptions, and design features of TRIP. Although many elements eventually appeared in the final plan, six stand out as critical or, at least, as distinctive.

First, the program was comprehensive in that it applied statewide, was accessible to all individuals who desired public transportation, and (in principle) integrated all transportation systems already in place throughout the state with the new systems emerging from the TRIP demonstration. Of particular importance was the proposed linkup between rural areas and medium-density areas since many vital human services are situated in population centers and are far removed from individuals living outside these centers. Statistically, West Virginia is the most rural state east of the Mississippi River and, therefore, was an ideal test site for such a transportation program. Furthermore, transit availability had declined steadily in recent years due to the pullout of carriers from low-profit, rural routes.

A second key feature of TRIP was its provision of a direct user subsidy in the form of transportation coupons that were analogous to food stamps. Eligible users—low-income, elderly, or handicapped persons—purchased an $8 book of TRIP tickets each month through regional welfare offices. The actual cost of these tickets, discounted at a rate proportional to the user's household income and assets, averaged slightly over $1. These tickets were directly exchanged in lieu of cash for transportation services on all certified carriers. They could also be accumulated and then spent at a later time, especially on interstate carriers. Eligible users who required more frequent travel (e.g., weekly medical treatments) could request additional books of tickets at the same discounted rate. Providers of transportation services in the state—this included virtually every public carrier—redeemed the tickets at face value. Thus, providers received revenues from the program in the form of an indirect, but not a guaranteed, subsidy. Since the subsidy was on the user side, there was a built-in incentive for providers to deliver adequate services if they wished to attract user patronage.

During the planning phase, it was immediately recognized that limiting the user subsidy to one public transportation mode would severely restrict the travel potential of the ticket-eligible elderly and handicapped. These individuals required as flexible a choice in travel destination as the general population. To arrive at this capability, virtually every mode of carrier—including rail, intercity bus, intracity bus, and taxicab—was established as a certified TRIP provider. This transit mix not only met the needs of the ticket user but also prevented the creation of a new special-population system exclusive of the general population and its rider revenues. Vehicles purchased through the TRIP demonstration became the property of already existing providers or governmental transportation authorities.

The most far-reaching structural feature of the TRIP demonstration was its regional planning and implementation concept. Previous legislative and executive actions had divided West Virginia into 10 geographic regions with authority over community and economic planning and development. Each region was required to develop a regional transportation plan in order to receive capital and operating grants from the TRIP central office. In principle, these plans integrated the transportation services in the region and fulfilled the unique transportation needs in the region, including systems for the elderly and handicapped.

In order to coordinate and direct regional transportation plans and to operate the subsidy or ticket system, a TRIP central office was established in the West Virginia Department of Welfare. This office approved regional plans, distributed capital grants, provided technical assistance through transportation experts, and monitored the impact of the program across the state. Twenty-seven welfare offices within the 10 planning and development regions processed individual applications for the ticket disbursement program.

Because of this organizational arrangement, TRIP became the first statewide program of its kind in the nation. A transportation system emerged that targeted the transportation problems of the low-income elderly and handicapped as well as serving the transportation requirements of the general public. Transportation for special populations was not outside the general system or confined to special-purpose vehicles; it was integrated through user subsidies with public carriers. Thus, the experience of TRIP has important implications for the future development of public transportation, particularly for rural areas. As a unique, large-scale effort with substantial state and federal support, the pilot program could help to shape the development of rural transportation programs at both state and national levels.

VI. Evaluation of the Transportation Remuneration Incentive Program

The two major objectives of West Virginia's Transportation Remuneration Incentive Program were: (a) to provide dependable and conveniently accessible public transportation to the residents of the state and (b) to provide transportation subsidies to the low-income elderly and low-income handicapped—two groups most likely to need some form of public subsidy to improve their mobility—that would enable them to purchase at reduced rates books of TRIP tickets that could be used for intrastate and interstate travel.

Given the importance of the program both in meeting the more immediate transportation needs of the people of the state (particularly the low-income elderly and low-income handicapped) and in potentially shaping the long-run development of transportation policy, it was considered essential to document the outcomes of TRIP and to understand the factors influencing those outcomes. Accordingly, in January 1975, the West Virginia Department of Welfare contracted with the Office of Research and Development of West Virginia University to conduct a comprehensive longitudinal study of TRIP (Phase III TRIP Evaluation, 1977). This evaluation, now concluded, had as its major purposes the study of the impact of TRIP on: (a) eligible users and eligible nonusers; (b) service agencies and the clients of these agencies; (c) transportation providers throughout the state. Other aspects of the evaluation consisted of (a) studies designed to generate information on the public's receptivity to the program and the general need for public transportation among the state's households; (b) field staff surveys concerned with measuring the effectiveness of procedures used to implement and maintain the program; (c) an overall benefit–cost analysis of TRIP; (d) several special studies dealing with strategies for client recruitment and enrollment, travel behavior among the TRIP eligible populations, informal transportation networks, factors motivating change from private to public transportation, marketing rural public transportation, and factors related to low ridership of the TRIP buses.

Specifically, the study of the impact on the eligible users and eligible nonusers (the Assessment Area Surveys) focused on travel behavior and attitudes, access to services, quality of life, and acceptance and usage of TRIP. The study of TRIP's impact on agency services (the Agency Impact Studies) focused on client use of TRIP, agency caseloads, characteristics of agency users, travel behavior of agency clients, effectiveness of client services, agency outreach, and benefits and costs of agency services. The final major component of the evaluation study (Survey and Analysis of the Providers) sought to determine the nature and condition of existing public transportation in the state, the providers' awareness of and attitudes toward TRIP, and the impact of TRIP on the providers.

The methodological design of the major components of the evaluation was based on both longitudinal and cross-sectional surveys of samples of program users and nonusers and a statistically representative sample of the households of West Virginia. Specifically, there were four major elements within the design: (a) longitudinal and cross-sectional interview surveys of TRIP eligible users and eligible nonusers in seven "assessment area" counties; (b) 10 case studies of selected service agencies potentially subject to the influence of TRIP; (c) a longitudinal mail questionnaire survey of a statistically representative sample of West Virginia households; (d) personal interview and mail questionnaire surveys of all public transportation providers in West Virginia. Additional elements of the design were an overall benefit–cost study of TRIP, a longitudinal interview survey of TRIP staff members, a client recruitment and enrollment study, and one or more small sample studies of private and public transportation usage and the informal transportation networks used by the elderly and handicapped.

The design was based on a concept of sequential outcomes that a successful program would be expected to generate among program users. The outcomes in the order in which they would be expected to occur were: (a) awareness of the program; (b) receptivity to the program; (c) enrollment in the program; (d) use of the program; (e) increased mobility of users; and (f) improvement in the quality of life of program users (including improved access to agency services).

In essence, the design was intended to generate measurements of each of these six expected outcomes. The measurement and assessment of outcomes was based largely on comparisons made at three or more points in time of the behavior, attitudes, and personal circumstances and characteristics of program users and nonusers in seven counties. Specifically, the comparisons were of the ownership and use of private transportation, travel activities in access to and use of public transportation, attitudes toward public transportation and TRIP, and personal characteristics. By tracing changes in these behaviors, attitudes, and circumstances among TRIP users over a 3-year period, and by comparing them to changes among nonusers of TRIP, it was possible to determine the impact of TRIP on the personal welfare of users.

Similarly, the tracing of change over a 3-year period in the need for public transportation and in awareness and acceptance of TRIP among a representative sample of the state's citizens provided a measure of the support for and impact of TRIP on persons other than those eligible to use the program's ticket system. The monitoring of selected service agencies over time provided some important measures of the impact of TRIP on agency caseloads, services, and client welfare. The study of the changes in all the individuals and institutions touched by TRIP was the major thrust of the evaluation.

Thus, the evaluation constituted a comprehensive, multifaceted effort to document the activities of TRIP and to weigh its outcomes. At the present time, a substantial amount of information has been generated not only about TRIP but also about the role of public transportation and its potentials and problems in a rural state. Despite the somewhat preliminary nature of some of the findings included in Section VII of this chapter, the data that are included should provide a fund of useful information. Because of the tentative nature of some of the analyses, caution in interpretation needs to be exercised; it is possible that additional conclusions might be drawn from certain analyses to be completed in the future.

VII. Results of the Transportation Remuneration Incentive Program

A. Administration of the Ticket System

1. Publicity and Recruitment

Awareness of TRIP was especially low among the target group populations. Initial participant awareness stemmed mainly from contact with welfare or referral agencies. There was an early emphasis on publicity via mass media or community organizations. Efforts spent on publicizing TRIP to the general population and to the target population in particular were insufficient to meet the promotional needs of the program. Direct contacts were limited to individuals on SSI and related lists. The field staff cited the unavailability of other potential client rosters. Later enrollees, however, did indicate initial awareness through direct contact.

Awareness of the program seemed to be related to one's mode of travel; users of public transportation were *more* likely and users of private vehicles were much *less* likely to know about the program. Some awareness of the program came about simply because of contact with TRIP vehicles.

2. Enrollment

Enrollment in the ticket subsidy program was lower than expected. However, those who did enroll maintained an active status. Perhaps the estimate of enrollment rate (within a given time period) was too high. Any major behavioral change requires both *directed promotional efforts* and *time*. Without *specific promotional efforts* to decrease the critical period between program implementation and enrollment, the process of dissemination (from awareness to adoption) may well outlast the time alloted to demonstrate the program.

There was no evidence to suggest that eligibility requirements were problematic, except for the difficulty of arriving at a consistent definition of *handicapped*. Apparently, some changes were made in income level and household income requirements during the program.

The delay in systems implementation limited the analysis of the statewide impact of TRIP on both providers and eligible participants. Also, at the time of the analysis, TRIP had not been implemented in the more rural regions of the state, and, therefore, one important target population was not served and was not fully included in the data. In addition, feeder lines and vehicles were not established; these were considered critical to success in the rural transportation aspect of the program.

Both administrators and staff reported that delays in implementation significantly deterred recruitment and subsequent enrollment in the program. Delays probably served only to *increase* skepticism about the innovation and thus probably contributed to the lack of acceptance and usage. It is possible to speculate about, but impossible to directly calculate, the negative effects of the delays on the future success of the program.

Personal characteristics of the eligible population reduced its effective size. Pre-TRIP estimates of the TRIP eligible population (based on income and age data) were most likely too high. Survey data revealed that up to 20% of the eligible sample was not able to travel outside the home on a regular basis or could do so only with personal assistance and door-to-door service that was not possible with conventional transit or, in some instances, even with taxicabs.

Overall, no problems were evident with respect to ticket application, purchasing, and distribution. Most tickets were purchased through welfare offices rather than other ticket operations in the community. In the first year, a significant percentage of applicants had long waits for receipt of tickets after their applications were approved. This delay seems to have disappeared subsequently.

3. Staff Organizations, Procedures, and Attitudes

Apparently, Area Office Administrators regarded TRIP as a very low priority responsibility. Staff were not specifically selected or trained for the program. There was a high turnover of personnel early in the program, but this subsided during the second and third years. No guidelines handbook was available to direct staff publicity and recruitment activities. Unfortunately, a highly developed and deliberate campaign specific to the target group was necessary but not in effect.

Most staff members were favorable toward the concepts of the program, although some questioned its location in welfare agencies. The attitude of many TRIP supervisors was more consonant with the welfare caseload philosophy of decreasing rather than increasing case rolls. Frustration, lack of support, and lack of resources resulted in a generally negative attitude.

Transportation specialists were not hired by TRIP until the second and third years. There were some indications that a lack of continuity (and expertise) occurred when RRC International, Inc., the initial consultants for the program, pulled out. Too much reliance on RRC for management and decision making was probably the cause.

B. Travel Behavior and Use of TRIP

1. Changes in the Frequency of Travel

The participants in TRIP traveled more frequently and regularly because of TRIP to grocery and other shopping stores, church, medical facilities, and friends and relatives. This pattern consistently emerged over the three years of the evaluation. Eligible *nonparticipants* indicated that they would also travel more frequently to these same places if public transportation were available to them; however, they also expressed the need for more "nonessential" travel.

Separate studies of travel behavior conducted during the evaluation confirmed the fact that these destinations accounted for almost all of the travel activity by persons in the TRIP eligible population. Frequency of travel to various types of social service, training, and medical agencies displayed virtually no change. This outcome was apparently due to the large number of tickets required to travel to these facilities.

2. Changes in Mode of Travel

Participants increased their use of both buses and taxicabs; however, taxicab utilization displayed a relatively larger increase. During the same period, nonparticipants relied increasingly on their own or others' private vehicles. The data suggest that participants who had previous experience with buses continued to rely on and ride them, and did so at a much higher rate; these individuals accounted for most of the increase in bus utilization. Taxicabs attracted a larger segment of participants who, prior to TRIP, had not relied on public transportation. These participants subsequently reduced their frequency of travel with friends and others. Eligible nonparticipants were much more likely to own or have access to a private vehicle either in their own or another household.

3. Changes in Travel Destinations

No dramatic change in travel destinations, or new destinations, was evident, except for perhaps travel to church and church-related activities. In general, participants tended to increase their frequency of travel to those places to which they already frequently traveled for such purposes as shopping, visiting, and medical treatments. From the data collected, it is not possible to discern whether participants, because of the ticket subsidy, were able to change *where* they shopped, obtained medical care, etc. It is important to note that a wider implementation of TRIP, especially in the more rural areas, might have resulted in different findings here. The potential for change, however, was apparent; for example, although almost 25% of the clients in the agency sample were eligible for the program, only a much smaller fraction enrolled in the program, and even fewer used tickets to reach the various types of service agencies.

4. Ticket Use and Adequacy

Enrollment in the program was not a sufficient condition for *participation* in it. By 1977 almost two-thirds of the enrollees were *active* users, a gradual increase from the 50% figure reported in 1975. Over 90% of those participants who utilized the program remained active. One-fourth of the enrollees had not purchased tickets or exchanged them for transit services. Nonuse of tickets was highly related to the unavailability of public transportation and, to a much lesser degree, to the accumulation of tickets for long-distance trips, even though virtually none of the users in the samples reported such trips. Over one-half of the participants stated a need for additional ticket books (from two to five) in order to meet their monthly travel requirements (to their most frequently traveled destinations). Studies at the agencies found that many enrollees did not use their tickets because of the large number of tickets required to get to the particular agency.

5. *Opinions about TRIP, Need for Travel, and Reasons for Using the Program*

Participants and nonparticipants alike expressed very positive feelings about the specific aims of the program and also indicated general support for the provision of public transportation in the state.

Over the three years of the program, larger percentages of participants reported that they traveled as much as they needed, but many still specified an additional need for more travel and greater transportation availability. In contrast, nonparticipants, over the same time period, stated a diminished need for public transportation services.

Enrollees in the program viewed it as a way to save money, help them in some unspecified way, and provide a means of transportation. The major incentive for utilizing the program was the discount value of the tickets; that is, reduced spending on transportation. Other benefits reported by participants included increased mobility and elimination of the need for another automobile or dependence on others for transportation.

6. *Factors Associated with the Use of TRIP*

Enrollees in the program came from a population of eligible persons who were involved with other similar government services and learned about the program through direct or indirect contact with welfare agencies. Participants were for the most part already using public transportation, especially buses, and resided close to bus routes. These persons lacked access to funds for private transportation. They were also relatively mobile and traveled outside their homes. Eligible nonparticipants had much more access to alternative transportation or had physical disabilities that prohibited their use of conventional public transportation. These individuals also reported that the cost of TRIP reduced its attractiveness, especially for those persons who traveled at no cost with friends and relatives. Participants indicated that they would like to see major improvements in the availability and accessibility of public transportation and in the size of the monthly allocation of ticket books.

C. Provider System

1. *Types of Providers*

Providers were for the most part small, rural, and marginal operators. With the exception of urban-centered providers, they appeared to be small businesses with an owner–operator and one or two helpers. The providers operated one or two vehicles (usually private rather than commercial models) and served restricted areas.

2. Quality of Provider Service

Virtually none of the participants reported any on-board problems. However, participants felt that the buses should travel more often and closer to their homes. Almost all noted inconvenient schedules or a lack of service during certain hours or days of the week.

There was also the problem of routes. Many participants, when asked about where they wanted to travel more, mentioned trips to visit friends and family. These destinations, often removed from major business or service sectors, were not aligned with bus routes. Adequate access to family and friends by public transportation was probably impossible by conventional transit configurations.

Another major criticism, from a physical standpoint, was the difficulty in using a bus. Buses are hard to board, the seats are uncomfortable, the stops too short. This seems to reflect the problems the aged have in coping with a system designed for younger age groups.

3. User Reliance on Taxicabs

As noted earlier, there was a greater utilization of taxicabs over buses among TRIP participants. Several factors seem to explain this differential use. Taxicab service was relatively more available to users, even before TRIP, and continued to be more available because of the delays in bus implementation. Taxicab service was a more familiar mode for many of the participants who had previously depended on rides from friends and relatives in private vehicles. In addition, some of our results suggest that bus transit was simply not convenient, or, for that matter, not possible, for many types of trips that necessitated carrying packages (e.g., shopping). Taxicab service also did not require the user to be aware of schedules or routes. In some instances, the waiting time for a return bus was especially lengthy. Finally, some participants were physically incapacitated to a degree that prohibited bus travel and required personalized assistance (by the driver) and door-to-door service.

4. Impact of TRIP on Providers

TRIP had a minimal impact on providers. Only those providers whose existence depended upon a public grant seemed to feel any large impact from TRIP. The fractionation of transportation providers into small, private operators diluted and reduced the impact of the program until it failed to make a substantial contribution to the providers' operations.

Although they were least likely to be materially assisted by TRIP, the smaller operators were the most enthusiastic. Larger firms located in the population centers accepted TRIP but were less enthusiastic. Most were of the opinion that TRIP ticket users were not new riders but old patrons who went from cash use to ticket use. Consequently, the impact of TRIP on the providers (particularly with regard to ridership) was small. Most were highly critical of the delay in ticket reimbursement. This was especially true of the smaller operators who could not afford the cash flow delay.

For the most part, the providers did not view TRIP as a catalyst for the advancement of their industry. Their views, however, did seem to reflect agreement with the more altruistic nature of the program.

D. Conclusions

The assessment area, agency impact, travel behavior, and small sample studies all seem to indicate a preference for personally arranged transportation rather than scheduled transportation. New users of public transportation seem to prefer taxicabs over buses (where there is a choice). Nonusers mentioned their own or others' personally arranged transportation as the reason for nonparticipation in TRIP. The preference for personally arranged transportation and the predominance of one- and two-vehicle providers seem to have acted in concert as a single factor that reduced the impact of a transportation subsidy program and diluted the impact of TRIP among providers by spreading the benefits too thin. This preference for arranged transportation may also be linked to the types of trips made by eligible persons.

Lack of effective promotional efforts that were specific to the target groups contributed to lower than expected participation of the members of the target groups in the ticket subsidy program. This lack of effective promotional efforts also contributed to lower than expected growth in public transportation ridership among noneligible persons.

For those who did enroll, TRIP seems to be successful; users continue to remain active, purchase tickets, and increase their travel frequency. Maintenance of this behavior indicates that the system is probably effectively rewarding the users as was designed—by increasing their mobility and independence. Participants gain additional freedom in scheduling their trips and reducing their dependency on others for transportation. Many nonparticipants prefer and remain attached to informal transportation networks for their transportation needs.

The monthly ticket allotment appears to be inadequate for those participants residing in isolated areas served exclusively, or almost exclusively, by taxicabs.

E. Recommendations

Future staff hired by the TRIP Program at *all* levels should have prior experience (and credentials) with the technical, marketing, and operations aspects of public transportation systems. The early staff's limited expertise in the area of transportation probably contributed in part to the delays in program implementation. Supplemental and continuing in-service training on specific topics in transportation (e.g., recruiting, marketing, planning, route development) should remain an important administrative function.

Promotional strategies that are specific to the target groups should be developed with an allowance of sufficient resources for an intensive statewide campaign. Contingencies that would promote both efficient, creative recruitment efforts on the local level and their diffusion to other regions should be enacted concurrently. These and other procedures should be incorporated into a manual utilized by all TRIP staff personnel.

Related to the previous recommendation is a requirement to set specific objectives concerning the transportation needs of the eligible population. This would involve a determination of how many (and what kinds of) trips would be subsidized and to what degree. Thus, some measure of adequacy of performance could be calculated for the program.

A more realistic estimate of the size of the eligible target population needs to be made. This is critical if the coverage of the program is to be assessed. The information gathered in arriving at this estimate could also prove to be valuable in pinpointing the characteristics of presently eligible persons who might eventually enroll and participate in TRIP or in similarly subsidized transportation programs.

Much more coordination must be brought about between TRIP and other community agencies acting to provide transportation services to the TRIP eligible population. Such efforts would presumably increase the effectiveness of the transportation sector.

The TRIP central staff should provide technical assistance to regional transportation systems. Included could be direct training on such topics as marketing surveys, scheduling and routing, recruitment strategies, and the design of incentive programs to increase ridership.

A more extensive economic and behavioral study of variations of the present ticket allocation system is needed. This study would analyze the impact on transportation and travel behavior of varying parameters of the discount value, eligibility requirements, and monthly ticket allotment. It would also be important to consider other subsidy strategies; for example, trip allotment versus ticket allotment.

Regional systems should implement evaluation and feedback procedures in order to monitor enrollment rates and ridership. These data should be used dynamically to alter and modify the transportation program.

The feeder systems originally planned for the rural areas need to be implemented and evaluated. The assessment of the impact of TRIP in rural areas is seriously limited by the present absence of feeder routes and carriers, especially with regard to TRIP's provision of transportation to the more isolated communities in the state.

The relatively greater utilization of taxicabs over buses by many of the participants suggests that further planning is needed concerning the types of vehicles deployed in TRIP. Future vehicles might have a smaller seating capacity and offer more personalized service to various destinations.

Additional demonstrations of other transportation delivery systems are necessary. Several planned alternatives, including a postal bus and a health transporter, did not materialize, thus obviating the possibility of evaluating the feasibility of such alternative systems. Other possibilities include the distribution of van or van-type vehicles to social service agencies, service contracts with taxicab companies, work-pool vans, and subsidies to individuals to provide more informal transportation services.

The extensive utilization of informal transportation networks (i.e., riding with friends and family outside the household) by the TRIP eligible population requires additional study. Such research should determine the appropriate relationship between transportation services provided by TRIP and those provided by informal networks.

Finally, marketing strategies aimed at the TRIP noneligible population should be explored. Ultimately, the financial success of the program rests on attracting the general population into using public transportation systems. The provider data collected in the present evaluation underscores this problem. The ticket eligible segment of the population can never carry the entire burden of the cost of public transportation. It is hoped that research efforts being conducted in other states and at the federal level will provide some of the technology to increase public transportation utilization and efficiency.

F. Implications

Probably the most important finding of the TRIP demonstration project is that public transportation presents physical and psychological barriers to the elderly that may discourage them from using it. Availability of transit vehicles is a necessary but far from sufficient element in the ultimate success of a transportation program. Cost to the rider is also only partially related to program utilization. The functional relationship between the transportation system and the potential client needs careful analysis. It is a large behavioral step when an individual shifts from private to public transportation. This step must be divided into smaller movements; each subdivision should then be examined for its potential to promote or block the client's transition into the system. The initial experiences an individual has with the system are probably the most crucial. An early failure or aversive experience greatly reduces the likelihood that the individual will approach the system again.

The transportation environment in which an individual is living prior to the introduction of the new system determines to a large degree his subsequent adaptation to the new system. Many elderly participate in informal transportation networks that provide them not only with convenient and inexpensive mobility opportunities but also with social benefits. Conventional public transportation competes poorly against these networks; however, if properly designed, they could complement them and thus enhance the elderly's overall mobility. How, when, and where one travels can be viewed as behavior subject to a socialization process. Everett (1978) and Danish (1977) envision developmentally focused training programs that would teach both the young and old effective travel behavior skills. Such programs could alter present travel behavior (less reliance on the automobile) and promote alternative modes of travel such as walking and bicycling. Driver education in the school system could be replaced by comprehensive courses emphasizing efficient travel behavior. Community-based programs for the elderly could include life skills training, part of which involves coping with public transportation. These experiences would expand perceptions of the transportation environment across the life span and change one's values toward mobility and life-style.

The notion of special transportation programs for special populations is not viable given the real cost of convenient and comfortable transportation. Transportation systems, if they are to be effective and efficient, must serve the general public. TRIP is one example of how a general public system can provide special services to target populations. Other designs are possible and should be tested. In the long run, integrated transportation systems delivering adequate service to all populations represent the best answer to the mobility crisis.

Like most demonstration programs, TRIP highlighted the practical need for more facts and fewer assumptions about the impact of human service intervention. Before the program was started, many decision makers believed that it would create a TRIP-fare monster similar to food stamp welfare programs. This did not happen for a variety of reasons. For example, the size of the potential eligible population was grossly overestimated; transportation-disadvantaged individuals adapt to their situation through informal transportation arrangements; transportation is *not* analogous to food; and so on.

I wish to close this chapter with a passage, which for me is biblical inpiration, from Alice Rivlin's (1971) *Systematic Thinking for Social Action:*

On balance, I believe the advantages of social experimentation far outweigh the disadvantages, and that the federal government should follow a systematic experimentation strategy in seeking to improve the effectiveness of social action programs. The process will not be easy or quick or cheap. Nor can one look forward to an end to it. . . . The process of developing new methods, trying them out, modifying them, trying again, will have to be continuous. But unless we begin searching for improvements and experimenting with them in a systematic way, it is hard to see how we will make much progress in increasing the effectiveness of our social services [p. 107].

The TRIP demonstration project follows the spirit of Rivlin's exhortation. Rational–intuitive social planning proceeds faster and in the correct direction if guided by the road signs of systematic intervention and evaluation.

REFERENCES

Ashford, N., & Holloway, F. M. Transportation patterns of older people in six urban centers. *The Gerontologist,* 1972, *12,* 43–47.

Bell, W. G., & Olsen, W. T. An overview of public transportation and the elderly: New directions for social policy. *The Gerontologist,* 1974, *14,* 324–330.

Bissonnette, K. K. *Incentive, enrollment, and travel behavior: A study of a special transportation program for the elderly and handicapped.* Unpublished doctoral dissertation, West Virginia University, 1978.

Burkhardt, J. E. *The transportation needs of the rural poor.* Bethesda, Md.: Resource Management Corp., 1969. (NTIS No. PB-185-253)

Burkhardt, J. E. *A study of the transportation problems of the rural poor.* Bethesda, Md.: Resource Management Corp., 1972. (NTIS No. PB-208-158)

Carp, F. M. Walking as a means of transportation for retired people. *The Gerontologist,* 1971, *11,* 104–111.

Carp, F. M. The mobility of older slum-dwellers. *The Gerontologist,* 1972, *12,* 67–65. (a)

Carp, F. M. Retired people as automobile passengers. *The Gerontologist,* 1972, *12,* 66–72. (b)

Carp, F. M. Transportation. *The Gerontologist,* 1972, *12,* 11–16. (c)

Culter, S. J. Transportation and changes in life satisfaction. *The Gerontologist,* 1972, *12,* 155–159.

Danish, S. J. Human development and human services: A marriage proposal. In I. Iscoe, B. C. Bloom, & C. D. Spielberger (Eds.), *Community Psychology in Transition.* New York: Halstead Press, 1977.

Everett, P. B. *Contributions of psychology to transportation planning and management: The status quo and the future.* Paper presented at the meeting of the Eastern Psychological Association, Washington, D.C., April 1978.

Falcocchio, J. C., & Cantilli, E. J. *Transportation and the disadvantaged.* Lexington, Mass.: Lexington Books, 1974.

Gelwicks, L. E. *Transportation and its influence upon the quality of the older person's relation with the environment.* Unpublished manuscript, 1970. [Cited in H. M. Golden. The dysfunctional effects of modern technology on the adaptability of aging. *The Gerontologist,* 1973, *13,* 136–143.]

Golden, H. M. The dysfunctional effects of modern technology on the adaptability of the aging. *The Gerontologist,* 1973, *13,* 136–143.

Gurin, D. *The physical mobility of the poor: An introductory overview.* Cambridge, Mass.: Harvard University Press, 1969. (NTIS No. PB–190–981)

Hyde, J. L., & Cohen, S. H. *An analysis of travel behavior in a low income, handicapped or elderly population.* Paper presented at the meeting of the Eastern Psychological Association, Washington, D.C., April 1978.

Office of Research and Development, West Virginia University, *Phase III TRIP Evaluation.* Morgantown, 1977.

Patton, G. V. Age groupings and travel in a rural area. *Rural Sociology,* 1975, *40,* 56–63.

Revis, J. S. *Transportation for older Americans: A state of the art report.* Washington, D.C.: Institute of Public Administration, 1975. (NTIS No. PB–247–958)

Revis, J. S., Eckman, A., Coit, R., Davidson, J., Revis, B., & Rechel, R. *Planning handbook: Transportation services for the elderly.* Washington, D.C.: Institute of Public Administration, 1975. (NTIS No. PB–247–958)

Rivlin, A. M. *Systematic thinking for social action.* Washington, D.C.: Brookings Institution, 1971.

Sundeem, R. A., & Mathiew, J. T. Fear of crime and its consequences among elderly in three urban communities. *The Gerontologist,* 1976, *16,* 211–219.

State of West Virginia, Department of Welfare. *TRIP Development Plan.* Charleston, 1974.

CHAPTER 8

Effects of Nutritional Supplementation and Early Education on Physical and Cognitive Development[1]

M. G. HERRERA
J. O. MORA
N. CHRISTIANSEN
N. ORTIZ
J. CLEMENT
L. VUORI
D. WABER
HARVARD SCHOOL OF PUBLIC HEALTH
BOSTON, MASSACHUSETTS

B. De PAREDES
COLOMBIAN INSTITUTE OF
FAMILY WELFARE
BOGOTA, COLOMBIA

M. WAGNER
INSTITUTE OF NUTRITION
JUSTUS LIEBIG UNIVERSITY
GIESSEN, WEST GERMANY

I. Introduction

During the period since 1930, it has become apparent that the physical and psychological development of malnourished children reared in poor environments is stunted (Scrimshaw & Gordon, 1968). Because of the relative feasibility of ameliorating malnourishment somewhat independently of other components of the "culture of poverty," a greater understanding of the relationship between malnutrition and intellectual development is of importance to health policy planning. Since 1965 increasing attention has been paid to other characteristics of the child's early en-

[1] This research was supported in part by the Colombian Institute of Family Welfare; NICHHD Grant No. 3R01–HD06774; the Ford Foundation, Grant No. 740–0348; the Justus Liebig University, Giessen, West Germany; and the Fund for Research and Teaching, Department of Nutrition, Harvard School of Public Health.

149

vironment that interact with malnourishment and determine cognitive competence. In addition to nutritional supplementation, health care and enhancement of the social environment have been used in attempts to prevent cognitive retardation and school failure (Barnes, Moore, & Pong, 1970; Coursin, 1967; Eichenwald & Fry, 1969; Elias, 1976; Hegsted, 1972; Kallen, 1971; Latham & Cobos, 1971; Pollitt, 1969; Ricciuti, 1970, 1977; Scrimshaw, 1967; Winick, 1970).

In 1920 Jackson and Stewart showed that starvation in weanling rats reduced brain weight irreversibly. Other investigations using rats and mice have shown diminished cell division and delayed myelination in the central nervous system (CNS) as a result of starvation during the critical period of rapid brain growth (Chase, Dorsey, & McKhann, 1967; Dobbing, 1964, 1966, 1968; Dobbing & Widdowson, 1965; Guthrie & Brown, 1968; Howard & Granoff, 1968; Winick, Fish, & Rosso, 1968; Winick & Noble, 1966). Severe protein deficiency in the presence of normal caloric intake has been shown to cause degeneration of neurons in the central nervous systems of pigs and dogs (Platt, Heard, & Stewart, 1964) and may result in irreversible neurological abnormalities (Platt *et al.*, 1964; Stewart & Platt, 1968). On the other hand, small but significant differences in brain cortex weight and depth have been found among groups of weanling rats fed *ad libitum* but subjected to different degrees of environmental stimulation. Among humans, it has been found that quasi-starvation causing the clinical picture of marasmus results in reduced head circumference (Cordano, Baertl, & Graham, 1963), lower brain weight (Brown, 1966), and electroencephalogram (EEG) disturbances (Engel, 1956; Nelson, 1959). However, the confounding of social and health variables cannot be disregarded in the interpretation of these observations.

The incidence of low birth weight (< 2500 gm) varies with socioeconomic status. This relationship has been documented across social classes and within relatively homogeneous lower-class populations. On the other hand, maternal nutritional status is also associated with birth weight (Frisancho, Klayman, & Matos, 1977). Low birth weight, in turn, is associated with perinatal mortality, neurological disorders, mental retardation, and poor school performance (Churchill, Neff, & Caldwell, 1966; Francis-Williams & Davies, 1974; Wiener, Rider, Oppel, & Harper, 1968; Willerman & Churchill, 1967). Malnourished or low birth weight infants elicit different patterns of care from their mothers because of their own behavioral and physical characteristics (Chavez, Martinez, & Yaschine, 1974; Lewis & Lee-Painter, 1974; Scarr-Salapatek & Williams, 1973). These associations suggest, but do not prove, a causal sequence leading from maternal malnutrition to early mortality, morbidity, and cognitive retardation.

Malnourished and previously malnourished children have been found to perform less well than control subjects in a variety of tests of psychological functioning (Barrera-Moncada, 1963; Cabak & Najdanvic, 1965; Champakam, Srikantia, & Gopalan, 1968; Chase & Martin, 1970; Cravioto & DeLicardie, 1970; Cravioto & Robles, 1965; Klein, 1969; Monckeberg, 1968; Pollitt & Granoff, 1967; Rajatasilpin, Suepsaman, & Yamart, 1970). However, it is necessary to use caution in the interpretation of these findings (Cravioto & Robles, 1965; Kallen, 1971; Pollitt, 1969) because the relationship between malnutrition and defective psychological development is confounded by health and social factors that covary with nutrition and may themselves affect psychological development. For example, Stoch and Smythe (1963, 1967) found significant differences in psychological test scores between malnourished Cape colored children in South Africa and a control group selected from the same urban area. However, malnourished subjects also lived in poorer houses and experienced more family instability, strife, parental absenteeism, and unemployment than the control subjects. Brockman (1968), working in Lima, Peru, compared the cognitive development of children who had recovered from malnutrition with that of tall children from the same geographic area who were accepted as adequately nourished controls. Significant differences were found between the psychological test scores of the two groups. However, Pollitt and Ricciuti (1968), contrasting short children with tall children from the same poor neighborhoods, found that the short children had shorter mothers as well as larger numbers of siblings, less educated mothers, lower birth weights, and less stable homes.

The environmental and social background of malnourished children may differ significantly from that of well-nourished children living in the same impoverished neighborhood. For example, Graham and Morales (1963) found that families of children suffering from *kwashiorkor* and *marasmus* lived in more crowded conditions, had lower incomes, and had a higher proportion of illegitimacy in contrast with average families living in the same slums. Cravioto and Robles (1965) reported that low birth weight infants in a rural Guatemalan village came from larger families with older mothers who had fewer years of schooling. McLaren (1966) showed that malnourished children were more often than not the result of closely spaced pregnancies.

Malnutrition and disease are known to coexist in children of deprived populations (Scrimshaw, Taylor, & Gordon, 1959). Malnutrition and infection are synergistic, and serious difficulties are encountered in assessing their relative contributions to retarded intellectual development.

Social class differences in cognitive competence and school performance have been reported (Deutsch, 1973; Monckeberg, Tisler, Toro, Gattas, & Vega, 1972; Weinberg, Dietz, Penick, & McAlister, 1974). Physical and social characteristics of the environment related to both social class and cognitive development have been proposed as intermediate variables: richness of the physical environment (Biber, 1970; Kramer & Rosenblum, 1970; Manosevitz, 1970), opportunity for free and varied play (Lewis & Goldberg, 1970; Richardson, 1974), parental verbal competence (Bing, 1963; Deutch, 1963; Hess & Shipman, 1967; Milner, 1951), parental attitudes and expectations concerning achievement (Bowlby, 1969; Bronfenbrenner, 1958; Kohn, 1963; Kohn & Carrol, 1960; Nosbet, 1961; Radin, 1971; Riskin & Faunce, 1970; Tulkin & Kagan, 1972; Young, 1970), family size (McLaren, 1966; Wray & Aguirre, 1969), and maternal age and responsiveness (Yarrow, 1964). Similar factors are thought to mediate differences in intelligence scores found between urban and rural children (Klineberg, 1963; Peluffo, 1964). Our own findings in Colombia (Christiansen, Vuori, Mora, & Wagner, 1974) and those of Klein and collaborators (Klein, Kagan, Freeman, Yarbrough, & Habicht, 1972; Klein, Yarbrough, Lasky, & Habicht, 1974) in Guatemala disclose differences in cognitive development that are related to family socioeconomic characteristics even within what appear to be homogeneously poor populations. Cross-cultural studies have posited the effects of heredity and culture on mental development test scores (Christiansen & Livermore, 1970; Goodnow, 1970; Klineberg, 1963; Lesser, Fifer, & Clark, 1965; Sears, 1970). Among the cultural factors, parental attitudes and characteristics of the verbal and physical environments appear to be most significant. Such factors may be responsible for diminished competence or may simply reflect less opportunity to acquire the skills measured by the tests. Variations in attitudes toward problem solving, particularly in structured test situations, may also play a role.

Food supplementation has been used to reduce the natural relationships among nutritional, social, and environmental factors that may affect cognitive development. An association has been found between supplementation and intellectual development scores at ages 1 through 5 in malnourished populations; language and verbal skills have been most sensitive. Prenatal supplementation appears to explain most of the variance in scores (Freeman, Klein, Kagen, & Yarbrough, 1977). Supplemented children have been found to be more active than unsupplemented children, and the mothers of supplemented children have been found to be more responsive to their needs (Chavez *et al.,* 1974).

Interventions designed to enrich the social environment appear to have immediate and long-range beneficial effects on mental competence. Retarded institutionalized children placed in responsive home settings have exhibited long-lasting improvements in cognitive development in contrast with controls (Skeels, 1966), and it seems likely that nutrition played a significant role in some of these studies. Malnourished children from the poorest socioeconomic strata in Cali, Colombia, who were enrolled in a health, nutrition, and preschool education program at age 3 showed improvement in cognitive competence (McKay, Sinisterra, McKay, Gomez, & Lloreda, 1978). Multiply deprived Korean infants reached normal levels of intellectual competence after being adopted into American middle-class families (Winick, Meyer, & Harris, 1975). Such findings suggest that nutritional rehabilitation and environmental stimulation may *both* be necessary to mitigate the negative effects of deprived environments.

In animal experiments, the detrimental effects of malnutrition on behavior are especially severe among subjects reared in isolation. Environmental and social enrichment reduces the behavioral consequences of malnourishment (Elias & Samonds, 1974, 1977; Frankova, 1974; Levitsky & Barnes, 1972).

The findings summarized in this introductory section suggest the following hypotheses:

1. Behavioral competence is determined by genetic endowment and its somatic expression (CNS organogenesis), but the most important factor is cumulative experience through interaction with the physical and social environment.
2. Physical and social characteristics of the early environment and particularly caretaker–infant interaction are primary determinants of cognitive development.
3. Malnutrition among underprivileged populations is one of a series of continuously interacting social, environmental, and biological variables that lead to subnormal development.
4. Malnutrition may influence the development of cognitive competence in the following ways:

   a. Through apathy and unresponsiveness, which, in turn, impair interaction with both the physical and social environments. From an early age, responsiveness of the infant is a determinant of the stimulation he receives from his caretaker and from the objects in his environment. Unresponsive children elicit less attention; thus, a negative cycle is established. Similarly, negative labeling of the child due to malnutrition-related unresponsiveness and disease, negative body image, or subnormal physical development also interferes with social interaction.

   b. Malnutrition is associated with increased morbidity due to infectious disease. Infectious disease may affect mental development through CNS damage, but it is more likely to do so by reducing or altering interaction with the environment and caretakers.

c.Malnutrition during pregnancy and early life may have a direct detrimental effect on CNS development.

A prospective study was designed to test these hypotheses, utilizing food supplementation and early environmental stimulation in a sample of families at high risk of malnutrition. Nutritional status and home social environment were selectively altered. Selection bias was avoided by *random assignment* of subjects to experimental and control groups. A health-care program provided for all study groups permitted surveillance of morbidity and reduced program drop-out rates. Longitudinal follow-up studies permitted measurement of health, nutrition, and social variables during and beyond the period of intervention. This allowed quantification of changes in relevant nontreatment variables occurring naturally or as consequences of the intervention program. The design also permitted evaluation of the effects of food supplementation programs of various durations, which were initiated at different developmental stages, on health, physical and cognitive development. In addition, it provided for assessment of early stimulation effects by themselves or in combination with food supplementation.

II. Design of the Bogota Project

The experimental design of the Bogota Project consisted of a dual intervention study of children at risk of malnutrition extending from the sixth month of gestation through 3 years of age. Pregnant women whose families and offspring were the subjects of study were selected from the population in the southern barrios of Bogota, Colombia, on the basis of two criteria: Mothers were in the first or second trimester of pregnancy and families had one or more children under 5 years of age of whom at least 50% were malnourished.[2] The first criterion was adopted in order to begin the study during the period of fetal development known to be the most sensitive to maternal nutritional intake. The purpose of the second criterion was to select a sample for study that was at risk of malnutrition.

The study area, with a population of over 100,000, is served by two municipal health centers, one of which was used as the study field station. Four surveys of the entire zone made at 6-month intervals were completed

[2] Malnutrition was defined as less than 85% in weight-for-age according to Colombian standards.

in October, 1974, and yielded information from which 522 families who met the selection criteria were identified. Procedures, possible risks, and benefits were explained, and only those families who freely consented to participate were enrolled. Ninety-six (17%) of the eligible families were not enrolled: 39 because of change of address, 34 due to abortion, and 23 because they chose not to participate. Sociological data from 57 of the 96 families compared with similar data from the participating families showed no significant differences, thus arguing against selection bias in enrollment. The 456 families who enrolled were randomly assigned to six experimental groups as shown in Figure 8.1. After random assignment to the experimental groups, no significant differences were found among the groups in family income, maternal education, maternal age, type of dwelling, or neighborhood of residence. All groups were given a uniform obstetrical and pediatric health-care program. Subjects were observed longitudinally by repeated measurement of nutritional status, intellectual functioning, and a number of concomitant social and health variables (see Table 8.1).

The experimental groups created by the design could be combined in several ways for analytical purposes (see Figure 8.1):

1. Until time of birth, Groups A, B, and A_1 merge as the control groups receiving no supplementation; groups C, D, and D_1 together represent the supplemented sample. The design is a simple randomized trial with a treatment and control group.
2. After birth, groups A, A_1, D, and D_1 constitute a two-component factorial experiment that allows assessment of simple and interactive effects of supplementation and stimulation.
3. Groups A, B, C, and D permit study of the effects of supplementation at different ages.

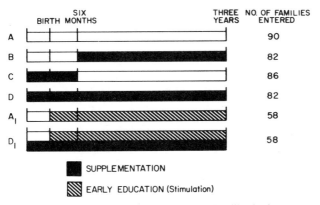

Figure 8.1. Intervention schedule for 456 families is shown.

Table 8.1

Schedule for Mother, Child, and Family Measurements

Measurements	Months of pregnancy				Birth	15 Days	Months after birth								
	5	6	7	8			2	3	4	7	9	13	18	24	38
Mother															
Medical history and examination		X	X	X											
Biochemical determinations	X	X	X												
Dietary survey	X	X	X												
Characteristics of delivery					X										
Morbidity survey						every 2 weeks during pregnancy; 6 months of lactation									
Child															
Anthropometry					X	X	X	X	X	X	X	X	X	X	X
Medical and neurological examination					X	X	X				X			X	X
Psychological tests					X	X				X		X	X	X	X
Biochemical determinations					X				X	X					X
Dietary survey					X								X		X
Morbidity survey							every 2 weeks throughout study								
Family															
Sociology questionnaire	X													X	X
Dietary surveys	X			X		X				X		X	X	X	X
Caretaker–child interaction observations									X	X		X	X	X	X

4. Group A by itself constitutes a sample for ecological study since the only intervention it receives is free medical care and measurements.

A. The Health-Care Program

The health-care program was designed to provide all study groups with uniform preventive care and treatment of disease, to obtain health information on the pregnant mother and infant under study, and to provide an incentive for families to remain in the study. Three components comprised the health-care program:

1. *Obstetrical and medical care for the mother.* During pregnancy, mothers were given an initial medical and obstetrical examination and were requested to return monthly. After delivery, medical care was provided upon request. All medical services at the station, including laboratory tests and prescribed medicines, were provided free of charge.

2. *Maternity services.* Deliveries were attended at the maternity service of a university hospital. Free transportation to the hospital was provided, and preferential admission of study cases was assured.

3. *Pediatric care.* All children under 7 years of age in the study families were enrolled in a pediatric care program, and prescribed medicines and laboratory examinations were provided free of charge. Medical care was standardized as much as possible. The one pediatrician in charge did not know which families were supplemented, and he was encouraged to deal with any clinical problem as he would have ordinarily.

B. The Food Supplementation Program

Food supplements were provided in amounts sufficient to meet a substantial proportion of the recommended dietary allowance (RDA) for each member of the family over 1 year of age (see Table 8.2). Supplements were given to Groups C, D, and D_1 from the time of enrollment. The program of supplementation shown in Table 8.3 was implemented for children below 1 year of age. All children *weaned* before 6 months of age in Groups C, D, and D_1 were provided with whole dry milk in the following amounts:

1. Children younger than 2 months of age received 1 pound per week (64 gm dry milk daily).
2. Children from 2 to 5 months received 2 pounds per week (128 gm dry milk daily).

Starting at 6 months of age, all children in Groups B, D, and D_1 were

Table 8.2

Nutrient Composition of the Supplement [a] Provided for Members of the Family over 1 Year of Age

Source	Grams	Calories (No.)	Proteins (gm)[b]	Fat (gm)	CHO (gm)	Calcium (mg)	Iron (mg)	Vitamin A (I.U.)	Thiamin (mg)	Riboflavin (mg)	Niacin (mg)	Vitamin C (mg)
Dry skim milk	60	214	21.6	.6	30.6	720	.40	18	.18	1.18	.66	3.6
Enriched bread	75	233	8.4	2.6	43.9	133	1.28	3	.11	.21	.47	.5
Vegetable oil	20	176	0	20.0	0	0	0	0	0	0	0	0
Total		623	30.0	23.2	74.5	853	1.68	21	.29	1.39	1.13	4.1
Additional bread for mother	75	233	8.4	2.6	43.9	133	1.28	3	.11	.21	.47	.5
Additional vitamins for mother		—	—	—	—	160	10.20	6000	5.00	5.00	30.00	100.0
Total for mother		856	38.4	25.8	118.4	1146	13.16	6024	5.40	6.60	31.60	104.6
Additional vitamins for the child		—	—	—	—	—	7.50	1110	—	—	—	—
Total for child over 1 year		623	30.0	23.2	74.5	853	9.18	1131	.29	1.39	1.13	4.1

[a] Sources (in percentages) of calories for child over 1 year from supplement:

Protein	120.0	19.2
Fat	208.8	33.3
CHO	298.0	47.5
Total	626.8	100.0

Sources (in percentages) of calories for mother from supplement:

Protein	153.6	17.8
Fat	232.2	27.0
CHO	473.6	55.2
Total	849.4	100.0

[b] Animal protein equals 25.2 gm (84%); vegetable protein equals 48 gm (16%).

Table 8.3

Nutrient Composition of the Supplement Provided for Children under 1 Year of Age

Source	Total grams	Calories	Proteins (gm)	Calcium (mg)	Iron (mg)	Vitamin A (I.U.)	Thiamin (mg)	Riboflavin (mg)	Niacin (mg)	Vitamin C (mg)
Under 2 months, weaned										
Dry whole milk (Nestogene new formula)	64	304	12.6	602	2.8	832	.17	.91	.38	2.6
RDA 0–2 months	—	480	8.8	400	6.0	1500	.20	.40	5.00	35.0
Percentage provided	—	63	143.0	150	47.0	55	85.0	227.0	8.0	7.0
From 2 to 5 months, weaned										
Dry whole milk	128	608	25.2	1204	5.6	1664	.33	1.82	.76	5.1
Commercial preparation	—	—	—	—	3.8	—	—	—	—	—
Total	—	608	25.2	1204	9.4	1664	.33	1.82	.76	5.1
RDA 2–5 months	—	770	14.0	500	10.0	1500	.40	.50	7.00	35.0
Percentage provided	—	79	180.0	241	94.0	111	85.0	364.0	11.0	15.0
From 6 to 12 months, all children (groups B and D)										
Whole dry milk	64	304	12.6	602	2.8	832	.17	.91	.38	2.6
Duryea[a]	36	124	10.1	162	2.5	720	0	.22	2.16	14.4
Commercial preparation	—	—	—	—	7.5	—	—	—	—	—
Total	—	428	22.7	764	12.8	1552	.17	1.13	2.54	17.0
RDA 6–12 months	—	900	16.2	600	15.0	1550	.50	.60	8.0	35.0
Percentage provided	—	48	140.0	127	85.0	103	34.0	188.0	32.0	49.0

[a]Duryea is a commercial weaning food made of rice, soybeans, opaque-2 corn, and milk.

provided with 1 pound of whole dry milk a week (16 oz. of liquid formula per day or 64 gm dry milk) and 250 gm of high protein vegetable mixture a week (Duryea, a food made of rice, soybeans, opaque-2 corn, and milk, which was donated by Corn Products). All children in Groups C, D, and D_1, regardless of whether or not they were breast fed, were given Duryea (250 gm every 2 weeks) starting at 3 months of age (see Table 8.3). Supplementation ended for Group C at 6 months of age. After 1 year of age, all children in Groups B, D, and D_1 took part in the food supplementation regimen for all members of the family (see Table 8.2).

Between the ages of 3 months and 6 months of age, children in Groups C, D, and D_1 were given 18.8 mg of ferrous sulfate daily. Beginning at 6 months of age, children in groups B, D, and D_1 were given a daily dose of 37.5 mg of ferrous sulfate. After 1 year of age, they also received oral doses of 200,000 I.U. of vitamin A every 6 months.

To minimize nonnutritional aspects of the supplementation program, food was distributed weekly in a locale resembling a neighborhood shop rather than at the health center. This reduced contact between supplemented and nonsupplemented mothers.

1. Instructions for Use of the Supplement

The first time supplements were given and periodically thereafter, a nutritionist taught the mother how to prepare the dry milk and other foodstuffs. The nutritionist emphasized hygienic handling, storage, and the amounts of milk and other supplements that should be consumed by pregnant women and infants. Early weaning was discouraged. Practical demonstrations repeated as often as needed were followed by household visits.

2. Monitoring and Assessment of Supplement Use

Several measures were used to monitor consumption of the supplement. To discourage sale of the foodstuffs, at least in the original containers, the return of the containers in which the food was packed was required prior to provision of the next allotment. Families were also visited unexpectedly so that we could check on the presence of an appropriate amount of the supplement in the home.

C. The Infant Stimulation Program

One goal of the infant stimulation program was to stimulate learning and development of the target child through direct intervention by a trained visitor. This goal was a means of pursuing the second, more important goal: to modify caretaker–child interaction so that stimulation would become self-sustaining in the absence of intervention personnel.

The infant stimulation program was based on the work of Lambie and his collaborators (Lambie, Jeffs, Miller, Jackson, & Court, 1972). During the first 3 years of life, the child's family was visited twice weekly by a specially trained paraprofessional home visitor (a secondary school graduate with experience in teaching) who interacted with the child and his principal caretaker. Each visitor was assigned six to eight families, thus ensuring continuity of contact. In addition to a program supervisor, there were three coordinators, each of whom was responsible for five home visitors. The coordinators and program supervisor provided ongoing training to the visitors through group and individual discussions and by monitoring visits and reviewing visit plans. Both the program supervisor and the coordinators acted as home visitors themselves in order to remain in close contact with field issues. A tentative written plan was made before each visit, and after every session the visitor prepared a written report of her observations and recommendations for the next visit.

The infant's behavior during and between visits was discussed with the caretaker; suggestions and ideas from the caretaker were encouraged. Questions were asked by the visitor about the development and behavior patterns of the child to encourage interest in, and sensitivity to, the child and his evolving needs. Gradually, the visitor played a less direct role, and the caretaker assumed the primary role of stimulator and interactor. This transfer was considered important to the effectiveness of the stimulation program because no effort, regardless of how well executed, can have real influence if contact is limited to 2 hours weekly.

The program did not restrict its focus to training in specific skills but emphasized general problem-solving abilities and use of diverse roles. There was, however, a repertoire of suggested activities appropriate to different developmental stages that were intended to extend and reinforce certain behaviors.

The visitor was viewed not as an educational specialist but as a flexible and sensitive observer who assumed specific interactive and supportive roles in order to help further the child's development. Although the home visitor lacked information on the child's test performance, she decided when to introduce each new activity and when to switch from one to another based on her continuing experience with the child.

Other children, especially siblings, were allowed to participate in "play" sessions. Visitors made every effort to limit contacts to the domain of cognitive functioning of the target infant and his siblings, referring health and other questions to the project physician. Materials available in most homes were utilized as toys: newspapers and magazines, bottles and cans, keys, beans, etc.

The delivery of the infant stimulation intervention was monitored by means of a specially designed instrument for assessing visitor–caretaker–child interaction and through supervision by program coordinators and the program supervisor.

III. Summary of Current Results of the Bogota Project

A. *General Characteristics of the Study Sample*

Table 8.4 summarizes descriptive data on initial sample characteristics of supplemented and unsupplemented groups. Ninety percent of the study sample lived in grossly inadequate housing. Nearly 60% of the families occupied a single room, and only 15% had more than two rooms. Fifty-two percent of the families (ranging in size from 2 to 16 with a mean of 5.1) slept with more than two per bed. The father lived with, and was the principal wage earner in, 95% of the families. Seventy percent of the employed fathers were unskilled or skilled manual laborers with seasonal employment.

One-third of the families had no running water in the house, and over one-third had no garbage collection. Twenty percent had no public sewerage. Educational level of the parents was very low; 11% of the mothers had no formal education, and only 8% had progressed beyond the

Table 8.4

*Initial Comparability in Selected Social Variables
for the Experimental Groups*

Social variables	Unsupplemented ($N = 229$)	Supplemented ($N = 225$)
Family size	5.8 ± 2.5	5.2 ± 2.0
Proportion of migrant families	75.5%	73.3%
Proportion of families with fathers present	95.6%	95.6%
Number of rooms	1.7 ± .9	1.6 ± .9
Area per person (m²)	3.2 ± 1.8	3.5 ± 1.9
Mother's age (years)	26.6 ± 6.1	25.8 ± 5.4
Mothers with less than 3 years education	40.6%	39.6%
Family income (U.S. $ monthly)[a]	57.40 ± 29.02	53.37 ± 25.73
Per capita income (U.S. $ monthly)[a]	8.86 ± 5.10	8.63 ± 3.96
Age of youngest child (months)	22.1 ± 12.0	21.0 ± 11.6
Mother's daily calorie intake	1621 ± 655	1622 ± 635
Mother's daily protein intake (gm)	37.0 ± 22.9	35.6 ± 19.2

[a] Average exchange rate is: $1 (U.S.) = $25.50 (Colombian).

primary level. Eight percent of the fathers had no formal education, and 17% had some education beyond primary school. Twelve percent of the mothers were unable to read at all, and 35% read only with difficulty.

The mean interval between prior pregnancies was 21 months. Mean weight of the mothers at entry into the program was 54 ± 6.8 kg at a gestational age of 24.8 ± 3.6 weeks. Mean height was 149.8 cm with a range of 133–165.

Initial maternal nutritional intake estimated by the 24-hour recall method was one standard deviation or more below recommended calorie and protein allowances for pregnant Colombian women. The nutrient gap was particularly large for protein, but it was also significant for calories and other nutrients.

In summary, the study sample consisted of poor urban migrants living in crowded, unsanitary conditions with an average income of $40 per month (in U.S. dollars) and a mean parental educational level of 3 years of schooling. At the time of recruitment, the diets of the pregnant women in the study were clearly deficient, especially in protein.

B. Effects of Nutritional Supplementation during the Third Trimester of Pregnancy on Maternal Diet, Maternal Weight Gain, and Birth Weight

Results of the Bogota Project regarding the effects of nutritional supplementation on maternal diet, maternal weight gain, and birth weight have been published by Mora, Navarro, Clement, Wagner, de Paredes, and Herrera, 1978; and Mora, de Parades, Wagner, Navarro, Suescun, Christiansen, and Herrera, 1979. The following is a summary of these results.

Of the 850 calories provided to pregnant women in the supplemented group, 490 were ingested. However, 360 of these calories replaced calories consumed in their presupplementation diet. Of the 39 gm of protein provided as daily supplementation, 26 were actually consumed; 6.8 gm of these 26 gm represented replacement of protein in the usual diet. Therefore, the net daily increments achieved with supplementation were 133 calories and 19.6 gm of protein.

This small but significant increase in dietary intake resulted in a 95 gm difference in birth weight between unsupplemented and supplemented male subjects ($p < .05$). However, there was no supplementation effect on birth weight among females. The effect on birth weight was greater in males supplemented for 13 weeks or longer. Moreover, birth weight effects were associated with the rate of weight gain during the last trimester of pregnancy.

Although the study was not designed to assess the effects of treatment on mortality, the results showed that stillbirth, neonatal mortality, and perinatal mortality rates among the supplemented group were approximately half of those recorded in the control groups (Mora, Clement, Christiansen, Suescun, Wagner, & Herrera, 1978).

C. The Influence of Presupplementation Diet on Supplement Utilization and Birth Weight

The presupplementation dietary intake and socioeconomic characteristics of the families may influence utilization of supplements and their biological effects (Christiansen, Mora, Navarro, & Herrera, in preparation). In order to examine these relationships, the study sample was stratified according to initial dietary intake and expenditures on food. The median values were used to divide experimental and control groups into two categories: high initial diet (> 1500 cal or > 30 gm protein) and low initial diet (< 1500 cal or < 30 gm protein). No significant differences in birth weight between supplemented and unsupplemented subjects were found among the low initial dietary intake groups. Significant differences were observed among the groups with a high initial diet (see Table 8.5).

Figure 8.2 summarizes initial mean calorie and protein intake by treatment group according to initial level of calorie consumption. As expected, no differences were present between treatment and control groups. The

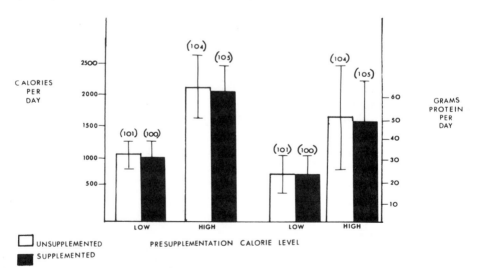

Figure 8.2. Presupplementation calorie and protein intake are shown in high and low presupplementation calorie subsamples.

Table 8.5

Children's Birth Weight (gm) among Supplemented and Unsupplemented Mothers
within Dietary Subcategories

Maternal Dietary intake/24 hr before supplementation	Supplemented (S)			Unsupplemented (US)			S–US	p
	$\bar{X}$	SD	N	$\bar{X}$	SD	N		
calories								
1500+	3012	412	105	2892	425	103	120	<.01
1500−	2913	360	100	2932	363	101	−19	NS
protein (gm)								
30+	3015	380	107	2914	413	105	101	<.05
30−	2905	371	93	2913	398	98	−8	NS

high initial diet subset had an initial mean intake of approximately 2000 calories (a value close to the RDA, given the weight and height of the women), whereas protein was deficient at 45 gm/24 hours. On the other hand, the low initial diet subset was severely deficient in calorie (1200) and protein (23 gm) intake. Figure 8.3 shows the result of the dietary survey after 2 months of treatment. In the high initial diet subset, supplementation significantly increased mean protein intake from 45 to 62 gm but did not influence calorie intake. In the low initial diet subset, supplementation significantly increased both protein and calorie intake. However, achieved levels remained markedly inadequate: 1680 calories and 45 gm protein/24 hours. When consumption of supplements was examined, no significant differences between high and low initial diet groups were observed (see Table 8.6). They differed, however, in the extent to which they substituted supplements for their initial diet. The high initial diet group did not increase calorie intake and mostly utilized high protein supplements to replace low protein staples in the home diet. In the low initial diet group, net supplementation occurred for both calories and protein, indicating that there was less substitution.

D. Supplementation Effects on Newborn Behavior

Because supplementation effects on birth weight were sex-related, newborn nutritive sucking data were analyzed in a series of three-way ANOVAs (Supplementation × Sex × Age) in which the repeated measures

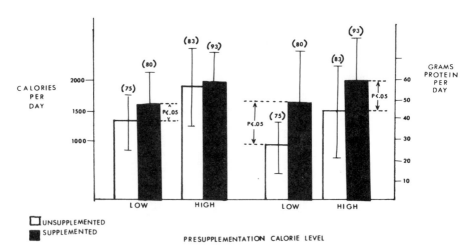

Figure 8.3. Calorie and protein intake after 2 months of supplementation are shown in high and low presupplementation calorie subsamples.

Table 8.6

Use of the Supplement at 8 Months of Pregnancy
within Initial Dietary Strata

Nutritional variable		N	Calories/Day		Proteins (gm/day)	
			$\bar{X}$	SD	$\bar{X}$	SD
Initial calories/day	1500+	78	490	335	28	18
	1500−	96	553	347	29	17
Initial grams protein/day	30+	78	503	340	28	18
	30−	96	542	346	29	17

at 24 and 30 hours were over the last factor (Vuori, Navarro, Christiansen, Mora, & Herrera, in press). As shown in Table 8.7, a significant supplementation main effect appeared for total dextrose intake and for intake per suck. Babies born to unsupplemented women consumed more dextrose than those born to supplemented women. A Supplementation × Sex interaction effect for intake per suck reflected higher consumption among unsupplemented than among supplemented boys; among girls the difference was not significant. Tests on simple effects showed that girls in the unsupplemented group sucked at a faster rate than boys ($p < .01$), whereas in the supplemented group sex differences were not signifcant.

E. Effects of Nutritional Supplementation during the Last Trimester of Pregnancy on Visual Habituation at 15 Days

Tests of the effects of nutritional supplementation on visual habituation were carried out when the infants reached 15 days of age (Vuori, Mora, Christiansen, Clement, & Herrera, 1979). The baby was placed on a bed lying on his side so that he faced a slot in the wall of an enclosure through which the stimuli were presented. The standard stimulus, a 2 × 2 black and white checkerboard that measured 15 × 15 cm, was presented for eight 60-second trials separated by 10-second intervals. The discrepant stimulus, a 6 × 6 checkerboard, was then presented for a 60-second period (see Friedman, 1972). Total fixation time, number of fixations, fret–cries, and limb movements per trial were recorded by two observers who were blind to the infant's treatment group. Habituation rate was defined as fixation time at $T1$ persisting at $T8$ ($T1–T8$ divided by $T1$). Dishabituation rate was similarly defined ($T9–T8$ divided by $T9$). The fixation data were also

Table 8.7

Nutritive Sucking in Full-term Infants at 24 and 30 Hours after Birth

	Males		Females	
	Unsupplemented (N=64)	Supplemented (N=63)	Unsupplemented (N=63)	Supplemented (N=60)
24 hours				
Sucks/minute	37.0 ± 13.2	41.4 ± 13.6	42.4 ± 12.4	39.5 ± 15.4
Dextrose consumption (ml)	14.8 ± 5.9	13.9 ± 6.3	16.9 ± 7.7	14.6 ± 6.2
Consumption/suck (ml)	.68 ± .35	.35 ± .31	.66 ± .52	.62 ± .32
30 hours				
Sucks/minute	40.8 ± 11.4	42.4 ± 11.4	47.2 ± 15.5	43.5 ± 15.1
Dextrose consumption (ml)	17.0 ± 7.4	13.8 ± 6.2	16.4 ± 7.1	15.1 ± 6.0
Consumption/suck (ml)	.67 ± .30	.53 ± .31	.58 ± .37	.60 ± .34

analyzed using a Supplementation × Sex × Trial analysis of variance in which factors were assumed to be fixed and repeated measures over the last factor.

Figures 8.4 and 8.5 summarize the data for boys and girls, respectively. More supplemented infants (70%) displayed habituation ($T1–T8$) than unsupplemented ones (56%) ($p < .05$). Habituation rate was significantly higher in supplemented females than in unsupplemented ones ($p < .01$), although this difference was not significant in males.

The analysis of variance on habituation revealed a main effect for trials ($p < .001$), a Supplementation × Trials interaction ($p < .001$), and a Supplementation × Sex × Trials interaction ($p < .05$). The Supplementation × Trials interaction was due to group differences mainly at $T1$ and $T7$. In comparison with the supplemented babies, the unsupplemented ones displayed a shorter fixation time at $T1$ ($p < .001$) and a longer one at $T7$ ($p < .001$). The unsupplemented babies moved more during the habituation trials ($M = 11.80$, $SD = 6.85$) than did the supplemented ones ($M = 10.19$, $SD = 5.53$; $t(242) = 2.03$ $p < .05$). Supplemented girls grew fussier and cried significantly more during the habituation trials ($M = 4.13$, $SD = 4.49$) than did unsupplemented girls ($M = 2.26$, $SD = 3.65$; $t(117) = 2.42$, $p < .01$).

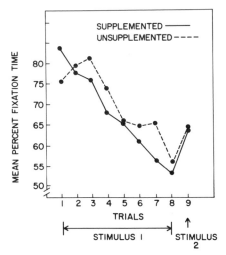

Figure 8.4. Mean percent fixation time per trial is shown for supplemented versus unsupplemented male infants. Stimulus 1 was a 2 × 2 checkerboard; Stimulus 2 was a 6 × 6 checkerboard.

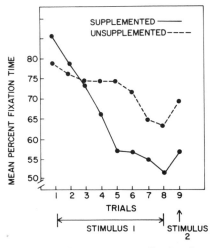

Figure 8.5. Mean percentage fixation time per trial is shown for supplemented versus unsupplemented female infants. Stimulus 1 was a 2 × 2 checkerboard; Stimulus 2 was a 6 × 6 checkerboard.

F. Supplementation Effects on Newborn Responsiveness to
   Aversive Stimulation

At 2 weeks of age, clear differences appeared between supplemented and unsupplemented infants with regard to responsiveness to aversive stimulation (Vuori, Navarro, Christiansen, Mora, & Herrera, in press). More unsupplemented (39%) than supplemented (23%) infants became irritable in the course of the testing session ($p < .01$) and needed quieting by experimental soothing procedures. No differences between groups were observed in response to the soothing or "caretaking" procedures.

In response to experimental aversive stimulation, unsupplemented infants exhibited a higher number of cries both to nipple removal [$F(1, 216) = 7.44, p < .01$], and to a cold disk placed on the abdomen [$F(1, 034) = 13.52, p < .001$]. Comparison of decrements (i.e., linear slopes) in proportion of infants crying over time (in six consecutive intervals) showed that the group differences in the total number of cries were partly due to the unsupplemented infants crying for a longer time rather than to individual phonations of shorter duration. Supplemented girls recovered from crying in response to the cold disk at a faster rate than unsupplemented ones [$F(1, 8) = 5.98, p < .05$].

G. Effect of Supplementation and Stimulation on
   Performance on the Griffiths and Einstein Tests

1. The Griffiths Test

The Griffiths test samples a wide range of behavior. A general quotient is used to incorporate five subscales: personal–social, speech–language, eye–hand coordination, locomotor, and performance. As part of this study, the effects of supplementation and stimulation on test performance were measured (Waber, Ortiz, Christiansen, Clement, Mora, Wagner, & Herrera, in preparation). Because systematic differences were found among scores obtained by different examiners, the data were corrected before analysis by means of a multiple regression equation computed with examiner, nutrition, stimulation, sex, and interactions as dummy variables. This procedure was carried out for every test score of every age group. The beta-weights for the examiner term were then subtracted from every score obtained by a given examiner as a correction factor.

Table 8.8 shows means and standard deviations as well as statistically significant F-tests and t-tests for the six groups on each of the five Griffiths subtests; it also shows the general quotient for each of the four ages when testing was carried out. A four-way repeated measures analysis of variance (Nutrition × Home education × Sex × Age) was computed using the first four groups, for which treatment had been constant throughout the study.

Table 8.8

Descriptive Statistics for the Griffiths Test by Subscale and Treatment Group

		Months			
		4	6	12	18
Locomotor					
Unstimulated/Unsupplemented	(N=67)	99.0 (24.7)[1a2]	105.4 (14.8)[a]	94.2 (16.5)	96.6 (15.8)
Unstimulated/Supplemented	(N=67)	106.8 (25.9)	108.5 (18.8)	94.6 (12.9)	101.1 (12.7)
Stimulated/Unsupplemented	(N=43)	102.8 (24.8)	105.9 (20.4)	94.5 (15.4)	97.4 (17.5)
Stimulated/Supplemented	(N=51)	113.3 (25.8)[a]	114.4 (17.2)[a]	101.4 (19.6)	104.8 (15.8)
Supplemented >6 months	(N=63)	105.4 (22.8)	111.8 (16.2)	98.5 (11.7)	102.5 (13.2)
Supplemented <6 months	(N=75)	109.1 (23.1)	107.8 (14.9)	95.7 (14.2)	97.9 (14.9)
Personal-social					
Unstimulated/Unsupplemented	(N=67)	103.2 (13.6)[bc]	87.9 (17.0)	102.5 (13.6)	94.4 (10.0)
Unstimulated/Supplemented	(N=67)	104.8 (14.3)[e]	95.0 (17.3)	98.9 (12.5)	99.3 (12.3)
Stimulated/Unsupplemented	(N=43)	111.7 (11.8)[b]	96.4 (16.9)	98.3 (11.1)	99.5 (11.9)
Stimulated/Supplemented	(N=51)	113.4 (12.8)[cde]	95.8 (12.5)	104.2 (11.7)[b]	99.0 (16.1)
Supplemented >6 months	(N=63)	104.7 (15.9)[d]	92.7 (18.1)	101.4 (11.7)	96.6 (9.3)
Supplemented <6 months	(N=75)	107.4 (12.7)	95.1 (17.2)	96.7 (11.6)[b]	95.6 (10.1)
Speech-language					
Unstimulated/Unsupplemented	(N=67)	101.0 (20.5)[a]	95.9 (11.3)	100.7 (11.8)[b]	90.0 (8.6)[cd]
Unstimulated/Supplemented	(N=67)	107.2 (18.8)	95.9 (13.6)	102.2 (13.8)	93.9 (11.3)
Stimulated/Unsupplemented	(N=43)	112.8 (19.1)[a]	97.8 (9.1)	105.8 (13.0)	98.2 (10.6)[c]
Stimulated/Supplemented	(N=51)	109.2 (17.3)	100.5 (5.6)	109.2 (12.0)[b]	99.0 (11.1)[d]
Supplemented >6 months	(N=51)	108.2 (20.0)	97.2 (11.6)	102.1 (13.1)	92.9 (9.5)
Supplemented <6 months	(N=75)	107.3 (18.2)	98.8 (9.5)	102.5 (11.6)	94.5 (9.1)

171

Table 8.8 (cont.)

		Month			
		4	6	12	18
Eye-hand					
Unstimulated/Unsupplemented	(N=67)	94.0 (16.6)	91.9 (14.6)[a]	96.3 (12.7)[a]	95.4 (7.4)
Unstimulated/Supplemented	(N=67)	94.1 (12.2)	96.1 (13.0)	99.9 (12.1)	95.8 (7.8)
Stimulated/Unsupplemented	(N=43)	93.1 (13.5)	97.3 (13.7)	100.0 (10.6)	97.2 (9.8)
Stimulated/Supplemented	(N=51)	94.8 (15.9)	99.3 (8.9)[a]	103.9 (9.7)[a]	97.1 (8.5)
Supplemented >6 months	(N=63)	94.6 (15.9)	95.7 (12.2)	99.1 (11.5)	96.3 (7.1)
Supplemented <6 months	(N=75)	97.6 (13.9)	85.5 (13.7)	98.0 (12.3)	95.2 (7.1)
Performance					
Unstimulated/Unsupplemented	(N=67)	104.9 (18.0)	104.0 (17.5)[a]	94.3 (16.1)	98.9 (11.2)
Unstimulated/Supplemented	(N=67)	105.1 (17.0)	108.0 (16.1)	97.7 (12.8)	98.3 (10.5)
Stimulated/Unsupplemented	(N=43)	104.0 (11.9)	105.2 (17.6)	97.0 (8.9)	97.1 (10.0)
Stimulated/Supplemented	(N=51)	107.0 (14.4)	108.5 (14.6)	98.5 (9.8)	97.6 (9.9)
Supplemented >6 months	(N=63)	104.7 (17.9)	110.7 (17.4)	101.0 (12.0)	99.6 (10.4)
Supplemented <6 months	(N=75)	109.1 (17.8)	113.0 (17.1)[a]	97.0 (11.5)	98.2 (9.2)
General quotient					
Unstimulated/Unsupplemented	(N=67)	100.4 (13.0)[b]	97.0 (11.3)[a]	97.6 (11.8)	95.1 (7.6)
Unstimulated/Supplemented	(N=67)	103.6 (12.6)	100.7 (12.4)	98.6 (9.6)	97.7 (8.1)
Stimulated/Unsupplemented	(N=43)	104.9 (11.3)	100.5 (12.7)	99.3 (8.1)	97.9 (9.9)
Stimulated/Supplemented	(N=51)	107.5 (12.1)[b]	103.7 (8.3)[a]	103.4 (9.6)	99.5 (9.3)
Supplemented >6 months	(N=63)	103.5 (13.0)	101.6 (11.6)	100.4 (8.5)	97.6 (6.9)
Supplemented <6 months	(N=75)	106.1 (12.2)	102.0 (10.5)	98.0 (9.5)	96.3 (7.6)

[1] Numbers indicate mean (and standard deviation).
[2] Superscript letters indicate pairs of means within each column that differ significantly from each other by t-test.

Only those children tested on at least three of the four testing occasions were included in the analysis. The analysis is thus based on data from 141 subjects.

Nutritional supplementation enhanced scores on the locomotor [$F(1, 133) = 9.34$, $p = .003$], personal–social [$F(1, 133) = 5.29$, $p = .024$], eye–hand coordination [$F(1, 133) = 4.01$, $p = .048$], and performance [$F(1, 133) = 6.69$, $p = .01$] subscales and on the general quotient [$F(1, 133) = 7.47$, $p = .008$]. The stimulation program increased scores on the personal–social [$F(1, 133) = 6.87$, $p = .01$], speech–language [$F(1, 133) = 16.92$, $p = .001$], and eye–hand coordination [$F(1, 133) = 3.71$, $p = .057$) subscales as well as on the general quotient [$F(1, 133) = 4.65$, $p = .03$].

2. The Einstein Test

Table 8.9 shows means and standard deviations as well as statistically significant F-tests and t-tests for the three scales of the Einstein test. Means for both maximum scores achieved and stage levels derived from the scores are presented. The prehension scale was given to children at 4 and 6 months, and the object and spatial scales were given at 4, 6, 12, and 18 months. Four-way repeated measures analyses of variance (nutrition $\times$ stimulation $\times$ sex $\times$ age) were computed for each scale. These analyses were based on 195 individuals for the prehension scale and 125 individuals for the object and spatial scales (Waber *et al.*, in preparation).

Treatment effects appeared almost exclusively on the prehension subscale. Stimulated children achieved a higher maximum score [$F(1, 187) = 12.58$, $p < .001$] as well as a higher stage level [$F(1, 187) = 11.45$, $p < .001$] than did those who had not received the education treatment. The interaction of nutrition and stimulation was statistically significant; the group receiving both treatments achieved the highest maximum score [$F(1, 187) = 4.00$, $p = .047$] and highest stage level [$F(1, 187) = 4.23$, $p = .041$]. Interaction of stimulation and age was significant for maximum score achieved [$F(1, 187) = 9.53$, $p = .003$] and for stage level [$F(1, 187) = 9.09$, $p = .003$]; it was also significant for the maximum score of the spatial scale [$F(1, 187) = 3.10$, $p = .027$]. These interactions reflected a decline in the treatment effect with age or a possible ceiling effect. Since the scores were not normalized at each age, there was a large effect of the factor age for every scale, which presumably reflected the association of stage progression with chronological age.

IV. Summary and Discussion

The Bogota Project was designed to study the single and interactive effects of environmental and nutritional variables on the physical and

Table 8.9

Descriptive Statistics for the Einstein Test by Subscales and Treatment Group

			Months		
		4	6	12	18
Prehension					
Unstimulated/Unsupplemented	$(N=67)$	2.79 $(.24)^{1a2}$			
Unstimulated/Supplemented	$(N=67)$	2.86 (.20)			
Stimulated/Unsupplemented	$(N=43)$	2.92 $(.10)^a$			
Stimulated/Supplemented	$(N=51)$	2.91 (.17)			
Supplemented > 6 months	$(N=63)$	2.79 (.26)			
Supplemented < 6 months	$(N=75)$	2.87 (.20)			
Substage					
Unstimulated/Unsupplemented	$(N=67)$		2.98 (.08)		
Unstimulated/Supplemented	$(N=67)$		2.99 (.005)		
Stimulated/Unsupplemented	$(N=43)$		2.99 (.005)		
Stimulated/Supplemented	$(N=51)$		2.99 (.005)		
Supplemented > 6 months	$(N=63)$		2.98 (.08)		
Supplemented ≤ 6 months	$(N=75)$		2.99 (.005)		

Unstimulated/Unsupplemented	(N = 67)	2.88 (.99)	3.68 (.52)	5.33 (.86)	6.38 (.49)
Unstimulated/Supplemented	(N = 67)	3.08 (.70)	3.71 (.35)	5.12 (.93)	6.23 (.76)
Stimulated/Unsupplemented	(N = 43)	3.01 (.80)	3.62 (.25)	5.30 (.77)	6.23 (.66)
Stimulated/Supplemented	(N = 51)	3.17 (.48)	3.71 (.31)	5.35 (.73)	6.01 (.69)
Supplemented > 6 months	(N = 63)	2.93 (.95)	3.56 (.89)	5.47 (.79)	6.31 (.51)
Supplemented < 6 months	(N = 75)	2.94 (.93)	3.69 (.35)	5.32 (.96)	6.29 (.69)
Spatial substage					
Unstimulated/Unsupplemented	(N = 67)	.58 (1.55)	3.61 (.47)	5.92 (.68)	6.70 (.20)
Unstimulated/Supplemented	(N = 67)	1.25 (1.63)	3.53 (.77)	5.92 (.55)	6.66 (.28)
Stimulated/Unsupplemented	(N = 43)	1.04 (1.13)	3.66 (.08)	6.08 (.47)	6.61 (.33)
Stimulated/Supplemented	(N = 51)	.94 (1.35)	3.67 (.06)	6.08 (.44)	6.64 (.18)
Supplemented > 6 months	(N = 63)	1.15 (1.56)	3.60 (.67)	6.02 (.56)	6.68 (.15)
Supplemented < 6 months	(N = 75)	1.27 (1.62)	3.62 (.45)	6.00 (.52)	6.70 (.14)

[1] Numbers indicate mean (and standard deviation).
[2] Superscript letters indicate pairs of means within each column that differ significantly from each other by t-test.

cognitive development and health of children. Food supplementation and early environmental stimulation were used in a sample of families at high risk of malnutrition in order to alter selectively nutritional status and home environment. Subjects were randomly assigned to experimental and control groups. A health-care program, provided for all subjects, permitted surveillance of morbidity and reduced the drop-out rate. Health, nutrition, and social variables were measured longitudinally, facilitating quantification of change in relevant variables occurring naturally or as consequences of the intervention.

Results as of 1979 show significant effects of nutritional supplementation during pregnancy on maternal weight gain, perinatal and neonatal mortality, and birth weight among males. These effects were observed in spite of significant substitution of the supplement for the initial diet, which reduced the net increment in food intake. This finding implies that the treatment was not purely nutritional since the intervention served to free family resources for satisfying other material needs. Further study of the intrafamily decision-making processes that led to this practice is crucial to the future of any food supplementation or other intervention programs for families at high risk of malnutrition. The findings raise a number of questions that should be addressed by further analysis of the data.

No significant differences in birth weight in response to supplementation were found among the half of the sample with low initial dietary intake (less than 1500 calories or less than 20 gm of protein per day). In contrast, significant differences as a result of supplementation were observed in the sample half with high initial dietary intake. In the latter group, supplementation increased net intake of protein but not of calories thus suggesting that protein was the limiting factor. This observation is in keeping with those of Edozien, Switzer, and Bryan (1976) in the United States and Higgins (1971) in Montreal, but it is in conflict with the findings of Lechtig, Yarbrough, Delgado, Habicht, Martorell, and Klein (1975) in rural Guatemala, who found calories to be the significant factor.

The absence of supplementation effect on birth weight in the low initial diet group could be explained by the deficient calorie and protein intake even after supplementation. The low initial diet set probably represented the most malnourished women in the sample. Their increments in calorie and protein intake may have been channeled to replenishment of maternal energy and protein stores instead of to the fetus. Another possibility is that part of the extra calories consumed by the low initial intake group were utilized to increase the level of physical activity. The latter explanation would be in keeping with the findings of Viteri (1977) and his colleagues, who demonstrated an increase in spontaneous activities (such as walking and visiting relatives and friends) among cane cutters who received food supplementation. Regardless of the reason, the results suggest that a certain threshold of calorie and protein intake must be surpassed in order to affect offspring birth weight among severely deprived women. The results further suggest that when calorie intake is not severely limited, increments in protein intake have a significant effect on birth weight. From the point of view of policy planning, these findings call attention to a subset of women in urban poverty areas who are severely deprived nutritionally. Significant improvement of their nutritional status may be necessary before supplements can be expected to affect the birth weight of their offspring.

The increased consumption of dextrose by unsupplemented newborns is consistent with the heightened responsiveness to food among malnourished newborns in animal species (Hseuh, Blackwell, & Chow, 1970; Smart, 1971). Food intake during the first day of life has also been reported to be higher in human infants with low Apgar scores than in controls (Dubignon, Campbell, Curtis, & Partington, 1960). The fact that differences in dextrose intake between supplemented and unsupplemented infants were observed only among boys is in line with the supplementation effects on birth weight.

At 15 days of age, food supplementation had an effect on the neonate's ability to respond to and process visual information. In comparison with babies in the randomly assigned unsupplemented control group, the babies of supplemented mothers displayed stronger responses to stimulus onset, as indicated by longer initial fixation and a more rapid habituation to stimulus repetitions. These findings are consistent with previous research on the effects of pre- and perinatal risk variables upon newborn attention (Lewis, Bartels, Campbell, & Goldberg, 1967; Sigman, Kopp, Permelee, & Jeffrey, 1973; Stechler, 1964) and on differences in cardiac-orienting response and habituation between 1-year-old malnourished and well-nourished infants (Lester, 1975).

Differences in attention between supplemented and unsupplemented infants may be maturational in nature. Sigman *et al.* (1973) found that orienting response magnitude was the most sensitive indicator of attentional differences between neonates at various levels of neurological maturation.

Unsupplemented infants responded more irritably than supplemented infants to both the general testing situation and the aversive stimulation. Unsupplemented infant response both to interruption of nonnutritive sucking and to a cold stimulus on the abdomen was characterized by more cries and slower recovery than were observed among supplemented infants. The most commonly reported behavioral manifestation of pre- and perinatal malnutrition in animal species is heightened emotional responsiveness to moderately stressful stimulation (Levitsky & Barnes, 1970; Smart, 1971). In humans, extended irritable response to moderately aversive stimulation (such as that displayed by the unsupplemented infants) has been found to be associated with risk factors such as maternal narcotic addiction (Strauss, Lessen-Firestone, Starr, & Ostrea, 1975) and lower socioeconomic status (Bell, Weller, & Waldrop, 1971). Moreover, heightened emotional responsiveness to nipple removal and to cold disc application appears to be predictive of diminished social responsiveness and activity at 4 and 8 months of age (Birns, Barten, & Bridger, 1969; McGrade, 1968).

Both interventions—nutritional supplementation and stimulation—had modest but statistically significant effects on the children's performances on the Griffiths Test. Greatest improvement was shown by the group that received both treatments. All scores declined with age, which is the typical pattern among children raised in impoverished environments (Monckeberg *et al.,* 1972). Different interventions influenced different behavioral domains measured by the Griffiths Test. Nutritional supplementation had its primary effect on those scales that reflect motor functioning (locomotor and performance), whereas educational stimulation primarily affected linguistic development (speech–language).

In summary, the Bogota Project thus far has shown that the effects of deprivation can be ameliorated by both nutritional supplementation and psychological stimulation. With the exception of the reduction of mortality, which must be interpreted cautiously given the small number of observations, treatment effects were of modest magnitude. Each intervention appears to have influenced specific domains of behavior, and the data suggest that concurrent administration of both modes of intervention increases their effectiveness. Further analysis of the data is likely to disclose features of the family environment that independently influence physical and cognitive development. Furthermore, characteristics of the family that are associated with heightened susceptibility to the beneficial effects of treatment may be identified. It appears unlikely that any single intervention will by itself ameliorate the development of children raised in severely deprived environments. Multifaceted interventions addressing a range of needs would be more likely to succeed.

REFERENCES

Barnes, R. H., Moore, A. U., & Pong, W. G. Behavioral abnormalities in young adult pigs caused by malnutrition in early life. *Journal of Nutrition,* 1970, *100,* 149–155.

Barrera-Moncada, G. *Estudios sobre alteraciones del crecimiento y del desarrollo psicologico del sindrome pluricarencial (kwashiorkor).* Caracas, Venezuela, Editora Grafos, 1963.

Bell, R. Q., Weller, G. M., & Waldrop, M. F. Newborns and preschoolers: Organization of behavior and relations between periods. *Monographs of the Society for Research in Child Development,* 1971, *36*(1–2, Serial No. 142): 1–145.

Biber, B. Goals and methods in a preschool program for disadvantaged children. *Children,* 1970, *17,* 15–20.

Bing, E. Effect of child-rearing practices on development of differential cognitive abilities. *Child Development,* 1963, *34,* 631–648.

Birns, B., Barten, S., & Bridger, W. H. Individual differences in temperamental characteristics of infants. *Transactions of the New York Academy of Sciences,* 1969, *31,* 1070–1082.

Bowlby, J. *Attachment and loss.* New York: Basic Books, 1969.

Brockman, L. *The effects of severe malnutrition on cognitive development in infants.* Unpublished doctoral dissertation, Cornell University, 1968.

Bronfenbrenner, U. Socialization and social class through time and space. In E. E. Maccoby, T. N. Newcomb, & E. L. Hartley (Eds.), *Readings in social psychology,* 3rd ed. New York: Holt, Rinehart, 1958.

Brown, R. E. Organ weight in malnutrition with special reference to brain weight. *Developmental Medicine and Child Neurology,* 1966, *8,* 512–522.

Cabak, V., & Najdanvic, R. Effect of undernutrition in early life on physical and mental development. *Archives of Diseases in Children,* 1965, *40,* 532–534.

Champakam, S., Srikantia, S. G., & Gopalan, C. Kwashiorkor and mental development. *American Journal of Clinical Nutrition,* 1968, *21,* 844–852.

Chase, H. P., Dorsey, J., & McKhann, G. M. The effect of malnutrition on the synthesis of a myelin lipid. *Pediatrics,* 1967, *40,* 551–559.

Chase, H. P., & Martin, H. P. Undernutrition and child development. *New England Journal of Medicine,* 1970, *282,* 933–939.

Chavez, A., Martinez, C., & Yaschine, T. The importance of nutrition and stimuli on child mental and social development. In J. Cravioto, L. Hambraeus, & B. Vahlquist (Eds.), *Early malnutrition and mental development.* Uppsala, Sweden: Almqvist & Wiksell, 1974.

Christiansen, N., Mora, J. O., Navarro, L., & Herrera, M. G. *Effects of nutritional supplementation during pregnancy upon birth weight: Influence of pre-supplementation diet.* Manuscript in preparation.

Christiansen, N., Vuori, L., Mora, J. O., & Wagner, M. Social environment as it relates to malnutrition and mental development. In J. Cravioto, L. Hambraeus, & B. Vahlquist (Eds.), *Early malnutrition and mental development.* Uppsala, Sweden: Almqvist & Wiksell, 1974.

Christiansen, T., & Livermore, G. A comparison of Anglo-American and Spanish-American children on the WISC. *Journal of Social Psychology,* 1970, *81,* 9–14.

Churchill, J. A., Neff, J. W., & Caldwell, D. F. Birth weight and intelligence. *Obstetrics and Gynecology,* 1966, *28,* 425–429.

Cordano, A., Baertl, J. M., & Graham, G. G. Growth sequence during recovery from infantile malnutrition. *Journal of Pediatrics,* 1963, *63,* 698–699.

Coursin, D. B. Relationship of nutrition to central nervous system development and function: Overview. *Federation Proceedings,* 1967, *26,* 134–138.

Cravioto, J., & DeLicardie, E. R. Mental performance in school age children. *American Journal of Diseases of Children,* 1970, *120,* 404–410.

Cravioto, J., & Robles, B. Evolution of adaptive and motor behavior during rehabilitation from kwashiorkor. *American Journal of Orthopsychiatry,* 1965, *35,* 449–464.

Deutch, M. The disadvantaged child and the learning process: Some social, psychological and development considerations. In A. H. Passow (Ed.), *Education in depressed areas* (Vol. 11). New York: Columbia University Press, 1963.

Deutsch, C. P. Social class and child development. In B. Caldwell & H. Ricciuti (Eds.), *Review of child development research* (Vol. 3). Chicago: University of Chicago Press, 1973.

Dobbing, J. The influence of early malnutrition on the development of myelination of the brain. *Proceedings of the Royal Society of London,* Series B, 1964, *159,* 503-509.

Dobbing, J. The effect of undernutrition on myelination of the central nervous system. *Biology of the Neonate,* 1966, *9,* 132-147.

Dobbing, J. Vulnerable periods in developing brain. In A. N. Davidson & J. Dobbing (Eds.), *Applied neurochemistry.* Oxford: Blackwell Scientific, 1968.

Dobbing, J., & Widdowson, E. M. The effect of undernutrition and subsequent rehabilitation on myelination of rat brain as measured by its composition. *Brain,* 1965, *88,* 357-366.

Dubignon, J., Campbell, D., Curtis, M. G., & Partington, M. W. The relation between laboratory measures of sucking, food intake, and perinatal factors during the newborn period. *Child Development,* 1960, *40,* 1107-1119.

Edozien, J. C., Switzer, B. R., & Bryan, R. B. *Medical evaluation of the special supplemental food program for women, infants and children (WIC).* School of Public Health, University of North Carolina, Chapel Hill, N.C., 1976.

Eichenwald, H. F., & Fry, P. C. Nutrition and learning. *Science,* 1969, *163,* 644-648.

Elias, M. F., & Samonds, K. W. Exploratory behavior and activity of infant monkeys during nutritional and rearing restriction. *American Journal of Clinical Nutrition,* 1974, *27,* 458.

Elias, M. F., & Samonds, K. W. Protein and calorie malnutrition in infant cebus monkeys: Growth and behavioral development during deprivation and rehabilitation. *American Journal of Clinical Nutrition,* 1977, *30,* 355-366.

Elias, M. F. Malnutrition in infancy and intellectual development. In K. F. Riegel & L. A. Meacham (Eds.), *The developing individual in a changing world* (Vol. 2). Chicago: Aldine Press, 1976.

Engel, R. Abnormal brain wave patterns in kwashiorkor. *Electroencephalography and Clinical Neurophysiology,* 1956, *8,* 512-522.

Francis-Williams, J., & Davies, P. A. Very low birth weight and later intelligence. *Developmental Medicine and Child Neurology,* 1974, *16,* 709-728.

Frankova, S. Interaction between early malnutrition and stimulation in animals. In J. Cravioto, L. Hambraeus, & B. Vahlquist (Eds.), *Early malnutrition and mental development.* Uppsala, Sweden: Almqvist & Wiksell, 1974.

Freeman, H. E., Klein, R. E., Kagan, J., & Yarbrough, C. Relations between nutrition and cognition in rural Guatemala. *American Journal of Public Health,* 1977, *67,* 233-239.

Friedman, S. Newborn visual attention to repeated exposures to redundant vs. novel targets. *Perception and Psychophysics,* 1972, *12,* 291-294.

Frisancho, A. R., Klayman, J. E., & Matos, J. Influence of maternal nutritional status on prenatal growth in a Peruvian urban population. *American Journal of Physical Anthropology,* 1977, *46,* 265-274.

Goodnow, J. Cultural variations in cognitive skills. In J. Helmuth (Ed.), *Cognitive studies.* New York: Bruner Mazel, 1970.

Graham, G. C., & Morales, E. Studies in infantile malnutrition: Nature of the problem in Peru. *Journal of Nutrition,* 1963, *79,* 479-487.

Guthrie, H. A., & Brown, M. L. Effect of severe undernutrition in early life on growth, brain size, and composition in adult rats. *Journal of Nutrition,* 1968, *94,* 419-426.

Hegsted, D. M. Deprivation syndrome of protein-calorie malnutrition. *Nutrition Reviews,* 1972, *30,* 51-54.

Hess, R. D., & Shipman, V. C. Cognitive elements in maternal behavior. In J. P. Hill (Ed.), *Minnesota symposia on child psychology* (Vol. 1). Minneapolis: University of Minnesota Press, 1967.

Higgins, A. *Montreal diet dispensary study in nutritional supplementation and the outcome of pregnancy.* Washington, D.C.: National Academy of Sciences, 1971.

Howard, E., & Granoff, D. Effect of neonatal food restriction in mice on brain growth, DNA and cholesterol, and on adult delayed response learning. *Journal of Nutrition,* 1968, *95,* 111–121.

Hsueh, A. M., Blackwell, R. Q., & Chow, B. F. Effect of maternal diet in rats on food consumption of the offspring. *Journal of Nutrition,* 1970, *100,* 1157–1163.

Jackson, C. M., & Stewart, C. A. The effects of inanition in the young upon the ultimate size of the body and of the various organs in the albino rat. *Journal of Experimental Zoology,* 1920, *30,* 97–128.

Kallen, D. J. Nutrition and society. *Journal of the American Medical Association,* 1971, *215,* 94–100.

Klein, R. E. *Performance of malnourished in comparison with adequately nourished children on selected cognitive tasks* (Guatemala). Paper presented at the annual meeting of the American Association for the Advancement of Science, Boston, December 1969.

Klein, R. E., Kagan, J., Freeman, H. E., Yarbrough, C., & Habicht, J-P. Is big smart? The relation of growth to cognition. *Journal of Health and Social Behavior,* 1972, *13,* 219–225.

Klein, R. E., Yarbrough, C., Lasky, R. E., & Habicht, J-P. Correlations of mild-to-moderate protein–calorie malnutrition among rural Guatemalan infants and preschool children. In J. Cravioto, L. Hambraeus, & B. Vahlquist (Eds.), *Early malnutrition and mental development.* Uppsala, Sweden: Almqvist & Wiksell, 1974.

Klineberg, O. Negro–white differences in intelligence test performance: A new look at an old problem. *American Psychologist,* 1963, *18,* 198–203.

Kohn, M. L. Social class and parent–child relationships: An interpretation. *American Journal of Sociology,* 1963, *68,* 471–480.

Kohn, M. L., & Carrol, E. E. Social class and the allocation of parental responsibilities. *Sociometry,* 1960, *23,* 372–392.

Kramer, Y., & Rosenblum, L. A. A response to "frustration" in one-year old infants. *Psychosomatic Medicine,* 1970, *32,* 243–257.

Lambie, D. Z., Jeffs, M., Miller, N. M., Jackson, L., & Court, W. *A curriculum of materials for infant education* (Carnegie Infant Education Project, preliminary version). Ypsilanti, Michigan: High/Scope Educational Research Foundation, 1972.

Latham, M. C., & Cobos, F. The effects of malnutrition on intellectual development and learning. *American Journal of Public Health,* 1971, *61,* 1307–1324.

Lechtig, A., Yarbrough, C., Delgado, H., Habicht, J-P., Martorell, R., & Klein, R. E. Influence of maternal nutrition on birth weight. *American Journal of Clinical Nutrition,* 1975, *28,* 1223–1233.

Lesser, G. S., Fifer, G., & Clark, D. H. Mental abilities of children from different social-class and cultural groups. *Monographs of the Society for Research on Child Development,* 1965, *30*(4), 1–115.

Lester, B. M. Cardiac habituation of the orienting response to an auditory signal in infants of varying nutritional status. *Developmental Psychology,* 1975, *11,* 432–442.

Levitsky, D. A., & Barnes, R. H. Effect of early malnutrition on the reaction of adult rats to aversive stimuli. *Nature,* 1970, *225,* 468–469.

Levitsky, D. A., & Barnes, R. H. Nutritional and environmental interaction in the behavioral development of the rat: Long-term effects. *Science,* 1972, *176,* 68–71.

Lewis, M., Bartels, B., Campbell, H., & Goldberg, S. Individual differences in attention: The relation between infant condition at birth and attention distribution within the first year. *American Journal of Diseases of Children,* 1967, *113,* 461–465.

Lewis, M., & Goldberg, S. Perceptual cognitive development in infancy: A generalized expectancy model as a function of the mother–infant interaction. *Annual Progress in Child Psychiatry and Child Development,* 1970, 26–46.

Lewis, M., & Lee-Painter, S. An interactional approach to the mother–infànt dyad. In M. Lewis & L. A. Rosenblum (Eds.), *The effect of the infant on its caregiver.* New York: Wiley, 1974.

McGrade, B. J. Newborn activity and emotional response at eight months. *Child Development,* 1968, *38,* 1247–1252.

McKay, H., Sinisterra, L., McKay, A., Gomez, H., & Lloreda, P. Improving cognitive ability in chronically deprived children. *Science,* 1978, *200,* 270–278.

McLaren, D. S. A fresh look at protein–calorie malnutrition. *Lancet,* 1966, *2,* 485–488.

Manosevitz, M. Early environmental enrichment and mouse behavior. *Journal of Comparative and Physiological Psychology,* 1970, *71,* 459–466.

Milner, E. A. A study of the relationship between reading readiness in grade one school children and patterns of parent–child interaction. *Child Development,* 1951, *22,* 95–112.

Monckeberg, F. Effect of early marasmic malnutrition on subsequent physical and psychological development. In N. S. Scrimshaw & J. E. Gordon (Eds.), *Malnutrition, learning and behavior.* Cambridge, Mass.: M.I.T. Press, 1968.

Monckeberg, F., Tisler, S., Toro, S., Gattas, V., & Vega, L. Malnutrition and mental development. *American Journal of Clinical Nutrition,* 1972, *25,* 766–772.

Mora, J. O., Clement, J., Christiansen, N., Suescun, J., Wagner, M., & Herrera, M. G. Nutritional supplementation and the outcome of pregnancy: Perinatal and neonatal mortality. *Nutrition Reports International,* 1978, *18,* 167–175.

Mora, J. O., de Paredes, B., Wagner, M., Navarro, L., Suescun, J., Christiansen, N., & Herrera, M. G. Nutritional supplementation and the outcome of pregnancy: Birth weight. *American Journal of Clinical Nutrition,* 1979, *32,* 455–462.

Mora, J. O., Navarro, L., Clement, J., Wagner, M., de Paredes, B., & Herrera, M. G. The effect of nutritional supplementation on the calorie and protein intake of pregnant women. *Nutrition Reports International,* 1978, *17,* 217–228.

Nelson, G. K. The electroencephalogram in kwashiorkor. *Electroencephalography and Clinical Neurophysiology,* 1959, *11,* 73–84.

Nosbet, J. Family environment and intelligence. In A. H. Halsey, J. E. Floud, & C. A. Anderson (Eds.), *Education, economy, and society.* New York: Free Press, 1961.

Peluffo, N. La nozione de conservazione del volume e la operazion di combinacione come indice di soilippo del pensioro operatio in vaggetti apparterenti ad ambienti fisci e socioculturali diversi. *Rivista di Psicologia Sociale e Archivo Italiano di Psicologia Generale e del Laboro,* 1964, *31* (2–3), 99–132.

Platt, B. S., Heard, C. R. C., & Stewart, R. J. C. Experimental protein–calorie deficiency. In H. N. Munro & J. B. Allison (Eds.), *Mammalian protein metabolism* (Vol. 2). New York: Academic Press, 1964.

Pollitt, E. Ecology, malnutrition, and mental development. *Psychosomatic Medicine,* 1969, *31,* 193–200.

Pollitt, E., & Granoff, D. Mental and motor development of Peruvian children treated for severe malnutrition. *Revista Interamericana de Psicologia,* 1967, *1,* 93–103.

Pollitt, E., & Ricciuti, H. *Biological and social correlates of stature among children living in the slums of Lima, Peru.* Unpublished data, Cornell University, 1968.

Radin, N. Maternal warmth, achievement motivation and cognitive functioning in lower class preschool children. *Child Development,* 1971, *42,* 1560–1565.

Rajatasilpin, A., Suepsaman, B., & Yamart, V. Intellectual development and its relationship to the nutritional status among school children. *Journal of the Medical Association of Thailand,* 1970, *53,* 788–792.

Ricciuti, H. N. *Adverse social and biological influences on development:* In H. McGurk (Ed.), *Ecological factors in human development,* Amsterdam: North-Holland, 1977.

Ricciuti, H. N. Malnutrition, learning, and intellectual development: Research and remediation. In F. F. Korten, S. W. Cook, & J. I. Lacey (Eds.), *Psychology and the problems of society.* Washington, D.C.: American Psychological Association, 1970.

Richardson, S. A. The background histories of school children severely malnourished in infancy. In I. Schulman (Ed.), *Advances in pediatrics.* Chicago: Yearbook Medical Publishers, 1974.

Riskin, J., & Faunce, E. E. Family interaction scales: Theoretical framework and method. *Archives of General Psychiatry,* 1970, *22,* 504–537.

Scarr-Salapatek, S., & Williams, M. L. The effects of early stimulation on low birth weight infants. *Child Development,* 1973, *44,* 94–101.

Scrimshaw, N. S. Malnutrition, learning and behavior. *American Journal of Clinical Nutrition,* 1967, *20,* 493–502.

Scrimshaw, N. S., & Gordon, J. E. (Eds.), *Malnutrition, learning, and behavior.* Cambridge, Mass.: M.I.T. Press, 1968.

Scrimshaw, N. S., Taylor, C. E., & Gordon, J. E. Interaction of nutrition and infection. *American Journal of Medical Science,* 1959, *237,* 367–403.

Sears, R. Relation of early socialization experiences to self concepts and gender role of middle childhood. *Child Development,* 1970, *41,* 267–290.

Sigman, M., Kopp, C. B., Parmelee, A. H., & Jeffrey, W. E. Visual attention and neurological organization in neonates. *Child Development,* 1973, *44,* 461–466.

Skeels, H. M. Adult status of children with contrasting early experiences. *Monographs of the Society for Research in Child Development,* 1966, *31*(3, Serial No. 105), 1–65.

Smart, J. L. Long-lasting effects of early nutritional deprivation on the behavior of rodents. *Psychiatria, Neurologia, Neurochirurgia,* 1971, *79,* 443–452.

Stechler, G. Newborn attention as affected by medication during labor. *Science,* 1964, *144,* 315–317.

Stewart, R. J. C., & Platt, B. S. Nervous system damage in experimental protein–calorie deficiency. In N. S. Scrimshaw & J. E. Gordon (Eds.), *Malnutrition, learning and behavior.* Cambridge, Mass.: M.I.T. Press, 1968.

Stoch, M. B., & Smythe, P. M. Does undernutrition during infancy inhibit brain growth and subsequent intellectual development? *Archives of Diseases in Children,* 1963, *38,* 546–552.

Stoch, M. B., & Smythe, P. M. The effect of undernutrition on subsequent brain growth and intellectual development. *South African Medical Journal,* 1967, *41,* 1027–1030.

Strauss, M. E., Lessen-Firestone, J. K., Starr, R. H., Jr., & Ostrea, E. M., Jr. Behavior of narcotics-addicted newborns. *Child Development,* 1975, *46,* 887–893.

Tulkin, S. R., & Kagan, J. Motor–child interaction in the first year of life. *Child Development,* 1972, *43,* 31–41.

Vuori, L., Mora, J. O., Christiansen, N., Clement, J., & Herrera, M. G. Nutritional supplementation and the outcome of pregnancy: Visual habituation at 15 days. *American Journal of Clinical Nutrition,* 1979, *32,* 463–469.

Vuori, L., Navarro, L., Christiansen, N., Mora, J. O., & Herrera, M. G. Food supplementation of pregnant women at risk of malnutrition and newborn responsiveness to aversive stimulation. *Developmental Medicine and Child Neurology,* in press.

Waber, D., Ortiz, N., Christiansen, N., Clement, J., Mora, J. O., Wagner, M., & Herrera, M. G. *Effects of nutritional supplementation and psychosocial stimulation on cognitive development of children up to 18 months of age at risk of malnutrition.* Manuscript in preparation.

Weinberg, W. A., Dietz, S. G., Penick, E. C., & McAlister, W. H. Intelligence, reading achievement, physical size, and social class. *Journal of Pediatrics,* 1974, *85,* 484-489.

Wiener, G., Rider, R. V., Oppel, W. C., & Harper, P. A. Correlates of low birth weight: Psychological status at eight to ten years of age. *Pediatric Research,* 1968, *2,* 110-118.

Willerman, L., & Churchill, J. A. Intelligence and birth weight in identical twins. *Child Development,* 1967, *38,* 623-629.

Winick, M. Nutrition and mental development. *Medical Clinics of North America,* 1970, *54,* 1413-1429.

Winick, M., Fish, I., & Rosso, P. Cellular recovery in rat tissues after a brief period of neonatal malnutrition. *Journal of Nutrition,* 1968, *95,* 623-626.

Winick, M., Meyer, K., & Harris, R. Malnutrition and environmental enrichment by early adoption. *Science,* 1975, *190,* 1173-1175.

Winick, M., & Noble, A. Cellular response in rats during malnutrition at various ages. *Journal of Nutrition,* 1966, *89,* 300-306.

Wray, J. D., & Aguirre, A. Protein-calorie malnutrition in Candelaria, Colombia: Prevalence: Social and demographic factors. *Journal of Tropical Pediatrics,* 1969, *15,* 76-98.

Yarrow, L. J. Separation from parents during early childhood. In M. L. Hoffman & L. W. Hoffman (Eds.), *Review of Child Development Research* (Vol. 1). New York: Russell Sage Foundation, 1964.

Young, H. B. Socioeconomic factors in child development. *Bibliotheca Nutritio et Dieta,* 1970, *14,* 43-63.

CHAPTER 9

Is Genetic Counseling Intervention?[1]

STEPHEN S. AMATO

WEST VIRGINIA UNIVERSITY MEDICAL CENTER
MORGANTOWN, WEST VIRGINIA

Genetic counseling is certainly an intrusion that attempts to intervene in the lives of others. Although in some instances it may be a positive intervention, in other cases it may not even be a welcome encounter. The substance of this chapter is that genetic counseling *is* intervention but that this affirmative answer must be extensively qualified.

I. What Is Genetic Counseling?

Genetic counseling is a process of communication. It involves a complex number of factors concerning the patient, the family, and the disease or condition. It presupposes or is dependent upon an accurate and complete diagnosis (if that is possible). Because the patient very often does not understand the disease, counseling should also include a review of the diagnosis and a discussion of the nature of the condition, the prognosis, treatment modalities, and alternatives. (If these have been covered previously, they should still be reviewed briefly.) Genetic counseling, by its

[1] Research for this chapter was supported in part by a grant from The National Foundation March of Dimes.

185

LIFE-SPAN DEVELOPMENTAL PSYCHOLOGY
Intervention

nature, includes an assessment of the recurrence risk and the rationale for arriving at the stated risk; it also should include the possibilities for prenatal diagnosis. In addition, but not as an afterthought, it should include a discussion of the impact of the disease upon the family and the individual. Genetic counseling represents the communication of factual information to the family; it also should facilitate the family members' progress to a more homeostatic state in terms of their coping process and the reduction of nonfunctional responses such as guilt. Genetic counseling is a therapeutic intervention, and, as with any interpersonal relationship, it is rarely neutral and is probably viewed as either good or bad from the perspective of the client–patient. It is definitely not decision making for other people. Unfortunately, patients are often referred so that the counselor can "set them straight" about the family decision. The expectation is that the counselor will advise a "good" course of action.

In general, geneticists see their success in terms of altering the reproductive behavior of patients in a "reasonable direction" and reducting the number of persons in the population afflicted with genetic diseases or genetic vulnerability to disease. Although geneticists perceive themselves as nondirective (and present themselves as such in questionnaires and publication), they also indicate strong feelings and opinions about genetic diseases (Sorensen & Culbert, 1977).

The dichotomy of nondirective genetic counseling versus strong feelings about genetic disease has the potential for producing a situation in which the geneticist engages in unconscious persuasion of patients to do what society in general, through the medium of the counselor, thinks is "right."

The geneticist must realize that strongly held opinions will flavor the information presented to the patient. As long as the individual counselor recognizes this human response, he can still do humane and effective genetic counseling.

II. The Setting for Genetic Counseling

Most genetic counseling is conducted in the setting of a medical center, and, because of the time and complexity of the history taking and specialized examinations required, there are generally several people involved in the process. Two general models exist: one involves an encounter with the entire group at one time; the other involves more individual encounters with a sequence of professionals. The actual interpretation or counseling may be done in a small or large group, and many centers combine a group approach with a more personal type of session. In a consumer evaluation questionnaire sent to our patients, virtally all families who had experienced the group counseling in another medical center or in the satellite clinic where it was practiced in our region said they preferred the individual, more personal setting. In fact, altering the format of the satellite clinic in the region that had used the group format increased the number of referrals (apparently, persons who made the referrals disliked the rather public group format) and increased the percentage of patients keeping their appointments.

In our clinics, various specialists see the family in sequence, but only one person is involved with the interpretation and counseling. Each family is assigned a genetics associate (a person with a master's degree in a related area and an internship in medical genetics) who assists in obtaining a data base, performs counseling, provides follow-up, and also serves as a patient advocate in the process. In most genetics clinics, major counseling emphasis is placed upon risks of occurrence and recurrence (Lubs & de la Cruz, 1977). Little or no time may be spent on discussing the feelings the experience evokes or even the emotional impact of the condition upon the family. With the constraints of time, the latter items unfortunately are not perceived as being essential to genetic counseling and may be omitted. However, these factors are of great significance to the family and drastically affect how the patient perceives the genetic information received. Several sessions help clarify and reinforce the genetic content of the counseling and aid in establishing a more traditional patient–professional relationship. Genetic counseling that does not take these factors into consideration is probably an academic exercise for the counselor but is not very helpful for the counselees.

III. Who Does Genetic Counseling?

In 1979 there was no current comprehensive index of practicing genetic counselors, but a detailed study conducted by Sorensen in 1973 (and published in Sorensen & Culbert, 1977) provides a profile of geneticists at that time. Approximately 80% of geneticists were physicians, and the majority of these were pediatricians (64%); 16% were internists, 5% were in obstetrics, and 5% were in pathology; 8% of these physicians also held a research degree (an M.D.–Ph.D.). The remainder of those practicing genetic counseling were geneticists with Ph.D. degrees (11%), nurses (2%), or from various other disciplines (7%). It is probable that a survey taken in the late 1970s would show a much higher proportion of persons in the latter category. This has been necessitated by the increased awareness and demand for genetics services. The development of graduate programs to prepare genetic counselors has provided nonphysicians who partially fill this need. Although the general data are not available, it is probably safe to say that the majority of genetic counselors function primarily at medical centers and as tertiary referral resources. Generally, and unfortunately, the practicing primary physician who is in the ideal position to do genetic counseling is uncomfortable with it or inadequately trained to do it. Perhaps a brief review of the history of medical genetics will clarify why genetic services are not yet integrated into general medicine and why difficulties have arisen within the lay community concerning the intent of geneticists.

Until the 1960s, medical genetics could explain few human diseases. Human genetics also carried the stigma of selective breeding of humans to "improve" the human race. Such plans were frequently proposed, and in 1865 Francis Galton formalized this concept and called it *eugenics*. Eugenics was used to further questionable political and social goals, and the resulting mistrust and subsequent rejection of eugenics were quite inhibitory to the growth of human and medical genetics. Eugenics still evokes strong negative reactions from the general population (Howard & Rifkin, 1977) as well as from the scientific community. Fortunately, other branches of genetics were able to thrive, and these gave the United States preeminence in agriculture and animal science.

The modern upsurge in human genetics was initiated by the discovery of the correct chromosome number in humans in 1956 and the discoveries of chromosome abnormalities shortly thereafter. Subsequent years have been accompanied by enormous progress through the synthesis of molecular biology, biochemistry, genetics, and medicine. The first modern medical geneticists were physicians and scientists working in research laboratories at medical centers. Because medical genetics grew out of laboratory activity, the perception of genetics is still primarily one of scientific endeavor rather than of medical practice, even though most practicing genetic counselors have been physicians (80%) (Sorensen & Culbert, 1977).   The prevailing model was, and still is, that of a physician-scientist interested in laboratory aspects of genetics and limiting his research to a relatively small group of esoteric diseases or to basic laboratory investigation. The process of genetic counseling is a by-product of these primary activities and interests. However, we have reached the point at which medical genetics must be perceived as an integral part of the practice of medicine. This is not to say that only physicians can do genetic counseling, but merely that it should be considered an appropriate activity for primary physicians as well as geneticists with other training. In 1973–1974, Sorensen's study (1977) found that the average time spent in genetic counseling was about 8 hours per week. No doubt, a 1979 survey would show that genetic counselors spend considerably more time in this activity, but it would also show that more counseling is done by health professionals other than physicians.

IV. How Do Patients Get to a Genetic Counseling Unit?

The practicing physician is the person who most often encounters the potential genetic problem. The problem may be real, or it may be imagined. It may involve fertility, pregnancy, age, a positive family history, a birth defect, or any of a long list of possible difficulties. The family may have perceived the problem and requested medical advice that lead to a referral to the genetics unit by a referring physician or agency. Sometimes the family has read about the genetics services and refers itself. Although some families are dissuaded from seeking genetic services by newspaper articles, the popular press is probably responsible for the vast increase of the use of genetic services, especially prenatal diagnosis.

With the exception of population screening, most genetics units see a patient because something has already happened. Parents who may have been anticipating the birth of a child are confronted by a birth defect representing a discrepancy between expectations and reality; thus, they need assistance. Although numerous articles have emphasized the preventive nature of genetic counseling (e.g., Leonard, Chase, & Childs, 1972), we actually do more to prevent repeat events than to prevent the initial event. However, this process of post facto, but early, intervention can be very beneficial. The birth of an infant with a congenital defect is a catastrophic event to the parents, but frequently only the technical aspects of the problem concern the physician. Medicine has concentrated on rescue tactics to save the infant. Under these circumstances of crisis, medical information given to the family is piecemeal. This increases the family's stress, and the overall chances for marital discord are greatly increased. If the infant survives, the risk for child abuse can be considerably increased. Under these circumstances, the family having a child with a birth defect is at significantly increased risk for separation or divorce when compared to a peer group. Because more than 80% of the families we see in our clinics already have an affected individual, our role includes assistance with that individual as well as prevention of recurrence.

V. Problems in the Application of Genetic Counseling

The eugenics movement persists in modern medical genetics because there is often an assumed correct or better choice that provides an available alternative for parents. Unfortunately, one couple's decision represents a negligible event in the general health of the population. In spite of this realization, medical genetics is often seen as an answer to the prevention of many diseases. The real benefit of genetic counseling seems to come to the family. Society benefits from the family's ability to cope with the existing problem rather than from a dramatic reduction of disease in the population.

There can be numerous uncertainties in genetic counseling relating to diagnosis and recurrence risk, but these uncertainties can be described in words that the family will understand. Certain statistical concepts that may be helpful in an academic discussion of risks can become absurd in a clinical situation when they are substituted for a verbal description of the uncertainty. The emphasis in counseling should be on communication; to enhance communication, the geneticist must be sensitive to the mental state of the patient. Statistical calculation, beyond a certain point, means little to a patient. In effect, if an event is possible, the alternatives may seem to be two-fold to confused people—either it will happen or it will not. This is not a subtle point; however, it is one frequently made by clients, although it is ignored by geneticists because it does not fit the reality of the situation. In order to avoid the patient's retreat into this simplistic haven, the counselor must emphasize clear communication.

Geneticists are beneficiaries of an information explosion in cytogenetics, biochemical and molecular genetics, somatic cell genetics, etc. and have developed a complex jargon for professional communication. The jargon is of little use in the communication of reports to referring physicians, who are generally undertrained in genetics (often because the scientists-geneticists are not skilled in communicating with medical students in their classes). The technical jargon is also a problem in communicating with the family.

Another problem in the practice of genetic counseling has been the lack of follow-up. Frequently, genetic counseling is represented by a single encounter, although numerous studies have shown this to be of little use to the family.

VI. How Does One Assess the Effect of Genetic Counseling?

Genetic counseling grew out of the patient's need to understand specific data about himself or his family. Geneticists needed to document their efforts to see if they had made a difference in the decision making of the family. Possibly because most geneticists are in academics, the main type of instrument used in evaluation of counseling effectiveness has been the quiz type of questionnaire. (How many patients knew that Tay-Sachs disease was autosomal recessive? What was its recurrence risk? What was the gene frequency in Ashkenazi Jews as opposed to Sephardic Jews as compared to white, non-Jewish Americans, etc.?) Success meant the patient could pass the test. Later, success was extended to mean that the patients had made the "correct" choice in their later reproductive behavior. Such studies obviously lend themselves to publication and provide positive feedback for the investigator.

Occasionally, a questionnaire–quiz asks about the individual's reaction to the genetic counseling experience. It seems obvious that the patient's reaction to the experience will dramatically affect his retention of factual information and, in turn, his decision making, for the latter is dependent upon perceptions and feelings rather than facts (although it is always the facts that concern us). The overall goal of genetic counseling seems to be a reduction in the number of children born with an inherited disease or with a genetic predisposition for the disease. Although this is commendable, most genetic diseases occur either as recessives—stemming from the union of two carriers who never knew they shared the same deleterious recessive condition—or as a new dominant mutation. At the present time, our role in primary prevention is minimal.

Since 1976, a detailed study of counseling has been conducted by the Department of Socio–Medical Studies at Boston University School of Medicine. Our clinic participated in it, and it has the potential to be an extremely valuable national study. Unfortunately, it soon became apparent that the precounseling questionnaire was antagonizing our patients, most of whom did not know why they were referred to our clinic and thought that "counseling" referred only to marital problems. (Many couples did have marital problems that made them defensive, and they were reluctant to discuss this at first.) The language and format of the precounseling questionnaire, which was designed to be presented with minimal preliminary discussion with the family, confused and alienated our patients, and most refused to participate. They were mistrustful of an invasion of their privacy.

I felt that our participation in the cooperative study had the potential to add a necessary dimension to the project. Our patients were predominantly from rural settings and lower socioeconomic groups and had relatively little formal education. Without representatives of such groups, the study could overrepresent the attitudes of patients who were able to manage the language and format of the requisite documents rather than the attitudes of "typical" patients. In spite of these problems, consumer evaluation and consumer participation in planning genetic services are essential. It is necessary that each genetic unit devise the means by which this can be accomplished. We must assess the outcome of our efforts, and we must decide what is the desired outcome of genetic counseling. Is it information retained by the patient, is it the success of the affected individual in realizing his or her maximum potential, is it a functional family, or is it the utilization of information to diminish the frequency of families with two occurrences of preventable birth defects? All of these are proper parts of the outcome of genetic counseling and should be included in assessing the outcome.

A case can be made for the cost effectiveness of helping the family to remain intact and to cope with the problem event while preventing repeated events. Studies of the effectiveness of genetic counseling have already established that single-encounter sessions are almost completely ineffective, no matter what criteria are utilized for assessment. The need for repeated contacts with affected families has increased the geneticist's awareness of the need to cooperate with community agencies to provide assistance to the family. This has also stimulated a more traditional doctor–patient relationship in which the geneticist feels responsibility for the patient's general care, health, and mental status.

VII. Recent Genetic Adventures and Misadventures

Because certain inherited diseases or types of birth defects are more common among specific subsets of the general population, and because a personally encountered type of problem is more apt to evoke an individual's involvement as an advocate, there have been many interest groups espousing research, education, and treatment aimed at their "favorite" genetic disease or condition. Thus, many genetic conditions compete with each other for funds. On the other hand, although "lumping" does seem logical and effective, the problems and anguish of the individual diseases can become diluted in a blanket type of program or appropriation. Federal and state governments should avoid funding a "disease of the month" for reasons of political expediency or even altruism; however, the impact and burden of the individual diseases must be kept apparent to legislators as well as to the general public.

Problems encountered in the many sickle cell anemia screening programs should serve as precautions for future population screening endeavors. Little attention was paid to education and informed consent prior to testing, and provision for follow-up counseling was poor. Data obtained from community health testing was used to discriminate against individuals with the sickle cell trait with regard to insurance, job opportunities, participation in athletics, etc. This early attempt at intervention, regardless of its sincerity or positive motivation, has made numerous groups, including the black population, wary of genetics and genetic intervention.

Since 1977, screening for hypothyroidism has been instituted in an increasing number of states. It would seem that this condition, which can be completely asymptomatic but can lead to impaired intellectual function, is a proper one for population screening; however, the programs are as yet too new for us to detect possible pitfalls. Certainly, appropriate follow-up, counseling, and treatment will be somewhat variable because these activities are left to the individual physician. It is hoped that these practitioners will respond with the judgment and knowledge their profession should have provided them. While we attempt to protect people from problems caused by genetic diseases, we must also protect them from the tragedy of misinformation and the prejudice of society.

Much of our activity in genetic counseling is educational. For example, when a child is born with cleft lip and cleft palate, we know the long-term problems are the development of articulate speech and good self-image. The feeding problems and surgical problems are surmountable, but the family immediately encounters the cosmetic problem and focuses on the facial appearance of the child. This is a pivotal period for the parents; their perception of the child and themselves can be altered appreciably by the way information about the birth defect is conveyed to them. Our own attitudes as well as the factual content of our counseling are of significance in our approach to patients.

VIII. West Virginia's Genetic Program: Birth Defects

Approximately one-third of all pediatric beds in the United States are occupied by the 10% of the population who have birth defects or complications of birth defects. In the United States the frequency of significant birth defects is about 2.5% (Center for Disease Control, 1978). In West Virginia it is slightly higher (3.4%), as determined by the State Bureau of Vital Statistics (1976). During the first year of life, an additional 6–8% of birth defects will become apparent. Of course, not all of these conditions are genetic, but the function of the geneticist and the primary physician is differentiating genetic from nongenetic causes of birth defects. In West Virginia approximately 12.9% of persons who die under the age of 20 do so from a birth defect; nationally, the figure is 10.9%. In West Virginia more people under 20 die from birth defects than from auto accidents!

Although statistics are presently available for only one year (West Virginia Bureau of Vital Statistics, 1976), the pattern of birth defects in West Virginia is very interesting. Of a total of 55 counties, 11 account for 1.2% of all births and 36% of all birth defects. Although it is not valid to make any generalizations based upon the statistics of a single year, the data warrant careful consideration. Some counties have birth defect frequencies exceeding 13%, and these include counties with large populations and metropolitan areas as well as sparsely populated rural areas. Thus, the increased frequency may not be due to random chance in a small population.

We need to investigate these matters, and we need to provide services aimed at evaluation, diagnosis, counseling, and treatment for these patients. Our challenge is to develop a genetics program that can alter the pattern and outcome of birth defects in West Virginia. The problem is solvable, and a successful parallel is available. In 1973 West Virginia was forty-nineth in infant mortality in the United States. By means of an aggressive perinatal program, the state improved significantly; in 1977 it was thirtieth in infant mortality. The state is manageable in terms of population (1.8 million in 1976), and the main medical–genetics resources are identifiable. The relevant agencies operate in cooperation rather than in competition. Funding for genetics has been from the March of Dimes, the West Virginia University Medical Center, the State Department of Health; and from the federal government through the National Genetic Disease Act.

This genetics program is built around several components. The first component is education, and to this end there were 47 programs for physicians, parent groups, teachers, and so on, in 1977. Capabilities for clinical and laboratory diagnosis were developed. A main genetics clinic was opened with an initial satellite clinic that has been expanded to two days per month, and other clinics are soon to be started. Our research has involved the applied problem of developing methods for altering the pattern of health care in a rural state. In general, educational programs aimed at large groups of physicians were ineffective. Programs aimed at smaller, local groups of physicians, care-giving agencies, and parent interest groups, together with newspaper articles, were more effective in producing referrals.

Continuation of referrals is dependent upon delivery of services that are perceived as satisfactory by patients and referring physicians. We aim to deliver rather extensive services of evaluation, diagnosis, treatment, and counseling. We must be aware of the families' reactions of shock, anger, guilt, embarrassment, depression, and isolation when confronted by a birth defect or genetic disease, and we aim to help the family through the process of adjustment. We avoid the antiquated model of talking to the family about institutionalization at the beginning (this is not really an alternative at first, anyway), because this fosters denial and has the potential to result in life-long rationalization. Instead, we help the family work through the process of coping so that they can act as advocates for their own children.

(Institutionalization may become relevant later if all resources fail, but it is not an alternative early in the process.)

IX. Prenatal Diagnosis

Early in the development of our program, many of our families had more than one affected individual. These were families that could have been helped to avoid recurrence of the disease condition. In addition to these families, some couples were in an increased empiric risk category. These included couples with a maternal age of 35 or a paternal age of 55. About three-fourths of the patients we see for prenatal diagnosis are at risk because of age, and one-fourth are at risk because of positive history.

Prenatal diagnosis includes counseling (involving the capabilities, limitations, and risks of the test along with background material about the techniques involved). We use ultrasonography and amniocentesis to eliminate the possibility of twins, measure the size of the fetus, locate fetal parts, and locate the appropriate "window" for amniocentesis. The latter technique involves placing a needle, under sterile conditions, into the amniotic sac and removing a small amount of amniotic fluid. This is not a terribly risky procedure if it is done carefully, but, like any invasive technique, it has the potential for morbidity and mortality for the fetus. Cells and fluid are removed and can be analyzed for chromosome composition and biochemical composition. The fluid can be analyzed for chemicals that may be present in unusual amounts. (Most often, we look for alpha-fetoprotein, which can be elevated in the presence of a neural tube defect or certain other abnormalities.) Approximately 4% of the patients we study have positive (abnormal) findings. Of our 12 positive findings to date, nine couples have opted for termination and three have elected to continue the pregnancy. A minimum of 10% of the couples we see were contemplating elective termination because of worry about a pregnancy late in life. From this data, we can see that amniocentesis is not tantamount to abortion. Prenatal diagnosis most often provides reassuring information to the parents, and this is so with approximately 96% of the patients we see.

A segment of the population tries to equate prenatal diagnosis with abortion and interprets modern medical genetics in terms of the old concept of eugenics. These people see geneticists as the embodiment of evil. They represent a vocal minority in the population of West Virginia and other states, and they can alter the climate for the practice of medical genetics. Rather than dismissing such interest groups as insignificant, it is worthwhile to maintain dialogue with them in order to emphasize the areas of common interest and to provide undistorted information about the practice of medical genetics and child advocacy for handicapped persons.

X. Conclusions

Do we intervene in people's lives? The answer is certainly yes. We intervened with newborn intensive care and infant transport in West Virginia, and we are attempting to do the same with genetics. We must recognize that it is more difficult to effect attitudinal change than to provide "rescue" medical service, but both can be accomplished. We must not overwhelm people with our technology; we must remember that parents see children as extensions of themselves and as their contribution to perpetuity. Genetic diseases and birth defects represent emotional problems that precipitate guilt and feelings of retribution for "past sins." We must be sensitive to these problems. Unfortunately, we do not have the opportunity for controlled experiments in the delivery of health care in West Virginia. We have no competing system to provide alternative genetic services for the people of the state, so it is our obligation to do the best we can. Genetic counseling in the long run will not be a function of an elite group, but a function of every physician. It will work best where there is an informed citizenry that demands the best kind of medical treatment.

REFERENCES

Center for Disease Control. *Congenital Malformations Surveillance Reports.* Washington, D.C., 1978.

Howard, T., & Rifkin, J. *Who should play God?* New York: Dell, 1977.

Hsia, Y. E. Appraisal of Counseling. In H. A. Lubs & F. de la Cruz (Eds.), *Genetic counseling.* New York: Raven Press, 1977.

Leonard, C., Chase, G., & Childs, B. Genetic counseling: A consumer's view. *New England Journal of Medicine,* 1972, *287,* 433–439.

Lubs, H. A., & de la Cruz, F. (Eds.). *Genetic counseling.* New York: Raven Press, 1977.

Sorensen, J. R., & Culbert, A. J. Genetic counselors and counseling orientation: Unexamined topics in evaluation. In H. A. Lubs & F. de la Cruz (Eds.), *Genetic counseling.* New York: Raven Press, 1977.

West Virginia State Bureau of Vital Statistics. Charleston: West Virginia Department of Health, 1976.

CHAPTER 10

Intervention in the Psychophysiology of Aging: Pitfalls, Progress, and Potential

DIANA S. WOODRUFF

TEMPLE UNIVERSITY
PHILADELPHIA, PENNSYLVANIA

I. Introduction

In an attempt to understand age changes in behavior, the psychology of aging has primarily involved the description of age-functional relationships over the life span. Beginning in the 1970s, however, geropsychologists recognized that some aspects of psychological aging had been described in sufficient detail so that hypotheses to explain these age changes could be generated; therefore, they called for an experimental psychology of aging (Birren, 1970) in which age-related variables would be manipulated and simulated (Baltes & Goulet, 1971). Still more recently, the call has been to extend experimental findings from the laboratory to life (Birren, 1974).

It is becoming very apparent that life-span developmental psychologists can initiate interventions that will affect the way life is lived and the age and time at which aging and death occur. Because of this tremendous responsibility, it is more important than ever that we carefully reflect on the manipulations we are attempting in order to make sure that we are optimizing the lives of those on whom we intervene. For this reason, it is important that we examine the pitfalls of past attempts at intervention, the

197

progress that we have clearly made in the 1970s, and the potential still remaining to be explored.

II. Pitfalls of Intervention Research

Perhaps because this chapter deals with psychophysiological intervention, I have taken a conservative stance. It is more apparent in psychophysiological interventions that we are dealing with life and death issues. However, many social and behavioral interventions often thought to be outside the realm of psychophysiology have psychophysiological implications and thus can determine life or death. Schooler and Rubenstein (see Chapter 6 of this volume) provide us with a definition of intervention, calling it activity that purposefully alters the course of events or behavior. What we often forget is that we can alter the course of events or behavior simply by *describing* the "pathology." An individual might be relegated to the back wards of an institution and expected to die on the basis of inappropriate measures and diagnosis. Thus, intervention is not simply a controlled experiment. Depending on one's perspective, intervention can affect the quality and quantity of life, or it can be very trivial in terms of its impact.

A. Jumping the Gun

It is my opinion that we have been in too much of a hurry to intervene for the sake of intervening. Science involves careful descriptive research, and it also involves explanation and modification (optimization) (Baltes, Reese, & Nesselroade, 1977). We should neither always experiment nor always rely on descriptive data. It has been pointed out that psychologists and other professionals have been too eager to experiment and intervene instead of developing descriptive strategies and looking more to guiding theoretical principles (Labouvie-Vief, 1973; Riegel, 1972; Woodruff, 1973). In an attempt to meet the urgent needs of society, we have become fascinated with experimentation and intervention. The problem is that attempts to perform experiments on human subjects have become the subject for debate concerning ethical questions. Thus, because of the risk of somehow damaging human subjects, particularly nonverbal infants and older individuals who have little choice or input on how to spend the last years of their lives, we avoid potentially stressful experimental manipulations. Of course, we must avoid pitfalls of the past in which inhumane experiments were performed on human subjects. At the same time, there are powerful design and analysis strategies that can be applied to descriptive developmental data and would permit us to make causal inferences about the variables involved (e.g., Achenbach, 1978; Baltes, Reese, & Nesselroade, 1977; Neale & Liebert, 1973; Wohlwill, 1973).

In the psychology of aging, it has been essential to demonstrate that phenomena that were once considered as indicating irreversible decline could be manipulated to simulate the behavior of younger organisms. However, it has also become possible to manipulate behaviors that are inappropriate for older people to learn. We geropsychologists have successfully managed to teach old people how to score better on intelligence tests, have enabled them to regain their "competence" by showing them how to solve problems in the manner that adolescents solve problems, and have improved their memory of paired associates by giving them verbal or visual cues. It cannot be denied that it was important to demonstrate empirically that older people could function as well as younger individuals during a period (the 1960s and early 1970s) when the aged were disparaged to the degree that "nobody over 30" was to be trusted. However, we now ask older people directly and indirectly to help contribute to our current understanding of the processes of aging. Since many of the older subjects refused to participate in intervention studies in which boring tasks were to be carried out, we have taken a new look at our procedures and designed ways to make tasks more interesting to the elderly. On such tasks, older individuals do perform more successfully, or at least as well as younger subjects (e.g., Baltes, Burgess, & Stewart, 1978; Labouvie-Vief, 1977; Plemons, Willis, & Baltes, 1978; Woodruff & Birren, 1972).

B. Reaction Time Studies: Pitfalls or Progress?

Many consider reaction time to be a rather uninteresting variable in psychology. Certainly, some of the reaction time tasks required of subjects do not engage their full attention, let alone their higher cognitive functioning. However, Sterns has discussed in this volume (see Chapter 14) and in other research reports (e.g., Sterns, Barrett, Alexander, Panek, Avolio, & Forbringer, 1977) the significance of even a few milliseconds when driving an automobile. Thus, human reaction time can become a life or death issue in the lives of elderly people (who die of accidental causes in far greater percentages than do adults between the ages of 30–65; U.S. Department of Health, Education and Welfare, 1970, 1974). Of course, this applies to the lives of individuals at all points in the life span as well. Some of my research has been directed at demonstrating the relationship between the slowing of behavior and the slowing of the electroencephalogram (EEG) alpha rhythm.

Since its discovery by Berger in the 1920s, the EEG alpha rhythm has been associated with the timing of behavior. Berger himself (1931) re-marked on the slowness of the EEG alpha rhythm in older adults. He believed that slowing was a function of senile dementia. Davis (1941) was the first to associate alpha slowing with normal aging processes. A number of cross-sectional studies of the EEG of healthy older adults have confirmed that the EEG alpha rhythm slows over the years between the thirties and the sixties about 1 or 2 Hz (cycles per second). Indeed, in a cross-sectional study, Surwillo (1963) has calculated EEG alpha slowing to occur at a rate of around .25 Hz per decade between the ages of 28 and 99 years. Similar results have been reported in longitudinal studies of EEG and aging (Obrist, Henry, & Justiss, 1961; Wang & Busse, 1969; Wang, Obrist, & Busse, 1970).

Although the major part of this chapter will deal with the adult portion of the life cycle, it is important to note that the EEG alpha rhythm changes in frequency and amplitude at several points in the life span. Lindsley (1936) was the first scientist in the United States to report data collection on the electroencephalogram. His data were collected on children and young adults, and he found that children had slower EEG alpha rhythms. Children also have slower reaction times than young adults (e.g., Surwillo, 1971, 1975). Thus, age changes in the EEG alpha rhythm provide a useful means of pointing out when significant changes in behavior and physiology occur.

On the surface, the attempt to train individuals to modify their brain waves—so that reaction time would be affected—may appear trivial, especially since changes in EEG frequency have affected reaction time by only around 10% or 20 msec (Woodruff, 1975). On the other hand, the literature on aging and EEG points so overwhelmingly to the "deterioration" of the central nervous system (CNS) that even a 20 msec change could be regarded behaviorally as well as statistically significant.

C. The Significance of Alpha Slowing

Investigators have reported four major changes in the brain wave activity of older adults. These include changes in frequency and abundance of alpha rhythm, changes in the incidence of fast activity, diffuse slowing (especially noted in institutionalized elderly), focal slowing, and abnormal activity in the temporal lobes (Marsh & Thompson, 1977, Obrist & Busse, 1965; Thompson & Marsh, 1973). The most reliable age change in EEG activity is the slowing of the dominant frequency, the alpha rhythm.

When an individual is awake but in a relaxed state (with closed eyes or otherwise lacking visual stimulation), the EEG recorded from surface electrodes placed over the occipital area contains easily detectable, large amplitude waves of 8–13 Hz. These are called alpha waves or alpha rhythm.

As mentioned previously, a domain of behavior in which alpha slowing may have significance is speed and timing. Consideration of the alpha rhythm as a timing mechanism for behavior began almost as early as the discovery of the human EEG; in a review of the early literature, Lindsley (1952) noted that Bishop (1933) and Jasper (1936) found relationships in animals between rhythmic cortical activity and brightness enhancement. At this time Lindsley made a distinction between alpha rhythm—the high amplitude rhythmic activity recorded in humans from scalp electrodes and most apparent in posterior leads—and alpha activity—the periodic waxing and waning in excitability of cortical cells that would not be recorded with scalp electrodes when large numbers of cells were not synchronized. Lindsley emphasized that alpha activity was always present in the brain even when alpha rhythm could not be recorded, and he suggested that a cycle of approximately 10 Hz as reflected in the alpha rhythm is the basic metabolic rhythm of brain cells. A large body of research literature has accumulated to support Lindsley's contention that the alpha frequency is related to excitability in the nervous system.

In a review of the literature pertaining to a periodic basis for perception and action, Sanford (1971) summarized the studies demonstrating relationships between alpha rhythm and the timing of a variety of behaviors by placing them in two major categories: studies related to alpha frequency and studies related to alpha phase. Along with two major strategies for measuring alpha–behavior relationships are two general rationales or hypotheses regarding the nature of the relationship. The more general hypothesis involving arousal suggests that brain wave frequency is associated with different states of consciousness and excitability of the cortex. Studies designed with this rationale often measure brain wave activity that is faster or slower than alpha bandwidths as well as measuring alpha; slow frequencies are associated with low arousal and slow reaction time, and faster frequencies are associated with higher arousal and faster reaction time. In those studies that attempt to relate behavioral timing to phases on the alpha wave, an excitability cycle hypothesis is used, and Sanford (1971) pointed out that there are two forms of this hypothesis. The first rationale suggests that the waxing and waning of excitability in the nervous system is marked by the alpha rhythm; it also suggests that signals input at points in the cycle close to the point of maximal excitability will be processed and responded to more quickly than signals input at less optimal points. The other hypothesis involving the concept of *perceptual moment* is more specific, making simple and precise predictions about reaction time. The notion is that stimuli are sampled at discrete intervals of time; longest reaction times will occur if a stimulus is presented when a new sample is just beginning, and shortest reaction times should occur when a sample is just about to end. Since the alpha cycle (lasting 100 msec for a 10 Hz alpha rhythm) is related to the points where the sample opens and closes, there is a strong relation between the phase at which a stimulus is presented and the time it takes for the subject to recognize that it has been presented. The subject cannot react to the stimulus until he perceives it; therefore, reaction time is a function of alpha phase, and the maximum difference between reaction times obtained in this way should be equal to the duration of one *moment* or *scan* (predicted to be around 100 msec for a full alpha cycle or 50 msec if the alpha half wave represents the *scan*) (Kristofferson, 1967). All of these hypotheses predict that slowing of alpha frequency would lead to slower perception and reaction, and sufficient data have accumulated so that an examination of both the arousal hypothesis and the excitability cycle hypothesis is warranted.

The finding that alpha activity could be manipulated in older individuals (Woodruff, 1975) suggested reversibility of "deterioration." It suggested plasticity in the older central nervous system (CNS). This work also demonstrated a relationship between EEG and reaction time. Presently, I am working to determine if age-related changes in the alpha rhythm affect behaviors other than reaction time—behaviors such as attention, mood, and information-processing. The aim of my current research is to answer puzzling questions about the significance of the slowing of the EEG alpha rhythm.

D. To Speed or Slow—That Is the Question

The typical interpretation of the fact that alpha frequency slows with age in that pathology is involved. The biological, decremental model of aging is invoked. Hence, when I attempted to train young and old subjects to produce EEG alpha rhythms slower and faster than their modal alpha frequency (Woodruff, 1975), it was anticipated that the production of faster alpha rhythms would be experienced in both young and old as a more pleasant state. Figure 10.1 illustrates the actual learning trials for young and old subjects. It can be seen in these data that old subjects took fewer trials to reach the criterion of producing slow waves. Young subjects were able to increase fast alpha rhythms in fewer trials. Anecdotal reports of the subjects suggested that slowing of alpha frequency (to produce more activity in the 7–9 Hz frequency bandwidths) was a pleasant experience. Neither the young nor the old subjects enjoyed producing faster activity as much as producing slow activity. (Subjects were unaware of the frequency for which they were reinforced.) The young subjects enjoyed producing brain waves in the dominant frequency range of the old subjects. This anecdotal finding has been reported to occur in at least one other laboratory (Duke University) by Larry Thompson (personal communication, May 1974). Thompson reported that some of his subjects refused to continue in the fast EEG condition. Subjects found slow modal alpha activity to be pleasant. Indeed, EEG activity in the 7–9 Hz bandwidth has been associated with creativity (Green, Green, & Walters, 1970). Both young and old subjects liked decreasing alpha bordering on the theta (4–7 Hz) range.

These data lead to another issue that is problematic in intervention research: What is the goal of the intervention? It seems that we always try to make the old more like young or adolescent individuals. A number of life-span developmentalists have highlighted behaviors that the aged perform better than younger subjects (Birren, 1969; Chandler, Chapter 4 of this volume; Labouvie-Vief & Chandler, 1978; Schaie, 1977). Very few scientists have studied the aged from the perspective of the aged themselves. Notable exceptions include G. Stanley Hall (1922) and Simone de Beauvoir (1972), who have written rather bitterly about the fate of aging. Certainly, the struggle and frustration of elderly cohorts in the 1960s and 1970s are expressed by Hall and De Beauvoir. Furthermore, the way society views aging at the present time makes it rather difficult to be old. Reflecting society's trend, psychologists have contributed to the dismal perspective of the aged. For example, developmental psychologists have standardized tests that are designed to measure children, adolescents, and very young adults. The apex of behavior on these tests is at best young adulthood (some are designed only for children). When older individuals deviate from the scores of the young, they are labeled as deficient. Deviation from norms standardized in younger samples is interpreted as decline. As of 1979, in developmental psychology we have almost no tests created from naturalistic observation of old people. This indicates that we need more descriptive data on the perspective of our elders.

Erik Erikson (1963) is perhaps one of the few life-span developmentalists who have tried to take an overview of life in terms of stages of development. His psychosocial life crises, along with the developmental tasks of Havighurst (1972), have implied that adults at different periods of adulthood are concerned with different issues. Social and cognitive behavior may be focused on different issues in a given cohort of 60-year-olds than in a cohort of 20- to 30-year-olds. This suggests that each age-stage may have its own relevant view; to compare across different ages and cohorts and to call some deviation from performance a decline is simply not valid. What was so clear with regard to race and sex in the 1960s is now becoming apparent with regard to old age. The difference is that almost all of us are going to be old—almost all of us will be in that minority group

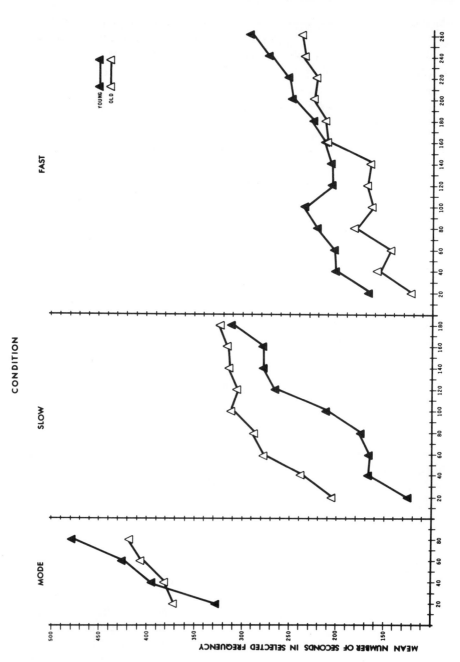

204

which is less respected and more poorly taken care of than any other group in the life span. Youth should not necessarily be the yardstick for old age. We need a great deal more descriptive data before we blindly intervene, lest our interventions be fatal.

E. Historical and Current Examples of the Problem of Haste in the Psychophysiology of Aging

According to Comfort's (1964) history of gerontological research, the first gerontological experiment was performed long before it was known that hormones existed. On June 1, 1889, the 73-year-old French physiologist Charles Brown-Sequard revealed that he felt rejuvenated because he had been experimenting on himself by injecting extracts from the testicles of monkeys. For this brave and pioneering work, Brown-Sequard was ridiculed and accused of senility. Although he said he felt 30 years younger, he died 5 years later at the age of 78.

Brown-Sequard's research was followed up by the Russian surgeon Voronoff, who transplanted chimpanzee testicles onto men. Considering the shock to the immune system, it is surprising that the patients survived.

Although both of these interventions were radical and seemingly absurd, many gerontologists still believe that hormones and the endocrine system hold the secrets of aging. Our attempts at intervention in the 1970s are not quite so radical; however, they might be considered equally laughable in future eras.

Another uncomfortable intervention was designed by Dr. Frederick Hoelzel in 1920. Hoelzel was convinced that overeating killed people early in the life span, and he was aware of the psychological problems of hunger pangs. Hoelzel's research aim was to discover a substance that would make people feel full. He first tried sand and commented, "I had no difficulty in swallowing moist sea sand seasoned with salt. The swallowing of about 4 oz. of sand made me feel as if I had eaten a meal. In fact it made me feel for a time that I had eaten too much . . . [quoted by Comfort, 1964, p.

Figure 10.1. Change in abundance of modal alpha frequency is shown for 10 young and 10 old experimental subjects who received biofeedback at three different brain wave frequencies (modal frequency, 2 Hz slower than modal frequency, 2 Hz faster than modal frequency). It is apparent that the task of producing alpha frequency 2 Hz slower than mode was carried out much more quickly than the task of producing alpha frequency 2 Hz faster than mode. This difference was significant at the .001 level of confidence. [Copyright © 1975, The Society for Psychophysiological Research. Reprinted with permission of the publisher from D. S. Woodruff, "Relationships among EEG alpha frequency, reaction time and aging: A biofeedback study." *Psychophysiology*, 1975, *12*, 673–681.]

91]." There was a problem with this diet. The sand was too heavy and irritating for repeated use. Hoelzel also tried glass beads, which had the same unfortunate consequences as sand. Finally, he discovered 'that using cellulose and psylluim seed avoided the drawbacks of the first two food substitutes. This filling is still currently used in some diet foods, and it appears that there are still some serious questions about whether the cellulose does more harm to the body than good.

At least Hoelzel and Brown-Sequard were gentlemen inasmuch as they experimented on themselves. In case we are lulled by historical examples into thinking that we are smarter today in the psychophysiology of aging, there are a few more recent examples of rejuvenating treatments. In the late 1960s, biological and behavioral scientists were interested in the question of whether RNA affected memory. Examination of the brains of accident victims of various ages led Hyden (1969) to demonstrate that there was less RNA in the brains of older subjects than younger subjects. Excited about the potential of a "memory drug," some researchers fed yeast RNA to old people in nursing homes, and the researchers claimed that the treated patients' memory improved. To follow up such work, we (Nordgren, Woodruff, & Bick, 1970) attempted to determine if RNA even got beyond the blood brain barrier in rats. The purpose of the study was to see if RNA worked as a nutrient to the brain, supplying substrates necessary to build more RNA. Rats were trained on a discrimination task to bar press. Their behavior was then examined after they had been injected with RNA (either whole RNA or the broken-down substrates of RNA) or a placebo. There were no behavioral differences between the rats injected with RNA and those treated with the placebo. We concluded along with many other laboratories that those who sought to establish a relationship between RNA and memory overclaimed the positive effects of RNA.

Hyperberic oxygen research also seems to have exaggerated the usefulness of this treatment on cognition and memory in adulthood. Thompson has published extensive attempts to replicate some of the earlier hyperberic research with more control over the experimental conditions (Thompson, 1975; Thompson, Davis, Obrist, & Heyman, 1976). He was unable to find changes in behavior or EEG as a function of hyperberic oxygen treatment.

Gerovital, a drug that may work as an antidepressant, is being tested in the United States after being used for years as a rejuvenation treatment by Anna Aslan and her colleagues in Rumania. Aslan shows pictures of her subjects before and after the treatment, and she claims that years are added to the life span, that baldness disappears, that wrinkles are eliminated, and that sexual potency returns. In the pictures, the subjects may look happier simply because this antidepressant drug makes them feel less depressed.

The common denominator of all of these treatments is to rejuvenate the individual, and many people flock to centers where such treatments are available and pay large sums of money for the treatment. The view of aging is so negative in Western society that miracle cures are sought. People are willing to believe a great deal to regain their youth. Their naivete typically leads to big disappointments. For this reason, intervention research must be taken very seriously. I feel that we should be more skeptical of the intervention procedure at the beginning of the project. At the same time, it is urgent that psychologists get involved in alleviating major problems in aging. It is time for us to start playing a more active role in making it possible for individuals to live out their later years in good psychological as well as physiological health.

III. Progress of Intervention Research

More progress in interventions to make life longer and of a higher quality in terms of education, health, and economic solvency has been achieved in the twentieth century than in any other time in human existence (Woodruff, 1977). To highlight some of this progress, human life expectancy will be used as an example.

Since 1900 science and technology have added 25 years to the average life expectancy. The gains in life expectancy are primarily in the earlier years (e.g., prevention of high infant mortality). This has resulted in increasing the percentage of middle-aged and older adults in the population of the United States, Europe, Japan, and the U.S.S.R. The advances have come primarily in the field of medicine, but we may be reaching a point at which medicine has to look to psychology for assistance in carrying out the work of helping people to live longer. Gains up to the present have been in the development of antibiotic drugs, sanitation, pasturization, health care to a greater percentage of the population, and childbirth practices. Major gains in life expectancy are presently available to individuals who can actually choose (consciously or unconsciously) to live longer. Physicians are now turning to psychologists to find out what gives life satisfaction in adulthood so that they can be more effective in improving health. Psychologists need to contribute in a number of areas concerning how to *motivate* people to take care of their health.

A. Factors in the Domain of Psychology that Affect Life Expectancy

Psychologists have made real progress in alleviating the hindrances to good health. The following pages give some examples of how psychologists have contributed.

1. Smoking

Without doubt, smoking has been shown to shorten life. It has been estimated that smoking two packages of cigarettes a day shortens life by at least 14 years. A great deal of psychological research has been invested in the problem of smoking, and the U.S. Department of Health, Education, and Welfare is now attempting to use psychological techniques in convincing people to quit. The efforts of scientists and the federal government have been remarkably successful in convincing individuals to stop smoking. Statistics from the American Cancer Society indicate that the percentage of individuals in the United States who smoke has dropped rather dramatically in the last decade. As can be seen in Table 10.1, the percentage of men over 21 who smoke has dropped from 52.4% in the mid-1960s to 39.3% in the mid-1970s. The only group in which there is an increase in smoking is teen-aged girls, for whom the percentage who smoke has increased from 22% to 27%. Many psychologists have been successful in helping people to quit smoking with the use of operant strategies and psychotherapy.

2. Diet

Nutrition is a complex field and one in which much more research needs to be carried out. There is little question that obesity shortens life expectancy. There is also general agreement that nutrition influences health and longevity. The maintenance of a moderate caloric intake with the proper balance of nutrients is a common feature in the life style of extremely long-lived individuals (Leaf, 1973). Furthermore, in animal research one of the very few manipulations that have worked to actually extend the life span of individual animals in the species has been to restrict caloric intake in early life (McCay, 1952).

In humans there is suggestive evidence that health and vigor, and even

Table 10.1

Percentage of Male and Female Smokers in Two Age Groups in 1964–1966, 1969–1970, and 1975 [a]

| | Age 21 and over | | Teen-aged | |
	Men	Women	Girls	Boys
1964–1966	52.4	32.5	—	—
1969–1970	42.2	30.5	22	31
1975	39.3	28.9	27	30

[a] Data are from the American Cancer Society.

greater life satisfaction, occur when normal body weight is maintained. Older individuals of moderate weight have fewer complaints and illnesses than their obese counterparts (Palmore, 1971). A most telling study was carried out by Olefsky, Reavan, and Farquhar (1974). They studied men and women who were mildly overweight and engaged them in a program to lose weight. The average weight loss was 24 pounds—a loss attainable by most without a great deal of sacrifice. This modest weight loss had profound metabolic consequences. Among the positive results, cholesterol levels fell from 282 mg/dl—far above the 250 mg danger level—to 223 mg, thus approaching the safe 200 mg level. Moderate changes in body weight and nutrition led to dramatic changes in risk factors for heart disease. Such data indicate that we do not have to undertake Herculean measures to extend our life expectancy. Simply losing 20 pounds can change many individuals from being at high risk for diseases to being safe from the dangers leading to major causes of death. Many social psychologists have been working on weight loss strategies and have successfully helped clients to lose weight. Life-span developmental psychologists could also contribute by identifying patterns of eating laid down early in life and their effect on weight in adolescence, adulthood, and old age.

3. Exercise

H. A. deVries, an exercise physiologist, demonstrated in both men and women that physiological efficiency was greater in experimental groups participating in a carefully planned exercise program than in nonexercising control groups (deVries, 1970, 1975; deVries & Adams, 1972; Adams & deVries, 1973). He also showed that a 15-minute brisk walk produced more muscle relaxation than 400 mg *meprobamite* (a commonly used tranquilizer pill supplied on prescription as either *Miltown* or *Equanil*). A decade after deVries' work, most programs for older individuals include an exercise component. Psychologists following up deVries' physiological work are finding that mood changes occur in those individuals who maintain an exercise regimen (Tredway, 1978). There is a need for psychologists to understand motivational aspects of maintaining regular exercise and to collect more empirical data on the psychological benefits of regular exercise.

4. Stress

Personality assessed with paper and pencil tests as well as with clinical evaluation appears to be as good a predictor of cardiovascular disease as cholesterol level, blood pressure, and smoking (Friedman & Rosenman, 1974; Woodruff, 1977). Psychologists are now using relaxation training, behavior modification, yoga, exercise, and meditation to help individuals with a high risk of cardiovascular disease to change and exhibit the personality traits of low-risk individuals, thus making *Type A* individuals into *Type B* individuals in terms of personality traits. Since it is possible that the Type A personality patterns may be engendered by social and environmental factors occurring early in life, there is a need for more information from life-span developmental psychologists who could empirically demonstrate the early life correlates of later onset of cardiovascular disease.

Several life-span developmental theories of personality center around the notion that successful adjustment involves mastering a series of stresses that confront the individual at various points in his or her life. These stresses have been variously called *psychosocial crises* (Erikson, 1963) and *developmental tasks* (Havighurst, 1972). In young adulthood, developmental tasks involve change and stress because the individual must find and develop an intimate relationship with a mate, establish himself or herself in an occupation, and bear and rear children. The stresses of middle age involve launching the children, establishing social and financial security, caring for aging parents, and adjusting to changing physical capacity and social status. In old age, change and stress are enormous as people face retirement, grief at the loss of friends and intimates, illness, and finally impending death. Stress is a part of life that cannot be escaped. However, greater longevity occurs when individuals learn to cope with stress effectively instead of avoiding it.

B. Other Significant Interventions in the Psychophysiology of Aging

In addition to extending life expectancy, there are a number of interventions in the psychophysiology of life-span development and aging that affect the quality of life. The three interventions to be discussed here are biofeedback, drug therapy, and assessment with computerized axial tomography.

1. Biofeedback Conditioning

Though the concept and technique of biofeedback has been extant since the development of electronic amplifiers for the study of physiological data, it has been a focus of major investigation only since the 1960s. The impetus of biofeedback research came from attempts to evoke autonomic responses through operant conditioning (see Miller, 1969, for a review) and from attempts to determine if subjects could discriminate and control various brain wave states (Kamiya, 1968). The reported success of these attempts encouraged researchers and clinicians to apply biofeedback techniques to a wide range of physiological functions and rates.

In 1962 Kamiya presented a paper suggesting that subjects could discriminate different states of their own EEG frequency; he later demonstrated that subjects could reliably learn to produce or suppress EEG activity in the bandwidths of the alpha rhythm (Kamiya, 1968). Subsequently, he reported that subjects could learn to control EEG activity in specific frequencies within the alpha rhythm (Kamiya, 1969), and he claimed that subjects could discriminate and be conditioned to produce frequencies as close together as .25 Hz (Kamiya, 1970). Numerous investigators report that they have replicated Kamiya's work (e.g., Beatty, 1971, 1972; Beatty & Kornfeld, 1972; Brown, 1970, 1971; Hardt, 1974; Kondo, Travis, & Knott, 1975; Travis, Kondo, & Knott, 1974; Walsh, 1974; Woodruff, 1975). Although aspects of these results have been challenged (e.g., Brolund & Schallow, 1976; Lynch & Paskewitz, 1971; Lynch, Paskewitz, & Orne, 1974; Paskewitz & Orne, 1973; Plotkin, 1976), sufficient data has accumulated to suggest that subjects can exert some control over their brain waves (Brolund & Schallow, 1976; Hardt & Kamiya, 1976).

Investigators reporting success with EEG feedback training have focused primarily on the alpha rhythm, and they have found that subjects can control the percentage of time in which they produce alpha rhythm. The typical procedure has been to place subjects in an electronic feedback loop that gives them information about presence of their alpha rhythm. Feedback has been visual, auditory, or both, and subjects have learned to control turning on and off short alpha bursts or to shift to greater periods of alpha.

The early work in this area stimulated considerable interest. It has been demonstrated that any number of visceral, glandular, and EEG responses can be operantly conditioned once discriminable cues are made available to the organism and appropriate reinforcers are determined. The potential clinical application of this technique has been considered, and in some instances demonstrated, for extensive clinical problems including essential hypertension, cardiac arrhythmia, tension and migraine headaches, anxiety and fear reduction, Raynaud's disease, reduction of pain, and problems of learning and attention—to name just a few (see Blanchard & Young, 1974; Budzynski, 1973; Shapiro & Schwartz, 1972, for reviews). Seminars on biofeedback techniques are attracting physicians, psychiatrists, physical therapists, and psychologists, and in some cases biofeedback is being incorporated into clinical practice.

The area of biofeedback research is not without its critics and controversies. There have been numerous problems in replication of EEG studies (as noted earlier) and of some of the earlier animal studies (Obrist, Black, Brenner, & Dicara, 1974). Self-control of cardiac functioning by means of operant techniques is believed by some to be more statistically significant than clinically useful (Blanchard & Young, 1973). Most unfortunately, the grandiose claims made for alpha training by commercial organizations precipitated an intense reaction on the part of many leading psychophysiologists that was generalized to other substantial research efforts in this area. This overzealousness on the part of commercial operations has subsided, however, and the persistence of respected researchers in working with biofeedback has been accepted by most as evidence that this approach merits serious investigation.

Thus, in addition to criticisms and controversies, there have been reliable findings reported, and the potential usefulness of operant techniques in the biofeedback framework is beginning to be given a fair test. Studies reporting absence of results from only brief training periods are in some cases being contradicted by studies of longer periods of training. Furthermore, some studies that extend procedures into clinical settings argue strongly that continued research and application must not be overlooked. For example, Weiss and Engel (1971) reported decreased preventricular contractions (PVCs) in four of eight patients in a ward setting during and immediately after heart rate training; moreover, three patients showed reduced frequency in a 21-month follow-up examination. All of the patients who successfully learned to decrease PVC's had at least 47 training sessions. Another study that supports this point is the finding by Sterman, MacDonald, and Stone (1973) that the enhancement of the so-called sensorimotor response in the EEG by operant procedures resulted in decreased frequency of seizures and reduced medication requirements in select patients with epilepsy.

As of 1979, the use of biofeedback techniques in aging research has been minimal. In a study described previously Woodruff (1975) demonstrated that the old performed as well as the young on a biofeedback task. Brannon (1976) demonstrated that alpha abundance could be increased with biofeedback in old subjects. In addition, Woodruff (1975) and Beatty, Greenberg, Deibler, and O'Hanlon (1974) demonstrated that biofeedback changes of EEG activity can lead to changes in performance. The significance of this work is all the more salient when viewed in the context of other research pertaining to EEG changes with age and to EEG and performance. Biofeedback manipulation of EEG in young and old adults may lead to insights about EEG–behavior relationships and resolve theoretical controversies revolving around the excitability cycle and arousal hypotheses. Biofeedback may also provide a means to intervene into deleterious age changes in performance.

2. Drugs

It is not within the scope of this chapter to mention all of the various drug treatments that have been successfully used to facilitate cognition and emotion and to alleviate pain and pathology in adulthood and old age. There is tremendous potential in the psychophysiology of aging to use biochemical methods to reduce disease and extend life in both quality and quantity. As mentioned earlier, responses to psychological stress are a major problem in adulthood and old age, and tranquilizing and antidepressant drugs are used extensively to alleviate symptoms of stress. Drugs to reduce high blood pressure and anticoagulant drugs are used to help the cardiovascular system to function more efficiently. Parkinson's disease can be relatively simply treated with substrates of neurotransmitters.

There are some biochemical changes in aging that may occur in individuals as part of normal aging processes. For example, Adelman (1975; Adelman, Britton, Rotenberg, Ceci, & Karoly, 1978) has demonstrated that the absence or the lower concentration of some enzymes leads to an imbalance that may induce diabetes in older individuals. The behavioral consequences of such age changes are not known. There is some evidence, however, that decreased availability of some biochemical substances does affect behavior in the aged.

A Nobel Prize was awarded in 1977 to Yalow, Guillemin, and Schally for their work on peptide hormone production of the brain. It has been demonstrated repeatedly that a number of short-chain polypeptide hormones such as melanocyte stimulating hormone (MSH) and adrenocorticotrophic hormone (ACTH) have a significant effect on brain–behavior relationships in humans and animals. A fragment of these peptides, MSH/ACTH 4–10, has been shown to be the behaviorally active core of each. The fragment appears to affect electrophysiological brain activity and to facilitate attention, learning, and memory in normal adult humans as well as in retarded adults (Kastin, Sandman, Stratton, Schally, & Miller, 1975; Miller, Harris, Van Riezen, & Kastin, 1976). This work has been extended in a sample of 13 older individuals (64–85 years old). In a double-blind study (Miller, Groves, Bopp, & Kastin, 1978) it was demonstrated that the injection of MSH/ACTH 4–10 resulted in a statistically significant increase in performance on the Benton Visual Retention Test in older subjects. Although blood, liver, free fatty acid, and urine profiles were not affected by MSH/ACTH 4–10 administration, visual memory showed a 30% improvement. However, there was great variability in individual performance; some subjects showed 100% improvement in the number of errors on the Benton scale, while others showed no improvement. It was concluded that cognitive functioning in some individuals may be related to decreased availability of neuropeptides to the aging brain. Given Adelman's (1975; Adelman *et al.,* 1978) finding that some enzymes used to break down complex molecules may not be available in the aging brain, it may be true that the enzymes involved in the breakdown of MSH and ACTH are less functional in later life. Another possibility is that there is a decreased availability of peptides to the aging brain.

The degree to which social and environmental influences contribute to age changes in biochemical processes is unknown. For example, in the study of depression, it is impossible at the present level of knowledge to separate the clear social and emotional losses that accompany aging in most societies from the biochemical changes. Biochemical changes might be due solely to physiological age change, due solely to physical, psychological, and social loss, or due to some combination of all of these factors. DeVries' (e.g., 1970, 1975) work with exercise physiology suggests that behavioral interventions such as exercise may have as significant effects as a pill (tranquilizer) and that moderate exercise may have fewer negative side effects than medication. Tredway's (1978) research makes it clear that participation in an exercise program can significantly affect mood. Participants were more cheerful, more energetic, less discouraged, and less tense after 15 weeks of an exercise program; moreover, the program appeared to facilitate social activity, thus having social as well as physiological and psychological effects.

3. Technological Advances in Assessment

Assessment is typically viewed as a descriptive procedure rather than an experimental technique. If intervention is defined as "activity that purposefully alters the course of events or behavior [Schooler & Rubenstein, Chapter 6 of this volume]," then assessment can be considered an intervention procedure. In the initial phases of the treatment, it is essential that proper diagnosis occur. Several new tools developed in the 1970s have tremendous potential for application on older populations. These measures allow us to visualize the brain structure of the *living* brain and to quantify brain response to stimulation. Even though all assessment tools have problems, these tools increase the level of certainty in assessment. One of these techniques, computerized axial tomography (CAT), is being used for diagnosis in older adults and in research on aging. The other technique, the event related potential (ERP), holds promise for future diagnostic use with the aging and is already in use at earlier points in the life span. ERPs are also being actively researched in laboratories across the country.

a. Computerized Axial Tomography. One of the major aims of research in the psychology of aging has been to pinpoint the parts of the nervous system in which age-related changes lead to the observed age changes in behavior. For the most part, this research has used behavioral measures to make inferences about the locus of age changes in the nervous system because direct measures of the nervous system were not available. Many of these studies implicated the central nervous system (CNS) as the locus of the major changes leading to behavioral deficits, but it has been difficult to validate or extend these inferences because the CNS is the most difficult part of the nervous system to measure. Clinical gerontologists and geriatricians have been faced with the same problem. In order to assess patients with behavioral disorders, they have had to use indirect measures of nervous system function or dangerous invasive techniques that involved risks and potential complications for their patients (e.g., angiography, pneumoencephalography). Computerized axial tomography is as safe and painless as any X-ray technique.

A significant minority of the aged population suffers from the gradual onset of impaired orientation, memory, judgment, and intellectual function. These are the classical symptoms of senile dementia, and prognosis for patients with this condition, which usually involves significant cerebral atrophy, is presently very poor. Behavioral symptoms of dementia may also result from treatable illnesses such as brain tumors, hemorrhages, or hypothyroidism; it is important to rule out these possibilities before diagnosing the case as senile dementia. Computerized axial tomography has been useful in this regard because it is a method of visualizing cerebral structures including the ventricular system and cortical sulci. The value of this technique in neurological assessment of patients of all ages is so great and has been recognized so rapidly that many hospitals throughout the country have installed the relatively expensive apparatus required for this procedure, even though it has become commercially available only since the mid 1970s. Thus, CAT scanning can be used in most large cities in the United States to assess geriatric patients showing symptoms of cerebral impairment, and it can be undertaken upon referral by the attending physician.

Figure 10.2 shows a patient being assessed with CAT. A rotating X-ray source takes over 28,000 readings in approximately 5 minutes. This usually consists of a scan that has viewed two continuous slices of brain tissue in a transaxial plane at a selected level. The entire procedure takes less than half an hour if the patient is cooperative and remains still.

The readings are processed by a computer that calculates 6400 absorption values in each slice. The computer calculates the density of tissue scanned by the X-ray beam, and different densities of tissue are translated into lighter or darker areas on a cathode-ray tube display. A Polaroid photograph is then taken of the display so that a permanent record can be assessed by a neuroradiologist or neurologist. The data are also stored on magnetic tape.

The resultant photograph is essentially a picture of a transaxial slice of the brain. The information obtained is directly related to the absorption characteristics of the tissue assessed, and these absorption characteristics

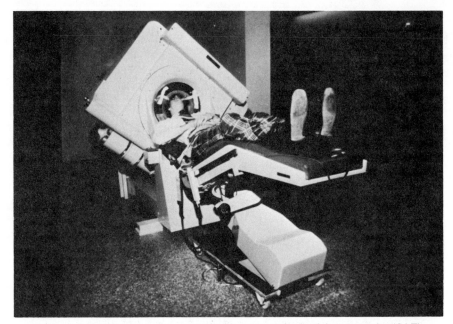

Figure 10.2. Patient is being assessed with computerized axial tomography (CAT).

are functions of the physical density and the atomic number of the elements present in the tissues. Bone and calcified areas that are dense look white in the computerized tomograms, grey matter of the brain looks gray, and the least dense areas, the ventricles, look almost black.

Figure 10.3 shows tomograms at two levels of the brain of a patient who came to the Baer Consultation and Diagnostic Center at the Philadelphia Geriatric Center. The patient, a man of 72, came to the center because he occasionally felt woozy, and he had experienced one episode in which he had forgotten what he was saying in the middle of a sentence. Since he is a very competent individual still holding a responsible position, he was concerned about this experience and wanted to know if he was neurologically impaired. The computerized tomogram along with the neurological, psychological, and psychiatric assessments of this man reassured him. All were normal, and the tomograms in Figure 10.3 show a normal old brain. The ventricles are small and hardly discernable, and no sulci are apparent.

The next computerized tomogram (Figure 10.4) shows a tumor in the right parietal area. The tumor shows up as a darker area, being less dense than neural tissue. This patient, a 71-year-old male, was assessed by the psychiatrist and the neurologist as moderately impaired, but his performance on psychological tests was normal. His neurological impairment is potentially treatable.

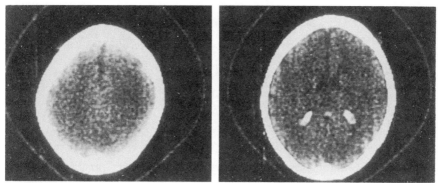

Figure 10.3. CAT scan of 72-year-old male shows the absence of brain pathology.

This is not the case for the patient whose tomogram is shown in Figure 10.5. She is an 83-year-old woman with a diagnosis of senile dementia. Neurological, psychiatric, and psychological assessment showed this woman to be moderately to severely impaired, and the CAT scan confirmed the diagnosis of senile dementia. The ventricles and a number of sulci are enlarged, indicating rather widespread cerebral atrophy characteristic of most senile dementia patients.

Huckman and his associates (Huckman, Fox, & Topel, 1975) at St. Luke's Medical Center in Chicago have devised and attempted to validate specific quantitative criteria for evaluation of cerebral atrophy and senile dementia. They have indicated that both enlarged ventricles and enlarged sulci are necessary for a reliable diagnosis of senile dementia, and they have provided numerical standards for the width of the ventricles at two points and for the width of the four largest sulci that can be considered atrophied (Huckman *et al.*, 1975). Huckman and his colleagues demonstrated that

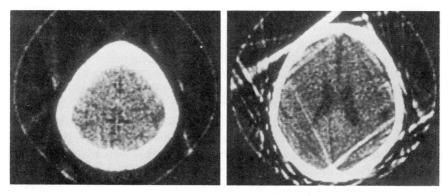

Figure 10.4. CAT scan of 71-year-old male shows tumor in the right parietal area. Tumor shows as darker area.

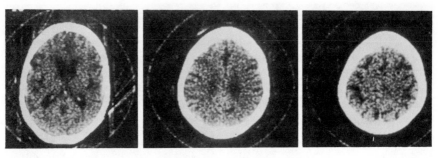

Figure 10.5. CAT scan shows 83-year-old woman with diagnosis of senile dementia. Ventricles and sulci are enlarged, indicating degeneration of brain tissue.

these criteria applied to tomograms yielded results as reliable as assessments based on pneumoencephalographic examination and pathologic examination at autopsy. These investigators also replicated the long-known observation that senile dementia is not always perfectly correlated with cerebral pathology. As has been noted in many pathologic studies of senile dementia, there are cases of behavioral dementia in which there is no apparent cerebral atrophy, and there are cases of cerebral atrophy in the absence of behavioral dementia. Thus, the same factors that limit pneumoencephalography and even pathologic examination of the brain also limit CAT scanning. Nevertheless, Huckman *et al.* (1975) reported that the expected incidence of atrophy in demented patients, as determined by sulcal and ventricular size with pneumoencephalography, was shown to be 85% in Gosling's report on 68 patients with senile dementia. With CAT scanning the incidence of atrophy was 80%, taking into account both sulcal enlargement and ventricular enlargement. Hence, in a great majority of senile dementia cases, CAT scanning is a safe method to confirm the diagnosis.

Computerized axial tomography is also useful in identifying treatable cases. In Huckman's group of 35 patients with a clinical diagnosis of senile dementia as determined by neurologists, CAT scans identified three patients who had potentially treatable illnesses (Huckman *et al.,* 1975) This 10% rate of potentially reversible cases clearly highlights the value of CAT in the assessment of senile dementia. The ability to "visualize" the living brain adds an additional degree of certainty to the diagnosis, and it may prevent unnecessary institutionalization of patients who show behavioral and neurological symptoms of senile dementia but actually have other treatable illnesses.

In a study of 15 elderly psychiatric patients residing in boarding homes in the Philadelphia area, Nathan, Gonzalez, and Laffey (1975) found clear relationships between severely demented patients and cerebral atrophy as assessed by CAT as well as relationships between patients with little evidence of dementia and normal computerized tomograms. However, they cautioned that patients in the middle range were more difficult to diagnose. For example, some patients without dementia had moderate atrophy, whereas other behaviorally demented patients showed no indication of atrophy on the tomogram. Nathan and his colleagues concluded that patients in this middle range should be candidates for further assessment and treatment attempts. They also concluded that CAT is an excellent new device that is relatively easy and safe to use, not only to judge the current status of the brain but also to monitor life changes within the patient to see what changes might occur that result in normal functioning or dementia. Nathan and his colleagues at Hahnemann Hospital in Philadelphia are following up their original CAT patients and extending their work to larger samples. Kaszniak (1976) has also demonstrated, in a group of 50 patients, that CAT scans predict behavioral changes.

Computerized tomography is an important new tool that is already useful in the assessment of aged patients and has additional potential as a research technique.

IV. Prospects for the Future: Event Related Potentials

Computerized axial tomography provides a picture of the neuroanatomical structure of the brain, but it does not represent the brain at various cognitive states. The CAT scan provides a view of the brain as if it were frozen at a given point in time. It does not identify differences in behavior as the brain carries out behavioral functions. A picture of physiological activity in the living brain is provided by electrical brain potentials (also called event related potentials or ERPs), and these measures are beginning to be applied to aged populations by research scientists. They might also be applied clinically to the aged to identify the locus of neurological impairment resulting in behavioral deficits.

Applying computer averaging techniques to brain electrical activity monitored with scalp electrodes (the same electrodes used to monitor the EEG), ERPs can be derived that reflect the response of the brain to externally presented stimuli in most sensory modalities. The cortical origin of these brain potentials is well established. There are many aspects of brain potentials that could be discussed in this chapter, for, depending on the sensory modality being stimulated and the nature of the stimulation, different potentials occur. ERPs vary as a function of the stimulus and the task, so there are, for example, visual evoked potential correlates of sensation, perception, and cognition.

The ERP that will be discussed briefly in this chapter is the human auditory evoked potential (AEP). (For a more comprehensive discussion of ERPs over the life span, see Klorman, Thompson, & Ellingson, 1978; Woodruff, 1978). Figure 10.6 represents the AEP to click stimuli at electrodes recording at the right hemisphere in the frontal, central, and occipital cortex. The characteristic waveforms at various latencies appear in most individuals, and the amplitude and latency of various waves provide information on the auditory pathway from the auditory nerve to the cortex. Thus, the AEP provides a means to map the parts of the CNS in which a problem might occur. Rather than discuss the whole AEP, I will limit my discussion to a very early aspect of the AEP—the activity occurring in the first 10 msec after stimulation. This very small (measured in tenths of millivolts) potential has been named the brain stem auditory evoked response (BAER). It provides information about hearing acuity, about the functional capacity of the auditory pathway through the brain stem, and about speed of conduction of neural impulses through this pathway. All of this information has particular application to the aging.

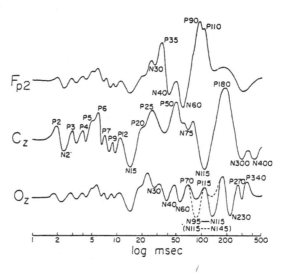

Figure 10.6. Schematic summary of the human AEP is shown as it would typically be recorded in a normal, awake adult subject not performing a specific task in relation to the click stimulus. Recording is referential to ears. A similar AEP would be recorded to click stimulation of both ears or to brief tone bursts. No amplitude calibration is shown since the P2-P9 complex is much smaller (typically .1–.5 μV) than later components (typically 1–20 μV) and for purposes of illustration is not drawn to the same amplitude scale. Components are not necessarily largest at the locations shown. Components N15, P20, N30, P35, a portion of N40, a portion of N60, N75, P90, and P110 are thought to be myogenic; all others are thought to be neurogenic. [From Goff, Allison, & Vaughan, 1978. Reprinted by permission.]

The BAER method of recording electrical activity of the human auditory nerve and brain stem auditory nuclei has been under development in laboratories in many parts of the world. In this method a click stimulus is used to evoke an electrophysiological response—the BAER—which is extracted from the EEG by means of computer techniques. The BAER history began in 1967 with the observation by Sohmer and Feinmesser that auditory nerve activity could be recorded from the human scalp. The actual BAER was discovered in 1971 when Jewett and Williston reported that in addition to the auditory nerve response, four more waves time-locked to the click stimulus could be recorded. They compared these waves to similar events recorded from animals and concluded that the human BAER permits one to trace the progress of click-induced neural activity through the human brain stem en route to the cortex. Laboratories in many parts of the world have since confirmed and extended these important discoveries. Much of this work is summarized in Figure 10.7, which represents the various waveforms of the BAER and the brain generators of the waveforms. This measure is one of the rare instances in which functional activity from known brain sites can be recorded. Anatomical mapping of the waves in animal and human autopsy data indicates that wave I originates in the auditory nerve, wave II is from the cochlear nucleus, waves III and IV are in the pons, wave V is in the inferior colliculus, and waves VI and VII are in the thalamus and thalamic radiations, respectively. Wave V is particularly well correlated with the intensity of the auditory signal in normal and pathological ears, and therefore it is useful diagnostically. The relationship between wave V latency and stimulus intensity is shown for normal ears in Figure 10.8, which indicates that a 60 dB signal has a wave V latency of 5.78 msec, that a 20 dB signal takes 8.08 msec to register at this level in the brain stem, and that a 10 dB signal is not detected in the nervous system of this subject. In subjects with impaired hearing, the latencies are longer.

The aspect of the BAER that has been used most frequently for clinical applications is the latency of wave V. Subjects with normal hearing produce, within narrow limits, the same wave V latency at a given click intensity. Hard-of-hearing patients deviate from these normal values in ways that are characteristic of their type of deafness (conductive, sensorineural). By comparing the latencies of the various waves of the BAER, it is also possible to detect lesions in the brain stem. Thus, localization of brain stem lesions due to trauma, cerebrovascular accidents, or progressively developing problems such as ischemia (insufficiency of blood flow) can be identified.

In addition to correlating with hearing ability in young adults with normal or abnormal hearing ability, wave V of the brain stem evoked potential shows changes in development. Figure 10.9 shows the decrease in latency with increasing age from infancy to age 42. The most rapid development of

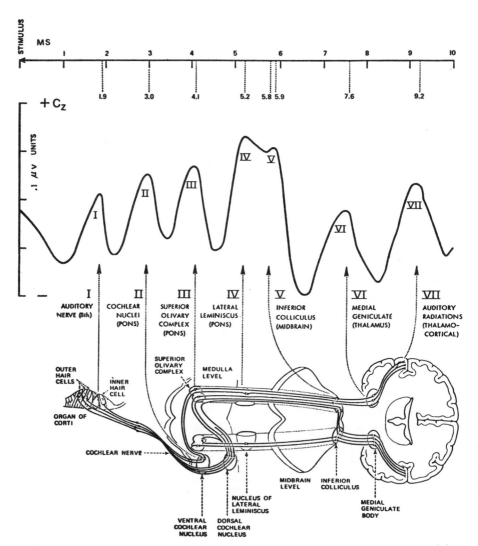

Figure 10.7. Diagram of normal latencies for vertex-positive brainstem auditory potentials (waves I through VII) evoked by clicks of 60 dBHL (60 dB above normal hearing threshold) at a rate of 10 per second. Lesions at different levels of auditory pathway tend to produce response abnormalities beginning with indicated components, although this does not specify the precise generators of the response; the relative contributions of synaptic and axonal activity to the response are as yet unknown. Intermediate latency (5.8 ms) between those of waves IV and V is mean peak latency of fused wave IV/V when present. C_{z+}, C_{z-} = vertex positivity, represented by an upward pen deflection, and vertex negativity, represented by a downward pen deflection. [From Stockard, Stockard, & Sharbrough, 1977. Reprinted by permission of Grass Medical Instruments, Quincy, Massachusetts.]

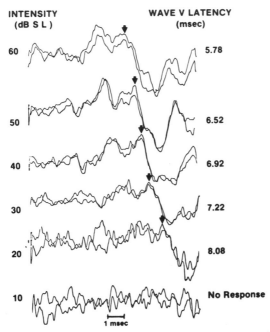

Figure 10.8. Typical normal brain stem auditory evoked responses (BAER) are shown at six intensities from an adult subject demonstrating hearing within normal limits. Note that the shift of wave V latency in milliseconds is a function of stimulus intensity. Each tracing represents the sum of 4096 responses to a .1 msec click, presented monaurally at the rate of 30 per second. Time base of each tracing is 10 msec. [From Sandlin & Mokotoff, 1976. Reprinted by permission.]

the auditory system occurs in the first 16 months, as reflected in the rapid decrease in wave V latency; adult values are reached around 16 months and maintained at least until middle age. Figure 10.10 shows potentials in a 5-week-old infant, a 7-month-old infant, and a young adult. Data on older subjects are not available; however, given the significance of this measure of the nervous system, it is clear that gerontologists could use the measure for clinical assessment and for research on age changes in the nervous system. Since Amadeo and Shagass (1973) demonstrated that these potentials are not different when the patient is awake or asleep, they are even being considered as a more reliable measure of brain death than the EEG.

In assessing the brain's response to an acoustic stimulus, the BAER technique provides objective data concerning the integrity of the cochlea, the auditory nerve, and the brain stem and thalamic auditory pathways. Although the brain stem auditory evoked response does not assess cortical response to an acoustic stimulus, coupling this measure with the cortical

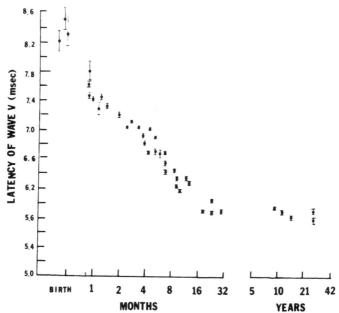

Figure 10.9. Latency of wave V to 60 dB clicks is represented as a function of age. Latencies decrease as subjects get older—particularly between the first postnatal month and 12–18 months after birth. At this time, the latency stabilizes and is similar to latency in childhood, adolescence, and young adulthood. Norms for older subjects are not available. [From Hecox, K., & Galambos, T. Brainstem auditory evoked responses in human infants and adults. *Archives of Otolaryngology,* 1974, *99,* 30–33. Copyright 1974, American Medical Association. Reprinted by permission.]

auditory evoked response (shown in Figure 10.6) provides us with a means of localizing auditory pathology.

Data on BAERs in old age would be useful for several purposes. Auditory acuity is known to decline with age, and the BAER provides information about the degree of hearing loss and the nature of the loss. This test can be used to differentiate conduction loss from sensorineural loss. Age changes in auditory acuity make adaptation in old age more difficult, and they have also been shown to be related to intellectual decrement. Granick, Kleban, and Weiss (1976) demonstrated that hearing loss in two separate samples of old subjects was related to intellectual deficit, and the impairment appeared to be more than simply a function of the fact that the subjects could not hear instructions or stimuli for the tests. Hearing loss was related to the performance measures of the test and not to the verbal measures. This result suggests that some mechanism that may be common to both the auditory apparatus and intellectual functioning is affected. By

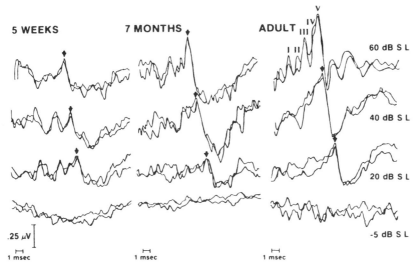

Figure 10.10. Typical brain stem auditory evoked responses (BAER) are represented for three age levels. Each tracing is the sum of 1000–2000 responses to a .1 msec click delivered monaurally 30 times per second at four intensities. Arrows indicate the peak of wave V. [From Hecox, K., & Galambos, T. Brainstem auditory evoked responses in human infants and adults. *Archives of Otolaryngology,* 1974, *99,* 30-33. Copyright 1974, American Medical Association. Reprinted by permission.]

measuring the auditory pathway with BAERs, the locus of the problem in both functions might be identified. No other measure is available that could provide such significant information.

Identification of the locus of neural events in which age changes affect hearing and intellectual processes could add to our understanding of the aging processes. The ability to detect problems in brain stem pathways might also lead to the alleviation of such problems. Cerebral ischemia is a major factor in the deterioration of central nervous system functions with age and produces some functional impairment long before clinical symptoms are even detectable. It has been proposed that vertebral–basilar artery insufficiency constitutes the most common form of chronic cerebrovascular disease, resulting in hindbrain ischemia (Meyer, 1975). Since hindbrain ischemia affects the brain stem, BAERs might be useful in the detection of this common problem, which can be alleviated through surgery. Thus, long before clinical symptoms are apparent, BAERs could be used in the identification and prevention of vertebral–basilar arterial insufficiency. Such early diagnosis could prevent strokes, debilitating or fatal falls, or hearing impairment—all of which are consequences of hindbrain ischemia. In addition, there may be many patients who have been diagnosed as having chronic brain syndrome and have been subjected to benign neglect when their symptoms could have been relieved by surgery. Normative data on BAERs in old age would provide information potentially crucial to early diagnosis.

We are at a point in research on brain potentials when we are beginning to map activity in the living, responding human brain. We are approaching a time when evoked potentials will yield neurophysiological data at all levels of the brain. We are developing safe, noninvasive measures that serve as windows into the functioning brain.

These windows, in the form of electrical brain potentials and computerized tomograms, can be used by gerontologists to answer some of the research questions they have asked for the last three decades. We now have available, reliable measures with which we can more accurately pinpoint parts of the nervous system that change with age. These techniques must also be taken from the laboratory to life and used in clinical settings to determine the most suitable treatments and living situations for the wide range of elderly individuals who present themselves for assessment and intervention.

REFERENCES

Achenbach, T. M. *Research in developmental psychology: Concepts, strategies, methods.* New York: Free Press, 1978.

Adams, G. M., & deVries, H. A. Physiological effects of an exercise training regimen upon women aged 52–79. *Journal of Gerontology,* 1973, *28,* 50–55.

Adelman, R. C. Disruptions in enzyme regulation during aging. In D. V. Parke (Ed.), *Enzyme induction.* Oxford: Plenum, 1975. Pp. 303–311.

Adelman, R. C., Britton, G. W., Rotenberg, S., Ceci, L., & Karoly, K. Endocrine regulation of enzyme activity in aging animals of different genotypes. *Birth Defects: Original Article Series,* 1978, *14* (1), 355–364. (Monograph)

Amadeo, M., & Shagass, C. Brief latency click-evoked potentials during waking and sleep in man. *Psychophysiology,* 1973, *10,* 244–250.

American Cancer Society. *1978 Cancer facts and figures.* New York, 1978.

Baltes, M. M., Burgess, R. L., & Stewart, R. B. *Independence and dependence in nursing home residents: An operant ecological study.* Unpublished manuscript, The Pennsylvania State University, 1978.

Baltes, P. B., & Goulet, L. R. Exploration of developmental variables by manipulation and stimulation of age differences in behavior. *Human Development,* 1971, *14,* 149–170.

Baltes, P. B., Reese, H. W., & Nesselroade, J. R. *Life-span developmental psychology: Introduction to research methods.* Monterey, Calif.: Brooks, Cole, 1977.

Beatty, J. Effects of initial alpha wave abundance and operant training procedures on occipital alpha and beta wave activity. *Psychonomic Science,* 1971, *23,* 197–199.

Beatty, J. Similar effects of feedback signals and instructional information on EEG activity. *Physiology and Behavior,* 1972, *9,* 151–154.

Beatty, J., Greenberg, A., Deibler, W. P., & O'Hanlon, J. F. Operant control of occipital theta rhythm affects performance in a radar monitoring task. *Science,* 1974, *183,* 871–873.

Beatty, J., & Kornfeld, C. M. Relative independence of conditioned EEG changes from cardiac and respiratory activity. *Physiology and Behavior,* 1972, *9,* 733–736.

Berger, H. Uber das Electren-kephalogramm des Menschen. III. *Archives of Psychiatry Nervenkr.,* 1931, *94,* 16–60.

Birren, J. E. Age and decision strategies. In A. T. Welford & J. E. Birren (Eds.), *Decision making and age.* Basel: Karger, 1969. Pp. 23–36.

Birren, J. E. Toward an experimental psychology of aging. *American Psychologist,* 1970, *25,* 124–135.

Birren, J. E. Translations in gerontology—from lab to life. *American Psychologist,* 1974, *29,* 808–815.

Bishop, G. H. Cyclic changes in excitability of the optic pathway of the rabbit. *American Journal of Physiology,* 1933, *103,* 213–224.

Blanchard, E. B., & Young, L. D. Self control of cardiac functioning: A promise as yet unfulfilled. *Psychological Bulletin,* 1973, *79,* 145–163.

Blanchard, E. B., & Young, L. D. Clinical applications of biofeedback training: A review of evidence. *Archives of General Psychiatry,* 1974, *30,* 573–589.

Brannon, L. J. *The effects of biofeedback training of EEG alpha activity on psychological functioning of the elderly.* Unpublished doctoral dissertation, Pennsylvania State University, 1976.

Brolund, J. W., & Schallow, J. R. The effects of reward on occipital alpha facilitation by biofeedback. *Psychophysiology,* 1976, *13,* 236–241.

Brown, B. B. Recognition of aspects of consciousness through association with EEG alpha activity represented by a light signal. *Psychophysiology,* 1970, *6,* 442–452.

Brown, B. B. Awareness of EEG-subjective activity relationships detected within a closed feedback system. *Psychophysiology,* 1971, *7,* 451–464.

Budzynski, T. B. Biofeedback procedures in the clinic. *Seminars in Psychiatry,* 1973, *5,* 537–547.

Comfort, A. *The process of aging.* New York: New American Library, 1964.

Davis, P. A. The electroencephalogram in old age. *Diseases of the Nervous System,* 1941, *2,* 77.

De Beauvoir, S. *The coming of age.* New York: Putnam, 1972.

deVries, H. A. Physiological effects of an exercise training regimen upon men age 52–88. *Journal of Gerontology,* 1970, *25,* 325–336.

deVries, H. A. Physiology of exercise and aging. In D. S. Woodruff & J. E. Birren (Eds.), *Aging: Scientific perspectives and social issues.* New York: D. Van Nostrand, 1975. Pp. 257–276.

deVries, H. A., & Adams, G. M. Electromyographic comparison of single doses of exercise and meprobamate as to effects on muscular relaxation. *American Journal of Physical Medicine,* 1972, *51,* 130–141.

Erikson, E. *Childhood and society* (2nd ed.). New York: Norton, 1963.

Friedman, M., & Rosenman, R. H. *Type A behavior and your heart.* New York: Knopf, 1974.

Goff, W. R., Allison, T., & Vaughan, H. G., Jr. The functional neuroanatomy of event related potentials. In E. Callaway, P. Tueting, & S. Koslow (Eds.), *Event related potentials in man.* New York: Academic Press, 1978.

Granick, S., Kleban, M. H., & Weiss, A. D. Relationships between hearing loss and cognition in normally hearing aged persons. *Journal of Gerontology,* 1976, *31,* 434–440.

Green, E. E., Green, A. M., & Walters, E. D. Voluntary control of internal states: Psychological and physiological. *Journal of Transpersonal Psychology,* 1970, *11,* 1–26.

Hall, G. S. *Senescence, the second half of life*. New York: Appleton, 1922.

Hardt, J. V. Alpha EEG responses of low and high anxiety males to respiration and relaxation training and to auditory feedback of occipital alpha. *Dissertation Abstracts International*, 1974, *35*, 1912B–1913B. (University Microfilms No. 74-19309)

Hardt, J. V., & Kamiya, J. Some comments on Plotkin's self-regulation of electroencephalographic alpha. *Journal of Experimental Psychology: General*, 1976, *105*, 100–108.

Havighurst, R. J. *Developmental tasks and education* (2nd ed.). New York: McKay, 1972.

Hecox, K. & Galambos, T. Brain stem auditory evoked responses in human infants and adults. *Archives of Otolaryngology*, 1974, *99*, 30–33.

Huckman, M. S., Fox, J., & Topel, J. The validity of criteria for the evaluation of cerebral atrophy by computed tomography. *Radiology*, 1975, *116*, 85–92.

Hyden, H. Biochemical aspects of learning and memory. In K. H. Pribram (Ed.), *On the biology of learning*. New York: Harcourt, Brace, & World, 1969. Pp. 67–125.

Jasper, H. H. Cortical excitatory state and synchronism in the control of bioelectric autonomous rhythms. *Cold Spring Harbor Symposium on Quantitative Biology*, 1936, *4*, 320–338.

Jewett, D. L., & Williston, J. S. Auditory evoked far fields averaged from the scalp of humans. *Brain*, 1971, *94*, 681–696.

Kamiya, J. *Conditioned discrimination of the EEG alpha rhythm in humans*. Paper presented at the meeting of the Western Psychological Association, San Francisco, 1962.

Kamiya, J. Conscious control of brain waves. *Psychology Today*, 1968, *1*, 56–60.

Kamiya, J. Operant control of EEG alpha rhythm and some of its reported effects on consciousness. In C. T. Tart (Ed.), *Altered states of consciousness*. New York: Wiley, 1969. Pp. 507–517.

Kastin, A. J., Sandman, C. A., Stratton, L. O., Schally, A. V., & Miller, L. H. Behavioral and electrographic changes in rat and man after MSH. In W. H. Gispan, T. B. van Wimersma Greidanus, B. Bohus, & D. deWied (Eds.), *Progress in brain research* (Vol. 42). Amsterdam: Elsevier, 1975. Pp. 143–150.

Kaszniak, A. W. *Effects of age and cerebral atrophy upon span of immediate recall and paired-associate learning in older adults*. Unpublished doctoral dissertation, University of Illinois at Chicago Circle, Department of Psychology, 1976.

Klorman, R., Thompson, L. W., & Ellingson, R. J. Event related brain potentials across the life span. In E. Callaway, P. Tueting, & S. Koslow (Eds.), *Event related potentials in man*. New York: Academic Press, 1978.

Kondo, C. Y., Travis, T. A., & Knott, J. R. The effects of changes in motivation on alpha enhancement. *Psychophysiology*, 1975, *12*, 388–389.

Kristofferson, A. B. Successiveness discrimination as a two-state, quantal process. *Science*, 1967, *158*, 1337–1339.

Labouvie-Vief, G. Implications of geropsychological theories for intervention: The challenge for the seventies. *The Gerontologist*, 1973, *13*, 10–14.

Labouvie-Vief, G. Adult cognitive development: In search of alternative interpretations. *Merrill-Palmer Quarterly*, 1977, *23*, 227–263.

Labouvie-Vief, G., & Chandler, M. J. Cognitive development and life-span developmental theory: Idealistic versus contextual perspectives. In P. B. Baltes (Ed.), *Life-span development and behavior*. New York: Academic Press, 1978. Pp. 182–210.

Leaf, A. Getting old. *Scientific American*, 1973, *229*, 44–52.

Lindsley, D. B. Brain potentials in children and adults. *Science*, 1936, *84*, 354.

Lindsley, D. B. Psychological phenomena and the electroencephalogram. *Electroencephalography and Clinical Neurophysiology*, 1952, *4*, 443–456.

Lynch, J. J., & Paskewitz, D. A. On the mechanisms of the feedback control of human brain wave activity. *The Journal of Nervous and Mental Disease,* 1971, *153,* 205–217.

Lynch, J. J., Paskewitz, D. A., & Orne, M. T. Some factors in the feedback control of human alpha rhythm. *Psychosomatic Medicine,* 1974, *36,* 399–410.

McCay, C. M. Chemical aspects of aging and the effect of diet upon aging. In A. Lansing (Ed.), *Cowdry's problems of aging.* Baltimore: Williams and Wilkins, 1952. Pp. 139–202.

Marsh, G., & Thompson, L. W. Psychophysiology of aging. In J. E. Birren & K. W. Schaie (Eds.), *Handbook of the psychology of aging.* New York: Van Nostrand-Reinhold, 1977. Pp. 219–248.

Meyer, J. S. *Modern concepts of cerebrovascular disease.* New York: Halsted, 1975.

Miller, L. H., Groves, G., Bopp, M. J., & Kastin, A. J. *A neuroheptapeptide influence on cognitive functioning in the elderly.* Paper presented at the Ninth Congress of the Society for Psychoneuroendocrinology, August 1978.

Miller, L. H., Harris, L. C., Van Riezen, H., & Kastin, A. J. Neuroheptapeptide influence on attention and memory in man. *Pharmacology Biochemistry and Behavior,* 1976, *5,* 17–21.

Miller, N. E. Learning of visceral and glandular responses. *Science,* 1969, *163,* 434–445.

Nathan, R. J., Gonzalez, C. F., & Laffey, P. Correlations between computerized transaxial tomography and the extent of dementia. Paper presented at the twenty-eighth annual meeting of the Gerontological Society, Louisville, Kentucky, October 1975.

Neale, J. M., & Liebert, R. M. *Science and behavior: An introduction to methods of research.* Englewood Cliffs, N.J.: Prentice-Hall, 1973.

Nordgren, R. A., Woodruff, D. S., & Bick, M. D. The effect of exogenous RNA on the retention of discriminative learning in the rat. *Physiology and Behavior,* 1970, *5,* 1169–1171.

Obrist, P. A., Black, A. H., Brenner, J., & Dicara, L. V. (Eds.). *Cardiovascular psychophysiology: Current issues in response mechanism, biofeedback and methodology.* Chicago: Aldine, 1974.

Obrist, W. D., & Busse, E. W. The electroencephalogram in old age. In W. P. Wilson (Ed.), *Applications of electroencephalography in psychiatry.* Durham, N.C.: Duke University Press, 1965. Pp. 185–205.

Obrist, W. D., Henry, C. E., & Justiss, W. A. Longitudinal study of EEG in old age. *Excerpta Medica International Congress Series,* 1961, *37,* 180–181.

Olefsky, J. M., Reavan, G. M., & Farquhar, J. W. The effects of weight reduction on obesity: Studies of lipic and carbohydrate metabolism in normal and hyperlipoproteinemic subjects. *Journal of Clinical Investigation,* 1974, *53,* 64–76.

Palmore, E. Health practices, illness and longevity. In E. Palmore & F. C. Jeffers (Eds.), *Prediction of life span.* Lexington, Mass.: Heath, 1971. Pp. 71–77.

Paskewitz, D. A., & Orne, M. T. Visual effects during alpha feedback training. *Science,* 1973, *181,* 361–363.

Plemons, J. K., Willis, S. L., & Baltes, P. B. Modifiability of fluid intelligence in aging: A short-term longitudinal training approach. *Journal of Gerontology,* 1978, *33,* 224–231.

Plotkin, W. B. On the self regulation of the occipital alpha rhythm: Control strategies, states of consciousness, and the role of psychological feedback. *Journal of Experimental Psychology: General,* 1976, *105,* 66–69.

Riegel, K. F. The influence of economic and political ideologies upon the development of developmental psychology. *Psychological Bulletin,* 1972, *78,* 129–141.

Riegel, K. F. History of psychological gerontology. In J. E. Birren & K. W. Schaie (Eds.), *Handbook of the psychology of aging.* New York: Van Nostrand-Reinhold, 1977. Pp. 70–102.

Sandlin, R. E., & Mokotoff, B. Brainstem auditory evoked response measurement. *Maico Audiological Library Series,* 1976, *14* (8).

Sanford, A. J. A periodic basis for perception and action. In W. P. Colquhoun (Ed.), *Biological rhythms and human performance.* London: Academic Press, 1971. Pp. 179–209.

Schaie, K. W. Toward a stage theory of adult cognitive development. *Journal of Aging and Human Development,* 1977, *8,* 129–155.

Shapiro, D., & Schwartz, G. E. Biofeedback and visceral learning: Clinical application. *Seminars in Psychiatry,* 1972, *4,* 171–184.

Sohmer, H., & Feinmesser, M. Cochlear action potentials recorded from the external ear in man. *Annals of Otolaryngology,* 1967, *76,* 427–435.

Sterman, M. G., MacDonald, L. R., & Stone, R. K. *EEG asymmetry and seizure modification following unilateral sensorimotor EEG biofeedback training.* Paper presented at the twenty-seventh annual meeting of the American Electroencephalographic Society, 1973.

Sterns, H. L., Barrett, G. V., Alexander, R. A., Panek, P. E., Avolio, B. J., & Forbringer, L. R. *Training and evaluation of older adult skills critical for effective driving performance.* University of Akron Department of Psychology and the Institute for Life-Span Development and Gerontology (Contract No. 223-822-0375). Andrus Foundation, August 1977.

Stockard, J. J., Stockard, J. E., & Sharbrough, F. W. *Mayo Clinic Proceedings,* 1977, *52,* 761–769.

Surwillo, W. W. The relation of simple response time to brain wave frequency and the effects of age. *Electroencephalography and Clinical Neurophysiology,* 1963, *15,* 105–114.

Surwillo, W. W. Human reaction time and period of the electroencephalogram in relation to development. *Psychophysiology,* 1971, *8,* 468–482.

Surwillo, W. W. The electroencephalogram in the prediction of human reaction time during growth and development. *Biological Psychology,* 1975, *3,* 79–90.

Thompson, L. W. Effects of hyperbaric oxygen on behavioral functioning in elderly persons with intellectual impairment. In S. Gershon & A. Raskin (Eds.), *Aging* (Vol. 2). New York: Raven Press, 1975. Pp. 169–177.

Thompson, L. W., Davis, G. C., Obrist, W. D., & Heyman, A. Effects of hyperbaric oxygen on behavioral and physiological measures in elderly demented patients. *Journal of Gerontology,* 1976, *31,* 23–28.

Thompson, L. W., & Marsh, G. R. Psychophysiological studies of aging. In C. Eisdorfer & M. Lawton (Eds.), *The psychology of adult development and aging.* Washington, D.C.: American Psychological Association, 1973. Pp. 112–148.

Travis, T. A., Kondo, C. Y., & Knott, J. R. Parameters of eyes-closed alpha enhancement. *Psychophysiology,* 1974, *11,* 674–681.

Tredway, V. A. *Mood effects of exercise programs for older adults.* Paper presented at the eighty-sixth annual meeting of the American Psychological Association, Toronto, September 1978.

U. S. Department of Health, Education and Welfare. Motor vehicle accident deaths in the United States—1950–1967. *Vital and Health Statistics* (Data from the National Vital Statistics System) Series 20, No. 9. Washington, D.C.: U. S. Government Printing Office, 1970.

U. S. Department of Health, Education and Welfare. Mortality trends for leading causes of death, United States—1950–1969. *Vital and Health Statistics* (Data from the National Vital Statistics System) Series 20, No. 16. Washington, D.C.: U.S. Government Printing Office, 1974.

Walsh, D. H. Interactive effects of alpha feedback and instructional set on subjective state. *Psychophysiology,* 1974, *11,* 428–435.

Wang, H. S., & Busse, E. W. EEG of healthy old persons—a longitudinal study: Dominant background activity and occipital rhythm. *Journal of Gerontology,* 1969, *24,* 419–426.

Wang, H. S., Obrist, W. D., & Busse, E. W. Neurophysiological correlates of the intellectual function of elderly persons living in the community. *American Journal of Psychiatry,* 1970, *126,* 1205–1212.

Weiss, T., & Engel, B. T. Operant conditioning of heart rate in patients with premature ventricular contractions. *Psychosomatic Medicine,* 1971, *33,* 301–321.

Wohlwill, J. F. *The study of behavioral development.* New York: Academic Press, 1973.

Woodruff, D. S. The usefulness of the life-span approach for the psychophysiology of aging. *The Gerontologist,* 1973, *13,* 467–472.

Woodruff, D. S. Relationships among EEG alpha frequency, reaction time and aging: A biofeedback study. *Psychophysiology,* 1975, *12,* 673–681.

Woodruff, D. S. *Can you live to be 100?* New York: Chatham Square Press, 1977.

Woodruff, D. S. Brain electrical activity and behavior relationships over the life span. In P. B. Baltes (Ed.), *Life-span development and behavior* (Vol. 1). New York: Academic Press, 1978. Pp. 112–179.

Woodruff, D. S., & Birren, J. E. Biofeedback conditioning of the EEG alpha rhythm in young and old subjects. *Proceedings of the 80th Annual Convention of the American Psychological Association,* Washington, D.C.: American Psychological Association, 1972. Pp. 673–674.

PART III

EDUCATIONAL AND DEVELOPMENTAL INTERVENTION

Intervention and Its Effects on Early Development: What Model of Development Is Appropriate?[1]

FRANCES DEGEN HOROWITZ
THE UNIVERSITY OF KANSAS
LAWRENCE, KANSAS

A discussion of intervention and its effects on early development at this time is propitious. We have just come through such an enormously productive period in the study of infant behavior and development that it is appropriate to say there has been a revolution in our thinking. This revolution is, however, only the latest act in a drama that has long featured the human infant as one of the central characters. The dramatic question—which is still unresolved—has been nature versus nurture; the contending scenarios represent the leading contestants for our theoretical loyalties regarding the question of how development happens.

I. A Brief Historical Overview

In May 1978, while I was preparing for an address at the Mid-Western Psychological Association—the association was celebrating its jubilee, its fiftieth year of meetings—I realized that the major theoretical orientations

[1] Partial support for the author and work reported in this chapter has come from grants from the National Institute of Child Health and Human Development and from the Bureau for the Education of the Handicapped.

235

LIFE-SPAN DEVELOPMENTAL PSYCHOLOGY
Intervention

regarding development and infants were already in place by 1930. Freud had elaborated upon the psychosexual stages and included the first 2 years of infancy as prime developmental periods among the first 6 years of life (Freud, 1917); Gesell had just published his book on infancy and human growth (Gesell, 1928); Watson had already conducted his classic experiments demonstrating conditioning in the young child (Watson & Raynor, 1920) and had staked out the behaviorists' position; Piaget had begun his studies of the sensorimotor development of his infant daughters (Brainerd, 1978). Although in the ensuing years these individuals would further elaborate their theoretical accounts and would contribute data relevant to their various positions, it is almost curious, given the empirical advances that have been made, that no major revisions of these basic theoretical orientations have been proposed in light of new data. It is a mark of persistence that we are still, in many ways, arguing the same arguments that so infused the emotions in the 1920s and 1930s.

Those emotions and the dramatic question to which I have alluded center around the question of "how development happens" and the enormous practical implications dependent upon the answer to that question. The nature–nurture controversy has focused insistently upon the human infant. In fact, much of the early research on infant behavior and development was motivated by the fact that the infant was thought of as a "proving ground" for the nature–nurture controversy. If you could show conditioning in infants, the argument for environmental control of development was reinforced; if you could demonstrate that training had no profound effects on response acquisition, then the arguments for maturational control of development were enhanced. Along the way some of the most sophisticated and some of the most controversial data were collected; moreover, some of the now classic studies of infants were completed (Appleton, Clifton, & Goldberg, 1975; Osofsky, 1979; Stone, Smith, & Murphy, 1973).

The nature–nurture controversy that dominated infancy research was declared a bitter draw by the end of the 1930s. Gesell's (1928) demonstrations using the co-twin control strategy were convincing only to the degree that the behaviors he chose to study, such as stair-climbing acquisition, had great developmental significance. Interestingly, the conclusions that Gesell drew regarding the inherent triumph of maturation over learning were not particularly informative about the controlling processes. On the other hand, the Iowa studies demonstrating the impact of environmental stimulation on development were so vulnerable to methodological critique that the results were not believed (Skeels & Dye, 1939; Skeels, Updegraff, Wellman, & Williams, 1938; McNemar, 1940). Had the results been accepted, Headstart, Upstart, and the Milwaukee and North Carolina type projects might well have been characteristic of the research of the 1940s instead of the 1960s and 1970s.

With the onset of World War II and the diversion of energies to other matters, there was very little infant research done during the 1940s and even until well into the 1950s. During this period, a whole generation of developmental psychologists was being trained, the technological advances spurred by war needs were making their way into behavioral laboratories, and new emphases in already established theories and orientations were about to make their mark on the American scene of developmental psychology, particularly in the area of infant behavior and development. In the latter part of the 1950s, four studies were published that had significant impact on what have come to be two major lines of research related to early behavior and development.

The first line of that research began in 1958 with the almost simultaneous publications by Fantz (1958) and Berlyne (1958), who demonstrated that infants would deploy their attention selectively to visual stimuli depending upon the patterning and complexity of the stimuli. The studies and the outpouring of subsequent research suggested that the human infant was processing stimulus information at a more sophisticated level than had been suspected. Discrimination was demonstrated in every sensory modality and was shown to be present in the first days of life; the newborn infant could also "learn" within simple laboratory conditioning paradigms (Appleton, Clifton, & Goldberg, 1975; Osofsky, in press; Stone, Smith, & Murphy, 1973). The world view about infants changed from thinking of the normal infant as a reflex-dominated organism to viewing the normal infant as coming into the world equipped to respond to that world in some selective ways. In the ensuing years an enormous amount of data have been generated about infant abilities; in turn, these data have generated a certain amount of awe about the competence of the human infant. These data and the formulations of Piaget have contributed to viewing the infant as an active participant in the discovery of stimulus information.

The second line of infant research also began in the 1950s with the publication of Harriet Rheingold's (1956) monograph in which she demonstrated that it was possible to modify the social responsiveness of infants in an orphanage by providing them with extra opportunities for mothering over an 8-week period. A companion publication by Kirk (1958), though it was not about infants but about retarded preschool children, provided an essential replication of the initial Skeels studies: Retarded children given an experimental preschool experience showed significant increases in level of functioning compared to children not provided with the preschool experience.

II. Educational Intervention in the 1960s and 1970s

In the 1960s, in a somewhat different arena, political pressures focused strongly upon the social problems produced by school failure. One possible avenue of social action might well have been influenced by the view that children fail in school because there is something wrong with the teaching in the school; therefore, let us fix the teaching and the school. An alternative view was that children fail in school because there is something wrong with the child and the child's background; therefore let us fix the background and the child. Obviously, we opted for the alternative view of fixing the child. Why? As Clarke and Clarke (1976) have pointed out in *Early Experience: Myth and Evidence,* part of the answer lies in the zeitgeist of deeply rooted beliefs about human development—namely the belief that early experiences are special experiences that not only lay the foundation for later development but also have a disproportionate impact on the course of development. In the 1960s the zeitgeist was supported by data and by fresh speculation: Skeels' early evidence and his dramatic follow-up of the children 30 years later (Skeels, 1966); Bloom's (1964) finding that half of an individual's intellectual competence was already determined by 4 years of age; Hebb's (1949) appealing theory claiming the prepotency of early learning, which likened the richness of early experience to a fat savings bank account from which one could draw the necessary financing of later learning; and mounting evidence that infants discriminate and process stimuli, which made plausible the idea that early enriched stimulation (and, conversely, relative deprivation) would have an impact on the developmental course and developmental outcome. Almost all of these studies and speculations referred to cognitive development, which was well suited to the concern with later school achievement problems. In the area of social–emotional development, Freudians and then Bowlby (1951) focused on maternal deprivation as producing disorders in attachment and in social and personality development. It is interesting that Yarrow (1961) and Casler (1961) reinterpreted some of the evidence for maternal deprivation effects back into the cognitive domain; this seems symptomatic of our tremendous preoccupation with intellectual achievement and cognitive functioning.

Much of what happened in the 1960s as a result of selecting the "fix the child" alternative was in the form of educational intervention programs that were a combination of "change the environment" and "fix the child." We all know that the public policy program was Headstart and that a concomitant line of intervention occurred in a variety of special intervention research projects, some of which antedated Headstart (see Horowitz & Paden, 1973). At first the results were encouraging, and many different kinds of programs appeared to have effects; then the results became discouraging as those effects faded when the programs ceased. The more intense the programs were, and the more they involved parents and families, the stronger and the more durable were the effects (Horowitz & Paden, 1973). But even the most intense programs (e.g., the Milwaukee Project) with some of the most dramatic gains have not been immune to slippage effects once the program has discontinued (see the report of the Milwaukee follow-up data in Clarke & Clarke, 1976).

The initial failure to find durable effects from educational intervention programs produced a variety of reactions. Early on, Jensen (1969) proclaimed, "We have tried compensatory education and it has failed [p. 1]," suggesting that genetic factors controlled intellectual development and environmental intervention could have little impact. Others claimed that the programs, were not intense or long enough or begun early enough. The response to this point of view was to recommend more programs in early infant stimulation. Those who still believed in compensatory education conceived of Follow Through as a further intervention in the school years in an effort to maintain Headstart gains. Nature versus nurture or the heredity–environment controversy took on new and emotional dimensions.

In the meantime, back at the laboratory and in the halls of medical centers, a more complex picture of the infant and development was beginning to emerge. Not only was it clear that the newborn infant entered the world with a more developed behavioral repertoire than had been thought, there also was an increasing recognition that the 9-month period of gestation did not occur in an entirely protected environment that was safe from external events and influenced only by the genetic factors unfolding in a benign or supportive sac. Instead, with regard to characterizing the influence of environment relative to genetic–biological factors, it became reasonable to claim that the only purely genetic moment was the moment of conception and that both adverse and positive environmental influences were functioning for 9 months prior to birth in the form of maternal behavior such as ingestion of drugs and alcohol, smoking, and nutritional habits. Correlative factors such as maternal age and education, along with the behavioral events, resulted in designation of risk categories to describe the expected status of the newborn infant. Concomitantly, there was a greater refinement in the descriptive classification of infants. No longer was it appropriate to talk about the premature infant versus the "term" infant. Gestational age and weight and even length became important combinatorial factors determining developmental status. Perinatal events such as length of labor, respiratory complications, and obstetrical medication were implicated, along with the other variables, in developmental outcome. However, no refinement of measurement of particular factors provided greater predictive power concerning the subsequent course of development. The more sophisticated our designations of the high-risk infant are, the more frustrating is our inability to make specific predictions.

All of the reviews of the literature (e.g., Sameroff & Chandler, 1975) and the major studies (e.g., Broman, Nichols, & Kennedy's [1975] National Perinatal Collaborative Study) focus their analyses not on specific process variables but on global descriptive variables summarized in terms of socioeconomic status and maternal education. Ramey, Stedman, Borders-Patterson, & Mengel (1978) have replicated this generalization by demonstrating that school failure could be predicted in a sample of a 1000 North Carolina first graders from information available at birth, namely the child's race and the mother's education. Additional predictors included birth order, age of mother, birth weight, the month that prenatal care began, and whether the child was of legitimate birth. These correlational data, as Ramey and his colleagues take pains to note, *do not* tell us about causal relationships.

The elusiveness of the causal relationships and the increasingly obvious absence of a complex enough theory of development have resulted in a general clouding of the whole picture concerning early development and effects of intervention. We now have completely contradictory claims being made with equal vehemence by respected laboratories and investigators.

The most unqualified claims are those propounded by Klaus and Kennell (1976), which are summarized in their book *Maternal–Infant Bonding*. In reviewing the evidence from their studies and those of others, they assert that there is a sensitive period immediately after birth and over the next few days in which the mother's attachment to her infant will occur if the infant and the mother are not unduly separated and if the infant is responsive to the mother. Indeed, it is the opportunity of mother and infant to be together immediately after birth that makes optimal use of this sensitive period. According to Klaus and Kennell (1976), separation in these crucial moments can result in affectional ties being "easily disturbed and . . . permanently altered during the immediate post-partum period [p. 52]." Furthermore, they view these early post-partum experiences as having "longlasting effects"; significant results detected 2 and 5 years later are attributed to extended contact during the first few minutes and days of life. Although many of the results of extended and early contact cited by Klaus and Kennell are in the realm of different parenting behaviors such as longer breast feeding, they claim that the effects on the child are pronounced—less infection, more weight gain, and, at 5 years, significantly higher IQs.

If Klaus and Kennell are correct, then an intervention as simple as providing mother and infant with immediate contact and with extended contact over and above the normal hospital routines has profound and permanent effects on development.

Burton White (1975) has offered us a less narrow period in which early experience results in long-lasting developmental influence. He claims that it all happens in the first three years of life and that subsequently the developmental course is unalterable. The effects of different environments, which he says are mainly a function of competent mothering, do not begin to manifest themselves until late in the second half of the first year of life. According to White, by 14 months of age the vector describing the developmental course becomes more defined and increasingly resistant to change; by 3 years of age the course can no longer be influenced. The theoretical claim that environmental variations are not very evident before the end of the first year of life is supported by the data from both the Milwaukee and the North Carolina projects; the infants enrolled from the first months of life in the experimental programs did not begin to show significant divergence from controls until about 12 to 14 months of age. Whether these findings support a particular model of development such as the one claimed by White or whether the first detection of difference is a function of the measurements used is not known. However, if White is correct, early intervention programs could—and, if done correctly, ought to—have an impact on not only the early course of development but also all subsequent development. The fact that the outcome data are not overly supportive of White's position could be easily countered by claiming that we simply do not know how to do the intervention.

On the other hand, the problem of evaluating effects of intervention may lie in our not knowing how and when to look for effects. There have been reports that support this idea from a self-formed consortium of former educational intervention researchers who have conducted a long-term follow-up of 14 infant and preschool experiments. In a preliminary report entitled *The Persistence of Preschool Effects,* Lazar (1977) gives results that indicate that although effects faded within two to three years after the programs ceased, the follow-up of the children—now in the latter part of elementary school, junior high, and high school—has resulted in a somewhat different picture. Compared to controls, the children involved in the experiment were less likely to be enrolled in special education classes, more likely to be in the appropriate grade for their age, and more likely to rate themselves as better than others in their school work. These effects do not appear to be correlated with length of program, whether the program was focused on infants or preschoolers, the age at which the program was begun, or whether the program was based at home or in a learning center. However, the home-based and the combined home-and-center-based children did seem to fare better than those who had only a center-based program in the initial analyses. Those who support the importance of early intervention programs have been very encouraged by these results, though firmer conclusions must await more complete analysis of the data.

It is possible that the effects of early intervention programs have an impact on a child immediately, but that the effects are not detectable for several years and reemerge only later. Are our measurements faulty, or is the U-shaped function a real one? Sidney Strauss (personal communication, 1978), at Tel Aviv University, has claimed that the U-shaped function may be more characteristic of behavioral development than was supposed, and he has identified many reports in the literature that note the U-shaped function. However, because there is no theory to account for the findings, many investigators dismiss the result as a chance occurrence. Strauss claims that it may be not a chance occurrence but a real phenomenon. If this analysis turns out to be valid, it will have important implications for how we think about the developmental course.

However, in the general area of cognitive and intellectual functioning, if there is a U-shaped function of effects from early to later performance, it does not show up in the correlational data. The fond hope of detecting true intellectual capacity via infant intelligence testing has long been abandoned because there is no correlation between measures of infant intelligence and later intellectual functioning. In Lewis' (1976) *Origins of Intelligence,* many of the authors attempt to account for this fact. Sandra Scarr-Salapatek's (1976) analysis claims that infant intelligence is different from later intelligence in that the human organism in the first 2 years of life is essentially primed to acquire certain kinds of intelligent behaviors that are consonant with primate evolutionary history, that these biases are programmed by the epigenotype, and that human environments guarantee the development of these behaviors through the provision of material objects that are assimilated to them. Although different environments might produce different rates of development, Scarr-Salapatek (1976) claims that all normal infants in normal environments ultimately acquire all that is to be acquired in sensorimotor intelligence: "All nondefective infants reared in natural human environments achieve all of the sensorimotor skills that Piaget has described [p. 185]." Furthermore, she says, "Differences in rates of sensorimotor development are not yet assignable to genetic or environmental causes, but they are relatively unimportant variations on a strong primate theme [p. 194]."

One conclusion that might be drawn from Scarr-Salapatek's analysis is that early intervention programs in the first 2 years of life would be expected to have an immediate impact on the rate of development but no long-term impact on developmental outcome. Yet, the terms *normal* and *natural* environments and *nondefective* infants are important qualifying concepts. What is a normal, natural environment, and what is a nondefective infant? Hunt and his colleagues (Hunt, Paraskevopoulos, Schickedanz, & Uzgiris, 1975) reported on the achievement of different levels of object permanence in five different environments ranging from middle-class American homes and an American intervention center for lower-class infants to Greek settings where infants were reared in a municipal orphanage, a special center, and at home. The range in achievement of the highest level of object permanence tested (three hidden displacements and reversal) was over 2 years among the environments. The children in the American parent–child center achieved the top level at a mean of 73 weeks of age, while the children in the Athens municipal orphanage achieved the same level of performance at a mean of 182 weeks of age; within the Greek samples there was a range of over 60 weeks difference between the home-reared infants and the orphanage infants. Are these nondefective infants in normal, natural environments? According to Scarr-Salapatek's analysis, the answer is yes because the infants from these obviously very different environments did achieve the top level of object permanence. Environmental variations may influence rate of attainment but not the attainment itself.

Thus, one could look at the data in terms of natural variations in environments and not attribute later developmental outcome to any impact of the natural variations; on the other hand, one could say that the municipal orphanage produced retardation, and thus intervention to change the environment is needed. Yet, why would one want to intervene unless one predicted from this early environment some clearly detrimental effects on later development? Are the babies who achieve top level object permanence at 182 weeks of age less happy and contented, and are they developing less well than babies who achieve that level of competence at 73 weeks of age? If they are not demonstrably unhappy, discontented, and discomforted, the only reason for undertaking intervention to change the rate of early development is if you have evidence or reason to believe that such "retardation" in the sensorimotor period predicts retardation and diminished functioning later on in the life span. It is just this lack of prediction within a normal, nondefective population that produced Scarr-Salapatek's analysis and some notable recanting in the last several years. Kagan (1976) and others have claimed resilience in psychological development and an essential discontinuity between infancy and subsequent development: "a slowing or retardation in the emergence of universal psychological competencies during the first two years as a result of environmental factors have no important implication for the eventual attainment of universal intellectual competences during pre-adolescence if the environment after infancy is beneficial to growth [p. 103]." The Clarkes, in whose book Kagan's article and comments appear (Clarke & Clarke, 1976), have selectively reviewed a large amount of the literature and offer a rather convincing analysis to suggest that early experience is not, in and of itself, more important than later experience, at least well into the childhood years. Or, to put it more graphically, the wedge of influence is not necessarily thickest and most profound in the early years, trailing off to thin impact in the preschool years. Rather, if there are adverse experiences in the first few years of life, the effect of those adverse experiences can be and often is offset by a change of circumstances and environment. Early intervention might be undertaken for humane reasons, but it is not warranted on the basis of the evidence; if such intervention is not undertaken during the early years, one cannot say the child is doomed to an inadequate level of functioning no matter what happens. The main implication that Clarke and Clarke (1976) draw from their review is that "the whole of development is important, not merely the early years. There is as yet no indication that a given stage is clearly more formative than others; in the long term all may be important [p. 272]." Thus, according to this view, early experiences do not necessarily set a course of development in motion that cannot be modified given (the Clarkes stress) a change of circumstances.

So where are we? The Clarkes call for a rethinking of our models of development, and I think this request would be well heeded. However, there is a danger that we will rethink ourselves into the same levels of simplicity that existed in the recent past, ignoring the increasing sophistication of our own data base concerning development and failing to critically examine our research strategies in light of our goals. I would like to make several analyses and suggestions in this regard.

III. Some Suggestions for Future Inquiries

First, the terms *intervention, normal environments,* and *nondefective children* must be entirely reexamined if we are to carry out research that has any chance of increasing our understanding of how development happens. What is an intervention? The notion of intervention assumes that there is a normal process that occurs and has a particular outcome unless special action is taken. At the level of the human species, is there an unintervened state? Is birthing a child in a hospital an intervention that somehow deflects the natural course of events and necessitates a further intervention of early infant–mother contact in order to restore the natural course? One gets the general feeling that this is what Klaus and Kennell (1976) are saying, although an informative and delightful journey through the anthropological records on child-bearing practices by Betsy Lozoff (1977) suggests otherwise. Unlike wild flowers, the human organism is dependent upon intervention in order to survive. Therefore, the questions we must ask are what interventions normally practiced have what effects, and is the imposition of special interventions that would not otherwise occur likely to change the outcome?

However, in order to answer these questions, one must ask further questions. Are variations in developmental outcome dependent upon differential values of variables involved in basic processes? Assuming that development is dependent upon the interaction or transaction of the organism and the environment, what equation including what variables will account for developmental outcome? Are the variables and the form of the equation the same for every domain of behavior? Are they the same in every period of development? To what extent are individual variations a function of individual difference parameters? It is not enough to appreciate or describe individual differences, we must understand how they fit into the lawful relationships. For example, do these individual difference factors change the form of the equation? How many equations account for how many different developmental outcomes? What are the functional relationships and how do changes in values of the variables involved in the functional relationships affect developmental outcome?

If the call to rethink our models of development results only in models that do not assume continuity, we will have lost an important opportunity. Given what we now know, it is time to attempt much more profound reformulations. First, there may be discontinuity at the gross level of the measurements we now make but continuity at more subtle levels. Second, continuities may be much more complex than our current models; U-shaped functions may occur more frequently than supposed in a variety of domains over different developmental periods. Third, our measurement abilities may be extremely gross compared to the level of analysis that will ultimately enable us to account for our phenomena.

At the University of Kansas, we have been working with neonatal assessment in an attempt to determine the relationship of individual differences and environmental interactions. Jean Dempsey (1977) and then Joseph Sullivan (1977) refined the Neonatal Behavioral Assessment Scale measures so that we can score the infant's modal behavior as well as the infant's best behavior. We have also added some scores that tell us, for example, whether the examiner found the infant had reinforcing value during the examination. In a study completed by Guilio Lancioni (1978), entailing repeated measures on 200 newborn infants, it became clear that the modal and best responsiveness to visual and auditory stimuli, the rapidity of build-up, and the general irritability of the infant accounted for 85% of the variance of the reinforcing value of the infant for the examiner. At 1 month of age, general irritability alone accounted for 51% of the variance.

Patricia Linn (Linn & Horowitz, 1978) has collected some preliminary data in which the independent evaluation of the reinforcing value of the infant predicts whether the infant will be held in close proximity to or away from the mother's body in observations taken during a feeding session in the hospital.

However, I believe it would be a mistake to be encouraged by these data into thinking that early relationships of variables will predict later behavior. There is no reason to expect prediction unless one can assume that the form and function of the relationships are stable. Everything we know about development should tell us that they are not stable; the challenge to understanding development is to discover the form and function of the equations that account for development and to determine how these forms and functions change over time. Furthermore, we ought to expect that there will be a variety of forms and functions, that the forms and functions may change at different points in development, and that some of the parameters that may qualify forms and functions in very profound ways are associated with individual differences.

What does all of this mean for evaluating the data related to intervention and its effects on early development? In a word, it means caution; in two words, extreme caution. We cannot draw any conclusions; only those tentative conclusions that push us to adopt more complex models and increasingly refined measurement strategies will be helpful. We need to be continually aware that human development, from birth to death, is possibly the most complex phenomenon on this planet and that only a healthy respect for how complex it is will permit us to adopt a long-term strategy for unraveling the processes. The critical questions are not about continuity and discontinuity but about process and about programmatic research strategies designed to illuminate process.

What does all of this mean for the task of informing social policy concerning intervention during the earliest years? Our basic scientific task is to specify the conditions that result in particular developmental outcomes, and we are a long, long way from that capability. However, we do know that there are a certain percentage of children who "don't make it"—whose developmental outcomes do not permit them to function in ways that result in their having a variety of options in our society. Early intervention, for many of the reasons cited by the Clarkes (1976), has been seen as a panacea; it is not. If it has long-term effects, those effects are not startling in light of our current ability to detect effects. Nor is early intervention an innoculation against future developmental problems. It has been observed that development is not a disease to be declared present or absent but a *process* in which the functional variables are probably changing over time. If we were interested in preventing vitamin C deficiency at 10 years of age, extra glasses of orange juice at 4 years would hardly seem to be a reasonable preventive strategy. Why do we wish to assume that the models that work for development are simpler than those in other domains? As long as there is no demonstrated or theoretical risk associated with early intervention programs, we do not know enough to abandon them. It is premature for us to make a final decision about the merits of early intervention as long as the complex ethical issues are taken into account and the families involved are not exploited. However, we do now know enough so that we ought not to expect that if we provide only early intervention programs we will not have to do anything else to benefit a child's development.

REFERENCES

Appleton, T., Clifton, R., & Goldberg, S. The development of behavioral competence in infancy. In F. D. Horowitz (Ed.), *Review of child development research* (Vol. 4). Chicago: University of Chicago Press, 1975. Pp. 101–186.

Berlyne, D. E. The influence of the albedo and complexity of stimuli on visual fixation in the human infant. *British Journal of Psychology,* 1958, *49,* 315–318.

Bloom, B. S. *Stability and change in human characteristics.* New York: Wiley, 1964.

Bowlby, J. *Maternal care and health.* Geneva: World Health Organization, 1951.

Brainerd, C. *Piaget's theory of intelligence.* Englewood Cliffs, N.J.: Prentice-Hall, 1978.

Broman, S. H., Nichols, P. L., & Kennedy, W. A. *Preschool I.Q.: Prenatal and early developmental correlates.* Hillsdale, N.J.: Lawrence Erlbaum Associates, 1975.

Casler, L. Maternal deprivation: A critical review of the literature. *Monographs of the Society for Research in Child Development,* 1961, *26* (2, Serial No. 80).

Clarke, A. M., & Clarke, A. B. D. *Early experience: Myth and evidence.* New York: Free Press, 1976.

Dempsey, J. *The measurement of individual differences in newborns.* Unpublished master's thesis, University of Kansas, 1977.

Fantz, R. L. Pattern vision in young infants. *Psychological Record,* 1958, *8,* 43–47.

Freud, S. Introductory lectures on psychoanalysis. In *The standard edition of the complete psychological works of Sigmund Freud* (Vols. 15 & 16). London: Hogarth Press, 1963. (Lectures originally published, 1917).

Gesell, A. *Infancy and human growth.* New York: Macmillan, 1928.

Hebb, D. O. *The organization of behavior.* New York: Wiley, 1949.

Horowitz, F. D., & Paden, L. Y. The effectiveness of environmental intervention programs. In B. M. Caldwell & H. N. Ricciuti (Eds.), *Review of child development research* (Vol. 3). Chicago: University of Chicago Press, 1973. Pp. 331–402.

Hunt, J. M., Paraskevopoulos, J., Schickedanz, D., & Uzgiris, I. Variations in mean ages of achieving object permanence under diverse conditions of rearing. In B. Friedlander, G. Sterritt, & G. Kirk (Eds.), *Exceptional infant* (Vol. 3). New York: Bruner/Mazel, 1975. Pp. 247–262.

Jensen, A. R. How much can we boost IQ and scholastic achievement? *Harvard Educational Review,* 1969, *39,* 1–123.

Kagan, J. Resilence and continuity in psychological development. In A. M. Clarke & A. D. B. Clarke (Eds.), *Early experience: Myth and evidence.* New York: Free Press, 1976. Pp. 97–121.

Kirk, S. A. *Early education of the mentally retarded.* Urbana, Ill.: University of Illinois Press, 1958.

Klaus, M., & Kennell, J. *Maternal–infant bonding.* St. Louis, Mo.: C. V. Mosby, 1976.

Lancioni, G. *A study of the stability & structure of the NBAs-K over the first month of life.* Unpublished doctoral dissertation, The University of Kansas, 1978.

Lazar, I. *The persistence of preschool effects.* Ithaca, N.Y.; Community Service Laboratory, Cornell University, 1977.

Lewis, M. (Ed.). *Origins of intelligence.* New York: Plenum, 1976.

Linn, P., & Horowitz, F. D. *The assessment of newborn hospital environments and their relationships to newborn behaviors.* Paper presented at the International Conference on Infancy Studies, Providence, Rhode Island, March 1978.

Lozoff, B. *The sensitive period: An anthropologic view.* Paper presented at the meeting of the Society for Research in Child Development, New Orleans, March, 1977.

McNemar, Q. A critical examination of the University of Iowa studies of environmental influence on I.Q. *Psychological Bulletin,* 1940, *37,* 63–92.

Osofsky, J. (Ed.). *Handbook of infant development.* New York: Wiley, 1979.

Ramey, C., Stedman, D., Borders-Patterson, A., & Mengel, W. Predicting school failure from information available at birth. *American Journal of Mental Deficiency,* 1978, *82,* 525–534.

Rheingold, H. The modification of social responsiveness in institutionalized babies. *Monographs of the Society for Research in Child Development,* 1956, *21* (2).

Sameroff, A., & Chandler, M. Reproductive risk and the continuum of caretaking casualty. In F. D. Horowitz (Ed.), *Review of child development research* (Vol. 4). Chicago: University of Chicago Press, 1975. Pp. 187–244.

Scarr-Salapatek, S. An evolutionary perspective on infant intelligence, species patterns and individual variations. In M. Lewis (Ed.), *Origins of intelligence.* New York: Plenum, 1976. Pp. 165–197.

Skeels, H. M. Adult status of children with contrasting early life experiences: A follow-up study. *Monographs of the Society for Research in Child Development,* 1966, *31* (3).

Skeels, H. M., & Dye, H. B. A study of the effects of differential stimulation on mentally retarded children. *Proceedings and Addresses of the American Association on Mental Deficiency,* 1939, *44,* 114–136.

Skeels, H. M., Updegraff, R., Wellman, B. L., & Williams, H. M. A study of environmental stimulation: An orphanage preschool project. *University of Iowa Studies in Child Welfare,* 1938, *15* (4).

Stone, J., Smith, H., & Murphy, L. (Eds.). *The competent infant.* New York: Basic Books, 1973.

Sullivan, J. W. *Kansas supplements to the Neonatal Behavioral Assessment Scale: A first look.* Unpublished manuscript, University of Kansas, 1977.

Watson, J. B., & Raynor, R. Conditioned emotional reactions. *Journal of Experimental Psychology,* 1920, *3,* 1–14.

White, B. L. *The first three years of life.* Englewood Cliffs, N.J.: Prentice-Hall, 1975.

Yarrow, L. J. Maternal deprivation: Toward an empirical and conceptual reevaluation. *Psychological Bulletin,* 1961, *58,* 459–490.

CHAPTER 12

The Preschool Child or the Family?:
Changing Models of Developmental Intervention

RALPH R. TURNER[1]
WEST VIRGINIA UNIVERSITY
MORGANTOWN, WEST VIRGINIA

DAVID B. CONNELL and ARTHUR MATHIS
ABT ASSOCIATES INC.
CAMBRIDGE, MASSACHUSETTS

Developmental psychologists who are interested in intervention theory, practice, and evaluation can gain valuable insights from Head Start. During the project's 15-year history, there have been a number of changes in its focus, direction, and support. A complex set of forces has produced changes in the nature of the program's underlying intervention model. The direction of this change has been toward increasingly comprehensive programming that involves the entire family rather than just the preschool child.

In this chapter, we present a retrospective view of Head Start and suggest that the underlying theme of changes in the program can be described by a set of dimensions that define general intervention strategies. Movement along these dimensions has meant movement away from a *treatment model* of intervention toward a *service model*. We further suggest that the role of developmental research is not one of guiding policymaking directly, but one of shaping the methodology and instrumentation of evaluation research designed to assess the effects of intervention programs that, in turn, may result in the modification of strategy. Finally, we present a

---

[1] Present address: Abt Associates Inc., Cambridge, Massachusetts.

LIFE-SPAN DEVELOPMENTAL PSYCHOLOGY
Intervention

detailed discussion of the Child and Family Resource Program, suggesting that it not only represents the prototype of the service model of intervention but also is a program that reflects the influence of developmental research both in intervention strategies and in evaluation design.

I. Head Start: A Retrospective View

Launched during the summer of 1965 in 11,000 centers at a cost of $83 million in federal funds, Head Start programs initially operated 6-to-8 weeks in the summer and served 550,000 economically disadvantaged children; full-year programs were launched on a small scale in 1965–1966. Implementation difficulties, shortages of trained staff, problems in finding suitable space, and funding uncertainties plagued the starting period. During this period, the "full-year" programs often operated only 4 to 6 months of the year. Like their summer counterparts, the extended programs varied greatly in approach and were particularly uneven in the provision of comprehensive services and in the type and extent of parent participation. In a context of uncertainty, program personnel tended to concentrate on what was perceived to be the primary goal of the program—educational services for preschool children.

In 1967 a set of 36 Parent and Child Centers (PCCs) were created based upon the joint proposal of the White House Task Force on Early Childhood Education under the direction of J. McVicker Hunt and the U.S. Department of Health, Education, and Welfare (HEW) Task Force on Early Childhood Development. The PCCs were to provide comprehensive services for children under 3 years of age, including health, nutrition, social services, and educational and supportive services for parents and other family members. The personnel involved in these programs were to work intensively with impoverished parents to assist them in strengthening and enhancing their efforts to be effective teachers and guardians of their children. Despite critical evaluations (Holmes, Holmes, Greenspan, & Trapper, 1973; Kirschner Associates, 1970) and a relatively high expenditure per family, the PCCs have survived. Several factors were involved, and an examination of them provides additional insight into developmental intervention. First, in the early 1970s the Office of Child Development (OCD) was struggling for its own survival. The PCCs were in place and were operating as one of the few programs for children under 3 and their families. The OCD needed programs to survive and could not afford, politically, to disband the PCCs (Steiner, 1976). Second, and more relevant to this chapter, the PCC staff responded to research-based criticism by stating, "This was to be a service program . . . the 'experimental' aspects of the program were to be innovations in content and delivery of service, not experimental research [Costello, 1970, p. i]." Thus, PCC laid important groundwork for responses to the critics who were beginning to use negative evaluation research results as a means to discontinue programs.

In 1969 the results published from a large post hoc evaluation conducted by the Westinghouse Corporation and Ohio University involving children from a national sample of Head Start centers had a major impact on Head Start (Cicarelli, Cooper, & Granger, 1969). Specifically, the Westinghouse Report stated: (a) that children who participated in Head Start summer programs did not score higher on measures of academic achievement, linguistic development, and personal–social development than children who did not participate; and (b) children attending full-year Head Start programs had better scores than nonparticipants in the first grade but did not have better scores than children in the second or third grades (this effect was particularly evident for black, inner-city, and southern children). The results indicating that the *parental* response to the program was overwhelmingly positive were less publicized, although they were perhaps equally important. The Westinghouse evaluation helped to shape the public and academic image of Head Start as a program whose effects were intended to be primarily in the area of school achievement. In fact, many of the recommendations following from the findings did find their way into Head Start policy. One exception was the suggestion that Head Start concentrate upon remediating specific academic deficiencies (Recommendation 2c). Although that recommendation did result in the establishment of the Head Start Planned Variation (HSPV) initiative, the vast majority of Head Start centers maintained an approach to services that included increased general learning opportunities for children, improved health and nutrition, and increased parental support for child development (Datta, 1975b).

In 1970 the first major evaluation concerned with the impact of Head Start upon communities was published (Kirschner Associates, 1970). Although the results of this evaluation were not widely publicized, the study documented that the program had influenced change in four areas: (a) increased involvement by the poor at decision-making levels; (b) increased employment of the poor as paraprofessionals; (c) increased emphasis on the educational needs of the poor; (d) modified health services and practices that served the poor more adequately and sensitively. Needless to say, this evaluation was received by Head Start administrators as an important endorsement of the program.

Partly in response to the Westinghouse study, Head Start was officially converted from a summer activity to a full-year project (although "full-year" remained somewhat loosely defined in practice) in 1970. The immediate impact was a drastic reduction in the number of children served, from an average 700,000 during the years 1966–1969 to about 400,000 from 1970–1978. In 1979 the program served only about 24% of the eligible population of children.

The Head Start Planned Variation initiative began in fall of 1969 as an attempt to systematically test curricula in sites that were not under the immediate control of the curriculum developers. The intent was to assess implementation, test the interaction of program effects and target population characteristics, and measure the long-term effects of specific academic approaches. Between 1969 and 1972, 12 sponsors participated in the program, as has been discussed in detail in a number of reports (cf. Rivlin & Timpane, 1975).

By 1972 a 3-year plan had been designed to introduce innovations and upgrade program quality. The Head Start Improvement and Innovation (I&I) effort has been one of the most comprehensive attempts to revitalize and redirect a major social program by the federal government. Policies regarding minimum length of the program year were developed, and Program Performance Standards were introduced that set forth basic requirements to be met as a condition of continued funding for the provision of services. Although it had always been expected that programs would deliver comprehensive services, no mandatory level of program activities in each component had ever been set forth, and there was no enforcement machinery to insure compliance. Recognizing the need for Head Start programs to tailor features of their activities to local conditions, the standards specified only those services required of all Head Start centers in the areas of education, parent involvement, social services, and health services (which included medical, dental, mental health, and nutrition). In addition, options were designated that permitted local centers to offer programs to their clients that differed from the 5-day week center-based model.

Head Start program initiatives beginning after the Westinghouse evaluation (1969) reflected the influence of that report. Specifically, the report recommended that more effective programs would result from: (a) intervention strategies that were of longer duration, perhaps extended down toward infancy and up to the primary grades; (b) variation in teaching strategies commensurate with specific characteristics of children; (c) training of parents to become more effective teachers for their children. Although these recommendations had been stated previously and had actually been implemented in part by the PCCs, they were now directly reflected in several influential demonstration programs: Parent–Child Development Centers (PCDC), Home Start, Child and Family Resource Program (CFRP), Project Developmental Continuity (PDC), the Bilingual-Bicultural Curriculum Development Project, and the Basic Educational Skills (BES) project. Figure 12.1 provides a comparison of these programs.

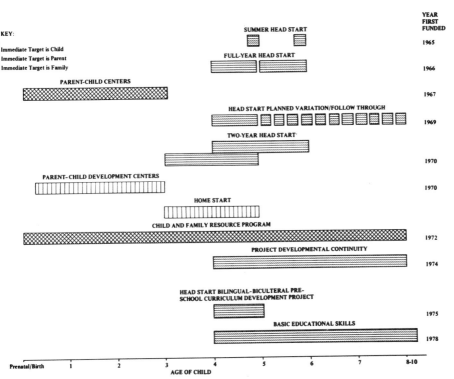

Figure 12.1. Previous Head Start-related intervention programs are compared. Summer, full-year, and 2-year Head Start programs are split into two age levels: entering Kindergarten and entering first grade. The Follow Through program was not under the direction of Head Start but was operated by the U.S. Office of Education.

In 1970 three PCCs were selected as research sites and renamed as Parent–Child Development Centers (PCDCs). Their aim was to develop programs for mothers and children from 3 to 36 months of age and to provide services that included: (a) guidance for child development and care; (b) health and nutrition education and guidance; (c) information about community resources; (d) social services.

In 1972, 16 Home Start projects were funded. Efforts were focused primarily upon parents rather than children, but they were generally concerned with the well-being of the entire family. Program services stressed the importance of health care and nutrition and emphasized the appropriate use of community resources. The program was expected to benefit parents, their preschool (and other) children, and even unborn children through improved parenting practices as well as improved family use of community services. By 1977 over 350 Head Start programs offered some form of home-based option.

In 1973, 11 Head Start programs received additional funds to incorporate program aspects of Head Start, PCC, and Home Start into a single program—the Child and Family Resource Program (CFRP). The program enrolled entire families with children from birth to 8 years of age and provided services to children and parents designed to promote their active and successful participation in the community. CFRP has been, and continues to be, carefully evaluated. As a result of these evaluations, which are described in detail in Section VI of this chapter, CFRP has been recommended to the Congress by the General Accounting Office (1979) as an intervention strategy that holds great potential for effective developmental intervention among low-income families.

In 1975 funds were allocated for 14 Project Developmental Continuity (PDC) planning grants. As a response to the discontinuity, often in physical location as well as in instructional flow, that is experienced by children as they move from Head Start through some early childhood (kindergarten) program and into elementary school, PDC was designed to provide continous, individualized instruction during that period. Each site developed multifaceted instructional packages that included education, handicapped mainstreaming, parental involvement, health, multicultural curricula, and nutrition.

Also in 1975, Head Start initiated a bilingual–bicultural strategy for programs serving Spanish-speaking children. The strategy included curriculum development, staff-training, technical assistance through a resource center, and research projects. Four curriculum models, each having as a foundation the principles of child development and the language and cultural needs of Spanish-speaking children, were developed. Each model incorporates both English and Spanish and is adaptable for use in multicultural settings as well.

Finally, in 1978 Head Start initiated the Basic Educational Skills (BES) project. This project is intended to synthesize Head Start and model programs approaches to promote and sustain long-range program enhancement of social competence (a child's effectiveness in dealing with his or her environment, school responsibilities, and life). The focus of BES is on increasing the intensity and specificity of proven Head Start activities and experiences that will lead to the acquisition of developmentally appropriate educational skills. The project links Head Start programs and public schools, together with strong parent involvement, in a collaborative effort to facilitate the child's learning experiences.

From the perspective just provided, one can detect Head Start's major underlying theme: From its inception in 1965, Head Start has been actively involved in broadening its program along a number of dimensions. This systematic change reflects changes in the concept of effective intervention that is held in the public (i.e., federal) sector and results from the combined input of basic developmental research, the outcome of evaluation research, and the influence of a host of Head Start advocates. Following a discussion of the dimensions along which program changes can be shown to have occurred, we will explore how the various forces combined to produce the currently held view of effective developmental intervention.

II. Alternate Models of Intervention

In Chapter 2 of this volume, Reese and Overton present an in-depth analysis of models, methods, and goals of intervention. We propose that there are two general models that reflect different views of intervention, only one of which Reese and Overton discuss. These models are not discrete but represent end points on a set of dimensions that describe intervention strategies. The "narrow" ends of these dimensions define the *treatment* model, which is best characterized by the features discussed by Reese and Overton. This is the model that is most familiar to academic professionals and from which most research and demonstration projects involving preschoolers were developed. The "broad" end of these dimensions describes the *service* model. Large scale, publically financed, intervention projects such as "basic" Head Start are derived from this model, which finds widespread support among practitioners and parents. Both models have been instrumental in shaping public policy toward developmental intervention. In this section we will examine the features of both models along with their underlying dimensions; we will then discuss the contributions of each model to a public policy of developmental intervention that increasingly reflects the acceptance of the *service* model as a guiding principle.

A. Treatment Model

Treatment, from our perspective, involves intervention in the experimental or quasi-experimental sense. Using this model, researchers develop intervention strategies that reflect a consistent theoretical foundation; this position reflects the notion that theory generates practice, which is discussed by Reese and Overton. The deficit and difference intervention models (cf. Reese and Overton) are subsumed under our treatment model, for both view the target, typically a single individual, as lacking something (deficit) or as possessing something that is not maximally functional (difference). In either case the treatment interventionist prescribes a series of events that is designed to change the individual in a specific way or for some specific purpose. As discussed by Horowitz and Paden (1973) and by Reese and Overton (this volume), the goal of these prescriptions may be to *enrich* the course of normal development by fostering "better" (e.g., faster, more complex) outcomes or, if the normal course of events seems destined to produce an unsatisfactory set of outcomes, to *prevent* such outcomes from occurring. Intervention programs that adhere to the treatment model generally can be distinguished by: (*a*) the specification of program activities by program planners; (*b*) the existence of specialized staff trained to deliver a specific treatment to each target in the program; (*c*) a focus upon a well-identified process or set of outcomes that serve as indices of program success; (*d*) an expectation that program benefits may be retained for long periods after the treatment ceases. Of course, few would argue that "pure" versions of such programs exist; experience has shown that uniform program implementation and treatment success with preschool children is not yet feasible. However, a number of early intervention programs were founded upon such principles, and proponents for the treatment model are still influential.

B. Service Model

In contrast, the service model maintains that intervention programs should provide specific services in response to the identifiable needs of individuals. This is the model that is frequently accepted by parents and by administrators and program staff members at the local and regional levels, and it is becoming increasingly influential among policy decision makers. In our view, this model does not fit directly into the Reese and Overton (this volume) characterizations since theory in the service model is often implicit. Although specific services—for example, intervention by a special education professional—may indeed follow from specific theoretical assumptions, the service model as an intervention strategy does not. As will be discussed in Section VI of this chapter, evaluation research designed to examine the effectiveness of this model often forces the explication of assumptions that guide the belief that a set of specific services put into a "black box" will result in specific outcomes from it. One could take the position that such a process represents the Reese and Overton (this volume) notion that "theory and practice interact reciprocally, each generating and generated by the other." As the underlying assumptions are made clear, they may well alter the practice of service delivery. At the same time, it is the practice that is guiding the explication of the theoretical assumptions.

The service model, then, concentrates on direct delivery or coordination of services that ameliorate or remedy specific client problems. Although long-term improvements are expected to follow from removal of problem situations, immediate short-term benefits are more highly valued in this model. Distinguishing characteristics of the model include: (*a*) the individualization of services to meet client needs; (*b*) the presence of experienced staff that are familiar with community problems and assistance agencies; (*c*) an emphasis upon an atheoretical approach that emphasizes process measures of success; (*d*) methods that facilitate or coordinate services instead of providing direct instruction or assistance.

III. Dimensions of Intervention Strategies

As was suggested earlier, one can conceive of a set of dimensions that describe different emphases in intervention strategies. The treatment model can be located at the narrow end of these dimensions, whereas the service model can be located at the broad end. This section presents a discussion of the dimensions along which the nature of programmatic intervention has moved. Although this discussion is not exhaustive, the dimensions presented do capture the major trends and provide the reader with a conceptual framework.

A. *Individualization*

The individualization dimension is concerned with the nature by which the program process and outcome goals are established. This process needs to be distinguished from individual instructional objectives, although these objectives may be included. In the traditional treatment program, the goals, set by the program planner, are generally uniform for the participants in the sense that all will move toward, if not actually achieve, them. In the service-oriented programs, the program personnel, together with the client, set *individual* goals that may vary greatly in content and comprehensiveness as well as in the target toward which they are directed and the means by which they are to be achieved. Thus, the scale of this dimension involves the origin of the program goals and moves this locus from the program planner toward the client. Two different enrichment programs that were derived from very different theoretical perspectives—the Bereiter–Englemann (1966) project and the Ypsilanti Perry Preschool Project (Weikart, 1970)—serve as good illustrations. In both programs, the planners developed goals and curricula that were designed to foster them. These were transported to the site and implemented by the program staff. Evaluation centered around a common question: Did the children who received the treatment obtain the goals? In contrast, the PCC and CFRP demonstration projects established goals that were arrived at mutually with the client and thus were individually tailored. However, when the client is active in the objective-setting phase, evaluation questions and criteria become considerably more complex. Although the Parent and Child Center (PCC) programs were obstensibly designed to assist mothers with children under 3 years of age, the actual nature and level of that assistance has varied from site to site and from client to client within individual sites. In the Child and Family Resource Program (CFRP) sites, the process by which goals are set is more routine, but individualization is clearly the course of action.

B. Target

A second dimension along which programs can be categorized involves the *target* of intervention. During the history of preschool intervention projects, the target has shifted from a primary focus upon the child, to a focus upon the parent as an agent for effecting change in the child, and, finally, to a focus on the entire family structure, which is seen as the environment in which the child is developing.

Child-targeted programs were prototypical in preschool intervention treatments and were the general model upon which basic Headstart was conceived. Demonstration projects such as those implemented by Bereiter and Englemann (1966) and Weikart (1970) explored specific kinds of intervention strategies based on the program planner's notions of how children develop. In the basic Head Start programs, some of these ideas were incorporated, but the typical education component was, and still is, eclectic in nature.

More direct parental involvement as a catalyst for change is seen in programs in which the parent is the primary target. These programs were designed with the intention of having an impact on the parent in order to have an impact on the child. The skills, abilities, and attitudes that were the targets of the programs were manipulated with an eye toward subsequent changes in child outcome measures. Although many intervention programs have involved home visitation and parental participation (e.g., Early Training Project, Gray & Klaus, 1970; Philadelphia Project, Beller, 1972), the Levenstein (1970) Verbal Interaction Project provides perhaps the purest example of parental targeting. As Bronfenbrenner (1974) states, "The [Levenstein] strategy involves a particular kind of experience that is focused in its purpose, sustained, sequential, and highly structural in cognitive, social, and motivational terms. . . . First, Levenstein's strategy has as its *target* not the child as an individual, but the mother–child dyad as an interactive system. Second, the principle and direct agent of intervention becomes not the tutor, but the mother [p. 26]." A second example of a parent-targeted program was reported by Gordon (1971). The model involved phased sequence in which family-centered intervention was begun during the first 2 years of life; preschool components were introduced on a limited basis and expanded as the child neared preschool age. Throughout the program, the parent was targeted and functioned as the primary agent of intervention for the child.

Programs focusing on the *family,* as the third target, view it as the arena in which the child develops and interacts. Family-targeted programs contain project objectives that have an impact on each family member's development, not just the child's. The primary example of this approach is the Child and Family Resource Program (CFRP). The intent of CFRP is to provide support services to each member of the family, either directly or indirectly. A detailed description of the CFRP program follows in Section V of this chapter, but a few examples here will serve to illustrate the point. Family services have been developed that involve direct counseling and assistance as well as referral to community agencies. Parent involvement includes direct parent participation in the early childhood education component as well as parent education on a wide variety of subjects including child development and nutrition.

C. Scope

Preschool intervention projects range in scope from narrow, involving a single process, to comprehensive, involving several processes that are targeted for intervention. The Bereiter–Englemann program (1966), for example, focused on the acquisition of tools for academic learning—verbal and numerical symbols. The Verbal Interaction Project (Levenstein, 1970) concentrated on parent–child verbal interactions. On the other hand, the Philadelphia Project (Beller, 1972) sought to improve performance across a range of processes involving both intellectual functioning and socioemotional functioning. Still wider scope is found in the comprehensive CFRP project, which contains several targets for each of the four service components: family services, early childhood education services, parent involvement services, and health and nutrition services.

D. Uniformity of Implementation

Programs can be categorized according to their standardization of each of the implementation sites. On one end of the scale, identical versions of the program, or planned variations of that program, are implemented at the same level at all of the sites. On the other end, the particular program components may be designed by, and implemented in, each of the individual sites. Head Start Planned Variation (Datta, 1975a) demonstrates the uniform pole. Three waves of Head Start children (in 1969, 1970, and 1971) were involved—some 2000 children each year. About one-third of the children attended regular Head Start classes and the other two-thirds attended classes supervised by 12 curriculum sponsors. Each sponsored program was implemented uniformly at the sites under the control of that sponsor. In contrast, regular Head Start programs are provided with uniform performance standards and guidance, but the actual program implementation is at the discretion of the local head teachers and project directors.

E. Types of Service Delivery

The final dimension characterizes the types of services that the project delivers. At one pole, the services are delivered directly, whereas at the other, there is a coordination of the services that are available from the community. The Parent–Child Development Center (PCDC) project is designed to provide direct services by the program staff, including guidance of child development and care, maternal–child health and nutrition educational sessions and services, and activities, classes, and special lectures on a wide variety of topics of interest and concern to the parents. In contrast, the CFRP staff provides a minimum of direct service. Rather, staff members serve as resource persons—"superfriends"—that know who can get what done for whom. Armed with a comprehensive list of agencies and contacts, they coordinate services for all members of the family across all content areas, including academic tutoring for the child and job training for the parent.

IV. Impact of Models on Intervention Policy Decisions

The increasing support for preschool intervention strategies that reflect the broad end of the proposed dimensions suggests that advocates of the service model have been more influential in the policymaking arena than those supporting the treatment model. In this section we will examine the impact of each model on the decision-making process and suggest that developmental theory, reflected in the treatment model, has had, and will continue to have, an impact, but that this impact is different from the one generally anticipated by basic developmental researchers.

The nature and dynamics of public policy formation have received widespread attention from a variety of social scientists, and we will not attempt an in-depth discussion here. Rather, we refer the interested reader to any of a number of sources—for example, Abt (1975), Anderson (1975), Dye (1978), and Jones and Thomas (1976)—and establish here a framework within which the treatment and service models are discussed.

Cook (1979) has suggested that the science community, including basic developmental researchers who advocate the treatment model, hold a "naive view" of the impact of research on decision making—namely the view that research findings become a guide or a blueprint for decision making and action. In fact, research findings are only one of several factors in a complex "debate" format that includes political considerations, social values, chance events, and the idiosyncratic preferences of the policy formulators. Research on knowledge utilization indicates that research findings function as a backdrop or frame of reference that raises the consciousness of the policymaker but does not directly influence the decisions (Caplan, 1977; Weiss, 1977).

The nature of knowledge utilization stems in part from the failure of basic research to deliver a "clean bottom line" (i.e., unequivocal results) to policymakers; little clean-cut developmental theory has emerged that *could* be used as a blueprint. The result is that policymakers do not *expect* research findings to be of direct use. The "set" for the treatment model is already negative. In addition, the various research and demonstration projects that were designed to test specific theoretical assumptions have had an impact on relatively few children and have had limited visibility. Moreover, the programs often had objectives that were different from those of the policymakers. Suchman (1967) suggested a series of questions that program evaluators ask, including "Who got the program?" and "What effect did the program have?" The policymakers are often politically interested primarily in who got the program (the service issue) and are not overly concerned with the magnitude of the effect (the treatment issue). As a result, the treatment model has not directly influenced policy decision making. At the same time, the nature of program administration—service delivery, in effect, for the majority of Head Start projects—has become increasingly complex.

As the definition of preschool intervention programs has broadened to include other family members and increasingly comprehensive services, the distinctions among programs have become obscured and their administration has become more complex. For example, Head Start required all grantees to insure that children receive health screening, assessment, and treatment where necessary. The Early Periodic Screening Detection and Treatment Program (EPSDT) is funded to provide just such services, and thus the role of Head Start grantees is to coordinate delivery. However, eligibility for EPSDT is determined by state agencies, whereas Head Start eligibility is federally determined. Children eligible for Head

Start may not be eligible for EPSDT and vice versa. Furthermore, at the present time EPSDT is not administered evenly within or between states, and frequently the services for which a child is eligible are simply not available. In order to provide the required services, the Head Start grantee must find funds or services elsewhere and, in the process, become an active, visible advocate for the service model.

At the same time, parents have had to become more involved in broadened programs. Historically, *parent involvement* has meant that parents should have a say in the specification and administration of the program, including the hiring of staff. As parent education models became popular in the early 1970s, parents were given a role in child stimulation and education. Warnings of potential program abuses of that role have been issued. Basically, critics view an emphasis on the parent-as-teacher model as a possible means of shifting responsibility in the case of program failure (Goodson & Hess, 1978; Schlossman, 1978). Hess and Jacks (1978) warn that parent education models may serve to undermine the confidence of parents in their parenting instincts, create a dependence upon the program for parenting advice, and generally diminish the authority of the family. Whether or not such fears are well founded, programs such as the PCCs and CFRP have given priority to individualization and delivery of services, thus establishing parents as partners in program design. As a result, the level of parent involvement in preschool intervention programs has been increasingly raised during the years between 1965 and 1979. Along with that increased involvement has come political responsiveness; policymakers interested in "who got the program" recognize the level of parental satisfaction in Head Start. In 1979, service model advocates (parents and administrators) were instrumental in blocking a reorganization plan that would have moved Head Start to the proposed Department of Education—a move viewed by some as potentially changing the focus of Head Start to that of a preschool readiness program.

Throughout the history of Head Start, administrators at the national and regional levels have dealt with a decentralized program having great variation from site to site. Since the early 1970s, the development of administrative procedures to maintain program accountability (as distinct from financial accountability) and to signal problem areas while not threatening valuable program diversity has been a major effort, resulting in the development of Head Start Performance Standards (discussed previously) and of the Self-Assessment Validation Instrument (SAVI). SAVI procedures require each grantee to submit a self-assessment for each area of the Performance Standards. On a 3-year schedule, a team of technical assistance specialists and regional HEW staff conduct an intensive review of SAVI items at the Head Start sites. Discrepancies are noted and technical assistance is scheduled when necessary.

As programs become even more diverse, the challenge for administrators is to specify meaningful standards that apply to each Head Start center yet do not eliminate the ability of Head Start to shape the program to meet local needs. In addition, increased program diversity increases the difficulties involved in providing adequate training and technical assistance to local staff. Assistance staff must be familiar with both local conditions and required procedures.

Thus, the service model advocates have been relatively more influential in the policymaking arena for several reasons. First, the majority of Head Start projects are supported by public funding agencies that are service oriented and, as a result, serve many more children and are more visible while doing so than are research and demonstration projects. Second, as the administration of these projects has become more complex, the administrators and parents have become increasingly active and effective in presenting their needs in the policymaking "debate." Finally, the results of the research and demonstration initiatives have not been clean-cut and have not played a direct role in the decision-making process. However, recent results from longitudinal research (Lazar, 1978) have shown that participants in intervention programs were more likely to be found in the correct grade in the later elementary school years and were less likely to have been recommended for special education. These effects *combined* with overwhelming parental support have resulted in a resurgence of support for Head Start (Palmer, 1979).

Developmental research and theory will have an increasingly influential, if indirect, role in the design of evaluation research efforts. Growing out of the pressure for accountability in social programs, evaluation research provides a framework for a linkage between the treatment and service models. Suchman (1967) has argued that just such a link is the key to progress in intervention strategy development: "Action programs in any professional field should be based upon the best available scientific knowledge and theory of that field. Since such a knowledge base is the foundation of any action program, the evaluation researchers who [systematically test] some theoretical proposition rather than a set of administrative practices. . .make the most significant contribution to program development [p. 170]."

Cohen (Chapter 7 of this volume) presents a comparison between experimental and evaluation research that provides insights into how such a linkage might be formed. In the same manner that traditional experimental research methods provide evidence that confirms or disaffirms underlying theoretical propositions, evaluation research methods provide evidence for the effectiveness of an intervention strategy. In both cases, the results are used to modify the assumptions. As developmental intervention programs have broadened, the need for more complex research design has become clear. Individualization within programs as well as site-to-site variations have made imperative the task of linking individual *process* (the interactions of a client with the program) with the *outcomes*. It is no longer sufficient simply to count the services delivered or to test children's pre- and post program participation. Furthermore, the range of both process and outcome variables has become enormous as programs have incorporated parents and families as intervention targets. Such topics as parent knowledge and use of community services, family capacity for independence, and family coping skills are now regions of evaluation interest.

Developmental research findings are contributing to the design of intervention strategies and to the development of evaluation instrumentation that is sensitive to the kinds of change the intervention is designed to promote. Research in social competence provides a good example. The promotion of social competence has been taken up by Head Start as a developmental objective (Zigler & Trickett, 1978). Much of the recent research has been directed toward operationalization of the concept and developing assessment techniques that are ecologically valid and, therefore, are prime candidates for inclusion in evaluation designs (see Kohn, 1977). The results of these evaluation efforts can be fed back into both intervention strategy design and theory modification. However, such a linkage requires increased awareness of evaluation research results by developmental researchers.

An important example of the use of developmental research findings to design and implement intervention and evaluation strategies is found in the Child and Family Resource Program.

V. The Child and Family Resource Program: Model and Objectives

The Child and Family Resource Program (CFRP) is a national Head Start demonstration program and is part of the Head Start Improvement and Innovation efforts to develop models for providing developmental services and support to families with young children. The CFRP enrolls eligible low-income families whose children are under 8 years of age; a particular emphasis is placed on children from birth to 3 years and on children from 5 to 8 years who have entered public school. CFRP also includes traditional Head Start classroom education and services for preschool children. Not only does the program serve a broader age range of children than Head Start, it also focuses on the entire family rather than just on the child and works through the family to promote healthy growth and development for children. Perhaps the most distinctive features of CFRP are its emphasis on a comprehensive assessment of each family's strengths and needs and its creation of an individualized program developed with the family for services obtained through CFRP.

In addition to offering the full range of educational, health, and social services provided through Head Start, CFRP also provides

1. Comprehensive individual assessment of family and child needs based on consultation with the family.
2. Preventive, treatment, and rehabilitative services as required for individually diagnosed medical, dental, nutritional, and mental health needs of children up to 8 years of age.
3. Family support services including emergency services, individual and group counseling, referral services, and family planning assistance.
4. Prenatal medical care and educational services for pregnant mothers.
5. Developmental services for families and children, including
   a. Programs to assist parents in promoting the total development of infants and toddlers through age 3 (*The Infant-Toddler Component*)
   b. Preschool comprehensive Head Start services for children ages 3 to 5 in the *Head Start Center*
   c. Programs designed to ensure smooth transition for children from preschool into the early elementary grades (*The Preschool-School Linkage Component*)
   d. Group activities and family development programs for parents
   e. Special programs for children with handicapping conditions

Once a family is enrolled in CFRP, the assessment process is begun with family members. The CFRP staff takes the major share of responsibility for identifying services and activities the family wants from CFRP. CFRP staff members then employ a variety of strategies to secure for families the desired services. They work directly with CFRP family members, particularly with parents and children between birth and age 8; they work indirectly on behalf of families by coordinating or advocating better services for particular families. They also work with community agencies to improve services in general for low-income families and to develop needed services not already available in the community. Interactions among CFRP staff, families, and the community are therefore complex and interrelated. Families influence the particular set of services they get from CFRP; CFRP influences the family directly and indirectly by affecting the way the family interacts with the community. The community influences the services provided by the CFRP and constitutes the environment in which families rear their children. Through their coordination work, CFRP staff members also influence the services available and families' access to them. CFRPs have one other source of influence: National CFRP Guidelines and direction from the national CFR Program Office in the Administration for Children, Youth, and Families (ACYF). CFRP in operation involves four sets of actors and the relationships among them: families, CFRP staff and program operations, the local communities in which CFRPs operate, and ACYF's national policies toward CFRP. Each of these is represented by a box in the model shown in Figure 12.2.

A. Community–CFRP Link

The CFRP is expected to *coordinate* existing community services in order to avoid duplication and to develop new services as needed by participating families. Therefore, the CFRP staff members must be involved with the social, political, and economic structure of the community both as advocates for low-income families in general and as coordinators and facilitators of services for CFRP families.

B. Family–CFRP Links

Interactions between CFRP staff and families are basically of two types. CFRP staff members interact directly with family members by assessing their strengths and needs and then helping parents make plans for the services and activities they want. Direct interactions include center-based pro-

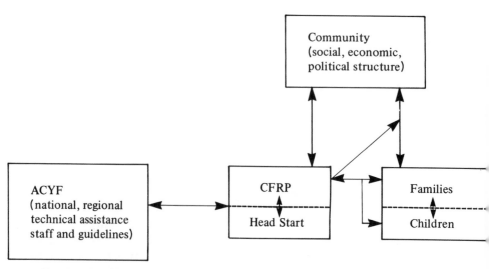

Figure 12.2. The Child and Family Resource Program model shows four sets of actors and the relationships among them.

grams to assist activities for mothers and infants, home visits to parents, Head Start services for preschoolers, group activities and family development education for parents, and prenatal medical care and educational services for pregnant mothers. CFRP's influence on children is considered to be "filtered" through interactions with the family in this model. That is, outcomes for children as a result of participation in CFRP depend primarily on the program's work with families rather than on intervention directly for children. In addition, CFRP influences the interactions between enrolled families and the community. The program builds upon the capabilities of existing services provided by other agencies; it assists and advises families about available resources and thereby reduces fragmentation and gaps in the delivery of relevant services.

C. ACYF–CFRP Link

ACYF has established *CFRP Guidelines* that identify general goals and specify minimum services to be provided (including those required by the Head Start Performance Standards). Local projects are also influenced by training and technical assistance staff and by staff from national and regional ACYF offices who advise and assist programs in meeting required standards. In turn, the projects provide feedback through these staff and through periodic reports upon the types of activities and resources that would be most responsive to the needs of the target families.

It is important to recognize that what distinguishes CFRP from traditional Head Start programs is not only the model of services and activities provided but also its underlying philosophy toward working with families and operating as a central source of services and support for them. This philosophy is expressed in CFRP's stated objectives:

1. To *individualize and tailor programs* and services to children and their families
2. To *link resources in the community* so that families may choose from a variety of programs and services but deal primarily with one resource center for all young children in the same family
3. To *provide continuity of resources and support* to families in order to guide the development of their children from the prenatal period through the early school years
4. To *enhance and build upon the strengths of the individual family* as a child-rearing system with distinct values, culture, and aspirations

It is this philosophy, as well as the mix of services offered, that CFRP was designed to test, demonstrate, and explore as a research and demonstration program.

VI. Evaluation of the Demonstration

Beginning in 1973, the CFRP was funded through Head Start grantees in 11 locations (one in each of the 10 HEW regions and one representing the Indian and Migrant Division) to demonstrate the feasibility of developing comprehensive approaches to providing child and family services within the framework of Head Start. Each program received about $125,000 per year for each of the demonstration years, and each was to serve between 80 and 100 families (see Table 12.1).

The present evaluation contract was awarded to Abt Associates Inc., (AAI) in October 1977. ACYF requires complex information about the effectiveness of CFRP in order to make policy decisions about the expansion of CFRP models or the expansion of some of their important features within Head Start. The broad policy questions posed by ACYF are these:

1. What should be the nature and extent of services provided to families in order to enhance their child's development?
2. What processes work best?
3. What should be the nature and extent of the continuity of services delivered to children?
4. For how long and through what processes should these services be delivered?

A. Study Sample

The primary research sample consists of families in six summative sites. In each of these sites, CFRP staff compiled a list of 100–120 families that were eligible for CFRP but not enrolled in it, with the condition that an infant under 1 year of age was a member of all recruited families. From the list of families in each site, 40 families were randomly selected for enrollment in CFRP; the remainder of the list formed the comparison group.

B. Evaluation Variables

Many evaluations of programs for children have been primarily input–outcome models in which outcomes for children were compared and related to background or entry-level characteristics and some relationship of these outcomes to the intervening program was assumed or hypothesized. In the CFRP evaluation, *inputs* include background variables for families and staff, community resources and demographics, descriptions of program organization, and information about regional and national ACYF guidance. Input variables describe the context in which the CFRPs

Table 12.1

Summary of CFRP Sites [a]

	Location/type	Number staff	Number families	Race (in percentages)			
				Black	Hispanic	Native American	White
Six summative sites							
New Haven, Connecticut	Urban	13	101	54	16	0	30
St. Petersburg, Florida	Urban	10	138	85	0	0	15
Jackson, Michigan	Rural and small town	12	102	30	5	0	65
Las Vegas, Nevada	Urban pocket, rural surround	13	82	50	10	10	30
Oklahoma City, Oklahoma	Rural	18	97	90	0	0	10
Salem, Oregon	Small town	22	110	5	0	10	85
Other program sites							
Modesto, California	Rural	4	80	0	100	0	0
Gering, Nebraska	Rural	25	108	0	54	14	33
Poughkeepsie, New York	Urban	8	80	50	0	0	50
Bismarck, North Dakota	Urban pocket, rural surround	18	99	4	0	9	87
Pottsville, Pennsylvania	Rural	21	141	4	0	0	96

[a] Data compiled from informal conversations with CFRP Project Directors in October 1977.

operate—the available resources and the characteristics of communities and variables served at any point in time.

Outcome variables are expected to capture the effects of CFRP participation. Families in the evaluation are being assessed in seven outcome areas (the last two areas apply only to families in CFRP):

1. Family circumstances
2. Maternal and child health
3. Parent–child relationships and interaction
4. Child development and achievement
5. Capacity for independence (use of community resources, coping strategies, affiliation with family and social networks)
6. Attainment of goals set by CFRP and staff
7. Family satisfaction with CFRP

Two remaining sets of variables used in this evaluation are *process* and *output*. Each category of variables represents one of two aspects of CFRP treatment: the services and activities delivered (output) and the processes and interactions through which the services are planned and delivered (process).

It is common for the term *process* to refer to a type of study rather than to a set of variables within the study. In the former sense, a process evaluation is one that identifies whether programs are providing the services for which they are mandated (Zigler & Trickett, 1978). In such a study the identification and description of services delivered is often the sole definition of program treatment. The nature and goals of CFRP, however, require a much more extensive definition of treatment. To be sure, CFRP is mandated to provide services and activities; but it is also guided by general goals that imply the importance of how services are provided as well as what services are provided. The most important of these general goals is individualization of services to families. Others include fostering independence for families, building on family strengths, and providing continuity of resources.

Output variables are the services and activities produced in general by program effort or obtained by specific families. Output and outcome variables are not the same. Examples of output variables include meetings, home visits, and immunizations—things received by families or provided by CFRP that can be counted. Outputs are important in identifying the pattern or emphasis of services in a particular project, whether they are direct or referral, group or individually oriented. They are also an important way of determining individualization.

Process variables may be of two types. First, there are those that refer to the transactions between staff and family members with regard to (*a*) the assessment and development of a program plan with each family; (*b*) the nature of staff activity with families, which can be categorized as primarily instrumental (doing things for the family), affective (listening or talking with the family), or a mixture (a home visitor teaching about child development); and (*c*) the functions and responsibilities assumed by staff and family in obtaining services or carrying out plans. Second, there are process variables that represent both programs activity in community advocacy and service coordination and activity in defining and maintaining the program itself. This last category includes setting goals or priorities for the program, maintaining staff communication and support, and arranging training and career development for staff.

The CFRP model and evaluation summarize the two major themes of this chapter. First, CFRP represents the end point of an evolution of Head Start programs on many dimensions, including individualization, comprehensiveness of service, orientation toward the family unit, and the provision of services through coordination and referrals. Second, the evaluation represents an extended effort to match research methods (and underlying theory) with program models. A new emphasis upon definition of process and linkage of process to outcome is evident. This pattern provides several points at which developmental theory can have direct input into the evaluation design. For example, each of the five outcome categories (family circumstances, maternal and child health, parent–child interaction, child development and achievement, and capacity for independence) represents a distinct conceptual domain, based on a body of theoretical and research literature in developmental, social, and clinical psychology. Similarly, several categories of congruence have been identified to assess staff-family relationship and congruence. Each of the categories—child-rearing style, perception of infant temperament and mother–infant interaction, and locus of control—draws upon developmental research.

VII. Concluding Comments

It has been our contention that changes in the nature of preschool intervention programs associated with Project Head Start reflect changes in the public view of effective intervention strategies. The characterization of these changes along a set of dimensions permits the dichotomization of two major intervention models. Developmental researchers advocate the treatment model since in their view it exemplifies how basic knowledge can best be utilized. However, in the practice of large scale intervention, which involves public policy formation, such as model has limited and indirect impact. It is the provision of services that is increasingly viewed as effective intervention by policymakers.

In our view, developmental research best contributes to intervention policy formation by directly influencing the nature of evaluation research conducted to determine the impact of the intervention programs. There are two direct and interrelated implications that follow from this position. First, services are becoming increasingly complex and individualized, and, as a result, evaluation research designs must necessarily become more complex as well. Much of the complexity results from a sharper focus on process and on process–outcome relationships. It is in this kind of design that developmental research can play an influential role. What is required is research that has both a special concern for interactive analyses (social competence research provides an excellent example) and a concern for ecological validity.

The second implication concerns the developmental researchers themselves. If the parallel analogy drawn between experimental and evaluation research is useful, and if the increased linkage between the two systems is mutually beneficial (as we think it is), then developmental researchers will need to develop increased competence in, and awareness of, evaluation theory, methods, and results. With these tools, developmental researchers will be in a better position to influence the design of intervention strategies and to modify developmental theory.

REFERENCES

Abt, C. L. (Ed.). *The evaluation of social programs.* Beverly Hills, Calif.: Sage Publications, 1975.

Anderson, J. E. *Public policy making.* New York: Praeger, 1975.

Beller, E. K. Impact of early education on disadvantaged children. In S. Ryan (Ed.), *A report on the longitudinal evaluations of preschool programs.* Washington, D.C.: U.S. Department of Health, Education and Welfare—Office of Child Development, 1972.

Bereiter, C., & Englemann, S. *Teaching disadvantaged children in preschool.* Englewood Cliffs, N.J.: Prentice-Hall, 1966.

Bronfenbrenner, U. *Is early intervention effective? Vol. II: A Report on Longitudinal Evaluations of Preschool Programs.* Office of Child Development, 1974. DHEW Publication No. (OHD) 74–75. Washington, D.C.: (HEW Publication No. (OHO) 76–30025)

Caplan, N. A minimal set of conditions necessary for the utilization of social science knowledge in policy formulation at the national level. In C. H. Weiss (Ed.), *Using social research in public policy making.* Lexington, Mass.: Lexington Books, 1977.

Cicarelli, V., Cooper, W., & Granger, R. *The impact of Head Start: An evaluation of the effects of Head Start on children's cognitive and affective development.* Westinghouse Learning Corporation, June 12, 1969, OEO Contract No. B89–4536.

Cook, T. *The utilization of evaluation research results.* Colloquium presented at West Virginia University, Morgantown, West Virginia, April 1979.

Costello, J. *Review and summary of a national survey of the Parent-Child Center Program.* Washington, D.C.: U.S. Department of Health, Education and Welfare—Office of Child Development, 1970.

Datta, L. Design of the Head Start Planned Variation experiment. In A M. Rivlin & P. M. Timpane (Eds.), *Planned variation in education: Should we give up or try harder?* Washington, D.C.: Brookings Institution, 1975. (a)

Datta, L. The impact of the Westinghouse/Ohio Evaluation on Project Head Start: An examination of the immediate and longer-term effects and how they came about. In C. Abt (Ed.), *The evaluation of social programs.* Beverly Hills, Calif.: Sage Publications, 1975. (b)

Dye, T. R. *Understanding public policy.* Englewood Cliffs, N.J.: Prentice-Hall, 1978.

General Accounting Office. *The Comptroller General report to Congress: Early childhood and family development programs improve the quality of life for low-income families.* Washington, D.C., 1979.

Goodson, B. G., & Hess, R. D. The effects of parent training programs on child performance and parent behavior. In B. Brown (Ed.), *Found: Long term gains from early intervention.* Boulder, Colo.: Westview Press, 1978.

Gordon, I. S. *A home learning center approach to early stimulation.* Gainesville, Fla.: Institute for Development of Human Resources, 1971. (Grant No. MH 16037-02)

Gray, S. W., & Klaus, R. A. The early training project: The seventh-year report. *Child Development,* 1970, *41,* 909-924.

Hess, R. D., & Jacks, L. L. *Experts and amateurs: Some unintended consequences of parent education.* Unpublished manuscript, 1978.

Holmes, M., Holmes, D., Greenspan, D., & Trapper, D. *The impact of Head Start Parent-Child Centers on children: Final report.* New York: Center for Community Research, 1973.

Horowitz, F. D., & Paden, L. Y. The effectiveness of environmental intervention programs. In B. M. Caldwell & H. N. Ricciuti (Eds.), *Review of Child Development Research* (Vol. 3). Chicago: University of Chicago Press, 1973.

Jones, C. O., & Thomas, R. D. (Eds.). *Public policy making in a federal system.* Beverly Hills, Calif.: Sage Publications, 1976.

Kirschner Associates, Inc. *A national survey of the impacts of Head Start centers on community institutions.* Washington, D.C.: U.S. Department of Health, Education and Welfare—Office of Child Development, 1970. (Project Head Start Contract No. B89-4638)

Kohn, M. *Social competence, symptoms, and underachievement in childhood: A longitudinal perspective.* Washington, D.C.: V. H. Winston, 1977.

Lazar, I. *Lasting effects after preschool: A report of the Consortium for Longitudinal Studies.* October 1978. U.S. Department of Health, Education and Welfare Publication No. OHDS 79-30178.

Levenstein, P. Cognitive growth in preschoolers through verbal interaction with mothers. *American Journal of Orthopsychiatry,* 1970, *40,* 426-432.

Palmer, F. Message from the President. *The Merrill-Palmer News,* Winter-Spring, 1979, i.

Rivlin, A. M., & Timpane, P. M. (Eds.). *Planned variation in education: Should we give up or try harder?* Washington, D.C.: Brookings Institution, 1975.

Schlossman, S. The parent education game: The politics of child psychology in the 1970's. *Teachers College Record,* 1978, *79,* 788-808.

Steiner, G. Y. *The children's cause.* Washington, D.C.: Brookings Institution, 1976.

Suchman, E. A. *Evaluative research: Principles and practice in public service and social action programs.* New York: Russell Sage, 1967.

Weikart, D. P. *Longitudinal results of the Ypsilanti Perry Preschool Project.* Ypsilanti, Mich.: High/Scope Educational Research Foundation, 1970.

Weiss, C. H. (Ed.). *Using social research in public policy making.* Lexington, Mass.: Lexington Books, 1977.

Zigler, E., & Trickett, P. K. IQ, social competence, and evaluation of early childhood intervention programs. *American Psychologist,* 1978, *33,* 789–798.

CHAPTER 13

Intervention for Delinquency: Art or Science?[1]

WILLIAM J. FREMOUW
WEST VIRGINIA UNIVERSITY
MORGANTOWN, WEST VIRGINIA

ANDREW L. REITZ
PRESSLEY RIDGE SCHOOL
PITTSBURGH, PENNSYLVANIA

I. Introduction

Juvenile delinquency describes a range of social problems from murder and gang warfare to truancy and running away from home. Although juveniles between the ages of 13 and 18 form only 10% of the population, the Federal Bureau of Investigation (1977) reports that in 1976 people under 18 years of age comprised 42% of the arrests for the Crime Index offenses: homicide, rape, robbery, aggravated assault, burglary, and auto theft. Furthermore, serious juvenile crime is rapidly increasing. From 1967 to 1976, the rate of juveniles arrested for violent crimes increased 98% compared to a 65% increase in arrests of people over 18. Youths under 18 years comprised 63% of vandalism and 52% of arson arrests. In addition, there were over 255,000 arrests for status offenses of curfew violations and running away. Overall, 25% of all arrests in 1976 were persons under 18

[1] Preparation of this chapter was partially funded by a grant from the Buhl Foundation.

years of age, and juvenile males were arrested four times more often than females. Conger (1973) estimated that one of every nine youths will be arrested and appear in juvenile court during adolescence.

Although most delinquency is viewed as a problem of adolescence, the origins of delinquency emerge in early childhood. A 20-year longitudinal study of 500 delinquent and 500 nondelinquent boys conducted by Glueck and Glueck (1950) revealed clear preadolescent roots for adolescent delinquency. Based on interviews and available records, 48.4% of delinquents began antisocial behavior before the age of 8, and another 49.8% began before reaching 14 years of age. Thus, only 1.8% of delinquent boys first began their antisocial careers after 13 years of age.

Although the roots of delinquency appear in childhood, the impact of early antisocial behaviors continues through adolescence into adulthood. A 30-year retrospective study of children treated at the St. Louis Municipal Psychiatric Clinic between 1924 and 1929 revealed that 60% of 176 juvenile delinquents were arrested as adults and their offenses were significantly more serious than those of other offenders (Robins & O'Neal, 1958). Glueck and Glueck (1968) also reported that 80.8% of delinquents had subsequent arrests between 17 and 25 years of age and that 60.7% of the delinquent group were again arrested between 25 and 31 years of age. Thus, juvenile delinquency is the middle period of a continuing conflict originating in childhood and extending into adulthood between an individual and the norms and laws of society.

The problem of juvenile delinquency has stimulated both research on its etiology and numerous treatment approaches. However, there has been little application of the basic research findings to the applied programs. Similarly, the questions raised from interventions with delinquents have not been addressed by the basic researchers. Therefore, the purpose of this chapter is to begin this overdue integration between basic and applied research. Based on program evaluation data on the major interventions for juvenile delinquency, this chapter will examine the implications of these findings for theories of delinquency and development. It will identify the assumptions of the etiology of delinquency that underlie the treatment approaches, summarize the interventions, and review empirical evidence of their effectiveness. The adequacy and utility of the treatment model then will be examined based on the available empirical evidence.

Unfortunately, the available program evaluation data is often difficult to interpret for the following methodological reasons:

1. First, most studies lack objective descriptions of the treatment population necessary to permit comparison and generalization of any results.

2. Second, random assignment of delinquents to either treatment or control groups is seldom practically or ethically possible. Therefore, most

evaluations are quasi-experimental designs without random assignment that compare the treatment program to comparison groups.

3. Although descriptions of the treatment model are available, the correspondence between the model and the actual treatment process is usually unknown in any multifaceted program. Therefore, a third problem is to determine the functional relationship between the specific interventions dictated by the model and the treatment outcome.

4. A fourth problem is the establishment of criteria for the evaluation of program effectiveness. Both the dimensions for evaluation and time period must be specified. The time period can vary from immediate, daily effectiveness to success 30 years after the program. Similarly, the relevant dimensions may range from changes in self-esteem or achievement to successful job performance or prevention of recidivism. Traditionally, most program evaluations use recidivism as the primary index of program success. Scales to quantify the severity of offenses have been developed and employed by Sellin and Wolfgang (1964) and Wolfgang, Figlio, and Sellin (1972). However, because recidivism only reflects a dichotomous negative outcome, other evaluators have begun to measure positive posttreatment adjustment in the areas of school success (Berleman, Seaberg, & Steinburn, 1972) or vocational adjustment (Shah, 1970). At this time, there is no generally accepted criteria for evaluating program success or failure.

II. Classification of Juvenile Delinquents

Questions of treatment effectiveness often focus merely on outcomes without specifying the treatment population. However, different programs cannot be compared unless they serve comparable youths. The label *juvenile delinquent* is a legal term that is applied to a heterogeneous group of adjudicated youths ranging from index offenders who have committed serious misdemeanors or felonies to status offenders whose only crimes are the violation of age-specific laws such as truancy or curfews.

To improve prevention and treatment programs, Hewitt and Jenkins (1946) first attempted to identify subtypes of juvenile delinquents. From clinical histories of child guidance clinics, Hewitt and Jenkins labeled the *unsocialized aggressive, socialized delinquent,* and *overinhibited* behavior patterns of children. Since this first typology, many others have been generated. The California *I*-level typology (Warren & Community Treatment Project Staff, 1966; Jesness, 1974) and the Differential Behavioral Classification system developed by Quay and Parsons (1971) are the two best developed and evaluated systems currently available. The *I*-level typology is based on a theory of sequential stages of interpersonal maturity proposed by Sullivan, Grant, and Grant (1957). The theory postulates seven stages that are signified by crucial interpersonal problems that must be resolved before further maturity occurs. Each stage of maturity is defined by the individual's perception of the relationship between self and others and the ability to understand personal and interpersonal events. Delinquents are theorized to be fixated at the second, third, and fourth stages. Based on clinical observations, nine clinical subtypes have been defined within these stages. Youths are classified based on responses to self-report measures and a clinical interview. The interrater reliability for the I levels is 88% agreement, and raters agree on 71% of the subtypes (Jesness, 1974). Table 13.1 summarizes the second, third, and fourth I levels and subtypes provided by Warren et al. (1966).

Jesness (1971) reports that in a sample of 1173 institutionalized delinquents, the most common subtypes are I_3 immature conformists (23.8%), I_3 manipulators (18.6%), I_4 anxious neurotics (15.2%), I_4 acting-out neurotics (13.8%), and I_3 cultural conformists (13.6%). Based on the classifications, experimental subjects of the same subtype were grouped and assigned to specific treatment programs. Subjects treated in homogeneous groups created fewer management problems and improved significantly more on self-report and behavioral measures of progress in the institution. Although these short-term outcome data support the predictive validity and utility of the I-level classifications, a 2-year follow-up revealed no significant differences in parole violations between experimental and control subjects. Both groups had a 65% recidivism rate. Smith (1974) found that boys at the three I levels significantly differed in performance on Raven's Progressive Matrices, verbal reasoning, and reading comprehension tasks.

Jesness (1975) provided further evidence for the validity of the I-level typology in a comparison of outcomes for 983 delinquents randomly assigned to either a behavior modification or transactional analysis program. The behavior modification project was significantly more effective for I_2 unsocialized passives, I_4 acting-out neurotics, and I_4 anxious neurotic delinquents than was the transactional analysis program. In contrast, the latter program produced significantly more improvement for I_3 cultural conformists and I_3 manipulators. The significant effectiveness of the behavior modification program for the least (I_2) and most (I_4) mature delinquents is intriguing. Basing their ideas on the ego developmental theory by Loevinger (1966), Frank and Quinlan (1976) proposed that behavior modification programs would be maximally effective for immature delinquents who need to test reality and to experience consistent consequences for their behavior. More mature delinquents such as the I_3 youths are predicted to need strong relationships with authorities and peers, which are more emphasized in transactional analytic or client-oriented programs. However, the effectiveness of the behavior modification program for the I_4 adolescents raises questions about the validity of

Table 13.1

Interpersonal Maturity Levels and Delinquent Subtypes [a]

Maturity Level 2 (I_2)

The individual whose interpersonal understanding and behavior are integrated at this level is primarily involved with demands that the world take care of him. He sees others primarily as "givers" or "withholders" and has no conception of interpersonal refinement beyond this. He has poor capacity to explain, understand, or predict the behavior or reactions of others. He is not interested in things outside himself except as a source of supply. He behaves impulsively, unaware of anything except the grossest effects of his behavior on others.

Subtypes: (1) Asocial, Aggressive (Aa) responds with active demands and open hostility when frustrated.

(2) Asocial, Passive (Ap) responds with whining, complaining, and withdrawal when frustrated.

Maturity Level 3 (I_3)

The individual who is functioning at this level, although somewhat more differentiated than the I_2, still has social–perceptual deficiencies that lead to an underestimation of the differences among others and between himself and others. More than the I_2, he does understand that his own behavior has something to do with whether or not he gets what he wants. He makes an effort to manipulate his environment to bring about "giving" rather than "denying" responses. He does not operate from an internalized value system but rather seeks external structure in terms of rules and formulas for operation. His understanding of formulas is indiscriminate and oversimplified. He perceives the world and his part in it on a power dimension. Although he can learn to play a few stereotyped roles, he cannot understand many of the needs, feelings, and motives of another person who is different from himself. He is unmotivated to achieve in a long-range sense or to plan for the future. Many of these features contribute to his inability to predict accurately the response of others to him.

Subtypes: (3) Immature Conformist (Cfm) responds with immediate compliance to whoever seems to have the power at the moment.

(4) Cultural Conformist (Cfc) responds with conformity to specific reference group, delinquent peers.

(5) Manipulator (Mp) operates by attempting to undermine the power of authority figures or to usurp the power role for himself.

Maturity Level 4 (I_4)

An individual whose understanding and behavior are integrated at this level has internalized a set of standards by which he judges his own and others' behavior. He can perceive a level of interpersonal interaction in which individuals have expectations of each other and can influence each other. He shows some ability to understand reasons for behavior, some ability to relate to people emotionally and on a long-term basis. He is concerned about status and respect and is strongly influenced by people he admires.

(Table 13.1 continues)

[a] This table summarizes the *I* levels and subtypes provided by Warren and the Community Treatment Project Staff (1966, pp. 53–54). [Reprinted by permission of Dr. Carl F. Jesness.]

Table 13.1 (Cont.)

Subtypes: (6) Neurotic, Acting Out (Na) responds to underlying guilt with attempts to "outrun" or avoid conscious anxiety and condemnation of self.

(7) Neurotic, Anxious (Nx) responds with symptoms of emotional disturbance to conflict produced by feelings of inadequacy and guilt.

(8) Situational Emotional Reaction (Se) responds to immediate family or personal crisis by acting out.

(9) Cultural Identifier (Ci) responds to identification with a deviant value system by living out his delinquent beliefs.

---

the developmental typology and the theoretical view that behavior modification programs are effective only for the least mature. These questions invite further replication and exploration of the interaction between *I*-level typology and treatment programs.

Whereas the *I*-level typology is based on a developmental theory, the Differential Behavioral Classification system (Quay & Parsons, 1971) was empirically developed by analyses of behavior ratings, self-report items, and life history variables. Factorial analyses of data from many studies (Quay, 1972) consistently identify the existence of the following four factors in both delinquents and other disturbed children: (*a*) unsocialized–psychopathic (aggressive, hostile, defiant, sensation-seeking); (*b*) neurotic–disturbed (anxious, socially withdrawn, guilty); (*c*) socialized-subcultural (peer-oriented, participative in group delinquent activity, defiant of adults); (*d*) inadequate–immature (passive, dependent, daydreaming). Depending upon the raters and data sources, interrater reliabilities vary among studies, but overall they appear to be adequately reliable (Quay, 1972).

The validity of this typology is supported by experimental research that has demonstrated predictable significant differences between the performance of psychopathic and neurotic subgroups on autonomic reactivity to auditory stimuli (Borkovec, 1970) and differences in the effects of perceptional isolation on preferences for novel and complex stimuli (Skrzypek, 1969). When Stewart (1972) reinforced delinquents to use aggressive and dependent verbs, the neurotics increased their use of dependency verbs, the subculturals increased their use of aggressive verbs, and the psychopaths decreased their use of both types of reinforced verbs. Akamatsu and Farudi (1978) reported that immature-inadequate delinquents performed more poorly on a pursuit rotor task after observing an adult model than after observing a peer model. For the socialized–subcultural group, the type of model did not affect performance. Gerard (1970) reported that the grouping of delinquents into homogeneous treatment subgroups reduced management problems and increased the therapeutic atmosphere. However, as in the Jesness study (1971), the preliminary follow-up data do not indicate significantly improved recidivism rates (Quay, 1975). The delinquents treated in homogeneous subgroups and the delinquents treated in heterogeneous groups both had a 30% recidivism rate after 1 year.

In summary, both classification systems are designed to categorize delinquents in order to match them better to appropriate treatment programs. Although the Differential Behavioral Classification system was empirically derived, the four behavior patterns appear to describe the three I levels theoretically posited by Warren *et al.* (1966). Descriptions of the I_2 level are similar to the unsocialized–psychopathic factor, the I_3 level corresponds to the inadequate–immature and socialized–subcultural factors, and the I_4 level is comparable to the neurotic–disturbed factor. In addition to evaluation of the comparability of these systems, the effects of treatment and time on the classification of the delinquents is an important, unexplored question. Since the I-level system is predicated on a developmental theory, delinquents who are successfully treated should demonstrate increasing levels of interpersonal maturity. If predictable improvements do not occur, then the I-level system would be better conceptualized as a trait typology instead of a developmental progression. Conversely, on the Differential Behavioral Classification system, movement from one factor such as immature to another factor such as neurotic would support a developmental instead of a trait approach to future delinquent classification efforts.

III. Treatment for Delinquency

Treatment programs for delinquency have ranged from projects to stimulate street gang business enterprises (Poston, 1971) to psychoanalytic residential treatment programs (Redl & Wineman, 1957). Since a comprehensive review of all treatment programs is beyond our scope here (see Cavan & Ferdinand, 1975, for a review), the remainder of this chapter will describe the major psychologically oriented interventions that have empirical evaluation data.

All treatment models acknowledge that delinquency is the product of an interaction between the person and the environment. However, the models differ in their relative emphasis on changing the person's mediational processes in terms of self-esteem or cognitive style or on changing the family or educational environment. From the perspective of the mediational model, delinquency is viewed as an understandable product of a youth's self-view and social perspective (Kohlberg, 1969). Therefore, the treatments attempt to alter these self and social perspectives. The environmental model views delinquency as a function of the person's previous learning history and current reinforcement contingencies. From this approach, treatments attempt to provide alternative reinforcement for appropriate behaviors and to teach academic and social skills that will increase the number of prosocial reinforcers available to the youths. The following discussion of interventions will be organized according to their emphasis on mediational or environmental determinants for delinquency.

A. Mediational Models

1. Youth Counseling

Historically, the Cambridge–Sommerville Youth Study was the first major methodologically adequate program for treatment and prevention of delinquency (Powers & Witmer, 1951). Based on a counseling–social work model of intervention, the project randomly assigned 650 5- to 13-year-old boys to either a control group or a group receiving individual tutoring and counseling for 5 years beginning in 1939. In addition to assisting the boys with individual personal and academic problems, the counselors focused on family problems in one-third of the cases. They also arranged for over 100 youths to receive medical or psychiatric services and for one-fourth of the youths to go to summer camps. The interventions that were provided, although not based on an explicit theoretical model, appeared to focus on improving the boys' self-images through a positive adult relationship and needed support services.

Both an initial follow-up (McCord & McCord, 1959) and a 30-year follow-up (McCord, 1978) revealed that the counseling project had no effect on the prevention of delinquency and adult criminality. In fact, the 30-year follow-up data from 506 men demonstrated that men in the counseling project were more likely to commit a second crime than those in the control group; they were also more likely to be treated for alcoholism, to manifest signs of mental illness and stress-related disease, to die younger, to have lower status occupations, and to be less satisfied with their work. These unexpected negative results are similar to deterioration effects produced by psychotherapy for some clients (Bergin, 1971). McCord speculates that the middle-class counselors may have inadvertently reinforced self-images of inadequacy and dependency and created unrealistically high expectations for the lives of the lower-class youths that led to later disappointments.

This significant follow-up study raises the perpetual question facing social activists: Is it better to have intervened and lost than never to have intervened at all? The implications suggest that unless the power of the intervention is great enough to offset the effects of the natural environment, a weak intervention may actually harm the recipient. For example, this occurs medically when consumption of less than a total series of penicillin treatments permits the disease to build immunities to medication and thus become more resistant to subsequent treatment. Unfortunately, unlike medical practitioners, we do not yet know what type and amount of counseling for youths at different ages or developmental levels is sufficient to produce positive growth. The long-term negative effects produced by counseling programs for some recipients are an important challenge to explain so that we can predict and control them in future interventions. The integration of a developmental framework such as the *I*-level typology may help to identify the types of boys that are most affected both positively and negatively by counseling programs. At this time, the Cambridge–Sommerville study stands as a symbol of ambitious delinquency intervention, rigorous evaluation, and the troubling fact that data from objective evaluation often provide a sobering contrast to the positive impressions and hopes of well-intentioned intervenors.

2. Therapeutic Wilderness Camping

Therapeutic camping is a growing but little publicized approach for treatment of delinquents and emotionally disturbed children. Proponents claim that camping experiences facilitate emotional growth, eliminate childish behaviors, alter attitudes, and increase independence (McNeil, 1957). The types of camping experiences range from day camp (Shniderman, 1974) and summer Outward Bound programs (Kelly & Baer, 1971) to year-round residential programs (Loughmiller, 1965).

Loughmiller, the major proponent of therapeutic camping, conceptualizes camping as an opportunity for challenges and experiences that stimulate development of positive self-esteem in adolescents. Their behavior problems are viewed as the products of their poor self-esteem and little interpersonal trust. While acknowledging the importance of a close relationship between each boy and his counselor, the camping treatment model places primary emphasis on the group process, which teaches a boy to live in a group with nine other youths who are dependent on each other for food, heat, and safety. Most decisions and responsibilities rest with the group as a whole. For many of the boys, these camps provide the first setting in which they are required to be responsible to a group for both their own behavior and the behavior of other group members. Loughmiller (1965) also emphasizes the importance of challenging outdoor experiences such as repelling or white-water canoeing for boys who have often failed in the past. It is assumed that the mastery of these tasks teaches the boy to realize his competence and to build self-confidence. Improvements in behavior are attributed to the development of a youth's positive self-image.

Initial evaluations generally support the claims of camping advocates. Rawson (1973) reported that following a summer camp program, boys had improved in self-esteem, attitudes toward school, parent ratings, and school grades. Mand and Green (1973) found that the staff rated 90% of the adolescents at Deveraux School as improved following a summer camp experience. Krippner and Weintraub (1971–1972) describe an 85% success rate for a year-round camping program in Georgia in which boys reside for an average of 2 years. A follow-up study of the Texas Salesmanship Club Youth Camps (1975) also indicates an 85% success rate. However, these results are inconclusive due to the absence of objective definitions of success and to the lack of control groups to determine the effect of maturation on improvement.

Better controlled evaluations also have begun to support the positive effects of camping programs for treatment of adolescents. Shniderman (1974) found that a group of 5½- to 11½-year-old boys who attended a day camp significantly improved on self and teacher ratings of social adjustment; however, improvement in parent ratings was nonsignificant relative to a matched control group. In a series of studies, Kelly and his associates have evaluated a 27-day Outward Bound program for delinquent boys. Kelly and Baer (1969) reported significant improvement in personality and self-concept measures of the participants. Gaston, Plouffe, and Chinsky (1978) also found that Outward Bound experiences produced significant improvement in self-esteem and interpersonal problem-solving skills relative to waiting list control groups.

In a comparison of boys who completed the Outward Bound program with a control group of boys who spent 9 to 12 months in an institution, Kelly and Baer (1971) found Outward Bound to be associated with a significantly lower recidivism rate. Furthermore, participants in the least challenging of the three Outward Bound programs evaluated had a significantly higher recidivism rate than those in the other two programs. However, another study comparing boys who went through the Outward Bound experience to a control group of institutionalized boys found no difference between the recidivism rates of the two groups (Kelly, 1974). Since these studies have incorporated comparison groups of institutionalized youths, the reported differences may be attributable to the negative effects of institutionalization and not only to positive effects of the camp programs.

Although the treatment model posits that improvement in self-esteem is the basis of other changes, the reported behavioral improvements cannot be automatically attributed to increases in self-esteem. Research on fear and anxiety has documented the independence of self-report measures such as those used to assess self-esteem and behavioral change (Lang, 1968) and has suggested that behavioral improvements often precede attitude changes (Bandura, Blanchard, & Ritter, 1969). Logically, the fact that wilderness camping does produce positive behavior change in delinquents does not necessarily confirm the assumptions that poor self-esteem is the cause of delinquency and that improvement in self-esteem mediates change. Longitudinal studies with repeated assessments are needed to determine whether improvements in self-esteem cause, result from, or are independent of behavioral changes. Since self-esteem or behavior change cannot be manipulated experimentally to determine causality, a cross-lagged panel design (Pelz & Andrews, 1964) could be used to study the correlations across time of changes in self-esteem and behavior. This type of research would help to resolve this recurring debate and clarify the theoretical focus of wilderness camping programs.

With regard to the year-round programs, a major issue is the impact and relevance of what boys learn during wilderness living when they return to their family, schools, and streets. Do improvements in self-esteem, problem solving, and social behavior equip boys to cope successfully with a complex urban environment? Equally important, what is the effect of infrequent family and heterosexual contact during adolescence on normal personal and social development? An evaluation project of the Pressley Ridge Camp (Fremouw, Byers, Brunts, & Hawkins, 1977) will help determine the long-term effects on academic, social, and community adjustment for adolescents who spend a mean of 17 months in a wilderness camp.

In summary, although the current evaluations of therapeutic camping share many of the same methodological limitations as other evaluations, the preliminary data appear to support the potential of therapeutic camping for delinquency treatment and raise issues for future research.

3. Developmental Approaches

Recent work has begun to explore verbal and cognitive-social development as central dimensions for the etiology and treatment of delinquency. Karoly (1977) suggests that delinquency can be conceptualized as an absence of self-management skills attributable to inadequate socialization. These deficits in self-management skills produce the impulsiveness and inability to defer gratification frequently observed in delinquents (Riddle & Roberts, 1977). Karoly states that the capacities of selective attention, long-term memory, time perception, and integration of an internal and external perspective are necessary to develop self-management. These capacities, in turn, require the development of certain language skills.

Supporting this view, White (1965) also proposes that the internalization of language is necessary to inhibit impulsive, associative responses to stimuli and to permit more logical cognitive processing of alternative responses. Associative processing is viewed as a rapid system based on stimulus–response learning relatively uninfluenced by verbal control. Thus, delinquents often make rapid responses such as hitting another person without considering the future consequences or social impact of their actions. Based on this analysis, Camp (1977) compared the use of verbal mediation for aggressive and normal boys. The results suggest that the differences in immature speech, reaction times, inhibition errors, and speed of responding during covert commands can be attributed to an ineffective linguistic control system of associative processing. However, because aggressive boys have demonstrated mediational ability by inhibiting responses to *overt* self-commands, the aggressive behavior is not simply the product of a *mediational deficiency* (Reese, 1962). Instead of not having any mediational skills, they fail to employ the skills present in their repertoires. Their failure to use verbal mediation consistently can be conceptualized as a *production deficiency* (Flavell, Beech, & Chinsky, 1966). In addition, these boys have a *control deficiency* (Kendler, 1972). Covert self-verbalizations do not control the aggressive boys' behavior, whereas overt self-verbalizations are effective. Thus, Camp (1977) concludes that aggressive boys are capable of verbal mediational responses but still rely on associative processes due to deficits in the production of effective mediational responses.

These results with aggressive boys invite replication with subgroups of delinquents to determine whether similar deficiencies in the verbal mediational process occur at the same point in the mediation–production–control sequence. If ineffective linguistic controls were also found for some delinquents, treatment programs to improve verbal mediation could be important for treatment of delinquency. Training to increase covert self-verbalizations has been effective in improving the performance of impulsive children on laboratory tasks such as Porteus mazes (Meichenbaum & Goodman, 1971) and in increasing prosocial behaviors of young aggressive boys (Camp, Blom, Herbert, & van Doorninck, 1977). However, self-instructional training has not been a widely applied intervention for older children in treating more socially relevant behaviors such as fighting or stealing. This promising approach awaits broader application and evaluation.

In a more explored area of developmental processes in delinquency, Chandler (1973) demonstrated that delinquents have an inability to view situations from the perspective of other people. This social egocentrism typically characterizes the social judgments of young children, but it is normally replaced in adolescence with a more relativistic, flexible cognitive style. The development of a role-taking perspective is assumed to be central to the socialization process and necessary for the development of social competence (Looft, 1972). To test the mutability of delinquents' social egocentrism, Chandler (1973) paid 15 delinquents to work in triads in a 10-week program during which they created and produced brief skits about people their age. Each triad wrote a skit, rotated through each of the three different roles in the skit, and received video feedback. The dramas and video films were designed to force the delinquents to assume different roles and to see themselves from other perspectives. In comparison with a no-treatment group and a placebo group that made documentary films, the training produced a significant improvement in role-taking ability; a follow-up showed that this development was associated with significant reductions in delinquent behavior. During the 18 months prior to the program, the experimental, placebo, and control groups committed a mean of 1.9, 2.5, and 2.0 delinquent offenses, respectively. In an 18-month follow-up, the experimental group committed a mean of 1.0 offenses compared to 2.1 and 1.8 offenses for the placebo and control groups.

In a replication and extension, Chandler, Greenspan, and Barenboim (1974) found that institutionalized emotionally disturbed children also were delayed in the development of their role-taking perspective and their referential communication skills. Forty-eight children who were delayed in the development of both referential and role-taking skills were divided into three groups that received (a) the role-taking training (Chandler, 1973), (b) training in accurate referential communication skills through communication games, or (c) no treatment. Both training groups significantly improved in role-taking abilities, and the communication training program also produced significant increases in referential communication skills. Behavioral ratings following training reflected a significant relationship between staff ratings and specific changes in role-taking and referential communication.

These results indicate that cognitive–social developmental deficits exist in delinquent and emotionally disturbed children and that these problems can be remedied through specially designed training programs. Although Glucksberg, Krauss, and Higgins (1975) conclude that the concept of role-taking skills has not been sufficiently defined to determine its relationship to referential communication skills, the results from the Chandler et al. (1974) study imply that referential communication skills and role-taking perspectives are hierarchically related. Apparently, the ability to perceive the role of another is necessary but not sufficient to translate the perspective into effective communication. The communication training program is sufficient to train both skills. Therefore, efficient interventions to facilitate social nonegocentrism should focus on training referential communication skills, and role-taking perspective will be acquired as a component of the training.

These experimental studies (Chandler, 1973; Chandler *et al.*, 1974) demonstrate that the reduction of social egocentrism improves behavior and lowers recidivism. Changes in social egocentrism could be monitored in existing programs to determine whether these results can be generalized; the importance of these changes could be explored in multifaceted programs such as therapeutic wilderness camping. If reductions in social egocentrism also discriminate between boys who succeed and fail in other programs, then social egocentrism could be a previously unidentified critical treatment dimension. The relationship between verbal mediation and role-taking perspective is another unexplored issue. If the production and control of verbal mediators were found to be necessary conditions for developing a role-taking perspective, then interventions for some boys would have to begin by increasing verbal mediational processes prior to applying Chandler's procedures. Unfortunately, these important studies by Chandler and their implications for treatment have remained relatively unnoticed by treatment planners.

B. Environmental Models

1. Educational Approaches

Because of the central role school plays in the development of children, and because of the reported relationship between school failure and delinquency (Cohen, 1955; Polk & Schafer, 1972), negative educational experiences are frequently considered central to the etiology of delinquency. The importance of school experiences in different formulations vary widely, but a model of the process can be abstracted that appears to be compatible with a majority of the current theories. Polk and Schafer (1972) refer to this model as the *goal attainment theory*. According to this model, delinquency develops in the following manner:

1. The child enters school in a situation in which school success and positive attention from both adults and peers are the primary reinforcers or motivators of behavior.
2. The child is not successful in school (the particular reason is not generally considered critical).
3. The child, as a result of poor school performance, receives little positive attention and much negative comment from both adults and peers for academically oriented behaviors.
4. Having failed to obtain approval from adults and "successful" peers, the child begins to seek approval from other "failing" peers through alternative, frequently inappropriate, behaviors.

5. This behavior pattern results in a cycle that further estranges the child from teachers and "successful" peers and causes the child to identify more closely with a subgroup of "failing" peers; in turn, this further escalates the inappropriate and delinquent behaviors.

6. The child gradually develops a new set of delinquent goals that are fostered by the new subgroup and are in direct opposition to the goals espoused by the school and society; this results in further delinquent behavior.

The preceding conception of the role that school failure plays in the development of delinquency has received widespread support in recent years. One indication of this support is the large number of school-oriented delinquency treatment and prevention programs that have been funded by a variety of local, state, and federal crime control agencies (most notably the Law Enforcement Assistance Administration) over the past 10 years. Most of these programs have been aimed at providing successful educational experiences for youths who presumably have experienced only failure. If a youth becomes delinquent primarily because of failure to perform adequately in school, then providing successful school experiences should be all that is necessary to eliminate delinquent behavior.

Although educationally oriented delinquency programs exist, little evaluative data are available on their effectiveness in either eliminating or preventing delinquency. One program that has systematically attempted to evaluate its own effectiveness is the Contingencies Applicable for Special Education (CASE) project (Cohen, Filipczak, Bis, Cohen, & Larkin, 1970). The CASE project began in 1965 as a 2-year program at the National Training School for Boys (NSTB), a correctional facility for delinquent male adolescents in Washington, D.C. During the 2 years of the project, 41 boys, ages 13–19, were treated for a mean of 8 months. The goals of the program were to increase the academic behaviors of the students and prepare them for return to the public school system. The program's primary component was a token economy system that was in operation during each class day. The students were awarded points for the successful completion of individualized academic assignments and could exchange them for a variety of activities and privileges.

A number of evaluative procedures were used, including success while residents were involved in the CASE program and success after discharge from the institution. Short-term program evaluation measures included the number of assignments completed, the amount of time spent studying, the number of points earned on the token economy, academic achievement scores, and IQ scores. Evaluation of postdischarge success was assessed by means of a 3-year follow-up study on resident recidivism.

Marked increases were reported for all of the in-program variables, including average achievement test increases of almost two grade levels per year and a mean increase of 12.5 points on standard IQ tests. However, the long-term evaluation of the program success, in terms of recidivism, is more difficult to interpret. Of the youths who had been in the CASE program for a minimum of 90 days and who could be located to assess follow-up success (27 of the 41 boys), 15 (56%) had been reinstitutionalized during the 3-year period. The vast majority of these residents (13) had been reinstitutionalized before the end of the first year. Unfortunately, no control group comparisons were conducted, so that interpretation of these data is difficult. When compared with Cohen and Filipczak's (1971) report of previous NTSB recidivism data of 76% during the first year following treatment, the results appear promising. However, compared with estimated national recidivism rates of 50–60% (Arbuckle & Litwack, 1960; Kennedy, 1964), the data are disappointing.

Overall, the data provide little support for a developmental theory of delinquency based on school failure. In spite of the evidence that the youths had been involved in a highly successful school experience, the program was unsuccessful in preventing further delinquent behavior from over one-half of the residents. However, the poor recidivism data do not necessarily invalidate the theory of delinquency based on school failure. For youths who are already delinquent, educationally centered treatment may be too late to reduce future delinquency. The fact that a successful educational experience is not sufficient to eliminate delinquent behavior in 16-year-old delinquents does not constitute definitive evidence that school failure is irrelevant to the development of delinquent behavior. To assess the effects of school failure on delinquency, we need longitudinal studies of high-risk preadolescents who have been exposed to a school failure prevention program. A number of delinquency prevention programs using primarily educational interventions have been implemented and have demonstrated significant effects on the academic and school-related behaviors of their clients (Burchard, Harig, Miller, & Amour, 1976; Cohen, Filipczak, Slavin, & Boren, 1971; Miller & Burchard, 1974). However, the major evaluation of these efforts awaits the collection of the long-term follow-up data necessary to demonstrate a causal relationship between school failure and delinquency.

Although school failure may play a major role in the development of delinquency, current delinquency treatment and prevention efforts generally treat the educational component as only one of many treatment foci. An exception to this trend toward more multifaceted programs is provided by recent treatment based on the assumption that learning disabilities are the cause of delinquency. The *learning disabilities model* (Berman & Siegal, 1975) also assumes that school failure is a critical component in the development of delinquency. More specific than the *goal attainment theory* (Polk & Schafer, 1972), the learning disabilities model identifies the cause of school failure as the child's particular learning disability. In addition, the model offers rich descriptions of how learning disabilities influence the child's early home and school behavior. Although several controversial studies report the incidence of learning disabilities to be between 32% and 90% in juvenile delinquent populations (Berman & Siegal, 1975; Compton, 1974; Duling, Eddy, & Risko, 1975), little conclusive data are currently available to support this model. Until serious definitional and assessment problems are resolved, it will be difficult to assess reasonably the efficacy of procedures based on a learning disabilities model of delinquency.

2. Residential Behavioral Approaches

A behavioral model of delinquency has formed the basis for a large number of rehabilitative and preventive programs for delinquents (Burchard & Tyler, 1965; Jesness & DeRisi, 1973; Karacki & Levinson, 1970; Patterson, 1974, Patterson, Cobb, & Ray, 1973; Patterson, Reid, Jones, & Conger, 1975; Schwitzgebel, 1964; Schwitzgebel & Kolb, 1964; Stuart, 1971; Stuart, Tripodi, & Jayaratne, in press; Wolf, Phillips, & Fixsen, 1972). The basic assumption is that all behavior, including delinquent behavior, is learned through reciprocal interaction between an individual and his environment (Bandura, 1969). Thus, delinquent behavior is viewed as a result of the failure of a youth's past environment to provide the instructions, examples, and feedback necessary to develop appropriate behaviors (Phillips, Phillips, Fixsen, & Wolf, 1971). Presumably, the failure to achieve desired goals using socially appropriate means results in the socially inappropriate behaviors labeled delinquent. Therefore, treatment programs based on this model generally focus on reducing disruptive delinquent behaviors while teaching new, socially appropriate behaviors.

The central feature of nearly all institutional and community based residential programs that operate from this model is a token economy (Kazdin & Bootzin, 1972). In a token system, a variety of privileges (e.g., store items, extra spending money, recreational activities, off-grounds passes, and occasionally consideration for discharge) are contingent upon a youth's progress through the various levels in the system and upon his or her point earnings over a specified period. Individual behavioral contracts (DeRisi & Butz, 1975; Jesness & DeRisi, 1973; Stuart, 1971) are often used as adjuncts to these token systems. Points and progress through the levels are generally earned for engaging in appropriate social and self-care behaviors and for progress in educational and vocational programs. Points are lost for engaging in inappropriate social behaviors and for rule infractions.

Braukmann and Fixsen (1975), in a review of the research on behavior modification with delinquents, have described two types of evaluative research: procedure evaluation and program evaluation. Procedure evaluation is conducted to evaluate the short-term effects of treatment procedures on residents while they are still participating in the treatment program. Program evaluation is conducted to evaluate the long-term effects of an entire program on the lives of those who have participated in it.

The purpose of procedure evaluation is "to provide immediate feedback to program administrators concerning the immediate effectiveness of particular aspects of a program [Braukmann & Fixsen, 1975, p. 209]." Presumably, the administrator can determine the effectiveness of the treatment procedures and use this data to revise procedures. Procedure evaluation research has focused on a wide range of target behaviors, including room cleaning (Fixsen, Phillips, & Wolf, 1972; Phillips, 1968; Phillips *et al.*, 1971), promptness (Phillips, 1968; Phillips *et al.*, 1971), aggression (Burchard & Barrera, 1972; Horton, 1970), language and conversation skills (Bailey, Timbers, Phillips, & Wolf, 1971; Liberman, Ferris, Salgado, & Salgado, 1975; Minkin *et al.*, 1976), classroom and study behavior (Bailey, Wolf, & Phillips, 1970; Phillips, 1968), self-care (Lattal, 1969; Liberman *et al.*, 1975), money saving (Liberman *et al.*, 1975; Phillips *et al.*, 1971), work behavior (Seymour & Stokes, 1976), and mealtime behavior (Doke, Feaster, & Predmore, 1977).

This research demonstrates that a wide range of the behaviors performed by delinquents can be modified using current treatment technology. However, a number of researchers (Burchard & Harig, 1976; Emery & Marholin, 1977) have questioned the relevance of the target behaviors modified in many studies to the problem of delinquency. The critical issue, according to Burchard and Harig (1976), is whether the target behaviors are "relevant in terms of the youth's ultimate adaptation to his natural environment. . .[p. 426]." In addition, as Emery and Marholin (1977) point out, "the relationship between the subordinate response (e.g., housekeeping, grooming, polite speech, job skills, academic repertoires, and negotiation skills) and the superordinate problem of delinquency (e.g., number of arrests, court contracts, future institutionalization) must be demonstrated empirically. It cannot be assumed to exist on an *a priori* basis [p. 867; emphasis added]."

Although procedure evaluation alone can answer a number of important questions about the efficacy of various behavior change procedures, it does not provide information on the relevancy of the target behaviors modified. Thus, the large amount of procedure evaluation literature from behaviorally oriented residential programs fails to address the question of whether the programs have long-term effectiveness. This question can be answered only when relationships between the long-term adjustment of delinquent clients and the training of certain behaviors such as promptness, social skills, and vocational skills have been evaluated.

Although behaviorally oriented programs are more data oriented than other approaches, their long-term program evaluations share the same methodological problems—specification of clients and procedures, adequate control groups, and outcome criteria—that are endemic to other evaluations of delinquency programs.

The Youth Center Research Project (Jesness & DeRisi, 1973; Jesness, DeRisi, McCormick, & Wedge, 1972) is one of the most adequate program evaluation projects reported in the literature. During this project, delinquent youths referred to the center were randomly assigned to either the Karl Holton School, a behaviorally based treatment program using both a token economy system and behavioral contracting, or to the O. H. Close School, a treatment program based on transactional analysis. One year follow-up data on the residents revealed little overall difference between the two programs; 31% of the O. H. Close School students and 32% of the Holton students had parole revoked. These data are somewhat more encouraging than parole violation rates for the two institutions prior to the implementation of the new programs (44% and 42%, respectively) and for two other California Youth Authority institutions (46%). Although there were no overall differences in recidivism between the behavior and transactional programs, Jesness (1975) reported significant differences in outcomes for subtypes of delinquents.

In their evaluation of another large, behaviorally oriented institution—the Robert F. Kennedy Youth Center—Karacki, Schmidt, and Cavior (1972) reported a 27% 1-year recidivism rate for graduates. This was compared to a recidivism rate of 33% for a random sample of youths discharged from other similar institutions.

A number of other program evaluation projects have been conducted without including comparison groups. Wagner and Breitmeyer (1975) reported a recidivism rate of 46% for the Program for Adolescent and Community Education (PACE) project, a behavioral program for both male and female juvenile offenders. Burchard and Harig (1976) reported a 1-year recidivism rate of 25–30% for the Intensive Treatment Program (ITP), a program for antisocial retarded youths. Finally, Cannon, Sloane, Agosto, DeRisi, Donovan, Ralph, and Della-Piana (1972) reported a recidivism rate of 58% at the Fred G. Nelles School for Boys, a program for adolescent male offenders.

The *teaching-family model,* an alternative to institutional care, was first developed at Achievement Place (Phillips, 1968) and has been widely adopted elsewhere. In this behavioral approach, six to eight youths live as a family unit with a carefully trained and supervised couple and continue to attend public school and utilize community resources. The program employs a type of token economy point system, includes a family government system, and places heavy emphasis on the development of academic and social skills. Because the teaching-family "parents" are the agents of change, the developers of the program have focused on intensive 1-year training and certification procedures for the parents. A preliminary follow-up study on a small group of Achievement Place residents (Braukmann & Fixsen, 1975; Fixsen, Phillips, Harper, Mesigh, Timbers, & Wolf, 1972) found that only 20% of the Achievement Place youths required further treatment in the year after discharge, compared to 50% of a sample of youths who had been candidates for the program. Data from a 5-year evaluation of 26 teaching-family homes and 31 comparable community homes should determine the success of the intensive teaching-family model relative to other community approaches (Jones, 1976).

In summary, very little controlled program evaluation has been done on residential behavioral treatment programs for delinquents. The results that are available are only mildly encouraging. Although such research findings do not necessarily suggest the inadequacy of the model, they clearly imply that its current application requires refinement. In view of the potency of the technology employed and of the impressive array of procedure research reported in the literature, Burchard and Harig (1976) conclude that the problem is not one of modifying behavior. Instead, the problem is to generalize the changes to the youths' natural environments. These authors suggest that the focus of treatment should change from residential settings to the youths' natural environments.

3. Nonresidential Behavioral Approaches

A wide variety of behavioral treatment and prevention programs for delinquents has been attempted in the natural environment. Programs using a behavioral contracting procedure as the primary focus of treatment have included the Family and School Consultation Project (Jayaratne, Stuart, & Tripodi, 1974; Stuart et al., in press), the Behavior Research Project (Tharp & Wetzel, 1969), and the Hartwig Project (Rose, Sundel, Delange, Corwin, & Palumbo, 1970). Additional programs have focused on recruiting participation in a community youth center activities program (Burchard, Harig, Miller, & Amour, 1976) and on employing delinquent youths as research assistants in a program aimed at curbing delinquency (Schwitzgebel, 1964; Schwitzgebel & Kolb, 1964). Finally, Patterson and his colleagues (Patterson, 1974, 1976; Patterson, Cobb, & Ray, 1973; Patterson, Reid, Jones, & Conger, 1975) have implemented a large-scale delinquency prevention project based on a multifaceted methodology referred to as the *social learning approach.*

Although the majority of programs designed to intervene in the delinquents' natural environment have failed to provide systematic data on the long-term effectiveness of their interventions, several programs have conducted some form of program evaluation research. Jayaratne *et al.* (1974) and Stuart *et al.* (in press) have reported data from two groups of delinquent and predelinquent youths referred to the Family and School Consultation Program. Each family in the program was assigned to a counselor who developed contracts between the youth, his family, and relevant school personnel to reduce the youth's specific behavioral difficulties in the school, home, and community. Evaluation data consisted of a number of measures of school performance as well as measures of home and community behavior. A 1-year follow-up showed that the treated youths performed better than the quasi-control group of program dropouts on school attendance, grades, and court contacts. However, even the treated youths showed deterioration from pretreatment levels on nearly all of the measures. In short, the treated youths did perform better than program dropouts, but instead of resulting in behavioral improvement, the program seemed capable of merely slowing the pace of behavioral deterioration.

Schwitzgebel (1964) and Schwitzgebel and Kolb (1964) reported the results of a treatment program that paid delinquent youths to participate as research assistants in a study to curb delinquency. For 9–12 months, the youths were paid to participate in interviews and in a variety of other group and individual activities. A 3-year follow-up study indicated that recidivism for a group of 20 treated youths was 35% compared to 45% for a group of matched controls. In addition, the treated youths were arrested significantly fewer times and spent less total time in jail than did the untreated youths.

The Social Learning Project (Patterson, Cobb, & Ray, 1973) at the Oregon Research Institute represents one of the more systematic delinquency prevention programs in operation. The social learning approach stresses the importance of a child's home and school social environments in the development and maintenance of deviant behavior. The treatment program focuses on changing these environments by modifying the behaviors of the important adults, including parents, teachers, and others who interact with the child on a regular basis.

Families are referred to the project by a variety of community agencies, including the juvenile courts, schools, and mental health clinics. The children, ages 5–14, are referred for serious conduct problems that generally include high levels of social aggression toward peers or adults. The family treatment package consists of the following: (*a*) study of a programmed text on child management techniques; (*b*) practice in defining, tracking, and recording a series of target behaviors; (*c*) participation in a parent-training group; (*d*) training in behavioral contracting; (*e*) optional booster sessions. When necessary, additional programs are implemented for the child in the school setting. School programs generally consist of a combination of a point system with reinforcers for appropriate classroom behavior and home-based contracts for school behavior. Both the families and the teachers are closely supervised throughout the training process to ensure that the procedures are being implemented in the prescribed manner.

Patterson (1976) has reported an evaluation study of the Social Learning Project based on data from 27 families who received at least 4 weeks of training. Approximately two-thirds of the boys showed marked reductions in deviant behavior as recorded by both direct observation procedures and the parent daily record. Six of the children showed increases in deviant behavior during the treatment program. Continued improvement was noted throughout the remainder of the follow-up study. The classroom data showed similar results. Although no control group was used for comparison, other studies (Walter & Gilmore, 1973; Wiltz & Patterson, 1974) have shown that control subjects generally do not improve and even show some tendency to deteriorate.

Patterson's social learning approach has been demonstrated to be a generally effective procedure for the treatment of aggressive boys. In addition, the approach may have broad implications for work with delinquents and predelinquents. However, the program's relevance to delinquency prevention cannot be assessed until additional research is conducted. First, it must be demonstrated that the children treated in the Social Learning Project are "children at risk" with regard to the development of delinquency; that is, a connection between Patterson's "conduct problem" boys and adolescent delinquents must be established. Second, it must be demonstrated that decreasing the boys' aggressive behaviors has some long-term effect on the probability of their becoming delinquent. Although it seems plausible that these relationships do exist, they await demonstration.

The conclusions drawn from the research on nonresidential behavioral programs are essentially the same as those drawn for residential behavioral programs. In short, the assumption that changing specific social or academic behaviors through reinforcement procedures will reduce future delinquent behaviors has yet to be proven clearly. Although the techniques for changing behaviors exist, and although some preliminary efforts are encouraging, the research has not determined which behaviors or combination of behaviors are critical for preventing or reducing delinquency.

Research on identifying the behaviors and the cognitive or social development processes necessary for successful adaptation by children may help identify areas for future behavioral interventions.

4. Family Interactional Approach

Glueck and Glueck (1950) demonstrated a strong correlation between the family and the development of delinquency. *They found that 50% fewer male delinquents had warm, loving mothers and fathers than did matched nondelinquent males.* In addition, the parents of the delinquents were generally more inconsistent or lax in disciplining their children, and twice as many parents of delinquent boys (compared to parents of nondelinquent boys) were extremely poor role models. Finally, Glueck and Glueck reported that significantly fewer delinquents than nondelinquents lived in a home with two parents present. In short, there are many familial variables that correlate highly with delinquency. Unfortunately, because many of these variables are difficult, if not impossible, to control, little information is available on the causal relationship between specific variables such as parental inconsistency or warmth and the etiology of delinquency.

Much of the work on nonresidential behavioral programs described here has focused on working with families. These programs have taught parents and teachers to provide appropriate, consistent consequences for children's positive and negative behaviors. Alexander and Barton (1976) has developed a related approach, called *family behavioral systems therapy,* which stresses the importance of adult–child communication patterns. Although this approach does not provide an explicit model for the development of delinquency, deviant family interactions appear to be the critical factor.

The implied model is based on a dichotomous analysis of family communication patterns (Gibbs, 1961). In this model, communication is viewed as either defensive (communication stifling) or supportive (communication enhancing). Using this analysis of communication as a basis, Alexander's (1973) interactional model makes the following four predictions:

1. Families of delinquents emit a higher ratio of defensive to supportive communications than do families of normal children.
2. The ratio of defensive to supportive communications in a delinquent family can be modified by treatment.
3. Once the family communication patterns are normalized through treatment, delinquency should decrease.
4. Families will continue to use their new patterns of communication with other children in the family, resulting in decreased sibling delinquency.

As the result of an ambitious research program, there is impressive evidence that all four predictions are accurate for families of status offense delinquents. Alexander (1973) compared the communication patterns of 20 delinquent families with 20 nondelinquent families. He found that the delinquent families emitted significantly more defensive communications than did the normal families. In addition, he found evidence that defensive communications are reciprocal in delinquent families but supportive communications are not. In normal families, the opposite is true; supportive communications are reciprocal but defensive communications are not.

Starting with the result that delinquent and nondelinquent families differ in communication patterns, Klein, Alexander, and Parsons (1977) developed a program evaluation paradigm to determine the functional relationship between the intervention of family behavioral systems therapy and its subsequent effects on delinquency. The model evaluated the primary, secondary, and tertiary prevention effects of the intervention. The three levels of evaluation assessed (a) the changes in family interaction at the end of treatment (tertiary prevention); (b) recidivism rates of the delinquents 6–18 months after treatment (secondary prevention); and (c) the rate of sibling delinquency 2½–3½-years following family intervention (primary prevention).

Parsons and Alexander (1971) first assessed the effects of treatment on delinquent families' deviant communication patterns. Forty families were randomly assigned to one of four treatment conditions: family therapy, family plus individual therapy, individual therapy, and waiting list controls. The results showed that the two groups of families that received family therapy significantly increased their supportive to defensive communication ratios relative to the other two groups. The assumption that delinquent communication patterns are amenable to treatment was demonstrated again in a study by Alexander and Parsons (1973). This study compared 46 families who received the family treatment package with 40 families who received client-centered or psychodynamic family therapy or no treatment. In addition to replicating earlier findings on tertiary prevention effects, this study found significantly lower recidivism rates at 12–18 months following treatment (secondary prevention) for the families receiving family therapy (26%) than for the other treatment groups (mean of 55%); the recidivism rate was also lower than the national rate (51%). Finally, Klein, Alexander, and Parsons (1977) compared the rate of sibling court contacts in the 2½–3½-year period following treatment (primary prevention) for the families in the four groups. Results showed that only 20% of the families who received family therapy had a second child who was referred to the juvenile court during the follow-up period, compared to a mean of 55% for the other treatment groups.

In summary, the well-controlled evaluation of Alexander's behavioral systems therapy for families of delinquents who have committed status offenses such as truancy or drinking has shown both statistically and socially important results. The assumption that improved family communication will reduce delinquency has clear support. To test whether this promising approach can be generalized, other studies should apply the family therapy program to the families of index offenders (which are often less stable) or to single parent homes. Even if the replication failed to produce similar results, family behavioral systems therapy would remain an important advance for the treatment of status offenders. Furthermore, the current results provide suggestions for further research on the relationship between family communication patterns and the etiology of delinquency. Research on the interaction between family communication styles and the development of academic skills, social skills, or mediational processes such as self-esteem and social egocentrism could provide important integration of theoretical approaches.

IV. Conclusion

After decades of efforts to understand, prevent, and treat delinquency, our art remains primitive for several reasons. First, there are relatively few intervention studies available. Second, most studies that do exist are poorly controlled. Third, those studies that are methodologically adequate often yield inconclusive results (e.g., Karacki *et al.,* 1972) or pessimistic results (e.g., McCord, 1978). Although most early efforts to treat delinquency have offered little insight into the normal developmental process, the studies that show that increases in role-taking perspective (Chandler, 1973) and family communication skills (Alexander & Parsons, 1973) are functionally related to reductions in subsequent delinquent behavior point toward important areas for further research. In addition, the Social Learning Project to reduce aggression in predelinquents (Patterson, 1976), the therapeutic wilderness camping (Loughmiller, 1965), and the teaching-family model (Phillips, 1968) appear to be promising approaches for continued development and evaluation. More major program evaluation projects with adequate control groups, procedural descriptions, client specifications, and outcome criteria—such as the 5-year project of the teaching-family model (Jones, 1976)—are needed to provide definitive answers about delinquency intervention. At this time, we can conclude only that delinquency interventions are based more on art than on science.

REFERENCES

Akamatsu, T. J., & Farudi, P. A. Effects of model status and juvenile offender type on the imitation of self-reward criteria. *Journal of Consulting and Clinical Psychology,* 1978, *46,* 187–188.

Alexander, J. F. Defensive and supportive communications in normal and deviant families. *Journal of Consulting and Clinical Psychology,* 1973, *40,* 223–231.

Alexander, J. F., & Barton, C. Behavioral systems therapy for families. In D. H. L. Olson (Ed.), *Treating relationships.* Lake Mills, Iowa: Graphic Publishing, 1976.

Alexander, J. F., & Parsons, B. V. Short-term behavioral intervention with delinquent families: Impact on family process and recidivism. *Journal of Abnormal Psychology,* 1973, *81,* 219–225.

Arbuckle, D., & Litwack, L. A. A study of recidivism among juvenile delinquents. *Federal Probation,* 1960, *2,* 44–46.

Bailey, J. S., Timbers, G. D., Phillips, E. L., & Wolf, M. M. Modification of articulation errors of pre-delinquents by their peers. *Journal of Applied Behavior Analysis,* 1971, *4,* 265–281.

Bailey, J. S., Wolf, M. M., & Phillips, E. L. Home-based reinforcement and the modification of pre-delinquents' classroom behavior. *Journal of Applied Behavior Analysis,* 1970, *3,* 223–233.

Bandura, A. *Principles of behavior modification.* New York: Hold, Rinehart, & Winston, 1969.

Bandura, A., Blanchard, E., & Ritter, B. The relative efficacy of desensitization and modeling approaches for inducing behavioral, affective, and attitudinal changes. *Journal of Personality and Social Psychology,* 1969, *13,* 173–199.

Bergin, A. The evaluation of therapeutic outcomes. In A. Bergin & S. Garfield (Eds.), *Handbook of psychotherapy and behavior change.* New York: Wiley, 1971.

Berleman, W. C., Seaberg, J. R., & Steinburn, T. W. The delinquency prevention experiment in the Seattle Atlantic Street Center: A final examination. *Social Service Review,* 1972, *46,* 323–346.

Berman, A., & Siegal, A. *A neurological approach to the etiology, prevention, and treatment of juvenile delinquency.* Unpublished manuscript, 1975.

Borkovec, T. D. Autonomic reactivity to sensory stimulation in psychopathic, neurotic, and normal juvenile delinquents. *Journal of Consulting and Clinical Psychology,* 1970, *35,* 217–222.

Braukmann, C. J., & Fixsen, D. L. Behavior modification with delinquents. In M. Hersen, R. Eisler, & P. Miller (Eds.), *Progress in behavior modification* (Vol. 1). New York: Academic Press, 1975.

Burchard, J. D., & Barrera, F. An analysis of timeout and response cost in a programmed environment. *Journal of Applied Behavior Analysis,* 1972, *5,* 271–282.

Burchard, J. D., & Harig, P. T. Behavior modification and juvenile delinquency. In H. Leitenberg (Ed.), *Handbook of behavior modification and behavior therapy.* Englewood Cliffs, N.J.: Prentice-Hall, 1976.

Burchard, J. D., Harig, P. T., Miller, R. B., & Amour, J. New strategies in community-based intervention. In E. L. Ribes-Inesta (Ed.), *The experimental analysis of delinquency and social aggressions.* New York: Academic Press, 1976.

Burchard, J. D., & Tyler, V. O. The modification of delinquent behavior through operant conditioning. *Behaviour Research and Therapy,* 1965, *2,* 245–250.

Camp, B. W. Verbal mediation in young aggressive boys. *Journal of Abnormal Psychology,* 1977, *86,* 145–153.

Camp, B. W., Blom, G. E., Hebert, F., & van Doorninck, W. J. "Think Aloud": A program for developing self-control in young aggressive boys. *Journal of Abnormal Child Psychology,* 1977, *5,* 157–169.

Cannon, D., Sloane, H., Agosto, R., DeRisi, W., Donovan, J., Ralph, J., & Della-Piana, G. *The Fred G. Nelles School for Boys rehabilitation system.* Salt Lake City: University of Utah, Bureau of Educational Research, 1972.

Cavan, R. S., & Ferdinand, T. N. *Juvenile delinquency.* New York: Lippincott, 1975.

Chandler, M. J. Egocentrism and antisocial behavior: The assessment and training of social perspective-taking skills. *Developmental Psychology,* 1973, *9,* 326–332.

Chandler, M. J., Greenspan, S., & Barenboim, C. Assessment and training of role-taking and referential communication skills in institutionalized emotionally disturbed children. *Developmental Psychology,* 1974, *10,* 546–553.

Cohen, A. K. *Delinquent boys.* New York: Free Press, 1955.

Cohen, H. L., & Filipczak, J. A. *A new learning environment.* San Francisco: Jossey-Bass, 1971.

Cohen, H. L., Filipczak, J. A., Bis, J. S., Cohen, J., & Larkin P. Establishing motivationally oriented educational environments for institutionalized adolescents. In J. Zubin & A. M. Freedman (Eds.), *The psychopathology of adolescents.* New York: Grune & Stratton, 1970.

Cohen, H. L., Filipczak, J. A., Slavin, J., & Boren, J. *Programming interpersonal curricula for adolescents (PICA)—project year three: A laboratory model.* Silver Spring, Md.: Institute for Behavioral Research, October 1971.

Compton, R. The learning disabled adolescent. In B. Kratoville (Ed.), *Youth in trouble.* San Rafael, Calif.: Academic Therapy Publications, 1974.

Conger, J. J. *Adolescence and youth.* New York: Harper & Row, 1973.

DeRisi, W. J., & Butz, G. *Writing behavioral contracts: A case simulation practice manual.* Champaign, Ill.: Research Press, 1975.

Doke, L. A., Feaster, C. A., & Predmore, D. L. Managing the "eat-and-run" behavior of adolescents via family-style dining. *Behavior Modification,* 1977, *1,* 73–92.

Duling, F., Eddy, S., & Risko, V. *Learning disabilities and juvenile delinquency.* Unpublished manuscript, Robert F. Kennedy Youth Center, 1975.

Emery, R. E., & Marholin, D. An applied behavior analysis of delinquency: The irrelevancy of relevant behavior. *American Psychologist,* 1977, *32,* 860–873.

Federal Bureau of Investigation. *Crime in the United States 1976.* Washington, D. C.: U.S. Government Printing Office, 1977.

Fixsen, D. L., Phillips, E. L., Harper, T., Mesigh, C., Timbers, G., & Wolf, M. M. *The teaching family model of group home treatment.* Paper presented at the meeting of the American Psychological Association, Honolulu, 1972.

Fixsen, D. L., Phillips, E. L., & Wolf, M. M. Achievement Place: The reliability of self-reporting and peer-reporting and their effects on behavior. *Journal of Applied Behavior Analysis,* 1972, *5,* 19–30.

Flavell, J. H., Beech, D. H., & Chinsky, J. M. Spontaneous verbal rehearsal in a memory task as a function of age. *Child Development,* 1966, *37,* 283–289.

Frank, S., & Quinlan, D. M. Ego development and female delinquency: A cognitive–developmental approach. *Journal of Abnormal Psychology,* 1976, *85,* 505–510.

Fremouw, W. J., Byers, E. S., Brunts, D. C., & Hawkins, R. P. Program evaluation of a therapeutic wilderness camp. In R. P. Hawkins (Chair), *Issues in program evaluation for adolescent treatment.* Symposium presented at the meeting of the Association for Advancement of Behavior Therapy, Atlanta, 1977.

Gaston, D. W., Plouffe, M. M., & Chinsky, J. M. *An empirical investigation of a wilderness challenge experience for teenagers: The Connecticut Wilderness School.* Paper presented at the meeting of the Eastern Psychological Association, Washington, D.C., 1978.

Gerard, P. Institutional innovations in youth corrections. *Federal Probation,* 1970, *34,* 37–44.

Gibbs, J. R. Defensive communications. *Journal of Communication,* 1961, *3,* 141–148.

Glucksberg, S., Krauss, R., & Higgins, E. T. The development of referential communication skills. In F. Horowitz (Ed.), *Review of child developmental research* (Vol. 4). Chicago: University of Chicago Press, 1975.

Glueck, S., & Glueck, E. *Unraveling juvenile delinquency.* Cambridge, Mass.: Harvard University Press, 1950.

Glueck, S., & Glueck, E. *Delinquents and nondelinquents in perspective.* Cambridge, Mass.: Harvard University Press, 1968.

Hewitt, L. E., & Jenkins, R. L. *Fundamental patterns of maladjustment: The dynamics of their origin.* Springfield, Ill.: State of Illinois, 1946.

Horton, L. E. Generalization of aggressive behavior in adolescent delinquent boys. *Journal of Applied Behavior Analysis,* 1970, *3,* 205–211.

Jayaratne, S., Stuart, R. B., & Tripodi, T. Methodological issues and problems in evaluating treatment outcomes in the family and school consultation project, 1970–1973. In P. O. Davidson, F. W. Clark, & L. A. Hamerlynck (Eds.), *Evaluation of behavioral programs in community, residential and school settings.* Champaign, Ill.: Research Press, 1974.

Jesness, C. F. The Preston typology study: An experiment with differential treatment in an institution. *Journal of Research in Crime and Delinquency,* 1971, *8,* 38–52.

Jesness, C. F. *Classifying juvenile offenders: The sequential I-level classification manual.* Palo Alto, Calif.: Consulting Psychologist Press, 1974.

Jesness, C. F. Comparative effectiveness of behavior modification and transactional analysis programs for delinquents. *Journal of Consulting and Clinical Psychology,* 1975, *43,* 758–779.

Jesness, C. F., & DeRisi, W. J. Some variations in techniques of contingency management in a school for delinquents. In J. S. Stumphauzer (Ed.), *Behavior therapy with delinquents.* Springfield, Ill.: Thomas Publishing, 1973.

Jesness, C. F., DeRisi, W. J., McCormick, P. M., & Wedge, R. F. *The youth center research project.* Sacramento, Calif.: California Youth Authority, 1972.

Jones, R. R. *Achievement Place: The independent evaluator's perspective.* Paper presented at the meeting of the American Psychological Association, Washington, D.C., 1976.

Karacki, L., & Levinson, R. B. A token economy in a correctional institution for youthful offenders. *Howard Journal of Penology and Crime Prevention,* 1970, *13,* 20–30.

Karacki, L., Schmidt, A., & Cavior, H. E. *The 1972 follow-up of Kennedy Youth Center releases.* Unpublished manuscript, Robert F. Kennedy Youth Center, 1972.

Karoly, P. Behavioral self-management in children: Concepts, methods, issues, and directions. In M. Hersen, R. Eisler, & P. Miller (Eds.), *Progress in behavior modification* (Vol. 5). New York: Academic Press, 1977.

Kazdin, A. E., & Bootzin, R. R. The token economy: An evaluative review. *Journal of Applied Behavior Analysis,* 1972, *5,* 343–372.

Kelly, F. J. *Outward Bound and delinquency: A ten year experience.* Paper presented at the Conference on Experiential Education, Estes Park, Colorado, October 1974.

Kelly, F. J., & Baer, D. J. Jesness inventory and self-concept measures for delinquents before and after participation in Outward Bound. *Psychological Reports,* 1969, *25,* 719–724.

Kelly, F. J., & Baer, D. J. Physical challenge as a treatment for delinquency. *Crime and Delinquency,* 1971, *17,* 437–445.

Kendler, T. S. An ontogeny of mediational deficiency. *Child Development,* 1972, *43,* 1–17.

Kennedy, R. F. Halfway houses pay off. *Crime and Delinquency,* 1964, *10,* 4–7.

Klein, N. C., Alexander, J. F., & Parsons, B. V. Impact of family systems intervention on recidivism and sibling delinquency: A model of primary prevention and program evaluation. *Journal of Consulting and Clinical Psychology,* 1977, *45,* 469–474.

Kohlberg, L. Stage and sequence: The cognitive developmental approach to socialization. In D. A. Goslin (Ed.), *Handbook of socialization.* Chicago: Rand McNally, 1969.

Krippner, S., & Weintraub, M. Anneewakee: A therapeutic community for emotionally disturbed boys. *Interpersonal Development,* 1971–1972, *2,* 121–129.

Lang, P. J. Fear reduction and fear behavior: Problems in treating a construct. In J. M. Shlien (Ed.), *Research in psychotherapy* (Vol. 3). Washington, D. C.: American Psychological Association, 1968.

Lattal, K. A. Contingency management of toothbrushing behavior in a summer camp for children. *Journal of Applied Behavior Analysis,* 1969, *2,* 195–198.

Liberman, R. P., Ferris, C., Salgado, P., & Salgado, J. Replication of the Achievement Place model in California. *Journal of Applied Behavior Analysis,* 1975, *8,* 287–299.

Loevinger, J. The meaning and measurement of ego development. *American Psychologist,* 1966, *21,* 195–206.

Looft, W. R. Egocentrism and social interaction across the life span. *Psychological Bulletin,* 1972, *78,* 73–92.

Loughmiller, C. *Wilderness road.* Austin: University of Texas, 1965.

McCord, J. A thirty-year follow-up of treatment effects. *American Psychologist,* 1978, *33,* 284–289.

McCord, J., & McCord, W. A follow-up report on the Cambridge–Sommerville youth study. *Annals of the American Academy of Political and Social Science,* 1959, *322,* 89–96.

McNeil, E. B. The background of therapeutic camping. *Journal of Social Issues,* 1957, *13,* 3–14.

Mand, C. L., & Green, L. An outdoor community for troubled adolescents. *Journal of School Health,* 1973, *43,* 8–17.

Meichenbaum, D. H., & Goodman, J. Training impulsive children to talk to themselves: A means of developing self-control. *Journal of Abnormal Psychology,* 1971, *77,* 115–126.

Miller, R. B., & Burchard, J. D. *The daily behavior card system: An experimental analysis of the effects of monitoring classroom behaviors.* Unpublished manuscript, University of Vermont, 1974.

Minkin, N., Braukmann, C. J., Minkin, B. L., Timbers, G. D., Timbers, B. J., Fixsen, D. L., Phillips, E. L., & Wolf, M. M. The social validation and training of conversational skills. *Journal of Applied Behavior Analysis,* 1976, *9,* 127–139.

Parsons, B. V., & Alexander, J. F. *Evaluation summary: Family groups treatment program.* Unpublished manuscript, Salt Lake County Juvenile Court, Utah, 1971.

Patterson, G. R. Interventions for boys with conduct problems: Multiple settings, treatments, and criteria. *Journal of Consulting and Clinical Psychology,* 1974, *42,* 471–481.

Patterson, G. R. Parents and teachers as change agents: A social learning approach. In D. Olson (Ed.), *Treating relationships.* Lake Mills, Iowa: Graphic Publishing, 1976.

Patterson, G. R., Cobb, J. A., & Ray, R. S. A social engineering technology for retraining the families of aggressive boys. In H. E. Adams & I. P. Unikel (Eds.), *Issues and trends in behavior therapy.* Springfield, Ill.: Thomas Publishing, 1973.

Patterson, G. R., Reid, J. B., Jones, R. R., & Conger, R. E. *A social learning approach to family intervention* (Vol. 1). Eugene, Ore.: Castellia Press, 1975.

Pelz, D. C., & Andrews, F. M. Detecting causal priorities in panel study data. *American Sociological Review,* 1964, *29,* 836–848.

Phillips, E. L. Achievement Place: Token reinforcement procedures in a homestyle rehabilitation setting for "pre-delinquent" boys. *Journal of Applied Behavior Analysis*, 1968, *1*, 213–223.

Phillips, E. L., Phillips, E. A., Fixsen, D. L., & Wolf, M. M. Achievement Place: Modification of the behaviors of pre-delinquent boys within a token economy. *Journal of Applied Behavior Analysis*, 1971, *4*, 45–59.

Polk, K., & Schafer, W. E. *Schools and delinquency*. Englewood Cliffs, N.J.: Prentice-Hall, 1972.

Poston, R. W. *The gang and the establishment*. New York: Harper & Row, 1971.

Powers, E., & Witmer, H. *An experiment in the prevention of delinquency: The Cambridge-Sommerville youth study*. New York: Columbia University Press, 1951.

Quay, H. C. Patterns of aggression, withdrawal, and immaturity. In H. C. Quay & J. S. Werry (Eds.), *Psychopathological disorders of childhood*. New York: Wiley, 1972.

Quay, H. C. Classification in the treatment of delinquency and antisocial behavior. In N. Hobbs (Ed.), *Issues in the classification of children* (Vol. 1). San Francisco: Jossey-Bass, 1975.

Quay, H. C., & Parsons, L. B. *The differential behavioral classification of the juvenile offender*. Washington, D. C.: U.S. Department of Justice, Bureau of Prisons, 1971.

Rawson, H. E. Residential short-term camping for children with behavior problems: A behavior modification approach. *Child Welfare*, 1973, *52*, 511–520.

Redl, F., & Wineman, D. *The aggressive child*. New York: Free Press, 1957.

Reese, H. W. Verbal mediation as a function of age level. *Psychological Bulletin*, 1962, *59*, 502–509.

Riddle, M., & Roberts, A. H. Delinquency, delay of gratification, recidivism, and the Porteus maze test. *Psychological Bulletin*, 1977, *84*, 417–425.

Robins, L., & O'Neal, P. Mortality, mobility, and crime: Problem children thirty years later. *American Sociological Review*, 1958, *23*, 162–171.

Rose, S. D., Sundel, M., Delange, J., Corwin, L., & Palumbo, A. The Hartwig project: A behavioral approach to the treatment of juvenile offenders. In R. Ulrich, T. Stachnik, & J. Mabry (Eds.), *Control of human behavior* (Vol. 2). Glenview, Ill.: Scott, Foresman, 1970.

Schwitzgebel, R. K. *Street corner research: An experimental approach to the juvenile delinquent*. Cambridge, Mass.: Harvard University Press, 1964.

Schwitzgebel, R. K., & Kolb, D. A. Inducing behavior change in adolescent delinquents. *Behaviour Research and Therapy*, 1964, *1*, 297–304.

Sellin, T., & Wolfgang, M. E. *The measurement of delinquency*. New York: Wiley, 1964.

Seymour, F. W., & Stokes, T. F. Self-recording in training girls to increase work and evoke staff praise in an institution for offenders. *Journal of Applied Behavior Analysis*, 1976, *9*, 41–54.

Shah, S. A. A behavioral approach to outpatient treatment of offenders. In H. C. Richard (Ed.), *Unique programs in behavior readjustment*. Oxford: Pergamon, 1970.

Shniderman, C. M. Impact of therapeutic camping. *Social Work*, 1974, *19*, 354–357.

Skrzypek, G. J. Effect of perceptual isolation and arousal on anxiety, complexity preference, and novelty preference in psychopathic and neurotic delinquents. *Journal of Abnormal Psychology*, 1969, *74*, 321–329.

Smith, D. Relationship between Eysenck and Jesness personality inventories. *British Journal of Criminology*, 1974, *14*, 376–384.

Stewart, D. J. Effects of social reinforcement on dependency and aggressive responses of psychopathic, neurotic, and subcultural delinquents. *Journal of Abnormal Psychology*, 1972, *79*, 76–83.

Stuart, R. B. Behavioral contracting within the families of delinquents. *Journal of Behavior Therapy and Experimental Psychiatry*, 1971, *2*, 1–11.

Stuart, R. B., Tripodi, T., & Jayaratne, S. The family and school treatment model of services for pre-delinquents. *Journal of Research in Crime and Delinquency,* in press.

Sullivan, C., Grant, M. Q., & Grant, J. D. The development of interpersonal maturity: Applications to delinquency. *Psychiatry,* 1957, *20,* 373–385.

Texas Salesmanship Club Youth Camps. *The wilderness way.* Dallas: Author, 1975.

Tharp, R. G., & Wetzel, R. J. *Behavior modification in the natural environment.* New York: Academic Press, 1969.

Wagner, B. R., & Breitmeyer, R. G. PACE: A residential, community oriented behavior modification program for adolescents. *Adolescence,* 1975, *10,* 277–286.

Walter, H., & Gilmore, S. K. Placebo versus social learning effects of parent training procedures designed to alter the behaviours of aggressive boys. *Behaviour Research and Therapy,* 1973, *4,* 361–377.

Warren, M. Q., & Community Treatment Project Staff. *Interpersonal maturity level classification: Juvenile diagnosis and treatment of low, middle, and high maturity delinquents.* Sacramento: California Youth Authority, 1966.

White, S. H. Evidence for a hierarchical arrangement of learning processes. In L. Lipsitt & C. Spiker (Eds.), *Advances in child development and behavior* (Vol. 2). New York: Academic Press, 1965.

Wiltz, N. A., & Patterson, G. R. An evaluation of parent training procedures designed to alter inappropriate aggressive behavior of boys. *Behavior Therapy,* 1974, *5,* 215–221.

Wolf, M. M., Phillips, E. L., & Fixsen, D. L. The teaching family: A new model for the treatment of deviant child behavior in the community. In S. W. Bijou & E. L. Ribes-Inesta (Eds.), *Behavior modification.* New York: Academic Press, 1972.

Wolfgang, M. E., Figlio, R. M., & Sellin, T. *Delinquency in the birth cohort.* Chicago: University of Chicago Press, 1972.

CHAPTER 14

Training and Education of the Elderly [1]

HARVEY L. STERNS
RAYMOND E. SANDERS
THE UNIVERSITY OF AKRON
AKRON, OHIO

I. Introduction

Since about 1970, a variety of factors have indicated that increasing numbers of older adults are participating in formal educational systems (see Birren & Woodruff, 1973; Schaie & Willis, 1978). This raises some practical and conceptual issues, at the heart of which is the fundamental question of whether the older adult is capable of profiting from formal education. For reasons of social policy and economics, the basis of this question is real, and it is found not only in the frequently cited negative stereotypes of older adults in our society but also in much of the basic research reporting the cognitive and intellectual performance of older adults to be deficient relative to that of younger adults. Furthermore, the answer to this question will undoubtedly be complex, for other questions (e.g., What is to be learned? How will the instructional experience be structured?) must be addressed at the same time. These complexities notwithstanding, we argue that the essential question concerning the "educability" of the older adult is most directly answered through research.

[1] The preparation of this chapter was partially supported by funds from the Andrus Foundation and the University of Akron Institute for Life-Span Development and Gerontology.

LIFE-SPAN DEVELOPMENTAL PSYCHOLOGY
Intervention

Education is the process of training and developing the knowledge, skill, mind, and so on, especially by formal schooling, teaching, and training. In accordance with this definition, it is our view that the question of older adult educability can best be answered through intervention research. An important consideration underlying the question of educability involves the criterion one adopts in attempting to determine to what extent a person is educable. Various criteria are possible, and each has its own associated assumptions and values. For the immediate purposes of this chapter, we have chosen to gauge educability by how much intervention research can modify older adult cognitive deficits. Since these "deficits" are most often inferred from performance comparisons between older and younger adults, it is apparent that for pragmatic reasons our criterion adopts young adult performance as an initial reference standard. (see Section IV).

Several factors contributed to our choice of criterion and its associated reference standard. First, the educational enterprise as it currently exists is clearly oriented toward the young adult population. Second, to the extent that the elderly do matriculate, there is evidence (Hiemstra, 1977–1978) indicating that they are interested in substantive curricula similar to those studied by the young. Third, the educational setting has been seen as a forum where old and young can become socially integrated (e.g., Birren & Woodruff, 1973). Taken jointly, these factors point toward the proposition that "age grading" of one sort or another may well be both undesirable and impractical, at least at the present time. It must be emphasized, however, that adopting young adult performance as a reference standard does not necessarily deny the possibility that there are qualities of cognitive functioning unique to the older adult (see, e.g., Schaie, 1975). This reference standard should be seen as a first approximation; more suitable reference points may be found in the future.

In the pages that follow, we first examine the philosophical presuppositions of education for the elderly raised by Moody (1976) and relate these presuppositions to conceptions of older adult cognitive functioning. Next, we review and comment on those intervention studies that have involved attempts to modify cognitive functioning in the elderly. Third, we argue that there is a continuing need for research that will more clearly explicate the characteristics of cognitive functioning in untrained elderly individuals, particularly as a preliminary to intervention. Finally, we discuss in general terms several educational implications we consider to be appropriate at this time.

II. Philosophical Presuppositions

The philosophical presuppositions of education for the elderly have been raised by H. R. Moody (1976). He presents four models of education of older adults representing four stages of development in our culture. Stage I, *Rejection,* is a product of the negative attitudes about aging prevalent in American society. Old age is seen as representing the antithesis of prevailing values of modern life, and it serves as a reminder of our mortality. The intrapsychic processes of repression and denial are recapitulated in the social institutions and mechanisms that our society has evolved to deal with the problems of aging. Examples of this are enforced segregation in nursing homes and retirement communities, mandatory retirement, neglect, and abandonment of older people. Education is *not* seen as justified since it makes little sense on economic grounds: Education is for the future, and there is little payoff from educating older adults.

Examples that extend this mode of thinking to the cognitive realm include discussions of inevitable decrements and notions that nothing can be done to improve functioning in older adulthood. "What do you expect from someone your age?" is indicative of this level of thought. This stage is exemplified by the notion of decline in cognitive functioning at all levels on all dimensions for everyone.

Stage II, *Social Services,* embodies the assumptions of the welfare state and interest group liberalism; it describes education for adults and older adults as a leisure time activity. At least for older adults, this attitude assumes prior disengagement from major social institutions. This level of thought is apparent in social responses that see unmet human needs as requiring the external intervention of public policy to deal with the casualties of industrialized society created by Stage I. Examples include transfer payments (food stamps, social security, welfare) as well as substantive programs for nursing homes, senior centers, etc. This mentality deals with "social problems" by developing a service that is done *for* someone, typically by a professional, certified person (nurse, social worker, physical therapist, etc.). Thus, the client is forced into a passive, recipient role. Our critique of this mentality does not deny the need for specialized services for selected groups of older people, but it does question the orientation and philosophy of the approach.

The characteristic educational mode of Stage II can be described as entertainment or keeping busy. The emphasis is on leisure time activities for the elderly as consumers and not as producers, in the mode of leisure, not the mode of work. There is an assumption of passivity and segregation. Older people are seen as *not* engaging in serious and meaningful involvement. Attention to older adults is in the name of conscience and political liberalism.

Extending this mode of thinking to the cognitive realm leads us to concepts such as age credit on intelligence tests and suggestions such as bigger print and more light. Issues extraneous to ability may be relevant here; the idea is that older adults can function but cannot function as well as younger people. The approach that is usually taken is to adapt the environment to fit the person.

Stage III, *Participation,* emphasizes that education can serve as a preparation for new active roles or as a political challenge to stereotypes of old age. The goal of this level of thought is to enable older people, as far as possible, to live their lives in contact with the mainstream of society and to pursue those activities associated with a normal life in that society. The answer is not to expand services but to radically restrict those institutions that have contributed to the problem despite their good intentions.

Participation suggests that meaningful, carefully selected activity is the fundamental criterion of successful aging. It suggests that the passivity inherent in the social services model is inappropriate for the majority of the older adult population. Education should be designed to offer a supportive environment and the opportunity to pursue second careers and personal interests; it should not focus on disengagement. The educational mode here is integration rather than segregation. Older people remain involved through second careers or volunteer services in whatever they choose to do. A key point is consciousness raising, which enables older adults to maintain a positive attitude toward themselves and their situation. The Harris Poll conducted for the National Council on Aging (1975) showed that older adults accept many negative stereotypes about aging for others but see themselves as exceptions. We must overcome this pluralistic ignorance present in our thinking, for it leads younger people to fear their own aging and leads many older adults into negative self-fulfilling prophecies. Stage III is the cutting edge of social reform; it entails sexuality, the right to work, and the opportunity to live in the mainstream of society. The extension to the cognitive domain is represented by the notion that there is plasticity in behavior during the older adult period. This level of thought emphasizes that alleviation and prevention are possible (see Baltes & Schaie, 1973; Birren & Woodruff, 1973). It involves the notion that special training approaches can be used to improve, compensate, or maintain levels of functioning. This approach does not deny biological change but entails understanding how to compensate for or improve existing levels of functioning. This is an active response. The training studies and approaches we discuss in this paper represent this level of thinking.

Stage IV, *Self Actualization,* describes old age as a period of potential psychological growth. It represents the older adult period as a special period (e.g., Erickson's [1950/1963] integrity versus despair) during which something is uniquely possible; that is, certain things are available only at this point in the life cycle. Issues of self-growth and personal satisfaction are paramount here. Disengagement may be required, but only for the sake of more meaningful activity. The older adult can be liberated from roles and involvement demanded by earlier work and child-rearing responsibilities. With regard to education, the challenge rests with the development of educational approaches that nourish psychological growth and allow older learners to bring a lifetime of experience to their studies.

In the cognitive domain, we are perhaps addressing the unique individual differences present regardless of age. We are addressing issues of creativity in older adults. Research concerning wisdom and knowledge in older adulthood would be an example of this level of thought.

The contention of this chapter is that we must first determine whether it is feasible to move away from Stages I and II in our conception of older adult education. To that end, we see research demonstrating modifiability and plasticity in older adult cognitive functioning as a key to opening the door to Stages III and IV. We feel that research on older adult cognition must fully explore what modifications are possible and specifically identify what processes are involved. As a first step, we see studies conducted in the traditional domains of cognitive research as the exploration ground. One looks to research demonstration for the evidence that training approaches can be facilitative. Therefore, we view this data base as a relevant approach to the issues of education for older adults.

III. Cognitive Training of the Older Adult

In this section, we review the studies that have examined the effects of training on older adult problem-solving performance. The rather limited number of these studies is somewhat surprising. Indeed, we suspect that if one were to compare the number of training studies to the number of articles that have issued exhortations for these studies, the latter would win easily. (However, we did not succumb to the temptation to make that comparison.)

Given the educational perspective of this chapter, our review of the cognitive training research is primarily intended to focus on the question of cognitive *potential* in adulthood; that is, the potential for older adults to profit from educational experience. It might be argued, of course, that the present research review is merely addressing the obvious, for the plasticity of older adult cognitive functioning has now been widely accepted. It is important to note, however, that assertions about plasticity have been typically, and uncritically, made on the basis of a very limited number of intervention studies. Furthermore, it is open to question whether the issue of plasticity in older adult cognitive functioning has been resolved to the satisfaction of all concerned. It is our opinion that a broad and critical review of older adult cognitive training studies is clearly warranted.

Because of their manipulative character, cognitive training studies are obviously relevant to theoretical efforts to explicate the causal factors underlying developmental ontogeny—an approach that has been persuasively spoken for by Baltes and Goulet (1971), among others. In what is perhaps the clearest case in point, the results of such studies have been frequently addressed to the issue of the relative contributions of biological decrement versus environmental impoverishment to older adult cognitive decline. Despite the heuristic value of this issue, our review of older adult cognitive training work is not specifically intended to examine critically whether cognitive deficits result from biological or environmental causes. By now it is abundantly clear that biological decrement models that posit universal, irreversible deficits are untenable. On the other hand, it is equally clear that the results of training investigations have not provided the unequivocal basis for discounting biological decrement of some sort. Thus, for the purposes of this chapter, we suggest an initially simpler framework to discuss training studies, which involves whether or not they can effectively promote improved cognitive functioning.

In the review that follows, the notion of "training" adopted is intentionally broad, and it includes manipulations that range from simple practice without feedback through the more highly structured procedures that the term ordinarily denotes. Our purpose in adopting such a broad interpretation was simply to allow as inclusive a research review as possible. On less pragmatic grounds, however, a distinction between practice and training should be made. Specifically, investigations involving practice reveal whether or not individuals spontaneously improve on task performance; the processes or strategies underlying any performance improvement are not dictated by the experimenter. On the other hand, in what is usually considered training, the experimenter provides at least some degree of input into the processes or strategies to be employed on a task.

A. Research Review

The majority of studies involving the training of older adult problem-solving performance have appeared in the literature since about 1973. Relevant studies prior to this date were few, and their results were not altogether convincing. An example of early intervention work is Crovitz's (1966) study using the Wisconsin Card Sorting Task, which demonstrated substantial differences between trained and untrained older adults. However, Crovitz's instructions concerning the nature of the task were so vague that her untrained subjects might have had little understanding of what the task involved. The preliminary training given to the experimental group may have simply clarified the nature of the solution to be sought and provided greater familiarity with the task materials instead of effecting any real reversal in a learning deficit.

Wetherick (1966) compared the effects of training on the ability of males of various ages to make inferences based on sequences of either all positive instances or both positive and negative instances. Although Wetherick found that the older men performed as well as the younger, he concentrated his discussion on a particular type of inferential error that was more frequently committed by the older subjects. Moreover, Wetherick's subject samples were matched on nonverbal intelligence, which makes it difficult to determine whether the overall comparability in performance across age groups was a result of training or of the matching procedure.

Not particularly successful was Young's (1966) attempt to train older adults on the Logical Analysis Device. Despite lengthy training and repeated demonstrations of the type of solution strategy demanded by the task, Young's elderly sample failed to show more than limited improvement. However, in light of the complexity of the Logical Analysis Device task, the inability of Young's elderly subjects to profit from training may well have reflected the inadequacy of the training.

In one of the more recent intervention studies, Hoyer, Labouvie, and Baltes (1973) sought to determine whether response-speed training would significantly enhance performance on a series of intellectual abilities tests. The two groups of subjects were respectively given practice and reinforced practice on speeded tasks involving cancellation, marking, and writing. Both of these groups showed reliable increases in speed on the training tasks, but they did not manifest superior abilities test performance relative to an untrained control group. However, the absence of transfer between the training and test tasks is not surprising if one considers the dissimilarities between those tasks.

Four experiments have examined the effects of training on Piagetian task performance—tasks on which the elderly had been previously found to exhibit some degree of decrement. The classification task, for example, is one in which subjects are evaluated with respect to their preferred mode of categorizing a set of stimulus items. Denney (1974) compared the classification task patterns of trained and untrained subjects who had previously grouped geometric stimuli according to criteria commonly observed in children. On the training stimulus set, modeling was found effective in promoting trained subjects to classify according to more mature similarity criteria more frequently than untrained controls; however, analogous training group superiority was not obtained in a test with mildly changed stimulus materials.

The 20-questions task represents a problem-solving situation in which the subjects' strategic approach is governed by their spontaneous tendencies to classify (Denney & Denney, 1973). Here, subjects are required to discover which item, out of a set of items presented, the experimenter has arbitrarily chosen as correct. To discover this item, subjects ask questions of any kind and in any order they wish; the only constraint is that the questions must allow yes or no answers. The most efficient strategy—constraint seeking—involves asking questions that test a class of items. Much less efficient, but more frequently used by the elderly (Denney & Denney, 1973), is the hypothesis-checking strategy in which questions test only a single item at a time. Whether modeling procedures would effect a change in older adults' question-asking strategies was investigated by Denney and Denney in 1974. Subjects who had previously asked no constraint-seeking questions were either provided with experimenter modeling or given additional question-asking experience. One modeling condition incorporated the experimenter's verbalization of the basis of the constraint-seeking strategy, whereas a second modeling condition did not. Relative to their practice control, both of Denney and Denney's modeling conditions evoked a reliable increase in the number of constraint-seeking questions.

Using Looft and Charles's (1971) perspective-taking task based on Piaget's mountain problem, Schultz and Hoyer (1976) investigated the effects of feedback training on spatial egocentrism. Two groups of subjects were given practice on a series of perspective-taking problems. One group received a combination of verbal and visual feedback following their responses, and the other group received no feedback; a third group included untrained control subjects. Half of the subjects in each treatment condition were tested immediately after training, and the other half were tested approximately 2 weeks after training. Included in the testing were a variety of transfer tasks. Analysis of the perspective-taking test scores revealed that the feedback-trained group was significantly superior to both of the other groups in the number of objective (i.e., correct) responses made; no difference was reported between the nonfeedback-trained and the control groups. In their analysis of error data, Schultz and Hoyer scored egocentric response errors separately from other wrong responses; they found that feedback training reduced the incidence of wrong responses but not the incidence of egocentric responses. In fact, very little egocentric responding was found in any of the three groups studied. Finally, no difference was found between those subjects tested immediately and those tested 2 weeks later, suggesting durability of the training; however, no transfer was evident between the training and transfer tasks on either occasion.

Hornblum and Overton (1976) presented nonconserving and partially conserving subjects with a variety of conservation tasks. Half of their subjects had received contingent feedback training (practice) on a conservation of surfaces task, whereas the remaining subjects were trained with no feedback. Of particular interest was Hornblum and Overton's finding of the rapidity with which their feedback-trained subjects' performance improved. During the training itself, feedback-trained subjects committed almost no errors after their initial incorrect response, and they were clearly superior to their control counterparts in this regard. This superiority of the feedback-trained group was also in evidence on four of the five transfer tasks administered.

In a doctoral dissertation at the University of Akron, Michael Christie (1980) applied a structured training sequence designed to increase performance on a formal operational task involving combinatorial thought. Based on an analysis of the combinatorial task, Christie identified a strategy that could lead to the systematic and efficient solution of such problems. His training procedure was developed in such a way as to address sequentially each of the components within this strategy. Christie's initial analyses indicate that the proportion of improvement in trained subjects is reliably greater than in control subjects.

In the area of concept problem solving, J. C. Sanders, Sterns, Smith, and R. Sanders (1975) administered a sequential training procedure developed to promote acquisition of an effective solution strategy for unidimensional concept identification problems. Combining operant and cumulative learning hierarchy principles, the training sequence contained a series of tasks arranged in order of increasing complexity. Furthermore, each of the component training tasks was aimed at enhancing a different aspect of problem solving, based on a task analysis of unidimensional concept identification problems. Training was given to two groups, with an extrinsic reinforcement system incorporated for one group but not for the other. Additional groups included controls as well as a group given practice with feedback. J. C. Sanders et al. (1975) found substantial and equivalent improvement in the training and reinforced training groups but only slight and nonsignificant performance increase in the practice and control groups. Similar results were reported by R. Sanders, J. C. Sanders, Mayes, and Sielski (1976) for a study in which structured training was given on a more complex bidimensional conjunctive concept identification task.

The extent to which enhanced unidimensional concept performance is durable over time and transferable across similar tasks was investigated by R. Sanders and J. C. Sanders (1978). In this study, subjects who had participated in the J. C. Sanders et al. (1975) unidimensional experiment were contacted a year later and asked to perform on a bidimensional conjunctive problem. In terms of their 1975 treatment group designations, the training group was found to be clearly superior to the reinforced training, practice, and control groups; there were no differences in conjunctive problem performance among the latter three groups. Thus, despite initially equivalent short-term training benefits, durability and transfer of improved performance were obtained with only the training group and not with reinforced training group. The absence of durability and transfer in the latter subjects was attributed to the extrinsic reinforcement system included in their training.

Because fluid abilities are presumed to be dependent upon the biological integrity of the individual, they offer a particularly interesting task domain for the assessment of modifiability of older adult performance. To that end, Labouvie-Vief and Gonda (1976) focused their training on an inductive reasoning marker of fluid intelligence, the Letter Sets Test. Raven's Progressive Matrices, another inductive reasoning task, was used as a transfer test. Performance on the training and transfer tasks was measured both immediately following training and after a 2-week interval. Labouvie-Vief and Gonda employed three training conditions. Two of the training conditions, cognitive training and anxiety training, were based on Meichenbaum's (1974) procedure designed to instill covert speech in order to provide effective self-regulation of problem solving. Whereas cognitive training was limited to strengthening self-instructional statements that would serve to guide subjects' solution efforts, anxiety training included additional self-instructions designed to aid subjects in coping with anxiety and failure and in emphasizing self-approval and success. A third training condition, unspecific training, consisted of subjects practicing on the Letter Sets Test with no instructions and, apparently, with no feedback. Labouvie-Vief and Gonda's results, albeit rather mixed, suggest that the inductive reasoning component of fluid ability can be modified through training and that the effects of training generalize over time and between related tasks. Furthermore, in comparing the efficacy of the different training conditions, Labouvie-Vief and Gonda concluded that unspecific training yielded the strongest effects.

Plemons, Willis, and Baltes (1978) have reported the successful improvement of performance on another fluid abilities task—Figural Relations. Their training program was developed on the basis of a task analysis of marker test items, and it included modeling. Furthermore, Plemons *et al.* constructed a hierarchy (from near–near through far–far) of transfer tasks according to both known factor loading patterns among the tasks and the degree of similarity they held with respect to the training program content. Several posttest sessions were held; the interval between the last two posttests was approximately 6 months in duration. Subjects' scores across the posttest sessions revealed, first, that the Figural Relations training program successfully enhanced performance on this fluid ability task. Second, degree of performance improvement on the various transfer tasks conformed to the transfer hierarchy delineated by Plemons *et al.,* indicating that their training did not merely promote general test-taking sophistication. Third, although performance differences between trained and untrained control subjects diminished over the posttest sequence, this was due to retest or practice effects in the control subjects rather than to performance loss in the trained subjects.

In a program of research that is almost unique for its focus on an applied problem, Sterns, Barrett, Alexander, Greenawalt, Gianetta, and Panek (1976) and Sterns, Barrett, Alexander, Panek, Avolio, and Forbringer (1977) have investigated the modifiability of information processing skills considered intrinsic to effective driver behavior in older adults. Based on an information processing model of driver decision making (Barrett, Alexander, & Forbes, 1977), structured training modules were developed for selective attention, perceptual style, and perceptual–motor reaction time. In constructing each of these modules, which were given over 4 days, Sterns and his colleagues sequenced the training so that it would result in performance improvement while holding error at a minimum. This attempt to promote learning was intended to circumvent performance-related difficulties, such as test anxiety and susceptibility to frustration, that are particularly evident in older adults. Briefly, the results of the Sterns *et al.* (1976, 1977) studies indicate that the older adult information processing skills measured in the studies generally can be improved and maintained over a 6-month period. However, a subsequent attempt (Sterns *et al.,* 1977) to apply an abbreviated training format was not as successful, indicating what may seem to be obvious—that too little training may not be enough.

B. Comments on Cognitive Training Research

Based on the preceding review of the existing cognitive training studies involving the aged, a number of observations appear to be warranted. First, with regard to the question of whether or not cognitive functioning in the elderly can be improved, we submit that the answer is affirmative. It is certainly true that methodological and design problems in some of the studies render their findings inconclusive, at best. Nevertheless, an adequate number of well-executed studies have successfully demonstrated improved functioning in a sufficiently wide variety of tasks that the reversibility of older adult cognitive deficit should no longer remain a point of contention. The efficacy of cognitive training, and the potential for older adults to profit from that training, are especially well documented in those studies (Plemons *et al.,* 1978; R. Sanders & J. C. Sanders, 1978; Sterns *et al.,* 1976, 1977) in which performance gain is shown to endure over considerable time spans and to generalize to other related tasks.

Second, reliance on task analysis (see Section IV) in developing a cognitive training program appears to be a strong "predictor" of the success of training with some tasks. This is particularly evident for the more complex tasks (e.g., J. C. Sanders *et al.,* 1975, R. Sanders *et al.,* 1976) in which practice with feedback fails to result in significant performance improvement. In a similar vein, the selection of transfer tasks to be administered following training might best be made on the basis of similarities between those tasks that are revealed through logical and empirical task analyses. Evaluations of whether training effects can be generalized across tasks having little or no overlap (e.g., Hoyer *et al.,* 1973) cannot be expected to provide adequate tests of transfer of training. On the other hand, logical analysis may not be helpful for other tasks such as conservation performance, in which simple practice with feedback suffices to promote improvement (e.g., Hornblum & Overton, 1976).

Third, a critical feature for those training procedures that require the separate training of different performance components appears to be the assurance that the more basic or subordinate skills are mastered before training progresses to the more complex or superordinate components. The most direct way to assure this is to establish performance criteria by which to regulate progression from one level or phase of training to the next (see J. C. Sanders *et al.,* 1975, R. Sanders *et al.,* 1976). Where no such assurance is made, as in the training by Young (1966), any gains on one component of performance could be easily mitigated by the premature introduction or intermixing of other performance components.

Fourth, the comparative efficacy of alternative training procedures remains virtually unexplored. Although the training studies reviewed here can be said to have employed a variety of training approaches (e.g., simple practice, practice with feedback, modeling, direct instruction in solution rules), only one study (Labouvie-Vief & Gonda, 1976) has reported data suggesting differential effectiveness of alternative training procedures. However, Labouvie-Vief and Gonda's conclusion that unspecific training (actually, practice) was superior to the more directive cognitive and anxiety training conditions must be viewed with some caution. On the one hand, it was noted earlier that Labouvie-Vief and Gonda's data were rather mixed, sufficiently mixed so that any conclusions about the differential efficacy of their training conditions should be regarded as tentative. On the other hand, Labouvie-Vief and Gonda's conclusion raises a more general issue that has generated some heat in the Piagetian training literature, namely, the issue of the relative effectiveness of tutorial versus self-discovery instructional approaches. In our view, one's conclusions about, and theoretical predilections for, a particular kind of training approach should be tempered by the nature and complexity of the tasks for which training is given. Particularly in older adults, we anticipate that training effectiveness will be moderated by the interaction between the individual's current level of functioning and the performance demands posed by a task. Therefore, research with the purpose of comparing alternative training procedures within a simplistic tutorial versus self-discovery framework is likely to result in data of limited information value.

Fifth, the results of the R. Sanders and J. C. Sanders (1978) investigation demonstrate that the durability and transfer of enhanced cognitive functioning cannot be taken for granted. Inasmuch as short-term training gains may or may not be maintained, a clear need for additional long-term follow-up research is indicated. Such investigations should not only include parametric evaluation of properties of training employed but also attempt to identify any moderating mechanisms that might contribute to the maintenance of improved performance in the period following completion of training.

Sixth, we conclude this section by arguing for continued research efforts in which the cognitive functioning of untrained older adults is assessed. A major premise underlying our argument is that such investigations are useful, indeed necessary, to the extent that they generate information beyond the mere demonstration of older adult deficits. That is, assessment research that yields more precise knowledge about the nature of these deficits provides the substantive basis for designing more effective training research. In this sense, there exists an intimate relationship between cognitive assessment and cognitive training investigations that remains to be more fully exploited. Therefore, in the following section, our discussion will focus on age-comparison research in which the problem-solving performance of older adults is assessed relative to that of younger adults. Because a number of research reviews (e.g., Knox, 1977; Rabbitt, 1977) are available, our discussion will not consist of a summary of existing studies. Instead, we believe that a more useful approach consists of highlighting those features of age-comparison studies that would contribute to a better understanding of adulthood cognitive functioning and that would carry over in a natural way to the training setting.

IV. Age-Comparison Research

As the heading of this section implies, we assume that the assessment of untrained older adult cognitive functioning will often be conducted through cross-sectional age comparisons with young adults. If past research provides any clue, it is reasonable to expect that age differences in performance will frequently be found; however, the cross-sectional nature of any such differences poses two issues. First, if one's objective is to explain age differences in performance, one must take into account the well-known finding that age and cohort effects are confounded in cross-sectional data (e.g., Baltes, 1968; Schaie, 1965). However, if the objective is to identify important characteristics of older adult cognitive functioning (as is consistent with the main focus of this chapter), the use of cross-sectional data is not inappropriate. It should be noted that the present assessment approach conforms to the descriptive, as opposed to the manipulative, side of research (e.g., Baltes & Goulet, 1971)—an approach that in isolation might be seen as "regressive." Nevertheless, we have already argued that intervention (manipulative) efforts will prove to be more effective when they are based on a more complete understanding of older adult cognitive functioning than is now available. In this sense, descriptive research continues to be important and is indeed compatible with, rather than independent of, manipulative research.

Once it is accepted that a more complete descriptive understanding of (untrained) older adult cognitive training is an appropriate goal, particularly as a preliminary step to training, one must deal with the second issue, which concerns the process of judging performance effectiveness or deficit. Making judgments about effectiveness necessarily requires a reference standard, and the more explicit the standard is, the better it is. For reasons we discussed in the introduction to this chapter, young adult performance can provide a useful reference standard, and it is one that is directly available when data are obtained cross-sectionally. The same young adult performance data also provide a reference standard by which to gauge the efficacy of, and progress within, any intervention procedure that may follow assessment.

There are two major features of age comparison that we strongly encourage for future studies: *task analysis* and reliance on *more direct measures* of subjects' problem-solving strategies. Each of these features will be discussed separately, and it will become clear that they are closely related. Their utility, which has become increasingly evident in discussions of children's cognitive development (e.g., Belmont & Butterfield, 1977), rests on their potential for revealing the strategies and strategy processes older adults use, or fail to use, in problem solving and other situations. It is this knowledge, not easily afforded by the more traditional measures of overall efficiency, that can serve to direct cognitive training in the elderly. Without this knowledge, one may well be in a position of training without knowing precisely what to train.

A. Task Analysis

Task analysis is the process by which performance on a given task is broken down into its components. For some tasks, these components may be identified through a logical analysis (e.g., Davidson, 1969; Siegler, 1976), whereas other tasks may require empirical identification based on analysis of patterns found in subjects' performance protocols (e.g., Gholson, Levine, & Phillips, 1972). Any task analysis that is initiated on a logical basis must, of course, be empirically validated. The objective of task analysis is to isolate the full range of performance components in a task; identification of the optimally efficient or "ideal" problem-solving strategy provides an additional standard against which subjects' performance can be evaluated. For some tasks, of course, suboptimal strategies may fail to contain all of the component processes that make up the ideal strategy, or they may not be organized in the most efficient manner. For other tasks, there may be different strategies possible (e.g., Gholson *et al.*, 1972).

Siegler's (1976) assessment of children's performance on the Piagetian balance scale task provides an excellent example of the utility of logical task analysis. Briefly, the balance scale task requires the subject to predict to which side, if either, a balance will tilt. The scale is constructed so that various combinations of weights can be placed on both sides of the fulcrum on any of four pegs. Thus, the side to which the balance tips is a function of the amount of weight per peg combined with the distance of the pegs from the fulcrum. The ideal strategy for these problems, called Rule IV by Siegler, involves multiplying the weight and distance from the fulcrum for each peg, adding these products across the pegs on each side of the scale, and then comparing the two sums; the balance should tip toward the side containing the greatest sum, or, if the sums are equal, it should not tip at all.

The key to Rule IV, and the reason it constitutes an ideal strategy for the balance scale task, is that subjects following that rule combine the critical variables, weight and distance, according to a cross-product principle. Use of this strategy would therefore result in errorless performance, regardless of the kind of balance scale problem presented.

Three additional rules have also been described by Siegler, the strategic properties of which were directly suggested by Rule IV. In Rule I, the most rudimentary of the rules, performance is considered to be determined by only one of the two dimensions; basing his rule on Inhelder and Piaget's (1958) work, Siegler assumed that the weight dimension would most often govern Rule I performance. In Rule II, subjects' decisions are assumed to include the distance dimension when the weights are unequal. Finally, Rule III performance is characterized by always involving both weight and distance, but the subjects have no principle available by which to resolve situations in which the weight and distance factors present conflicting cues.

Having devised the four-rule hierarchy of balance scale strategies, Siegler proceeded to construct various types of problems and predicted the performance pattern across the various problem types for each of the rule models. These problems were administered to 120 children (5–6, 9–10, 13–14, and 16–17 years old), each of whom was then classified as having used one of the four rule models in accordance with the performance pattern exhibited. Almost all (107) of the children could be unambiguously classified according to rule, thus documenting the empirical validity of the logically generated hierarchy. More important, however, the four-rule hierarchy resulting from Siegler's logical analysis provided a strategy classification measurement scheme for balance scale problem solving that proved to be more sensitive to the development of cognitive functioning than a more standard accuracy measure. That is, Siegler found that older children more frequently used the more advanced rules, but this trend was not as apparent in age comparisons of the number of correct predictions measure.

In the concept identification domain, Davidson (1969) has provided a comparable logical analysis for attribute identification problems of the type devised by Hovland (1952). Procedurally, these problems involve the simultaneous presentation of four stimulus instances—which are either all positive instances (i.e., examples of the concept to be discovered) or all negative instances (i.e., nonexamples of the concept)—that are used to identify a conjunctive or disjunctive concept solution. Thus, there are four different kinds of problems, based on the various combinations of type of instance (positive or negative) and type of concept rule (conjunctive or disjunctive) used. Davidson's logical analysis delineated the ideal solution strategy for each of these problems; the strategies are ideal in the sense that they lead to rapid, errorless problem solution.

R. Sanders, Beley, and Speroff (1977) have reported data documenting that young adults acquire and employ the solution strategies delineated by Davidson's logical analysis. Moreover, use of a verbalization procedure in their third experiment revealed an interesting "developmental" progression according to which the component steps of the ideal conjunctive, negative instance problem strategy are acquired. Within this progression is a hierarchy of strategy categories that is comparable to the hierarchy of rules Siegler (1976) proposed for the balance scale task. Although developmental investigation of Hovland-type problem performance is just beginning, it is expected that the hierarchy of strategy categories outlined here will also prove to be more informative about age differences in cognitive functioning than is the customary measure of time to solution.

The task analyses performed by Siegler (1976), Davidson (1969), and R. Sanders *et al.* (1977) are by no means the only task analyses available in the problem-solving literature. We have chosen to describe them in some detail in order to depict the general nature of the task analysis process, to illustrate its applicability to a wide variety of tasks, and to emphasize the utility of the task analysis approach. For example, it is clear that the ability to categorize an individual's performance according to a hierarchical strategy framework provides much richer information about that individual's present level of cognitive functioning than do general efficiency measures (solution–nonsolution of a problem, number of trials to solution, etc.). Thus, instead of simply demonstrating the occurrence of cognitive deficits in older adults, the use of tasks for which logical and empirical analyses have been conducted affords the possibility of more precise specification of what those deficits are. In turn, cognitive intervention procedures can be implemented with regard to the specific deficits identified, perhaps on an individualized basis.

The use of a task analysis approach to age-comparison research can lead to a better understanding of older adult cognitive functioning in another interesting way. Once older adult strategy deficits have been identified, at least tentatively, the investigator can alter instructional or procedural features of the task in order to prompt younger adults to perform similarly to the older adults (e.g., Baltes & Goulet, 1971). To the extent that one can closely simulate older adult performance in young adults, converging evidence concerning the nature of adulthood cognitive deficits will be gained. To our knowledge, no such attempt has yet been reported in the adulthood age-comparison literature on problem solving. Several studies (e.g., Belmont & Butterfield, 1977; Brown, Campione, Bray, & Wilcox, 1973) have successfully used this technique in assessing memory strategy performance in children and retardates.

B. Direct Strategy Measurement

The second feature of future age-comparison research that we wish to encourage pertains to the use of more direct measures of subjects' problem-solving performance. Again, the more direct measurement of what subjects do and do not do in their attempts to solve a problem was implicit in our discussion of task analysis. Nevertheless, it is important to reemphasize that insights into the nature of adulthood cognitive functioning are likely to be slow if undue reliance is placed on indirect, general efficiency measures of performance, particularly when the focus is on performance deficit. We now turn to the description of a problem-solving task in which more direct measurement of subjects' problem-solving processes and strategies is possible; the particular task we have chosen to discuss illustrates the potential value of direct measurement.

Within the hypothesis theory framework of human discrimination learning, Levine (e.g., 1966, 1969; Gholson, Levine, & Phillips, 1972) and his associates have developed the blank-trials probe procedure as a device for assessing the hypotheses subjects test while performing a discrimination learning problem. A blank-trials probe consists of a series of trials, inserted within a discrimination learning problem, during which no feedback is given after the subjects' responses. Because of the special (internally orthogonal) characteristics of the set of stimuli presented within a blank-trials probe, and because subjects maintain a hypothesis in the absence of feedback, the pattern of choice responses across the series of blank trials provides a direct measure of the hypothesis being tested by the subject.

Hypothesis theory characterizes the problem solver as actively testing hypotheses, maintaining a particular hypothesis if it results in correct responses, and rejecting it if it results in an error. The tendencies to maintain just confirmed hypotheses and to reject just disconfirmed hypotheses are found in young adults (e.g., Levine, 1966). However, several studies of children (e.g., Eimas, 1969; Gholson *et al.,* 1972) have shown a rather high probability for just disconfirmed hypotheses to be repeated, even though the children's performances were consistent with hypothesis theory in other essential respects. As this probability occurred at a close to chance level, the initial supposition was that children simply failed to remember just disconfirmed hypotheses. Hence, a memory deficit was implicated in children's discrimination learning, theoretically termed the *zero-memory assumption.*

As a consequence of their examination of the zero-memory assumption, Gholson *et al.* (1972) noted that the protocols of individual children revealed a variety of sequences according to which hypotheses were tested. Some hypothesis sequences, or *systems,* were sensitive to feedback and were collectively called *strategies;* the remaining systems, called *stereotypes,* were insensitive to feedback. The significance of this systems framework delineated by Gholson *et al.* is that it revealed that the tendency of young children to repeat just disconfirmed hypotheses was not due to poor memory but was the result of some children's adoption of a *stereotypic system.* Averaging across children using different systems, some strategic and some stereotypic, produced data that tantalizingly, but misleadingly, suggested memory deficit.

The point to be emphasized here is that Gholson and his associates' determination of the nature of young children's problem-solving "deficit" depended on the direct measurement of subjects' hypotheses. With hypothesis probe data, a comparable systems analysis of older adults' performance would be likely to yield more specific information concerning the hypothesis-testing deficits they display (Offenbach, 1974).

C. Commentary

It is clear that our illustrations of the use of task analysis and of direct measures of subjects' problem-solving strategies have been selected from the cognitive literature on children and young adults. Although the perspective of life-span research implies a sensitivity to conceptual and methodological advances across all segments of the life span, this chapter reflects our concern that investigators of adulthood cognitive functioning may often fail to capitalize on advances that occur outside this age domain. We have already argued that continuing research on older adult cognitive functioning is necessary. Combined with the approaches already available, such research promises to provide a substantive data base upon which to establish educational experiences for the older adult.

V. Implications for Education

A major theme of life-span psychology has been the contention that research on cognition in adulthood and old age has been descriptive and not sufficiently oriented toward intervention. A major task has been to challenge stereotyped assumptions about the irreversibility and fixed course of aging, and a concomitant goal has been to understand development through the modification of assumed antecedents in order to see what changes are produced in the developmental function. This exploration of modifiability has been the motivator of experiential and intervention research in adulthood and old age. As we have seen, such intervention-oriented work is beginning to appear in the literature, and there is growing support for the plasticity of human cognitive performance (Baltes & Goulet, 1971; Baltes & Labouvie, 1973; Baltes & Schaie, 1973, 1976; Sterns & Alexander, 1977).

During the 1970s we have also engaged in a tremendous growth in methodological sophistication in the field of life-span development, and we have seen a new cycle of insights on the limitations of these new methodologies (Baltes & Schaie, 1976; Botwinick, 1977; Horn & Donaldson, 1976; Schaie, 1965, 1977). There has been new information to support continuing abilities to learn in adults and older adults and continuing growth or stability of many dimensions of intelligence. In addition, this chapter has reviewed studies that provide examples of improved cognitive function.

Reviews of adult learning have summarized some of the knowledge that has become available in the 1970s (Birren & Woodruff, 1973; Knox, 1977; Schaie & Willis, 1978). To some extent, these reviews have captured the notion that past data set limits on our expectations and that we now have a more positive attitude regarding the older adult learner. We do not take the position that there is no decline in cognitive functioning, but we do support the view of Baltes and Schaie (1976) that it is not correct to believe in universal (for all people) and general (in all abilities) decline. Consideration must also be given to "large individual differences in adult change, multidimensionality, multidirectionality and the impact of biocultural, historical change [Baltes & Schaie, 1976, p. 722].''

Another major goal emphasized in the life-span literature is the development of a knowledge base that allows not only for "explanation but also for a priori (prevention) or a posteriori (alleviation) alteration or modification of developmental phenomena both on the level of intra- and interindividual differences dimensions [Baltes & Schaie, 1973, p. 376].''

The approach taken in this chapter has been that the first step toward changing attitudes and research approaches is to provide convincing research data. Manipulative experiments are the major tool for examining the validity of assumed causal relationships. The possibility of manipulating antecedents implies that age performance functions are not fixed and irreversible but are subject to modification. Short-term experiential manipulations are a first step toward isolating relevant dimensions for designing successful intervention strategies (Sterns & Alexander, 1977), and these intervention strategies include the educational enterprise. We propose, however, that a large number of researchers have not been involved in intervention research with older adults because they did not think it was possible. Moreover, even if researchers thought of intervention as a possibility, they did not know how to do it.

The role of education throughout the life span has been explored, and we are beginning to see some changes in attitudes toward adult and older adult education (Birren & Woodruff, 1973; Schaie & Willis, 1978). As schools embrace the nontraditional adult and older adult student to supplement enrollments, we are going through a period of "retroactive altruism." Whatever the reason is for this changing attitude and orientation, it must be seen as a positive step. But to make it a lasting phenomenon, founded on more than, for example, the economic pressures to which an educational institution may be subject, we need to obtain clear answers to the question of older adult educability. It is here that the major tasks and goals of contemporary life-span developmental psychology can, and are beginning to, contribute.

The growing success of training approaches in the laboratory and the use of specific methodological approaches to a better understanding of the nature of cognitive behavior are the key initial steps in educational intervention. Birren and Woodruff (1973), in an essay that we view as a manifesto for life-span education, call for such research examples in adulthood and old age. Their recommendations, which were presented in 1973 at the third life-span conference, are only now starting to come to fruition. According to Birren and Woodruff (1973), "To meet the needs of individuals in the last decades of the twentieth century, immediate action must be undertaken. Carefully planned strategies to alleviate existing deprivation as well as strategies to enrich and prevent deprivation will have to be developed on a large scale if educational institutions are to progressively serve society [p. 318]."

There can be little doubt that in our culture the expectancies and demands for older adults are different from those for adults; this is reflective of Moody's (1976) Stage II thinking. The nature of our educational response must be carefully considered. A major challenge is to move education to a higher level of response.

Reviews of adult learning approaches for application in the educational setting (Hickey, 1978; Knox, 1977; Schaie & Willis, 1978) indicate that our educational "technology" for this task is far from complete. Little or no research has been done in educational settings with older adults. There is a great need for carefully conceived research involving educational approaches that would build on methodologies developed in cognitive intervention studies.

A question might be raised regarding what all this research means in nonlaboratory situations. Clearly, current research calls into question the popular notion of inevitable decline in cognitive performance with age. What is also needed is a better understanding of cognitive functioning and its relationship to performance in everyday tasks. Our opinion is that we know little about the adult and older adult learner in more formal educational situations. As we see it, the initial need is to develop approaches to support the individual in existing educational environments, not to develop separate educational responses.

"If one follows the ancient literature of different civilizations, one soon discovers that the idea of lifelong learning is indeed a very old one and one could argue that lifelong learning was always going on in one form or another without it developing into an educational principle and often without it being a conscious act [McClusky, 1974, p. 101]." Because learning is natural for human beings at any stage in life, and because the need to learn something new always exists, it is puzzling that lifelong learning has taken so long to become an important concept in education.

There is an old rabbinical writing that goes something like this:

How long has a person the obligation to study Torah?
Till the day he dies.
Why so?
For as soon as man ceases to study he forgets.

REFERENCES

Baltes, P. B. Longitudinal and cross-sectional sequences in the study of age and generational effects. *Human Development,* 1968, *11,* 145–171.

Baltes, P. B., & Goulet, L. R. Exploration of developmental variables by manipulation and simulation of age differences in behavior. *Human Development,* 1971, *14,* 149–170.

Baltes, P. B., & Labouvie-Vief, G. Adult development of intellectual performance: Description, explanation and modification. In C. Eisdorfer & M. P. Lawton (Eds.), *The psychology of adult development and aging.* Washington, D.C.: American Psychological Association, 1973.

Baltes, P., & Schaie, K. W. On life-span developmental research paradigms: Retrospects and prospects. In P. Baltes & K. W. Schaie (Eds.), *Life-span developmental psychology: Personality and socialization.* New York: Academic Press, 1973.

Baltes, P. B., & Schaie, K. W. On the plasticity of intelligence in adulthood and old age: Where Horn and Donaldson fail. *American Psychologist,* 1976, *31,* 720–725.

Barrett, G. V., Alexander, R. A., & Forbes, P. J. Analysis of performance measures and training requirements for decision making in emergency situations. *JSAS Catalog of Selected Documentation Psychology,* 1977, *7,* 126. (Ms. No. 1623)

Belmont, J. M., & Butterfield, E. C. The instructional approach to developmental cognitive research. In R. V. Kail, Jr., & J. W. Hagen (Eds.), *Perspectives on the development of memory and cognition.* Hillsdale, N.J.: Earlbaum, 1977.

Birren, J. E., & Woodruff, D. S. Human development over the life span through education. In P. B. Baltes & K. W. Schaie (Eds.), *Life-span developmental psychology: Personality and socialization.* New York: Academic Press, 1973.

Botwinick, J. Intellectual abilities. In J. E. Birren & K. W. Schaie (Eds.), *Handbook of the psychology of aging.* New York: Van Nostrand-Reinhold, 1977.

Brown, A. L., Campione, J. C., Bray, N. W., & Wilcox, B. L. Keeping track of changing variables: Effects of rehearsal training and rehearsal prevention in normal and retarded adolescents. *Journal of Experimental Psychology,* 1973, *101,* 123–131.

Christie, M. Modification of combinatorial reasoning in the elderly. Unpublished doctoral dissertation, The University of Akron, 1980.

Crovitz, E. Reversing a learning deficit in the aged. *Journal of Gerontology,* 1966, *21,* 236–238.

Davidson, M. Positive versus negative instances in concept identification problems matched for logical complexity of solution procedures. *Journal of Experimental Psychology,* 1969, *80,* 369–373.

Denney, D. R., & Denney, N. W. The use classification for problem-solving: A comparison of middle and old age. *Developmental Psychology,* 1973, *9,* 275–278.

Denney, N. W. Classification abilities in the elderly. *Journal of Gerontology,* 1974, *29,* 309–314.

Denney, N. W., & Denney, D. R. Modeling effects on the questioning strategies of the elderly. *Developmental Psychology,* 1974, *10,* 458.

Eimas, P. D. A developmental study of hypothesis behavior and focusing. *Journal of Experimental Child Psychology,* 1969, *8,* 160–172.

Erickson, E. H. *Childhood and society.* New York: Norton, 1963. (Originally published, 1950.)

Gholson, B., Levine, M., & Phillips, S. Hypotheses, strategies and stereotypes in discrimination learning. *Journal of Experimental Child Psychology,* 1972, *13,* 423–446.

Hickey, T. Education in a human services context: A view from the research literature. In

M. Seltzer, H. Sterns, & T. Hickey (Eds.), *Gerontology in higher education: Perspectives and issues.* Belmont, Calif.: Wadsworth, 1978.

Hiemstra, R. Instrumental and expressive learning: Some comparisons. *Journal of Aging and Human Development,* 1977–1978, *8*(2), 161–168.

Horn, J. L., & Donaldson, G. On the myth of intellectual decline in adulthood. *American Psychologist,* 1976, *31,* 720–725.

Hornblum, J. N., & Overton, W. F. Area and volume conservation among the elderly: Assessment and training. *Developmental Psychology,* 1976, *12,* 68–74.

Hovland, C. I. A communication analysis of concept learning. *Psychological Review,* 1952, *59,* 461–472.

Hoyer, W. J., Labouvie, G., & Baltes, P. B. Modification of response speed deficit and intellectual performance in the elderly. *Human Development,* 1973, *16,* 233–242.

Inhelder, B., & Piaget, J. *The growth of logical thinking from childhood to adolescence.* New York: Basic Books, 1958; London: Routledge and Kegan Paul, 1958.

Knox, A. B. *Adult development and learning.* San Francisco: Jossey-Bass, 1977.

Labouvie-Vief, G., & Gonda, J. N. Cognitive strategy training and intellectual performance in the elderly. *Journal of Gerontology,* 1976, *31,* 327–332.

Levine, M. Hypothesis behavior by humans during discrimination learning. *Journal of Experimental Psychology,* 1966, *71,* 331–338.

Levine, M. Neo-noncontinuity theory. In G. Bower & J. T. Spence (Eds.), *The psychology of learning and motivation* (Vol. 3). New York: Academic Press, 1969.

Looft, W. R., & Charles, D. C. Egocentrism and social interaction in young and old adults. *Aging and Human Development,* 1971, *2,* 21–28.

McClusky, H. Y. The coming of age of lifelong learning. *Journal of Research and Development in Education,* 1974, *7*(4), 97–107.

Meichenbaum, D. Self-instructional strategy training: A cognitive prosthesis for the aged. *Human Development,* 1974, *17,* 273–280.

Moody, H. R. Philosophical presuppositions of education for old age. *Educational Gerontology,* 1976, *1,* 1–16.

National Council of the Aging, Inc. by Louis Harris and Associates, Inc. *The myth and reality of aging in America.* Washington, D.C.: The National Council of the Aging, 1975.

Offenbach, S. I. A developmental study of hypothesis testing and cue selection strategies. *Developmental Psychology,* 1974, *10,* 484–490.

Plemons, J. K., Willis, S. L., & Baltes, P. B. Modifiability of fluid intelligence in aging: A short-term longitudinal training approach. *Journal of Gerontology,* 1978, *33,* 224–231.

Rabbitt, P. Changes in problem solving ability in old age. In J. E. Birren & K. W. Schaie (Eds.), *Handbook of the psychology of aging.* New York: Van Nostrand-Reinhold, 1977.

Sanders, J. C., Sterns, H. L., Smith, M., & Sanders, R. E. Modification of concept identification in older adults. *Developmental Psychology,* 1975, *11,* 824–829.

Sanders, R. E., Beley, W., & Speroff, T. Transfer between conjunctive and disjunctive attribute identification problems. *Journal of Experimental Psychology: Human Learning and Memory,* 1977, *3,* 337–344.

Sanders, R. E., & Sanders, J. C. Long-term durability and transfer of enhanced conceptual performance in the elderly. *Journal of Gerontology,* 1978, *33,* 408–412.

Sanders, R. E., Sanders, J. C., Mayes, G. J., & Sielski, K. A. Enhancement of conjunctive concept attainment in older adults. *Developmental Psychology,* 1976, *12,* 485–486.

Schaie, K. W. A general model for the study of developmental problems. *Psychological Bulletin,* 1965, *64,* 92–107.

Schaie, K. W. Old wine into new bottles: A stage of theory of adult cognitive development. In

P. B. Baltes (Chair), *Cognitive behavior and problem solving.* Symposium presented at the meeting of the Tenth International Congress of Gerontology, Jerusalem, 1975.

Schaie, K. W. Quasi-experimental research designs in the psychology of aging. In J. E. Birren & K. W. Schaie (Eds.), *Handbook of the psychology of aging.* New York: Van Nostrand-Reinhold, 1977.

Schaie, K. W., & Willis, S. L. Life-span development: Implications for education. *Review of educational research,* 1978, *6,* 120–156.

Schultz, N. R., & Hoyer, W. J. Feedback effects on spatial egocentrism in old age. *Journal of Gerontology,* 1976, *31,* 72–75.

Siegler, R. S. Three aspects of cognitive development. *Cognitive Psychology,* 1976, *8,* 481–520.

Sterns, H. L., & Alexander, R. A. Cohort, age, and time of measurement: Biomorphic considerations. In N. Datan & H. W. Reese (Eds.), *Life-span developmental psychology: Dialectical perspectives on experimental research.* New York: Academic Press, 1977.

Sterns, H. L., Barrett, G. V., Alexander, R. A., Greenawalt, J. P., Gianetta, T., & Panek, P. E. *Improving skills of the older adult critical for effective driving performance* (final report). The University of Akron, Department of Psychology, July 1976. (Contract No. 223-822-0375, Andrus Foundation)

Sterns, H. L., Barrett, G. V., Alexander, R. A., Panek, P. E., Avolio, B. J., & Forbringer, L. R. *Training and evaluation of older adult skills critical for effective driving performance.* (Final Report) The University of Akron, Department of Psychology and the Institute for Life-Span Development and Gerontology, August 1977. (Contract No. 223-822-0375, Andrus Foundation)

Wetherick, N. E. The inferential basis of concept attainment. *British Journal of Psychology,* 1966, *57,* 61–69.

Young, M. Y. Problem-solving performance in two age groups. *Journal of Gerontology,* 1966, *21,* 505–509.

Author Index

Numbers in italics refer to the pages on which the complete references are listed.

Subject Index